Out of the House of Bondage

The Transformation of the Plantation Household

The plantation household was, first and foremost, a site of production. This fundamental fact has generally been overshadowed by popular and scholarly images of the plantation household as the source of slavery's redeeming qualities, where "gentle" mistresses ministered to "loyal" slaves. This book recounts a different story. The very notion of a private sphere, as divorced from the immoral excesses of chattel slavery as from the amoral logic of market laws, functioned to conceal from public scrutiny the day-to-day struggles between enslaved women and their mistresses, subsumed within a logic of patriarchy. One of emancipation's unsung consequences was precisely its exposure to public view of the unbridgeable social distance between the women on whose labor the plantation households relied and the women who employed them. This is a story of race and gender, nation and citizenship, freedom and bondage in the nineteenth-century South, a big abstract story that is composed of equally big personal stories.

Thavolia Glymph (Ph.D. Economic History, Purdue University) is an associate professor of African and African American Studies and History at Duke University. She has coedited two volumes of the award-winning *Freedom: A Documentary History of Emancipation* series and published scholarly articles in five book collections. Her current work focuses on a comparative study of plantation households in Brazil and the U.S. South, former Civil War soldiers in Egypt during Reconstruction, and a history of women in the American Civil War.

Out of the House of Bondage

The Transformation of the Plantation Household

THAVOLIA GLYMPH
Duke University

CAMBRIDGE
UNIVERSITY PRESS

CAMBRIDGE UNIVERSITY PRESS
Cambridge, New York, Melbourne, Madrid, Cape Town,
Singapore, São Paulo, Delhi, Mexico City

Cambridge University Press
32 Avenue of the Americas, New York, NY 10013-2473, USA

www.cambridge.org
Information on this title: www.cambridge.org/9780521703987

First published 2008
Reprinted 2010 (twice), 2011, 2012 (thrice)

A catalog record for this publication is available from the British Library.

Library of Congress Cataloging in Publication Data

Glymph, Thavolia
Out of the house of bondage : the transformation of the plantation household / Thavolia
Glymph.
    p. cm.
Includes bibliographical references and index.
ISBN 978-0-521-87901-9 (hardback) – ISBN 978-0-521-70398-7 (pbk.)
    1. Plantation life – Southern States – History – 19th century.   2. Women slaves – Southern
States – Social conditions – 19th century.   3. African American women – Southern States –
Social conditions – 19th century.   4. Plantation owners' spouses – Southern States – Social
conditions. – 19th century.   5. Women, White – Southern States – Social conditions – 19th
century.   6. Social distance – History – 19th century.   7. Households – Southern States –
History – 19th century.   8. Patriarchy – Southern States – History – 19th century.
9. Southern States – Social life and customs – 1775–1865.   10. Southern States – Race
relations – History – 19th century.   I. Title.
E443.G55   2008
307.72082′097509034–dc22   2007017918

ISBN 978-0-521-87901-9 Hardback
ISBN 978-0-521-70398-7 Paperback

*To the memory of my parents
and
for Sebastian, Morgan, and Kristal*

I *am* the Lord thy God, which have brought thee out of the land of Egypt, out of the house of bondage.

Exodus 20:2

Contents

Acknowledgments

I am happy to have this opportunity to acknowledge the support of colleagues, institutions, and friends that helped to keep the project that would become this book afloat. I have had the good fortune to work at institutions and with many wonderful colleagues whose own work deepened my understanding of the large processes and movements of history. Funding support from Duke University was critical to the final stages of the book's preparation. In addition, a year spent as a faculty Fellow with the John Hope Franklin Humanities Institute Seminar (2002–03) provided valuable time to revise what would become the first two chapters and, beyond that, a vibrant atmosphere of collegiality and interdisciplinary thinking. Archivists and research librarians at several institutions made the journey smoother. I wish to thank in particular Elizabeth Dunn and Eleanor Mills of the Rare Book, Manuscript, and Special Collections Library at Duke Libraries for their help generally and for locating and processing the cover illustration. My students, who over the years have listened patiently and often enthusiastically to my obsession with the nineteenth-century South, have been some of my most generous and formidable critics.

The opportunity to present some of the central ideas in this book at conferences and symposia meant access to a wider world of ideas and critiques that, in the end, helped to make the analysis sharper and the book much better than it otherwise would have been. I wish to thank the graduate students, colleagues, and institutions who sponsored these visits, and colleagues whose comments helped me to refine many of these ideas. Special thanks to Elsa Barkley Brown, for inviting me to give the annual address to the Southern Association for Women Historians during her year as president of the association; Elizabeth Fox-Genovese, for her invitation to speak at Emory; Sylvia Frey, for her invitation to give the National Endowment for the Humanities Lecture at the University of Richmond; Valinda Littlefield, for the invitation to give the Millercom Colloquium when she was still at the University of Illinois-Urbana; and Nan Woodruff, for her fateful invitation to speak at Penn State and the wonderful associations that would lead to. Nancy Hewitt, Ann Bowman, Laura

Woliver, Stephanie McCurry, Beverly Brock, David Brock, and Drew Gilpin Faust were always there with words of encouragement.

Susan Thorne, Darlene Clark Hine, and Karen Fields read the entire final draft, and each, in her own inimitable way, nudged me through the final year, tempering much needed constructive criticism with libations for the soul. Susan brought to the task a sharp theoretical eye and insights from her work and extensive knowledge in British history and the British Empire, along with uncommon friendship and humanity. Darlene read with an eye sharpened by a long, deep, and unsurpassed engagement with African American women's history, and the heart of a mentor. Her intellectual support was matched by a steady drum beat of unstinting kindnesses as I trudged through the final year of revising and editing. The genesis of this book, in fact, belongs to the long-ago conversations where Darlene, Kate Wittenstein, and I first began exploring the silences that surround black women's history. Karen Fields' generous offer to read the manuscript came as I was in the throes of final editing, and I am not sure which was more frightening to contemplate: the idea of having her read it or sending it before the public without her having done so. So, with what remained of my good sense, I accepted. Susan, Darlene, and Karen went far beyond the call of duty, providing gravity when that was needed, and, encouragement always. I have been richly rewarded by the insights of each of these scholars. To each, I am happily indebted. David Barry Gaspar provided invaluable comments on an early version of the manuscript. Stephane Robolin took valuable time from writing his dissertation to send me detailed written comments on an early version of Chapter 1.

This book found its wings at a crucial moment in my life, and I acknowledge with deepest gratitude individuals whose friendship, practical advice, good humor, steadfast support, and generosity helped to set it free and launch it, finally, out to the wider world. Their spiritual support and intellectual sustenance made an otherwise daunting year surmountable. Special thanks to Myrna and Emile Adams, Connie Blackmore, Joye Bowman, Daphne Davis, Sarah Deutsch, John Dittmer, Anita Earls, Lorin Palmer Fielding, Barbara Fields, Karen Fields, Marjorie Ford, John Hope Franklin, Gary Gallagher, Eugene D. Genovese, John Higginson, Darlene Clark Hine, William Hine, Vivian Jackson, Lori Leachman, Gerda Lerner, Valinda Littlefield, Kirsten Mullen, Sally Dalton Robinson, Julie Saville, Susan Thorne, and my THL comrades for saving a place for me. I also want to especially thank the many colleagues in the Departments of African & African American Studies and History at Duke for their support. Elizabeth Fox-Genovese did not live to see this book published but did know it was on its way and, I hope, how much her friendship and scholarship helped to sustain it.

Over the years, many others have shared laughter, intellectual comradeship, and time and have been constant in their faith in me and in this project. It would take more space than I have here to name them all, but there are a few I must name. Harold D. Woodman is among this number. I first read Woodman's work as an undergraduate student and decided then and there that I would study with him. At the time, I did not have the first clue about how to make this happen. But, clearly, I got that part figured out, which, fortuitously, also brought Darlene Clark Hine into my life. Hal's knowledge of the plantation South, I still think, is unparalleled. But I came to appreciate as much the breadth of his intellectual grounding and the greatness and generosity of his spirit. Ira Berlin brought me into the extraordinary world of the Freedmen and Southern Society Project. The experience of working as one of the editors on this project with Ira, Barbara Fields, Steven Hahn, Steven Miller, Joseph Reidy, Leslie Roland, Julie Saville, and the incomparable staff assistant at the time, Susan Bailey, was an incredible experience and a model of collegiality and collaborative scholarship.

This book will enter the wider world finally because of an exceptional and brilliant editor, Lewis Bateman. Lew understood what I was trying to do and shepherded this project with brilliance, and warmth. My thanks also to the copy and production editor, Elise M. Oranges; Mark Mastromarino, who prepared the index; Alisa Harrison, who provided valuable research assistance; and the readers for the Press for their votes of confidence. This is an occasion to also express my appreciation to Mrs. Mildred Moore of Cape May, New Jersey, for sharing and occasionally turning over her home to my family for brief summer retreats during the last years I worked on this book, to others in her family whose hospitality we enjoyed, and to Grace Plater for her always uplifting telephone calls and for caring deeply.

In the end, this book is indebted, first and foremost, to my parents. My father, known to all who knew and loved him as Luke, and my mother, whose mother memorably named her Pearl, gave me my first and most important lessons in southern history and the work of building free homes. They did not live to see this book published, but I think they would be pleased. One of the most rewarding parts of getting to this page is the occasion it presents to dedicate this book to my children, Sebastian, Morgan, and Kristal, whose love sustains and who have looked forward to this day as much as I. "I love you more."

And, finally, to John Coltrane, Nina Simone, Leadbelly, and Oleta Adams for knowing and reminding me of what it would take to get this done.

Thavolia Glymph
Durham, North Carolina

Abbreviations

BRFAL	Bureau of Refugees, Freedmen, and Abandoned Lands
DU	Duke University
LC	Library of Congress
LR	Letters Received
LS	Letters Sent
MDAH	Mississippi Department of Archives and History
NA	National Archives
NCDAH	North Carolina Department of Archives and History
RG	Record Group
SCDAH	South Carolina Department of Archives and History
SCHS	South Carolina Historical Society
SCL	South Carolinian Library
SHC	Southern Historical Collection

Introduction

At the deepest levels of a man's being it cannot make sense that he should voluntarily labor for those whose style of thinking declares them to be his enemies and whose triumph in the management of human affairs remain a persistent threat to the dignity of his person.

George Lamming

Tranquility and violence coexist.

Eric Hobsbawm

"The word *home* has died upon my lips."[1] Writing to her son in late June 1865, Mary Jones summed up one outcome of the Civil War. Decades later, Katie Rowe remembered another. "It was de fourth day of June in 1865 I begins to live."[2] Without slaves to do the work of her home, Jones's world, her home, was dead. In that death, Katie Rowe saw life and a future to claim as her own. As a former mistress and a former slave, Jones and Rowe stood opposite each other in 1865. Once connected by the institution of slavery, they now faced a common task: to build new lives on the ground of freedom. Both were transformed. This book recounts that transformation. It is a story of freedom and unfreedom, race and gender, and nation and citizenship in the world of the nineteenth-century American South. That big abstract story is composed of equally big personal stories, from a woman's right to choose the dress she will wear to her right to live.

The story properly begins before the war, when enslaved and slaveholding women related to each other on the ground of slavery. For Mrs. Jones, the home

[1] Mary Jones to Charles C. Jones, Jr., June 26, 1985 in *Children of Pride: A True Story of Georgia and the Civil War*, ed. Robert Manson Myers (New Haven: Yale University Press, 1972), p. 1275.

[2] Katie Rowe in *The American Slave: A Composite Autobiography, Oklahoma and Mississippi Narratives*, vol. 7 (Greenwood, CT: Greenwood Publishing Co., 1972), p. 284. Series hereafter cited by name of interviewee.

that died was, whatever else, a workplace. Enslaved women mopped its floors, dusted its mahogany tables, made its beds, ironed, wet-nursed, and bathed and powdered their owners. In its yard and outbuildings – from kitchens, smokehouses, loom and weaving houses to spring and ice houses, wood sheds, dairies, and chicken houses – enslaved women scoured dishes, made biscuits and pies from scratch, churned butter, turned vegetables cultivated in gardens they worked and freshly-killed chickens into breakfast, supper, and evening meals, and fruits into jams and jellies. They washed damask tablecloths and every piece of clothing their owners wore, raised and fattened the poultry, and fetched wood.[3] They were expected to do these things in silence and reverence, barefooted and ill-clothed.[4] These expectations formed part of the legitimized violence to which they were subjected. The story ends with a transformed plantation household and the emergence of free black and white homes. In the transformed plantation household, former mistresses could no longer command labor or deference. In the new black homes, black women found some privacy and the space to live fuller lives.

Ideas about what constitutes public and private, and differentiates them, are central to all of these matters. The notion of private/public assumes that the household is a family and thus private. This has made it difficult to see the household as a workplace and, beyond gender relations, as a field of power relations and political practices. Historians have long been interested in how questions of power and hegemony informed relations between slaves and slaveholders and between women and men. We have paid less attention to power relations between women.[5] My task is to reconstruct, as best I can, the day-to-day practices of domination and its responding discontents within the antebellum, wartime, and postbellum plantation households.

Historians have noticed and taken account of violence against slaves in the cotton, rice, sugar, and tobacco fields. Here it is easier to "see" because it took place in a "public" arena where cash crops were produced and came principally from the hands of men – masters, overseers, and slave drivers. Violence and power in the great house, the female side of domination, have not received nearly the commensurate attention. This neglect stems in part from

---

[3] Elizabeth Fox-Genovese, *Within the Plantation Household: Black and White Women of the Old South* (Chapel Hill: University of North Carolina Press, 1988), pp. 137–38; John Michael Vlach, *Back of the Big House: The Architecture of Plantation Slavery* (Chapel Hill: University of North Carolina Press, 1993); Deborah Gray White, *Ar'n't I a Woman: Female Slaves in the Plantation South*, rev. ed., New York: W. W. Norton, 1999).

[4] See, for example, Jacob Manson, *North Carolina Narratives*, vol. 15, pt. 2, p. 97.

[5] For an extended discussion of this point, see Chapters 2 and 3. The number of slaves who worked in and around plantation households has been estimated at around one-quarter of all slaves. But as Eugene D. Genovese writes, this is "guesswork honored by time and repetition" and such a large number is plausible only by adding to those whose duties were in the household, the small number of slaves owned by yeomen and slaves whose duties were strictly in the yard, such as gardeners and coach drivers (Genovese, *Roll, Jordan, Roll: The World the Slaves Made* [New York: Vintage Books, 1974], p. 328).

the fact that violence in the household took place within a supposed private domain and came from the hands of women. We must remember that the plantation household was also a workplace, not a haven from the economic world, that it was not private or made so by the nature of the labor performed within it or the sex of the managers. I take a lesson from nineteenth century southerners' own view of the home as a political space.[6] It is not home as an idea but flesh-and-blood practices that make it free or not, and public or private, or not.

Home as a political figure and space comes into focus only when a key misconception is set aside: that the household is a private space. Once the public character of the plantation household comes into full view, so, too, does its life as a "controlling context of power" and a second misconception, that plantation mistresses wielded little or no power.[7] Nothing could be further from the truth, which comes into focus when we notice that male dominance was not the controlling force within the plantation household. A third misconception interprets the aspirations and actions of black women on the basis of assumptions and questions that have framed the writing of the history of white women. Distinctions between modes of power are diminished. The fact that black and white women experienced different, and particular, modes of power within the plantation household becomes less visible. Just as plantation mistresses can be misconceived as more different than masters than the evidence shows, slave women can be misconceived as more like mistresses than the evidence shows.

If the authority of planter women is defined by the restrictions, legal and customary, imposed by white male authority, their power and violence disappear. On this view, the plantation household held freedom only for its male "white head."[8] Nothing bars the absurd conclusion that Mary Jones and Katie Rowe were equals by virtue of their femaleness. Indeed some scholars have challenged the idea of the southern lady that animated post-Civil War reminiscences, Lost Cause propaganda, and most historical studies prior to the mid-twentieth century. But their portrait generally depicts planter women as a silent abolitionist constituency and still, thus, as potent allies of slaves, and slave women in particular. Here were hardworking women so handicapped by patriarchy and paternalism that their lives more closely resembled those of enslaved women than the white men who were their fathers, husbands, and

---

[6] On sovereignty and everyday sites of power, see Patricia Yaeger, "Introduction: Narrating Space," in *The Geography of Identity*, ed. Patricia Yaeger (Ann Arbor: University of Michigan Press, 1996), p. 8; Nell Irvin Painter, "Soul Murder: Toward a Fully Loaded Cost Accounting," in Nell Irvin Painter, *Southern History Across the Color Line* (Chapel Hill: University of North Carolina Press, 2002).

[7] Quote is from E. P. Thompson, *Making History: Writings on History and Culture* (New York: The New York Press, 1994), p. 362.

[8] Lee Ann Whites, *The Civil War as a Crisis in Gender: Augusta, Georgia, 1860–1890* (Athens: University of Georgia Press, 1995), p. 18.

brothers; here were women who found in their own subjection the basis for an alliance with enslaved women.[9] Slaves rarely thought this.

Historians of southern women continue to work within a framework that gives such priority to patriarchy, paternalism, and a particular brand of domesticity, that these become paradigmatic for the study of black women in slavery and freedom. This reigning paradigm carries in its fold several unexamined foundational presumptions that work on several levels. Freedom for enslaved women has come to be understood as the right to patriarchy and its kindred domestic norms. As one scholar writes, freedom offered "black women the possibility of returning to the home," creating conditions in which black "women could be wives and mothers first and laundresses and cotton pickers second."[10] The contradictions, anachronisms, and foundational assumptions immediately begin to pile up on top of each other. The very phrase, "returning to the home," owes more to post-World War II discourse than to the realities of the post-Civil War era. It is also a diversion. Moreover, such analyses suggest that whatever claim black women had to domesticity was decidedly different from and trumped by white women's. The reigning ideology of domesticity did not call on white women to be wives and mothers *and* laundresses and cotton pickers. Indeed, for mistresses, it made work outside the home a disqualifying act.

White women wielded the power of slave ownership. They owned slaves and managed households in which they held the power of life and death, and the importance of those facts for southern women's identity – black and white – were enormous. In the antebellum period, white women were clearly subordinate in fundamental ways to white men, but far from being victims of the slave system, they dominated slaves.[11] The first part of this book studies the female face of slave owners' power. Its legacy for the Civil War and Reconstruction (and after) is the central focus of the second part. I begin by reconstructing the world of women in the plantation household. Cultural nostalgia sometimes

---

[9] This historiography has its modern roots in Anne Firor Scott's pioneering *The Southern Lady: From Pedestal to Politics, 1830–1930*, 25th Anniversary Edition (1970; Charlottesville: University of Virginia Press, 1995) and Catherine Clinton's *The Plantation Mistress: Woman's World in the Old South* (New York: Pantheon Books, 1982). For more recent elaborations of the thesis, see, for example, Leslie A. Schwalm, *A Hard Fight for We: Women's Transition from Slavery to Freedom in South Carolina* (Urbana: University of Illinois Press, 1997); Brenda E. Stevenson, *Life in Black and White: Family and Community in the Slave South* (New York: Oxford University Press, 1996); Brenda E. Stevenson, "Gender Convention, Ideals, and Identity among Antebellum Virginia Slavewomen," in *More than Chattel: Black Women and Slavery in the Americas* (Bloomington: Indiana University Press, 1996), pp. 183–90; and Marli F. Weiner, *Mistresses and Slaves: Plantation Women in South Carolina, 1830–80* (Urbana: University of Illinois Press, 1998), pp. 123–24; among others.

[10] Quotes are from, respectively, Jim Cullen, "'I's a Man Now': Gender and African American Men," in *Divided Houses: Gender and the Civil War*, ed. Catherine Clinton and Nina Silber (New York: Oxford University Press, 1992), p. 90, and Jacqueline Jones, *Labor of Love, Labor of Sorrow: Black Women, Work, and the Family from Slavery to the Present* (1985; reprint, New York: Vintage, 1995), p. 46. See also Whites, *The Civil War as a Crisis in Gender*, pp. 6–7.

[11] For an important corrective on this point, see White, *Ar'n't I a Woman?*, rev. ed., pp. 6–7.

gives priority to what Frederick Douglass called the "seeming" and Renato Resaldo "the elegance of manners," both of which in fact sit atop "relations of dominance and subordination."[12] Once we acknowledge that white women wielded the power of slave ownership, then our culture's fascination with slavery's and mistresses's seeming elegance and "veneer of manners" becomes visible as a dodge and can be cleared away. Not only did white women's violence, and their ownership and management of slaves make it impossible for black people to see them as ideal models of a "kind and gentle womanhood," but they resulted in specific practices of resistance. Chapters 1 and 2 investigate the female face of slaveholding power particularly as it was expressed through violence against enslaved women in the plantation household. Contrary to most interpretations, violence on the part of white women was integral to the making of slavery, crucial to shaping black and white women's understanding of what it meant to be female, and no more defensible than masters' violence. At the same time, white women's violence contradicted prevailing conceptions of white womanhood – and still does.

White women beat slave women and, more rarely, killed them in ways so disturbing that historians have judged them barbaric. Elizabeth Fox-Genovese writes of the "inherent injustice and inevitable atrocities" associated with white female violence. "In the heat of the moment," Jacqueline Jones notes, "white women devised barbaric forms of punishment that resulted in the mutilation or permanent scarring" of female slaves.[13] "In the course of reading plantation documents," Winthrop Jordan expressed surprise at finding so much evidence of white women's violence.[14] Still, Jordan was unable to see this violence as more than special cases or aberrations "by white women." In the main, historians have dismissed or minimized that womanly female violence. Mistresses "had in fact slapped, hit or even brutally whipped their slaves – particularly slave women or children," Drew Faust writes, despite the fact that the "exercise of the violence fundamental to slavery was overwhelmingly the responsibility and prerogative of white men. A white woman disciplined and punished as the master's subordinate and surrogate. Rationalized, systematic, autonomous, and instrumental use of violence belonged to men."[15]

[12] Frederick Douglass, *My Bondage and My Freedom*, (1855; reprint, New York: Dover 1969), p. 111; Renata Rosaldo, *Culture and Truth: The Remaking of Social Analysis* (Boston, MA: Beacon Press, 1989), p. 68. As Rosaldo also notes, "a mood of nostalgia makes racial domination appear innocent and pure" (Ibid). See also Achille Mbembe, "Necropolitics," trans. Libby Meintjes, *Public Culture* 15 (Winter 2003): 21–22.

[13] Fox-Genovese, *Within the Plantation Household*, p. 132; Jones, *Labor of Love*, pp. 26–27. Jones nonetheless views such violence as occurring in "the heat of the moment." Following this line of reasoning, Stephanie M. H. Camp argues that white female violence "was typically impulsive and passionate." (Camp, *Closer to Freedom: Enslaved Women and Everyday Resistance in the Plantation South* [Chapel Hill: University of North Carolina Press, 2004], p. 132.)

[14] Winthrop D. Jordan, *Tumult and Silence at Second Creek: An Inquiry into a Civil War Slave Conspiracy* (Baton Rouge: Louisiana State University Press, 1993), pp. 201–2.

[15] Drew Gilpin Faust, *Mothers of Invention: Women of the Slaveholding South in the American Civil War* (Chapel Hill: University of North Carolina Press, 1996), p. 63.

In part to preserve gentle feeling, mistresses generally defended their violence as heat of passion responses (even this demands investigation) and historians have tended to follow suit. However, as Eric Hobsbawm reminds us,
uncontrolled violence, "blind lashings," even when it does not kill, is "more
frightening, because both more random and cruel, inasmuch as this kind of violence is its own reward."[16] Whatever its degree or prevalence, white women's
violence was connected to and supported the larger culture of violence. The
notion of a gentle and noble white womanhood rode uncomfortably in tandem
with the ideology of domesticity that, with roots in Western Europe, came to
play an increasingly central part in how nineteenth-century white northerners
and southerners thought about themselves. In the South, white gender ideals
clashed with white women's domestic dominance.

Chapter 3 explores the interplay of notions of domesticity and ideologies of
race and slavery within the plantation household. Slaveholding women were
called on to make their homes and themselves models of domestic virtue but
depended on the work of slave women to accomplish these objectives. Southern prescriptive ideals asked them to "play the lady" *and* to be "domestic
manager," and judged them according to both yardsticks. Accomplishing this
required that they be both submissive and dominant. Their manners had to be
perfect and their households had to demonstrate attention to order, punctuality, and economy. Failure threatened their status as ladies and the institution
of slavery.

Success, in turn, depended on the cooperation of black women who notoriously refused to play their part. The ideology of domesticity required enslaved
women to work for the plantation household as if their own interests were
involved. Their failure to do so made it hard for mistresses to meet the emerging
standards of domesticity. Mistresses couched black women's noncooperation
as a refusal to be "better girls," in terms that suggested innate backwardness. This, not discontent under slavery, made them unalterably inefficient,
slothful, and dirty. This was the source of their "misbehavior" and could be
used to explain mistresses's violent responses and their inability to create the
ideal domestic home, to be "better girls" themselves. Violence against enslaved
women was thus justified. The disjuncture between these views and the fact
that beds got made, meals cooked, clothes washed and ironing done, floors
scrubbed, babies nursed, beds turned back, jams made, flies swatted, and much
more is glaring but not unexplainable. In the end, black women's noncooperation defined and marked the failure of southern domesticity and simultaneously the defeat of its accomplice, the ideology of a gentle and noble white
womanhood.

The Civil War made possible a sustained assault on the southern white
planter "home." From 1861 to 1865, slave women targeted the planter
household, the scene of "so much devilment," for destruction, desecration,

---

[16] Eric Hobsbawm, *Revolutionaries* (1973; reprint, New York: New Press, 2002), p. 253.

occupation, and transformation.[17] It is by now a commonplace of historical scholarship that domestic workers were often the first to flee slavery. Chapter 4 links their flight to the physical and psychological violence that had come from the hands of white women before the war rather than, in the way of much revisionist scholarship, to a desire on the part of enslaved women to mimic the gender ideals of the planter class. In their actions and words, slave women rejected the white household's symbolic and political meanings and its work. The transformation of the plantation household (and sometimes its literal destruction), with its claims to domesticity and civilization and violence, was a major goal of freedom as slaves understood it.

During and after the Civil War, mistresses fought to reestablish their claims to class and race privileges and to deny and turn back the efforts of black women to redefine the meaning of womanhood, freedom, family, home, and domestic economy. Black women won important victories and suffered defeats, but in the end they gained the larger victory. Slaveholding households great and small were irreversibly transformed and free black homes emerged.[18] What came to replace the antebellum plantation household was a hybrid formation, a cobbled-together patchwork of labor practices that bore the imprint of past experience and that carried the promises of freedom; the process which shaped this result was, in important respects, similar to that taking place simultaneously in the South's cotton and sugar cane fields. Subjected to a free labor market, former mistresses had to learn how to be employers and former slave women, employees. The meaning of southern womanhood also changed. None of these changes were guaranteed by the Union military victory or the constitutionally legislated emancipation that came in its wake. Remembering slavery, black women did not make the going easy. White women found the process demeaning and the loss of status appalling.

Chapters 5 and 6 unravel the particular initiatives on the part of freedwomen that fueled these changes and the adjustments in domestic work that transformed black and white homes and set them on a path to becoming free homes. These initiatives introduced mistresses to free labor practices – from bargaining, hiring, firing, and contracting for labor to accepting the right of employees to quit – however reluctant pupils they were – and to working for a living themselves. Former slave women took the lead in initiating these processes, but they too had much to learn. I mean to detail some of the precise forms this struggle took and how they guided the making of freedom and the remaking of southern womanhood. Though Reconstruction historiography has given the more prominent role to the more public battles over black freedom and citizenship, this struggle between women informed the other struggles as well – over land, family formation, wage labor in the fields, and black male

---

[17] Quote is from Charles Royster, *The Destructive War: William Tecumseh Sherman, Stonewall Jackson, and the Americans* (New York: Alfred A. Knopf, 1991), p. 344.

[18] Black homes, of course, remained under attack and faced new forms of, and more intense, violence. But this was precisely because they were free.

suffrage. It was part and parcel of struggles over the right to move about and to talk freely. The return of black women to domestic work was related to all of these battles. Where domestic work provided "ready cash," it could mean the difference between starvation and survival for fragile black household economies. The institution of a free wage economy in domestic work was inseparable from the larger struggles of emancipation.

Domestic workers, like field hands, fought to preserve privileges long established as virtual "rights." They tasked their labor – which some scholars mistakenly see as a postwar development – and determined a value for it that corresponded to their sense of a just rate. The very nature of slavery in the household and its management meant that mistresses often had little precise knowledge about such matters as how much time it took to wash or iron a certain amount of laundry. In slavery, there were wash days and ironing days, and the amount of work expected had been determined in large part by how much actually got done. Slave women had, themselves, over the course of time, set these standards. After slavery, they adapted the terminology of the task system used in field labor, made the calculations, and moved to put them in place: So many pieces of clothing or linen equaled so many tasks of washing and ironing.

As historians have shown, former mistresses were forced to do some or all of their own domestic work for a time, to take on for the first time in their lives the work slaves had previously done. Some became waged workers for the first time. Others founded mutual aid societies to help support themselves and their families.[19] They peddled old dresses to freedwomen; made and sold jams, preserves, and clothing; sewed for a living; taught in black schools; and took in boarders, not as a gesture of southern hospitality but to pay the bills. These and other endeavors signaled a radical shift in power and gender relations. When former mistresses went before the public to sell their wares in order to feed and clothe themselves and their families, *and to pay for their domestic help*, they acknowledged just how massive the break was. A change in the tone of admonitions from fathers and husbands on the dire necessity for change also marked the break. Former masters stressed with greater force than ever before the need to take domestic economy seriously. Yet, no matter how financially distressed they were, white women were determined to hold on to black domestic labor even when doing so required that they work to pay for it. The labor they got was not what they wanted or believed they were entitled to.

The end of slavery also brought another important development: The plantation household's façade of privacy was stripped away, fully exposing its public realm. Freedom gave black women the right to quit as it gave white women the right to fire them. It gave them the right to move about to seek other employment and to openly discuss the characters of their employers, to gossip about them. One achievement of gossip is to make the home more

---

[19] Ladies Mutual Aid Association (Charleston, SC), Handbill, ca. 1866 (43/0996), SCHS.

public, along with the abuses that take place there. Freedwomen who gossiped about white employers transmitted information about the personal and intimate lives of their employers as well as their character as employers and the work conditions in their homes. Slaves had always gossiped about the goings-on in plantation households. One of the important accomplishments of freedom was to multiply the number of witnesses and broadcast their testimonies at the moment and into the twentieth century. In forcing slave women to stay put in the plantation household, slavery by the same stroke veiled home truths. The mobility that accompanied emancipation tore away the veil. Speaking of the "scenes of cruelty" in the fields, Frederick Douglass made the sharp point that they were "enacted and witnessed."[20] The witnesses were slaves, he among them. In the ex-slave narratives we have many witnesses.

No longer legally bound to the white household after the Civil War, former slaves set out to demolish the residue of that attachment, which legislation was powerless to efface, as one of their first political acts. Former mistresses struggled to get along with free laborers whose "loyalty" they could no longer even pretend to command. Even when black women had no choice but to take employment in white homes, the terms upon which they did so changed radically. Sometimes, external appearances suggest otherwise, a sort of costumed continuity. The discontinuities become most apparent in actions such as former mistresses bargaining over how many pieces of laundry constituted a task. Such women would have been less inclined than scholars to find more continuity than discontinuity in the postwar plantation household. The costumes and the sets may have been old, but the dialogue and the actions were new.

Historians have chronicled the rich history of black people's claims to autonomy, from the reconstitution and formation of families and the establishment of their own educational, religious, and self-help organizations to the thirst for land and political rights. They have paid less attention to how such matters informed black women's quest for dignity as much as land, family rights, and religious freedom. The term "autonomy," today's watchword of freedom from the bottom up, often conceals more than reveals how people acted, what they sought to achieve in action, or the actual standards on which their actions were based. In demanding better pay and working conditions, respect, and an end to the power of white women to control their lives, freedwomen demonstrated their belief that freedom alone, without dignity, pride, and their own self-fashioned identity, was a dead end.

In historical scholarship, freedom is often reified as a "thing" or a "place" that one can "obtain" or "go to." But freedom is not separate from the understandings and intuitions of those who seek it, or live it. It is related to, but not congruent with, its official features deliverable by the actions of the state and certainly not subsumable under what E. P. Thompson called "the need for respect and status among working people themselves."[21] Whatever one

---

[20] Douglass, *My Bondage and My Freedom*, p. 92.
[21] Thompson, *Making History*, p. 362.

(validly) says about wages and political participation as "freedom," an authentically historical vision cannot be deemed adequate unless it can accommodate Virginia Newman's idea of freedom: "a blue guinea with yaler spots."[22] This was Newman's first "bought dress," and it represented, for her, control over her "whole life" and, concomitantly, the diminished control white people had over it. In the same way, black people's claim to leisure time eroded the customary practices that slaveholders had relied on to exact the fullest measure of their labor.[23]

A wide world of actions can be formulated as the needs of identity, or the requirements of a particular "identity."[24] Actions also testify to the fact that freedom had to be built. Freedom for mistresses was not a thing or place, either, but once again, a wide world of actions. Virginia Newman's purchase of a store-bought dress emancipated her from her former mistress's purview and control, a key component of planter women's antebellum identity. Freedom meant that white women lost the power of giving "gifts" like clothing (made, of course, by their purported beneficiaries, of cloth purchased by their labor), and hand-me-downs (purchased, again, with profits from the labor of slaves) or to "help" their slaves (with problems resulting from slavery itself).

The small aspects of the large status of slavery and freedom come into view with the actions of Virginia Newman. Chapter 7 explores the operation of small oppressions in the exercise of power and the struggles of black women to unweave the inequalities that were a part of everyday life. Understanding the theoretical and narrative divide that has often separated discussions of the transformation of the plantation household and the agricultural economy in the postwar South is as central to this task as understanding how white women's domination fit into larger repressions. The priorities of black women that led them to seek part-time work in white homes, to remove tasks previously done in white homes to their own, and to turn labor in their own homes to the production of products for the market and their families had repercussions for women who did not turn to domestic work as a source of income. Those priorities helped to make for labor shortages in domestic work that, in turn, led former masters and mistresses to attempt to force women whose contractual obligations were to field labor to work overtime in white homes without pay. In the end, black women's struggles were joined, whether they labored as field hands, domestic workers, or in their own homes. Former slaveholders,

[22] George P. Rawick, ed., *The American Slave: A Composite Autobiography* (Westport, CT: Greenwood Press, 1979); Virginia Newman, *Texas Narratives*, vol. 5, pt. 3, Supplement Series 2, p. 151. Slave narratives in this series are hereafter cited by the name of the interviewee.

[23] See E. P. Thompson, "Patrician Society, Plebian Culture," *Journal of Social History* 7 (Summer 1974): 383 and 391.

[24] For a salient and sobering analysis of the use and misuse of "identity" as a category of analysis and of practice, see Rogers Brubaker and Frederick Cooper, "Beyond 'identity,'" *Theory and Society* 29 (2000): 1–47, and Frederick Cooper, *Colonialism in Question: Theory, Knowledge, History* (Berkeley: University of California Press, 2005).

however, could only see pathetic attempts on the part of black women to emulate white women, "wild notions" of right and wrong.

The victories black women won in the first years of freedom, however, were not to last. Poverty, landlessness, peonage, discrimination, and violence forced them back to the fields and white homes on a full-time basis. The overthrow of Radical Reconstruction and the subsequent disfranchisement of black men further hurt their efforts to move out from under the power and control of white Southerners. Still, black women refused to surrender all that they had achieved. They continued to seek just wages for their work and held on to the right to leave employers who demanded that they surrender their right to mobility. The organization of domestic alliance associations in the twentieth century by white women, to teach black women to be "better girls," was a backhanded tribute to black women's tenacity and continued struggle.

This is a study about the power of mistresses and its meaning for how black and white women thought about unfreedom, freedom, work, gender, citizenship, and race. It departs from most studies of nineteenth-century southern women in its focus on the power white women exercised over black women during slavery. It accords a signal place and active role to planter women in the maintenance of the plantation household, and to black women in its destruction. It connects white women's exercise of power in the domestic realm to black women's understanding of the kind of freedom they wanted to have and build. In building freedom, former mistresses and former slave women looked to their own material and cultural history.

This book adopts the perspective of a wide geographical canvas. My argument also relies on the broad chronological sweep deployed here as well. Slavery was not a fixed social or cultural entity; social relations within the plantation household changed over time.[25] And the postwar transformation of the household was heavily influenced by memories, real as well as invented, of what slavery had entailed. Any regional study such as that attempted here must of necessity rely on the scholarship of others. To tell this story, I am building on two generations of scholarship in southern, U.S., and comparative women's history. I am particularly indebted to Elizabeth Fox-Genovese's conceptualization of the "household" as an analytical construct. I have also benefited from the growing and increasingly rich literature on middle-class domesticity in the northern United States and in Victorian Britain and the British Empire. The theoretical insights of a number of scholars working on questions of violence,

---

[25] They no doubt vary over space as well. I have not pursued this question or questions about regional or class variations in social relations in the household. This is the subject of my future work, which explores in greater detail how the geography of the plantation household affected and determined social relations within it. What I am trying to do here is something else altogether, to expose *norms* that informed southern households during slavery and after emancipation from which local variation will subsequently be measurable. I look forward to exploring in my own work, and the future work of others, local variations within the regional culture portrayed here.

gender, race, domestic economy, and British imperialism help to expose the domestic realm of the slave South.[26]

The domestic realm is a central theme of recollections of slavery compiled by the Works Progress Administration (WPA) slave narratives project, particularly those of black women. Former slaves held a very different view of the mistress than is conveyed in memoirs written by white Southerners and in many scholarly studies. Ex-slave narratives construct a place where, over the course of the antebellum period, female slaveholders in households large and small played an increasingly central role in the evolution of slave society, including the exercise of control over slaves. Long before the Civil War, slave women began the campaign that they hoped would reorder the plantation household and the ideologies of labor, race, class, and gender that undergird it, a struggle that intensified during the Civil War. This struggle had implications for the domestic world of postwar plantations – its battles over land, wages, and southern womanhood. Relations between southern black and white women in the postwar South would play out against those forged in slavery.

The interconnections between past and present, and between slavery and freedom, are apparent in the ex-slave narratives. Black survivors of slavery spoke openly and publicly of a nongenteel white womanhood that was at odds with the Lost Cause propaganda that, by the time they gave their interviews, had long since achieved hegemony in the North as well as the South.[27] The incongruence between what these ex-slaves said and the dominant authorized discourse must have occurred to Mildred Snead, a white interviewer for the WPA, during an interview with Harriette Benton. Snead was pleased to find before her a woman who looked as "one imagines an ex-slave woman to look." She made this observation in her notes: "Her skin is dark, she wears a white cap on her head, and her dress is very full and made of blue gingham, with a spotless white starched apron." Further confirming the impression, the former slave "gave a very broad smile" as Snead expected, or imagined, she should.[28]

Benton's way of talking about slavery, at least initially, may have as well encouraged Snead to believe that she had indeed found a good likeness of the imagined and widely romanticized original: Someone like Maum Mary Ann, described by a member of her former master's family as "fat and black, with clean white palms and a cheerful face." "I never saw her," Anne Simons Deas wrote, "without a large white apron and a bright-colored head-handkerchief." Benton, however, swiftly disabused her interviewer of her preconceptions, disrupting Snead's effort at validation with inconvenient talk of slavery's troublesome nature, including the heavy and outrageous demands that it had placed

[26] See, for example, Ingrid H. Tague, *Women of Quality: Accepting and Contesting Ideals of Femininity in England, 1690–1760* (Suffolk, UK: Boydell Press, 2002).

[27] White, *Ar'n't I a Woman?*, p. 24, n.1, p. 183, n.6, p. 184; Camp, *Closer to Freedom*, p. 7.

[28] Harriet Benton, in *The American Slave: A Composite Autobiography*, ed. George P. Rawick (Westport, CT: Greenwood Press, 1977), *Georgia Narratives*, Supplement Series 1, vol. 3, pt. 1, pp. 50–51.

on women, ending with this admonishment: "honey chile yo wouldn't of had a chance, you'se so little bit."[29]

There is in Benton's narrative a kind of ambiguity, as exemplified in the above quote. On one hand, it seemed to play to the continued sway well into the twentieth century of notions of white women's delicacy and black women's roughness. It might even seem to indicate a certain sympathy with such notions. In important respects, however, it is unambiguously revisionist. Whatever comfort Benton's clothing conveyed, her own words did not, ultimately, permit refuge in a comforting past. Her former mistress, she stated unequivocally, "user have her slaves beat jes' to hear 'em holler."[30] Snead must have then recognized her error. Neither the white cap on Benton's head nor the immaculate white apron wrapped around her body ensured compliance with racist ideals or guidance to the past or the present. In powerful language, Benton placed her former mistress distinctly outside the bounds of female gentility. And in charging her former mistress with distinctly unladylike behavior, with not just cruel but sadistic behavior, Benton would have known that she violated southern racial etiquette.[31]

In the end, Benton stood as the antithesis of the "rare find" hoped for by white interviewers, ex-slaves who, as one interviewer put it, were "contented in their memories of the sparkling, gay South, the bounty and joy of a sun-kissed land," and would look "back into those luxurious pre-war days" to "tell tales of the abundance, the high living, the excitement and the fast pace of the courtly and chivalrous men and gracious women of the old slaveholding South."[32] Ann Parker, despite appearing (like Harriette Benton at first glance) to fit the bill, also did not. When Parker assured her interviewer that "we ole 'uns still knows dat we is got ter be perlite to you' white ladies,"[33] the comment, again, was not unambiguous, at once acknowledging the protections and power accorded white women by dominant ideologies of class and race and denying them legitimacy. It called into question the idea that white women were innocent victims of those ideologies. Parker was clear about this: The arrangement of

---

[29] Benton, *Georgia Narratives*, Supplement Series 1, vol. 3, pt. 1, pp. 50–51; Anne Simons Deas, *Recollections of the Ball Family of South Carolina and the Comingtee Plantation* ([Summerville?] SC: privately published, 1909), p. 166. After the war, Maum Mary Ann renamed herself. At the age of 79, she became Mary Ann Royal. She died the following year, in 1866 (Edward Ball, *Slaves in the Family* [New York: Farrar, Straus and Giroux, 1998], p. 162).

[30] Benton, *Georgia Narratives*, Supplement Series 1, vol. 3, pt.1, p. 52. Snead's sense of racial superiority led her to mistake a black woman's smile and dress as an expression of political obtuseness, as confirmation of racial ideology.

[31] The "onus for acquiring racial etiquette," Charles Van Onselen reminds us, has always been on the subjugated. Charles Van Onselen, "Race and Class in the South African Countryside: Cultural Osmosis and Social Relations in the Sharecropping Economy of the South-Western Transvaal, 1900–1950," *American Historical Review* 95 (February 1990): 116.

[32] Esther de Sola, interviewer, at Lucy Thurston, *Mississippi Narratives*, Supplement Series 1, vol. 10, pt. 5, p. 2110.

[33] Ann Parker, *North Carolina Narratives*, vol. 15, pt. 2, p. 157.

racial matters in the South required her to pay homage to white women, but it was a forced and insincere homage, paid only because *"still . . . we is got ter"* (emphasis added).[34]

Clothing her political sense in a no doubt perfected command of satire, Parker mocked the notion that the ritual etiquette expected of her was founded in anything other than the power of white people to command it and, concomitantly, the idea that white women warranted a special grace. She thus challenged the symbolic and ideological equipment of southern racism. In charging former mistresses with violent, unladylike conduct, with manufacturing dehumanizing spectacles for sadistic pleasure, ex-slaves violated the South's racial creed; in making the charges before the faces of white women, they added to the aggravation.[35]

What slaves had to say about mistresses is often treated as disjointed, merely rambling, anecdotal tales, told in a language that itself is not "real."[36] Why this is so and what impact it has had on our understanding of slavery, Reconstruction, and southern women are important questions. Foregrounding the matter, of course, are questions concerning the reliability of the main body of extant slave testimony, particularly the WPA interviews conducted in the 1930s, which, in conjunction with slaveholders' records, are used in this study as central texts in the exploration of power in the antebellum and postbellum South.[37]

The state of repression under which black people continued to live into the twentieth century clearly influenced the testimony of many ex-slaves. Fear of white retaliation sometimes led black people to check the impulse to condemn slavery and slaveholders.[38] Still dependent on the goodwill of southern white

---

[34] As Jerrold Hirsch notes, white interviewers were anxious to have the narratives conform to romantic and mythic notions of the antebellum South. (Hirsh, "Toward a Marriage of True Minds: The Federal Writers' Project and the Writing of Southern History," in *The Adaptable South: Essays in Honor of George Brown Tindall*, ed. Elizabeth Jacoway et al. [Baton Rouge: Louisiana State University Press, 1991], pp. 148–75).

[35] Giving voice to such sentiments could still be deadly into the twentieth century. As one black woman stated in 1942, "To hit back or to do too much talking, you could get murdered. You just don't look a white woman in the face and tell her that she was doing you wrong." As quoted in Darlene Clark Hine, "Rape and the Inner Lives of Black Women: Thoughts on the Culture of Dissemblance," in Darlene Clark Hine, *Hinesight: Black Women and the Re-Construction of American History* (Brooklyn, NY: Carlson Pub. Co., 1994), p. 42.

[36] On the concept of "real" language used here, see Dale Spender, *Man Made Language* (Boston: Routledge & Kegan Paul, 1980).

[37] For an elaboration of this point, see Armstead L. Robinson, "The Difference Freedom Made: The Emancipation of Afro-Americans," in *The State of Afro-American History: Past, Present, and Future*, ed. Darlene Clark Hine (Baton Rouge: Louisiana State University Press, 1986), pp. 51–74, especially p. 57.

[38] C. Vann Woodward, "History from Slave Sources," *American Historical Review* 79 (April 1974): 470–81; John W. Blassingame, "Using the Testimony of Ex-Slaves: Approaches and Problems," *Journal of Southern History* 41 (November, 1975): 473–92; John Blassingame, "Introduction," in *Slave Testimony: Two Centuries of Letters, Speeches, Interviews, and Autobiographies*, ed. John W. Blassingame (Baton Rouge: Louisiana State University Press, 1977); Rawick, "General Introduction," *The American Slave*, pp. xii–xxi. See also the important

administrators of Depression-era federal assistance programs, black people would have been concerned not to offend them or their relatives, living or dead. Some ex-slaves saw the interviews as a means to win support in their efforts to obtain government relief, sometimes explicitly requesting food or clothing as a condition of giving the interview. Lucy Thurston's interviewer had no doubt that she had "bought Lucy's confidence" for the interview with dresses and other material things and "no mean amount of Dale Carnegies' [sic] miraculous system."[39] Most of the men and women interviewed in the 1930s were elderly. Some had only been days old when the Confederacy fell; others were children, teenagers, or young adults. Most were still poor.

The fact that most of the participants of the Federal Writer's Project were young children when freedom came has been cited by scholars as one of the major weaknesses of the narratives for understanding slavery, along with their advanced age at the time of the interviews. These factors are said to account for the sentimentalism in the narratives, the expressions of devotion and love for masters and mistresses. The continued reliance of many black people on the "good will" of southern whites did make some black people more cautious about criticizing a time still revered by southern white people. This situation often discouraged candor, but not completely. Indeed, Charles S. Murray, a white interviewer, believed that the WPA project in general was dangerous. He thought former slaves would be more candid than desirable. In a confidential

insights in Leon F. Litwack, *Been in the Storm So Long: The Aftermath of Slavery* (New York: Vintage Books, 1979), p. xiii, and Jordan, *Tumult and Silence at Second Creek*, pp. 129–33.

More recently, Walter Johnson has explained his decision to exclude the WPA narratives, but not the abolitionist narratives, from his study of the domestic slave trade as grounded in his finding "the rhetorical situation of the interview by a white recorder in the 1930s South to have been a great deal more inhibiting than that which characterized the production of the abolitionist narratives" (Walter Johnson, *Soul by Soul: Life Inside the Antebellum Slave Market* [Cambridge, MA: Harvard University Press, 1999], p. 11, quote at n.24, p. 226). It is important to keep in mind, however, that the Federal Writers Project took place not only against the backdrop of economic distress and state repression but also against the background of the rumblings of renewed freedom and citizenship struggles by black people. State repression weighed in on one hand, but the depression that left many hungry and homeless and placed the welfare of black people in the South at the mercy of white southern politicians and bureaucrats also had the effect of making the state a more effective and active agent of social change. (See Nan Elizabeth Woodruff, "African-American Struggles for Citizenship in the Arkansas and Mississippi Deltas in the Age of Jim Crow," *Radical History Review* 55 [Winter 1993]: 33–52.) This circumstance may have been equally critical in how ex-slaves interviewed in the 1930s put things, giving them somewhat more courage to speak out.

39 Lucy Thurston, *Mississippi Narratives*, Supplement Series 1, vol. 10, pt. 4, pp. 2115–2120, quote at p. 2115. What oral testimony tends not to record is the way in which people say things or how they say them. This goes beyond the important questions of "voice" raised cogently by Allen Isaacman to that of expression. Howard Russell, for example, heard an elderly slave woman "boast" of having nursed her master. He noted, however, that she did not smile in doing so. (Allen F. Isaacman, "Peasants and Rural Social Protest in Africa," in *Confronting Historical Paradigms: Peasants, Labor, and the Capitalist World System in Africa and Latin America*, ed. Frederick Cooper et al. [Madison: University of Wisconsin Press, 1993], pp. 224–25; Howard Russell, *My Diary North and South* [Boston, MA: Burham, 1863], p. 258).

note to his state director, he confessed that he "thought from the first it was a mistake to write these ex-slave stories." "The general run of negro," he stressed, "is only too glad of the opportunity to record his grievances."[40] To discount slaves' testimony wholesale would grant Murray's wish that no record of real events should outlive its real perpetrators and victims.

For many ex-slaves, the WPA interviews represented their only and last formal opportunity to speak openly about slavery and "ole missus" in particular. Recalling memories of events they had witnessed or learned of from a parent or grandparent, ex-slaves in the 1930s told a story of women in slavery that did not bespeak sisterhood across race or class lines or a gentle and noble white womanhood. One former slave, identified in the record only as "Granny," thought that anyone reticent to talk about such matters was simply just a fool. And she had no patience for those whose deadly poverty in the 1930s made them nostalgic for the Old South. About an acquaintance who had the habit of saying "he wish he was a slave again, den he'd hab clothes giv him an' he wouldn't have no food to fin," she said, "But me, I'd raver have my freedom an' a piece o' bread a day. I was a dog in dose days." And for her, the Old South was "nothin' to eat, an all day long work and plow, an allus [always] ole missus."[41]

Some former slaves spoke favorably of former mistresses. This book does not address these narratives directly, but their inclusion would not alter the central argument here that the institution of slavery was a joint production of masters and mistresses and that violence in the plantation household formed as important a part of that production as it did in the fields. Further, narratives in which former slaves address violent behavior on the part of slaveholding women are all the more significant in that they explicitly reject the protocols of proper racial etiquette, and do so at a time when speaking one's mind was still a dangerous enterprise for black people. The far safer path was to speak generously of former mistresses. Even narratives that attribute kind tendencies to mistresses are not unambiguous. They might begin, for example, with a glowing description of nice servants' quarters, plentiful food, and kindly

---

[40] Hirsh, "Toward a Marriage of True Minds: The Federal Writer' Project and the Writing of Southern History," pp. 148–75, quote at p. 166.

[41] Blassingame, ed., *Slave Testimony*, p. 540. See also, Mary Ellison, "Resistance to Oppression: Black Women's Response to Slavery in the United States," *Slavery and Abolition* 4 (May 1983): 56. Black people's candor did not always come as a surprise to white interviewers. Mrs. Charles E. Wells, interviewing ex-slave Adaline Montgomery in the 1930s, noticed that Montgomery hesitated when asked her father's name. Wells correctly surmised the source of the hesitation, writing: "I helped her out. He must have been a white man?" She may not have anticipated what she next heard, that the white man was one of her relatives. At any rate, Montgomery herself renounced the caution that Wells thought explained her initial hesitatation. Her good clothes, Montgomery stated, had come from "My old grandmother *on your side*." And she had been taught to write by "My aunty *on your side*." Adaline Montgomery, *Mississippi Narratives*, Supplement Series 1, vol. 9, pt. 4, pp. 1513–16. The emphasis is in the document as printed in the series. It is not clear, therefore, whether Montgomery pronounced the distinction in her statement or whether the emphasis was later added either by Wells or someone in the WPA offices.

masters and mistresses and end with comments that snap the narrative of paternalism apart. Vina Moore's narrative is like this. She began noting kind treatment, but before she was done, she was talking about the many slaves she knew who ran away and were hunted "jes lak horses er mules." Indeed, she who had been so well treated had run off herself. When she returned, she stated, her mistress was happy to see her, so much so that, "She didn't whip me."[42] Obviously, a beating by her mistress was not considered out of the question.

Arrayed in the literature of the antebellum and postbellum South as exemplars of a special kind of slavery and a special kind of womanhood, slaveholding women stood before slaves (and ultimately themselves) as "the bedrock upon which slavery rested."[43] Slaves experienced the power of slaveholding women as such. Mistresses could and did order slaves punished, and could and did themselves punish and sell slaves. Slaves often remembered their "missus" as cruel, ignoble, and racist.

In the final analysis, this study examines the day-to-day practices that exalted southern hierarchies of race, gender, and class and the day-to-day practices that assaulted them. It is about black women's struggles and the merger of two fights – that at the level of the state and at the level of the personal – on behalf of freedom and a new order in social relations and gender ideals. Freedom gave black women the right to be mothers, workers, friends, and companions. They also thought it gave them the right to citizenship and dignity. The Civil War left in its wake not only death and destruction but the promise of free homes for black and white southerners. Mistresses's households had to die if black women were to seek abundant life, and if white women, no less, were too. Former planter women and their descendents, however, found free homes difficult spaces to inhabit and the practices required to make them free, difficult to grasp.

This book is clearly not about black women only. It is also, necessarily, about white women. And this is consequential. It is only by looking at the two, separate and together, as recent scholarship in Southern women's history has demonstrated, that we can begin to understand what the sources tell us and see how certain ways of looking can muffle that understanding. Imagining that slavery only happened to black people and that the movement of black women from the plantation household and their efforts to transform it was only complicated for them is the first step in the wrong direction. It is to ignore, as Douglass wrote, "that slavery is *itself* an abuse; that it lives by abuse; and dies by the absence of abuse."[44]

[42] Vina Moore, *Texas Narratives*, Supplement Series 2, vol. 7, pt. 6, p. 2760; see also, Stevenson, "Gender Convention."

[43] Barbara J. Fields, "Who Freed the Slaves?" in *The Civil War: An Illustrated History*, ed. Geoffrey C. Ward (New York: Knopf, 1990), p. 181.

[44] Douglass, *My Bondage and My Freedom*, p. 436.

I

The Gender of Violence

We were taught to speak very low and to be delicate in our ways.

Kathleen Boone Samuels, ex-mistress

Oh, Lawd, let me see the end of it afore I die, and I'll quit my cussin' and fightin' and rarin'.

Chloe Ann [Hodges], ex-slave

She didn't never do anything to make us love her.

Annie Hawkins, ex-slave

I grieve that you will never know the tender tie that existed between mistress and servant.

Mary Norcott Bryan, ex-mistress

"Course I'se born in slavery, ageable as I am. I am a old time slavery woman and the way I been through the hackles I got plenty to say about slavery." This is how, in the 1930s, Lulu Wilson began her interview, establishing first her authority to speak about a system that, she said, had "no good in it" and, among other subjects, about the man and woman who had owned her:

Now, Missus Hodges studied 'bout meanness more'n Wash [Hodges] done. She was mean to anybody she could lay her hands to, but special mean to me. She beat me and used to tie my hands and make me lie flat on the floor and she put snuff in my eyes. I ain't lyin' 'fore Gawd when I say I knows that's why I went blind.[1]

Her former master, Wash Hodges, was "jes' mean, pore trash and he was a bad actor and a bad manager." He beat and starved the few slaves he owned and kept up a steady pattern of selling her mother's children. Still, for Lulu

[1] Lulu Wilson in *The American Slave: A Composite Autobiography*, ed. George P. Rawick, *Texas Narratives*, Supplement Series 2, vol. 10, pt. 9 (Westport, CT: Greenwood Publishing Co., 1979), p. 4194.

18

Wilson, the master was "jes' mean," but the mistress "*studied* 'bout meanness"[2] (emphasis added). For Wilson, the difference between a mean disposition and a mean imagination was not superficial.

Wash Hodges fits the well-known paradigm of the bad master. Though she appears regularly in manuscript sources and historical accounts, no such paradigm exists for the bad mistress. Mrs. Hodges, however, provides us with a useful starting place. Wilson's description of her is the virtual antithesis of the paradigmatic good mistress with whom we have become so familiar. This "good" mistress dedicated her life to the never-ending task of managing her household and caring for her family and slaves in sickness and in health. Her comeliness was due in no small measure to her ability to satisfy all who depended on her, to manage a household rent by inequalities of race and gender with seeming equanimity. This ability was taught, of course, but it was also believed to be inherent in the very nature of white women, "racially natural-ized," in today's shorthand. According to Kathleen Boone Samuels, "We were taught to speak very low and to be delicate in our ways." The mistress, as Maria Bryan put it, was a lady of delicacy and unmatched "gracefulness," as compared to the not-to-be envied "precision and primness of a northern fine lady, erect and stiff."[3]

The Old South, according to Belle Kearney, reared "men and women of high breeding" who "lived like the landed gentry of the British Isles from whom most of them had descended," dispensing lavish hospitality. Kearney offered romantic sketches of summer homes in Mexico and presented the comings and goings of her family as spectacular public affairs. "As the cavalcade journeyed, outriders were sent in advance; as they approached the coast, they blew their bugles. When the inhabitants, living on the roadside heard the blasts, they exclaimed, 'The Kearneys are coming.'"[4] The work of professional historians has often lent an air of scholarly respectability to this view. U. B. Phillips, one of the first historians to give it scholarly sanction, wrote approvingly of mistresses: "Her presence made the plantation a home; her absence would have made it a factory." Mistresses, quite simply, made the plantation a civilized place.[5]

Birthed in proslavery ideology and elaborated in prescriptive literature, southern white women's educational models, memoirs, and diaries of the

---

[2] Wilson, *Texas Narratives*, Supplement Series 2, vol. 10, pt. 9, p. 4193.

[3] Elizabeth R. Baer, ed., *Shadows on My Heart: The Civil War Diary of Lucy Rebecca Buck* (Athens: University of Georgia Press, 1997), p. xvii; Carol Bleser, ed., *Tokens of Affection: The Letters of a Planter's Daughter in the Old South* (Athens: University of Georgia, 1996), p. 20.

[4] Belle Kearney, "The Patrician Days of Madison County," typed manuscript copy, Belle Kearney Papers, SHC. Kearney is perhaps best known today for her work with women's suffrage, and less so for her opposition to black freedom.

[5] Ulrich Bonnel Phillips, *American Negro Slavery: A Summary of the Supply, Employment and Control of Negro Labor as Determined by the Plantation Regime* (Baton Rouge: Louisiana State University Press, 1966), p. 323. The work of Julia Cherry Spruill accomplished this for the colonial era. See Spruill, *Women's Life and Work in the Southern Colonies* (1938; reprint, New York: W. W. Norton, 1972), see especially pp. 64–84.

Old South, the iconic image of the southern lady became a fixture of post-Reconstruction white supremacist campaigns. Generations of white southerners born after slavery, but trained in the tattered ideology of class and racial superiority that they inherited, took up the cause and reconstituted it on new ground. The white home was reinvented as a highly gendered and racialized sanctuary. There, white women would continue to be "ladies" and managers of domestic spaces, both white and black. This message was conveyed in film, commercial product advertisements, federal programs, popular fiction, white women's social club agendas, and every sort of domestic efficiency and home alliance organization, whether targeted to black or white women. The props looked familiar as they juxtaposed clean white homes and smiling black servants appropriately attired in language and dress. This narrative (some spotty and scattered disclaimers aside) has been told for the most part as if there were no other, as if Lulu Wilson's, Harriet Robinson's, or Harriette Benton's did not exist. In the 1930s, looking back, Robinson said that her mistress was the "meanest woman I ever seen in my whole life," "a nigger killer." Harriette Benton, although a slave for only seven years, remembered her mistress as "a debil in her own way."[6]

The distance that separated the plantation memories of white southerners from the realities that called them forth was vast. Women like Samuels, Bryan, and Kearney helped to create one of the most powerful and influential icons of womanhood in American history: the plantation mistress. There have been other powerful and influential ideals of American womanhood but, arguably, none as coveted and admired.[7] Juxtaposing the claims of this ideal against the violence to which Wilson, Robinson, and Benton testified brings to fuller view the literal as well as grammatical antagonism in the conjoined usage of the adjectives "delicate" and "slaveholding." The power of the plantation mistress is exposed to view when we realize that in the American South, as elsewhere, the "domestic realm [w]as a site of power for women." It was also and therefore a site of struggle *between* women. For in the American South, no less than in more traditionally hierarchical societies, "rank could overcome the handicap of gender."[8]

This chapter analyzes the treatment of women and slavery in feminist historiography of the American South. Historiography and the memories on which

---

[6] Harriet Robinson, *Oklahoma and Mississippi Narratives*, vol. 7, pt. 1, p. 271; Harriet Benton, *Georgia Narratives*, Supplement Series 1, vol. 3, pt. 1, pp. 50–51.

[7] The most oft-cited example of this entrancement is Margaret Mitchell's *Gone with the Wind* (New York: Macmillan, 1936).

[8] Quotes are from Ingrid H. Tague, *Women of Quality: Accepting and Contesting Ideals of Femininity in England, 1690–1760* (Suffolk, UK: Boydell Press, 2002), p. 97. In addition to the work of scholars of Southern women, my thinking about this question has benefitted from the following works: Amanda Vickery, *The Gentleman's Daughter: Women's Lives in Georgian England* (New Haven, CT: Yale University Press, 1998); Leonore Davidoff and Catherine Hall, *Family Fortunes: Men and Women of the English Middle Class, 1780–1850* (Chicago: University of Chicago Press, 2002); and Achille Mbembe, *On the Postcolony* (Berkeley: University of California Press, 2001), 26–27.

it is built are difficult to disentangle, particularly in cases where the ideological work of those remembering the past is so charged for the historians recounting it. As the task of women's history has broadened over time from its initial ambition to recover women's agency to more recent efforts to broaden the class and especially the racial composition of the "community" of women one studies, women's historians have not had difficulty in relating these stories sequentially. Difficulties arise, however, when the stories of women of different backgrounds encounter one another. The plantation household was just such a site of contact between women whose access to power, privilege, and opportunity, much less food, clothing, and citizenship, was vastly unequal. Unfortunately, gender wielded as a primary category of historical analysis often obscures as much as it reveals of the nature of the social relations between free and enslaved, white and black women in the plantation household. This has made for a partial reckoning but a powerfully influential historiography.

Over the past three decades, historians have revisited the world romanticized in Lost Cause propaganda, overturning many of its most cherished shibboleths. The publication in 1970 of Anne Firor Scott's *The Southern Lady: From Pedestal to Politics, 1830–1930* was a pivotal historiographical moment.[9] Questioning the traditional portrait of elite southern women as fragile flowers, Scott found that neither patriarchal standards nor slavery freed or protected elite southern women from the grind of labor. Their lives, in this aspect, differed little from those of the vast majority of the world's women. If anything, the joining of patriarchy and slavery made the lives of mistresses harsher and more difficult overall. Whatever privilege they derived from membership in the master class did not translate into pampered and frivolous lives. They customarily rose at "five or six . . . to be in the kitchen when the cook arrived," and from there went about the "difficult, demanding, frustrating, and above all never-ending work" of "supervising and managing slaves," and such tasks as making "their own yeast, lard and soap."[10] In sum, the southern lady was "a hardworking, introspective, pious, versatile wife and mother who spent a good bit of energy trying to live up to the prescriptions set before her by men." The gap between the prescribed ideal and reality produced discontented women who chafed at marital norms and hypocrisies, educational exclusions and limitations, and, indeed, at the very institution of slavery. This discontentment, Scott argues, weakened southern patriarchy.[11]

---

[9] Glenda Gilmore likens Scott's work, for example, to "[t]he equivalent of *Origins* [C. Vann Woodward, *Origins of the New South*] in southern women's history." Glenda E. Gilmore, "Gender and Origins of the New South," *Journal of Southern History* 67 (November 2001): 773.

[10] Anne Firor Scott, *The Southern Lady: From Pedestal to Politics, 1830–1930*, 25th Anniversary ed. (1970; Charlottesville: University Press of Virginia, 1995), pp. 31–36, quotes at pp. 31 and 36.

[11] Jacqueline Dowd Hall and Anne Firor Scott, "Women in the South," in *Interpreting Southern History: Historiographical Essays in Honor of Sanford W. Higginbotham*, ed. John B. Boles and Thomas Nolen (Baton Rouge: Louisiana State University Press, 1987), pp. 467–68, quote at p. 467.

Scott's work directed new attention to the study of elite southern women, increasingly focused on gender relations, race, and class. This new round of scholarship promised a re-calibration of the standards by which mistresses would be studied and judged. In the wave of scholarship that followed, the frills of the plantation mistress gave way to the burden of dust and grime, household chores, and hard-headed management of slave labor and extended households. Jacqueline Hall and Anne Scott, for example, credit Catherine Clinton's *The Plantation Mistress* with providing "compelling evidence of the hard work performed by mistresses on even the largest of plantations."[12] Susanna Delfino and Michele Gillespie concur, writing that "few plantation mistresses escaped lives of duty, drudgery, and weighty responsibility. The ordinary planter's wife led a very demanding life, for she provided food, clothing, and care for an extended household comprised of family members and slaves."[13] In this revision, the southern belle has also been transformed. Carol Bleser finds in the letters of Maria Bryan "a testament to the falseness of our standard portrait of the 'typical' plantation daughter in the antebellum South. Although supported by the labor of her family's slaves and comfortable by virtue of her rank and privilege, Maria is not Scarlet, the pampered pet of a southern patriarch."[14]

There are at least two problems with this revisionist line of argument. It is true, of course, and Jacqueline Jones and Drew Faust, for example, quite rightly point this out, that mistresses did little actual work themselves.[15] Moreover, pampered pets are something of a straw man or straw animal as it were. In its general contours, the revisionist scholarship diverges surprisingly little from the view advanced by southerners like U. B. Phillips and Joel Chandler Harris at the turn of the twentieth century, emphasizing the demanding nature of the work of managing slaves. Joel Chandler Harris readily dismissed the idea "that the white woman of the South lived in a state of idleness during the days of slavery, swinging and languishing in hammocks while bevies of pickanninies cooled the tropical air with long-handed fans made of peacock tails" as no more than "fiction." Rather, he submitted, they were "the busiest women the

---

[12] Hall and Scott, "Women in the South," p. 466. The application of postmodern theoretical analysis has added another stiff wrinkle: the resurrection of "mammy" as a powerful icon of crossing. Here, as in traditional accounts, "old black mammy waddles to the rescue," permitting late-nineteenth-century "new white women" a linkage "to those southern ladies of old," allowing them to "cross the gender line between the white home and the larger world without directly challenging the symbol of the southern lady" and "be ladies" again. (Grace Hale, *Making Whiteness: The Culture of Segregation in the South, 1890–1940* [New York: Pantheon, 1998], pp. 102–6; quote is at p. 106.)

[13] Susanna Delfino and Michele Gillespie, "Introduction," in *Neither Lady nor Slave: Working Women of the Old South*, ed. Delfino and Gillespie (Chapel Hill: University of North Carolina Press, 2002), p. 3.

[14] Bleser, ed., *Tokens of Affection*, p. xiv.

[15] Jacqueline Jones, *Labor of Love, Labor of Sorrow: Black Women, Work and the Family from Slavery to the Present* (New York: Vintage, 1985), p. 25; Drew Gilpin Faust, *Mothers of Invention: Women of the Slaveholding South in the American Civil War* (Chapel Hill: University of North Carolina Press, 1996), pp. 77–78.

world has ever seen."[16] In short, the idea of the "southern lady" living happily and lazily in subjection to patriarchal authority was apparently already dead or moribund when, in 1906, Harris called it "fiction."

Feminist historians have added a crucial ingredient to this portrayal of the southern lady as hardworking and self-sacrificing: her suffering under the weight of the same patriarchal authority to which slaves were subjected. This is widely assumed to have encouraged her concern for the plight of other women, slaves among them, and to have fueled in the process a general ambivalence about slavery itself.[17] Slaves, writes Catherine Clinton, "generally saw the mistress of the plantation as a positive influence on the slave system," and those "most likely to remember well of her were the house servants, the male slaves, and those who lived on large plantations." By this view, the mistress emerges from slave testimony as the plantation authority figure who pled for better treatment of slaves, "as a white woman who tried to live up to the responsibilities of her position."[18] Fox-Genovese's argument that mistresses represented the "feminine face of paternalism that endowed the ownership of some people by others with whatever humanity it could muster" supports this position. Fox-Genovese qualifies this "core of truth," however, acknowledging that enslaved women did not believe this. One of the problems here is that scholars seem to be of two minds about the role mistresses played, at once judging them violent and good. And enslaved women in the household are at once co-conspirators in elevating the notion of mistresses as the "softer, female head of the household," even as they see through the veil of compassion. The ideology of paternalism joins these contradictory ideas.[19] The historiography also posits an affinity on the part of black women to the slaveholders' ideal of womanhood. If such

---

[16] Joel Chandler Harris, "The Women of the South," reprinted in Rev. J. L. Underwood, *The Women of the Confederacy* (New York and Washington: Neale Publishing Co., 1906), p. 36.

[17] See, for example, Marli F. Weiner, *Mistresses and Slaves: Plantation Women in South Carolina, 1830–1860* (Urbana: University of Illinois Press, 1998), pp. 74–87; George C. Rable, *Civil Wars: Women and the Crisis of Southern Nationalism* (Athens: University of Georgia Press, 1984); Catherine Clinton, *The Other Civil War: American Women in the Nineteenth Century* (New York: Hill and Wang, 1984); Catherine Clinton, *The Plantation Mistress: Woman's World in the Old South* (New York: Pantheon, 1982); Jean E. Friedman, *The Enclosed Garden: Women and Community on the Evangelical South, 1830–1900* (Chapel Hill: University of North Carolina Press, 1985); Brenda E. Stevenson, *Life in Black and White: Family and Community in the Slave South* (New York: Oxford University Press, 1996); Elizabeth R. Varon, *We Mean to be Counted: White Women and Politics in Antebellum Virginia* (Chapel Hill: University of North Carolina Press, 1998). Important exceptions include Elizabeth Fox-Genovese, *Within the Plantation Household: Black and White Women of the Old South* (Chapel Hill: University of North Carolina Press, 1999); Norrece T. Jones, Jr., *Born a Child of Freedom Yet a Slave: Mechanisms of Control and Strategies of Resistance in Antebellum South Carolina* (Hanover, NH: University Press of New England, 1990).

[18] Clinton, *The Plantation Mistress*, pp. 187–88. Using data from a study by Elizabeth Craven, Clinton concludes that Craven's analysis "matches in many ways the images projected by [white] women in their own testimonies." See also, for example, Weiner, *Mistresses and Slaves*, pp. 87–88.

[19] Fox-Genovese, *Within the Plantation Household*, pp. 132–35; Brenda E. Stevenson, "Gender Convention, Ideals, and Identity among Antebellum Virginia Slave Women," in *More than*

an affinity in fact existed, it performed the impossible feat of excluding black women, by definition, and yet somehow inspiring their allegiance, or at least diminishing their resistance. Unlikely, that made them allies of white women, a fitting complement to the notion of white women as the best friends slaves could hope to have.

So, not only do mistresses, unlike masters, remain essentially unsullied by the violence, indecency, and racism endemic to slaveholding societies, they are also widely assumed to be "soft" on the question of slavery, in spite of the virtual absence of anti-slavery activity among them.[20] Their "silence on this issue was demanded and enforced."[21] However, to read in their silence, abolitionist sympathies, is to offer an anachronistic crutch most never asked for nor believed they needed. Slaveholding women, Elizabeth Fox-Genovese suggests, "emerge from their diaries and letters as remarkably attractive people who loved their children, their husbands, their families, and their friends, and who tried to do their best by their slaves." However, she does not find their humanity incompatible with the fact that they "accepted and supported the social system that endowed them with power and privilege over black women."[22] Revisionist scholarship chronicles mistresses's hard work, their often abject misery, designs at resistance, and concern for the plight of slaves, all of which is viewed as evidence of a general ambivalence about slavery.

We should not be surprised to find ambivalence about owning other human beings, or to find its expression in acts of kindness or expressions of concern. However, paternalism was as much a justification of slavery as its opposite; it did not require nor did it usually accompany any criticism of the institution of slavery itself. Moreover, ambivalence in the plantation household, like all households, found expression in a wide variety of often contradictory emotions as well as the actions they informed: love and hate, duty and negligence, fear and confidence, comfort and rage, struggled for the upper hand, not only across the wide spectrum of white slaveholding women but within individuals as well.[23] Ambivalence, then, lends innumerable interpretive possibilities to slaveholding women's silence on the subject of slavery. Silence by its very nature neither

Chattel: Black Women and Slavery in the Americas, ed. David Barry Gaspar and Darlene Clark Hine (Bloomington: Indiana University Press, 1996), pp. 182–83.

[20] Clinton, *The Plantation Mistress,* p. 182; Fox-Genovese, *Within the Plantation Household,* p. 132. See also Carol Bleser, "Introduction," in *Tokens of Affection,* ed. Bleser; Suzanne Lebsock, *The Free Women of Petersburg: Status and Culture in a Southern Town, 1784–1860* (New York: W. W. Norton, 1984), and more recently, Weiner, *Mistresses and Slaves.* This argument was also made by Clement Eaton in 1964. "Southern women," he wrote, "seem to have been less convinced of the rightness of slavery than the men." For a spirited rejoinder, see Rable, *Civil Wars,* pp. 31–42.

[21] Clinton, *The Plantation Mistress,* pp. 181–82 and 187; see also pp. 109, 176–79, and 189, quote is at p. 181; Fox-Genovese, *Within the Plantation Household,* p. 243.

[22] Fox-Genovese, *Within the Plantation Household,* p. 243.

[23] See, for example, Nell Irvin Painter, "Soul Murder and Slavery: Toward a Fully Loaded Cost Accounting," in Nell Irvin Painter, *Southern History Across the Color Line* (Chapel Hill: University of North Carolina Press, 2002), pp. 15–39.

supports nor limits anyone among them. Ultimately, we can never be sure what it does or does not mean. Action, however, is of a different nature, and so mistresses's violence against slaves provides a useful lens through which to examine their feelings about slaveholding.

The testimony of former slaves is replete with bitter memories of violent acts committed by mistresses. As Norrece T. Jones writes, slaveholding women were "depicted frequently [by slaves and ex-slaves] as the most stringent and sadistic of the manor born." He describes the plantation household as a "war zone" where "spilling milk, breaking dishes, and a variety of other kitchen peccadilloes could and often did trigger barbaric responses from slaveholders throughout South Carolina."[24] Fox-Genovese reminds us of the "pervasive conflicts of everyday life" in which mistresses's "racism could take nasty forms."[25]

Yet, historians have subjected white women's silence to far greater scrutiny than their violence. Scholarly treatment of women's violence betrays the ways in which gender as a primary category of analysis depends on its absence. Southern women's history often replicates structurally, if not substantively, Lost Cause propaganda arguing white women's purported natural delicacy. The obvious and crucial difference is, of course, feminist historians' investment in a more racially inclusive women's history. It is, however, an inclusiveness predicated on the assertion that "the system of bondage ultimately involved the subordination of all women, black and white," which renders white women's power well-nigh invisible.[26]

While acknowledged, white women's violence is rarely analyzed as a central facet of their existence. The idea of the southern lady was a major component of the ideology of race and class that structured relationships in the antebellum South, and, like the ideology to which it clung, it was unstable and riddled with contradiction. Obviously, the very idea of a violent white womanhood was

---

[24] Jones, *Born a Child of Freedom Yet a Slave*, p. 116; U. B. Phillips documented only one case of "systematic and wholesale torture of slaves," on the part of a mistress, a case he considered an aberration. Phillips, *American Negro Slavery*, pp. 511–12.

[25] Elizabeth Fox-Genovese, "To Be Worthy of God's Favor: Southern Women's Defense and Critique of Slavery," 32nd Annual Fortenbaugh Memorial Lecture, Gettysburg College, 1992, p. 12.

[26] Jones, *Labor of Love*, p. 25. See also Clinton, *The Plantation Mistress*. Elizabeth Fox-Genovese has argued compellingly against this standard, but her cautionary remarks have not had the impact they deserve. See Fox-Genovese, *Within the Plantation Household*. Mary Chesnut's discussion of women's subordination in the antebellum South is arguably the most perceptive contemporary account from a white woman's point of view. See especially C. Vann Woodward, ed., *Mary Chesnut's Civil War* (New Haven, CT: Yale University Press, 1981), pp. 168–70 and passim. In the original journal Chesnut composed during the Civil War, she did not hedge the question of white women's complicity in the construction and maintenance of slavery. In the aftermath of war and emancipation, however, she would adjust considerably her original remarks. See Thavolia Glymph, "African American Women in the Literary Imagination of Mary Boykin Chesnut," in *Slavery, Secession, and Southern History*, ed. Robert L. Plaquette and Louis Ferleger (Charlottesville: University Press of Virginia, 2000), pp. 140–59.

antithetical to the reigning ideology and to gender ideals that equated power over slaves with white men. If white women's active participation as members of the master class in the construction and management of slavery is to be minimized or denied, then it becomes necessary to minimize or ignore the portraits lodged in the memories of former slaves. Those portraits add violence to the "lady's" repertoire. In the Old South, writes Drew Gilpin Faust, violence was for white men. Even though "slave mistresses had in fact slapped, hit, and even brutally whipped their slaves – particularly slave women or children," nonetheless, their "relationship to this exercise of physical power was significantly different from men's," and it was not "celebrated."[27] A corollary argument holds that slaves, themselves, "saw the master as the source of authority on plantations."[28]

Violence on the part of white women during and after slavery is not only considered different because of who wielded it, it is transformed and made different through a gendered analysis of power. The power of white men was unquestionably formidable and it was a more visible entity, recognizable in the most tangible of forms: property ownership; the vote; access to public office; control of civic life; the legal subordination of white women, slaves, and free black people; and the sexual abuse of black and white women. But since, "in fact," mistresses "slapped, hit, and even brutally whipped their slaves," it is plain that their power was neither invisible nor insignificant. Besides, that power was also recognizable in tangible forms similar to masters' even if in diminished capacity: the legal subordination of slaves to mistresses, and their own citizenship, civic, and property rights, all of which was visible to slaves.

The power of slaveholding women seemingly, then, is mistaken as powerlessness and taken less seriously, not because it was invisible or unrecognizable as such, but primarily because the prevailing ideology, then and now, presumes it not to exist. "White and black women's complex and frequently conflicted relations with the premier custodian of their own specific and different subordinations," writes Fox-Genovese, "lay at the core of their identities and in their everyday lives in innumerable particulars."[29] How, then, could violence and power come from the hands of gentle creatures set apart from

[27] Faust, *Mothers of Invention*, pp. 62–70; Drew Gilpin Faust, "'Trying to Do a Man's Business': Gender, Violence, and Slave Management in Civil War Texas," in *Southern Stories: Slaveholders in War and Peace* (Columbia: University of Missouri Press, 1992), pp. 175, 189, and 191 and passim. See also Fox-Genovese, *Within the Plantation Household*, pp. 132–33 and 201, and Fox-Genovese, "To Be Worthy of God's Favor." Even yeomen women, Stephanie McCurry writes, learned that "the hand of power was never designed for [them]." Stephanie McCurry, *Masters of Small Worlds: Yeoman Households, Gender Relations, and the Political Culture of the Antebellum South Carolina Low Country* (New York: Oxford University Press, 1995), p. 215. Delicacy was generally less of a requirement for white women and poor white women, but even here the ideal was influential.

[28] Clinton, *The Plantation Mistress*, pp. 189 and 187; Faust, *Mothers of Invention*, p. 70; Marli Weiner, *Mistresses and Slaves*, pp. 72–76, 88, and 123–124; Nancy D. Bercaw, *Gendered Freedoms: Race, Rights, and the Politics of the Household in the Delta, 1861–1875* (Gainesville: University Press of Florida, 2003), p. 53.

[29] Fox-Genovese, *Within the Plantation Household*, p. 101.

the masculine world of violence, or from women whose primary referent was the patriarchal power to which *they* were subjected? How, from women whose violence was "tempered by fear" of the enslaved and not "celebrated"? In fact, Frederick Douglass wrote, white women's violence "was generally condemned, as disgraceful and shocking." But, he cautioned, "it must be remembered, that the very parties who censured the cruelty of Mrs. Hamilton, would have condemned and promptly punished any attempt to interfere with Mrs. Hamilton's *right* to cut and slash her slaves to pieces."[30] That "*right*" went virtually unchallenged. The general confinement of mistresses to the more collapsed geography of the household has contributed to the sense that they were less purposeful and effectual in their acts of violence. In the enduring story of the Old South, mistresses gently ran households and nurtured their families, black and white. That they nonetheless engaged in violent behavior has confronted many historians with the vexing problem of what to call mistresses's violence, and how to explain it.[31]

Some scholars settle for the middle road: Some mistresses were kind, others cruel, and that is that.[32] "Both opinions," Brenda Stevenson argues, "hold some validity," for "if one is to credit the plantation mistress with having significant impact on the lives of slaves, then one must credit her with contributing to a system that was oppressive and harsh." In the end, historians typically retreat to the comforting assumption that mistresses could be no more than they were for fear of jeopardizing their privileged position. The "credit" for all of slavery and its abuses and inhumanity reverts to masters. As Stephenson writes:

Few were willing to risk their husbands' disapproval, or worse, in order to protect even their favorite slaves. As women, even as wealthy women, they did not have the power to challenge the profoundly entrenched institution. Bound by the precepts of their roles as obedient, submissive wives, slaveholding women acted principally as their husbands' representatives in the lives of slaves, not as independent, rebellious agents out to reconstruct or even to refine the system. Slaveholding men both designed and perpetuated chattel slavery.[33]

Stevenson's argument on the need for clarity about mistresses's contributions to the oppressive conditions of slavery deserves praise. The next step, assigning

[30] Weiner, *Mistresses and Slaves*, pp. 86 and 89; Frederick Douglass, *My Bondage and My Freedom* (1855; reprint, New York: Dover Pub., Inc., 1969), p. 150. See also Douglass's description of the transformation of Sophia Auld, his mistress in Baltimore (pp. 152–54); Weiner, *Mistresses and Slaves*, p. 86.

[31] For mistresses, there were no equivalents to the publicly sanctioned outlets for violent impulses that existed for white men – such as duels, patrols, militia, and war. For a comparative perspective, see Hilary McD. Beckles, "Taking Liberties: Enslaved Women and Anti-Slavery in the Caribbean," in *Gender and Imperialism*, ed. Clare Midgley (Manchester, UK: Manchester University Press, 1998), pp. 137–57; Hilary McD. Beckles, "White Women and Slavery in the Caribbean," *History Workshop Journal* 36 (Autumn 1993): 66–82.

[32] Weiner, *Mistresses and Slaves*, pp. 85–88.

[33] Stevenson, *Life in Black and White*, pp. 198–99. Debates in British women's and colonial history and feminist scholarship, especially on the question of "recuperative history," inform my thinking on this question. See, for example, Janet Haggis, "White Women and Colonialism: Towards a Non-recuperative History," in *Gender and Imperialism*, ed. Midgley, pp. 45–75.

them any significant degree of independent will or authority, is another matter. "Cotton was King, white men ruled, and both white women and slaves served the same master," Catherine Clinton writes.[34] Mistresses were not masters, true. But when women slaveholders acted in the affairs of the household, a great deal of evidence says that they acted on their own authority, and not simply as their husbands' representatives. A great deal of evidence suggests that when black women resisted the plantation household, they resisted the authority that mistresses exercised.[35] To act independently in all matters, mistresses did not have to be masters. (Nor did they have to be political, social, or civic equals of their husbands, fathers, and brothers.) Allegiance to slaveholding was the only prerequisite.[36]

In general, a silence surrounds white women's contributions to the basic nature of slavery, its maintenance, and, especially, one of its central tendencies, the maiming and destruction of black life. With the silence goes an apparent reticence to probe mistresses's participation in the abuse of power even though slave ownership conferred that power on all white persons. The great house, whether a six-columned mansion or a rude house of four rooms, was a space of slavery and, thus, of domination and subordination. Where the silence is sometimes broken, it is most often replaced by grammatical conventions that diminish white women's complicity in the system or that mitigate their capacity for moral discernment. Here, it is possible to see how "trivializing the problem of reactionary ideological formations serves to divert attention from those very forces."[37]

Some decades ago, Kenneth Stampp must have had in mind something truly hideous when he found this odd formulation: "Men and women, otherwise 'normal,' were sometimes corrupted by the extraordinary power that slavery conferred upon them."[38] Yet, violent behavior on the part of slaveholding women, or at their direction, is often excused or explained away as inconsequential and nonsystemic, as essentially unconnected to the culture of slavery, that is, nonessential to its operation. Rather, it is explained as variations of

---

34 Clinton, *The Plantation Mistress*, p. 35.

35 Fox-Genovese, *Within the Plantation Household*, pp. 110, 102, and 135, quote at p. 102. Fox-Genovese also argues that "the vast majority" of mistresses acted as "delegates of the master, or male authority," and that slave women's resistance in the household was a protest of the master's authority (Fox-Genovese, *Within the Plantation Household*, p. 110).

36 The habit of seeing any independent action or thought on the part of mistresses as having always to be linked to the question of abolition rather than allegiance to slaveholding, has played a part in obscuring the active engagement of mistresses in the maintenance of slavery. The questions are not unrelated, but the manner in which they are generally posed and linked contributes to an underestimation of the power of mistresses and their complicity in the making of the world of slavery.

37 Susan Thorne, "Fungusamongus: Or, An Imperial Idea without Enemies," *Journal of British Studies* 33 (Jan. 1994): 115–16. In part, as Susan Thorne writes, the problem lies in "restoring the essentially moral challenge of collusion to the center stage of our analysis of colonial as well as women's history" (p. 116).

38 Kenneth M. Stampp, *The Peculiar Institution: Slavery in the Antebellum South* (New York: Knopf, 1956), p. 182.

capriciousness and hysteria: "spontaneous outbursts of rage," expressions of temporary "petulance" (a mechanism that allowed mistresses to vent anger at their own subjection), or in other ways that suggest irregular rather than systemic behavior on the part of a subordinated member of the weaker sex. Cast this way, the violence that slaves suffered at the hands of slaveholding women appears less noxious, less an integral part of the complex and complicated goal of mastery, more a matter of ill humor, and a kind of tit for tat beyond the realm of historical investigation and analysis, more a problem in "human relations," than labor relations, and history.[39]

Attributing violence from the hands of white women to mere "petulance" or explaining it as "spontaneous outbursts" dislodges white women from their place at the slaveholder's table, even as it submerges their human and historical agency. What might be called the entrapment argument works similarly. Here, the mistress was "trapped within a system over which she has no control, one from which she has no means of escape."[40] Mistresses become passively submissive rather than active participants and initiators who "directly participated in and benefited from a labor system far more degrading than patriarchy at its worst."[41] This was not the mistress Douglass saw in Mrs. Hamilton's "brutal and revolting inflictions" on her slaves, Mary and Henrietta. And the "deeper shade" to her conduct affected him as much: "That almost in the very moments of her shocking outrages against humanity and decency, she would charm you by the sweetness of her voice and her seeming piety."[42]

The psychological and political needs of masters and mistresses to see themselves as honorable, just, and loved by their slaves no doubt encouraged a kind of blindness to inconsistencies that could be sated in expressions of ambivalence as well as justified by religious teaching, racist thinking, or paternalism. The same mistress who put out a female slave's eye at the dinner table, on Sunday mornings read the Bible to her slaves, punctuating the reading with pictures of the devil, who, she explained, punished slaves who stole or told lies.[43] Another

---

[39] See, for example, the recent intervention by Stephanie M. H. Camp (*Closer to Freedom: Enslaved Women and Everyday Resistance in the Plantation South* [Chapel Hill: University of North Carolina Press, 2004], pp. 42–43).

[40] Clinton, *The Plantation Mistress*, p. 35; Jones, *Labor of Love*, pp. 20–26. In a later work, Clinton partially revises this assessment, at least for the colonial period, writing that white women "were forced into full partnership in the building of the plantation South." Clinton, *Tara Revisited: Women, War, & the Plantation Legend* (New York: Abbeville Press, 1995), p. 29.

[41] Rable, *Civil Wars*, p. 31.

[42] Douglass, *My Bondage and My Freedom*, p. 149.

[43] Ida Henry, *Oklahoma Narratives*, vol. 7, p. 135. Such logic is still operative in parts of the country. In the late twentieth century, Alabama Governor Fob James, Jr., reintroduced chain gangs, used state money to send biology teachers a book on creationism, and encouraged the state's public school teachers to return to old-fashioned discipline. In a 1997 article entitled, with no obvious irony, "Different New South," James is quoted as advocating the following solution to the problem of youth violence: "A good butt-whipping and then a prayer is a wonderful remedy." *The New York Times*, August 29, 1997, A20.

former slave recalled that after beating her, her mistress would "read the Bible to me till I got qualified."[44]

These needs beg for historical explanations. Instead, we have too often accepted at face value contemporary efforts to explain them away. We are left simply with a slave society where "brutal and sadistic masters and mistresses did not represent the norm, but they did exist," where some were "irresponsible," some "psychopaths," and some "reasonably humane," where mistresses's violence is deemed "seldom calculated or premeditated." We are left with the unsatisfying proposition that "even more average and basically humane slaveholders had their share of bad moments of acute irritability. Typically, they wanted something; typically, the servants failed to measure up to the constant demand for steady, cheerful, reliable, total service; typically, blows fell."[45]

Anger in the heat of the moment does not necessarily, or generally, prompt people to gouge the offending party's eyes out, though it can do this, and worse. Why should it be that even brutality at the hands of white women that went beyond the "normal" level of slave punishment is deemed "seldom calculated or premeditated"? Supposing this was true, it would still miss the point. If, "in the heat of the moment a mistress might strike out with whatever was handy," she nonetheless had to be preconditioned to this kind of response. She lived in a world in which actions of this kind were accepted as understandable if not laudatory "slips." She also lived in a world that denied to her witnesses, particularly the slaves among them, the recourse to restrain or retaliate. And finally, she lived in a world that did not construe her actions as damaging to her reputation as *compos mentis*.

All societies recognize a continuum of violence and advocate distinctions between legitimate and illegitimate violence, criminal homicide and justifiable homicide, random violence and coordinated violence. The slave South was no different in this way. Historians have, unwittingly perhaps, adopted antebellum taxonomies that classify white women's violence against slaves as random or "normal" violence. Random, normal violence is defined as unpremeditated violence generally on a small scale. Its normalcy exists, theoretically, in its ordinariness and its unexpectedness.[46] Of course, this kind of violence was arguably of greater importance to the reproduction of slaveholders' power than violence of a more dramatic and less routine nature.

---

[44] Henry L. Swint, ed., *Dear Ones at Home: Letters from Contraband Camps* (Nashville, TN: Vanderbilt University Press, 1966), p. 42.

[45] Stampp, *The Peculiar Institution*, p. 182; Wilma King, *Stolen Childhood: Slave Youth in Nineteenth Century America* (Bloomington: Indiana University Press, 1995), p. 95; Fox-Genovese, *Within the Plantation Household*, pp. 132 and 201; Fox-Genovese, "To Be Worthy of God's Favor;" Genovese, *Roll, Jordan, Roll*, p. 333.

[46] A large body of literature on domestic violence examines this notion of normal violence. Random violence is explored in Joel Best, *Random Violence: How We Talk about New Crimes and New Violence* (Berkeley: University of California Press, 1999). See also, Melanie Perreault, "'To Fear and to Love Us': Intercultural Violence in the English Atlantic," *Journal of World History* 17 (March 2006): 71–93.

The ruling classes of slave societies resorted to large-scale violence and brutality only in the last analysis. Their day-to-day domination depended more on their slaves' knowledge that their mistresses and masters *could* kill them but also subject them to the constant experience of "normal" violence. Ria Sorrell's memory of the petty cruelties to which she was subjected haunted her long after emancipation. Her mistress "would hide her baby's cap an' tell me to find it. If I couldn't fin' it, she whipped me."[47] This kind of gratuitously perverse mental cruelty, with physical violence, reveals normative behavior in slave societies perhaps more clearly than "spontaneous" violence segregated from ordinary life by idiosyncratic moments of non-premeditation. Such occasional or spontaneous acts of violence can be said to be "premeditated" in the important sense that their randomness and, sometimes, unpredictability were far more effective reminders of what could happen than sustained predictable assaults would be, not least because it left, more often than not, valuable labor power standing, if subdued.

In the end, white women's agency has been profoundly underestimated.[48] While conceding that slaveholding women internalized the social values of the Old South and reaped the rewards of slave labor, historians have been less clear about the role mistresses played in the construction of these values and in disciplining slaves. By the outbreak of the Civil War, slaveholding women had become, in fact if not in law, central partners in slavery's maintenance and management, more solidly members of the ruling class in their own right despite whatever civil and social disabilities they suffered because they were not men. No doubt, being women made their part in the stewardship of slavery awkward and difficult at times, but that part was not untenable or resisted.

White women's gender subordination merits attention in its own right and for its own sake; its overthrow is part of human emancipation. To appreciate, however, that resistance to gender subordination stands distinct from opposing slavery, it is enough to do a thought experiment. If rich women in the Cotton Kingdom had gained equal rights with their men, how likely is it that they would have agitated for their slaves' emancipation? Without the ideological and historical screens that obscure the plantation household as a place where white women ruled, the practical world of violence by women and the threat of it comes into view. The point of the screens thus becomes immediately obvious, for the practical reality of routine domination is not easy to look upon.

---

[47] Ria Sorrell, *North Carolina Narratives*, vol. 15, pt. 2, pp. 300–302, quote is at p. 302; Genovese, *Roll, Jordan, Roll*, pp. 333–34.

[48] As shown by two studies of slave punishment that fail to mention white women at all, some scholars do not see white female power at all. See Stephen C. Crawford, "Punishments and Rewards," in *Without Consent or Contract. Technical Papers: The Rise and Fall of American Slavery*, 2 vols. *Conditions of Slave Life and the Transition to Freedom*, vol. 2, ed. Robert William Fogel and Stanley L. Engerman (New York: W. W. Norton, 1992), pp. 536–50; Charles Kahn, "An Agency Theory Approach to Slave Punishments and Rewards," in *Without Consent or Contract*, ed. Fogel and Engerman, pp. 551–65.

"Beyond the Limits of Decency"

Women in Slavery

Two-thirds of my religion consists in trying to be good to negroes because they are so much in my power, and it would be so easy to be the other thing.

Mary Boykin Chesnut, mistress

One day my mistress called fer me to come in to the house, but no, I wouldn't go. She walks out and says she is gwine make me go. So she takes and drags me in to the house. Then I grabs that white woman, when she turned her back, and shook her until she begged for mercy. When the master comes in, I wuz given a terrible beating with a whip but I did'ny care fer I give the mistress a good'un too.

Sophia Word, ex-slave

Nature has done almost nothing to prepare men and women to be either slaves or slaveholders.

Frederick Douglass, ex-slave

The plantation legend crafted before and after slavery enveloped mistresses in an aura of light and vulnerability, goodness and agreeableness, but slaves witnessed differently. Mandy Cooper failed to churn the milk fast enough and there was no butter for her mistress's noon meal. As punishment, she stated, "three white women beat me from angah [anger] because they had no butter for their biscuits and cornbread. Miss Burton used a heavy board while the missus used a whip."[1] She did not state what weapon the third woman used. Alice Shaw, assigned to fan flies and clear the table after dinner, dropped a dish. As punishment, her mistress beat her on her head. Clara Young did not always respond quickly enough to her mistress's summons. Her mistress lifted her dress and beat her.[2] Lila Nichols's mistress beat her whenever the baby

---

[1] Mandy Cooper in *The American Slave: A Composite Autobiography*, ed. George P. Rawick, *Alabama and Indiana Narratives*, vol. 6 (Westport, CT: Greenwood Publishing Co., 1972), p. 62. Hereafter cited by name of interviewee.

[2] Alice Shaw and Clara Young, *Mississippi Narratives*, Supplement Series 1, vol. 10, pt. 5, pp. 1921 and 2401.

chickens died and when she collected too few eggs from the chicken house. The same mistress, convinced that another female slave was trying to poison her, got up from her sick bed to strip and beat the woman, leaving her back "in gashes." She then ordered the slave woman chained until she had recovered sufficiently enough to be sold.[3]

Born into slavery in Virginia, sold to Georgia and later to Louisiana, Delia Garlic was a grown woman by the time of the Civil War. One of her former mistresses cruelly burned her. Blamed for an injury to the hand of her mistress's baby, Garlic said, her mistress "pick up a hot iron an' run it all down my arm an' han.'" The iron was hot enough to take "the flesh off when she done it." Another mistress beat her with a piece of stovewood.[4] In George Jackson's hell, the mistress "would jump me and beat me" whenever she was not satisfied with the way he weeded the garden.[5] Another former slave described her mistress as an "awful mean and exacting" woman who "used to beat me like I was a dog – hit me across the head with tongs or poker or anything." Her assigned work, "cleaning floors, polishing silver, wiping floors, waiting on the table, and everything," put her in the direct path of her mistress's power. Her mother, the cook, suffered as witness, helpless to intervene.[6]

Slavery, Delia Garlic concluded, "wuz hell."[7] And it was as much hell in the plantation household, where mistresses were principal perpetrators of violence, as it was in the cotton, tobacco, sugar, and rice fields. Violence permeated the plantation household, where the control and management of slaves required white women's active participation and authorized the exercise of brute or sadistic force. Mistresses became expert in the use of psychological and physical violence and, from their perch in the household, influenced the construction of antebellum slave society in its gender and racial dimensions.[8]

Hellish punishment did not require large transgressions. The young female slave whose mistress beat her like a dog also suffered for her inability to go up and down a wooden staircase noiselessly. Her mistress called her a "black bitch" and threatened to kill her for going up the stairs "like a horse." On

---

[3] Lila Nichols, *North Carolina Narratives*, vol. 15, pt. 2, pp. 148–49.

[4] Delia Garlic, *Alabama Narratives*, vol. 6, p. 130. The use of hot irons by mistresses to torture slave women is also documented in Theodore Weld, *American Slavery As It Is: Testimony of a Thousand Witnesses* (Westport, CT: Negro Universities Press, 1970), p. 26.

[5] George Jackson, *Ohio Narratives*, vol. 16, pt. 4, p. 46.

[6] Clifton H. Johnson, ed., *God Struck Me Dead: Religious Conversion Experiences and Auto-biographies of Ex-Slaves* (Philadelphia: Pilgrim Press, 1969), pp. 153–54. Slave children suffered violence and witnessed violence against their parents. See, for example, Frederick Douglass, *My Bondage and My Freedom* (1855; reprint, New York: Dover Publications, 1969), p. 93.

[7] Delia Garlic, *Alabama Narratives*, vol. 6, p. 129.

[8] On the need for studies of the psychological costs of slavery, see Deborah Gray White, *Ar'n't I a Woman? Female Slaves in the Plantation South*, rev. ed. (1985; New York: W. W. Norton, 1999), pp. 9–10, and Nell Irvin Painter, "Soul Murder: Toward a Fully Loaded Cost Accounting," in Painter, *Southern History Across the Color Line* (Chapel Hill: University of North Carolina Press, 2002), pp. 15–39.

another occasion, her mistress called her a "nappy-head bitch" and, though sick, mustered enough strength to "try to hit me."[9] Maria White's mistress beat the slaves in her household whenever their work displeased her. Austin Steward's mistress was "continually finding fault" and "frequently punished slave children herself by striking them over the head with a heavy iron key, until the blood ran." And even when not doing violence, she threatened violence. She "always kept by her side when sitting in her room," a cowhide whip, expecting, one imagines, to always find occasion to use it.[10]

Sometimes the punishments of hell required no transgressions at all on the slaves' part. One mistress used the occasion of instructing her children in spelling to beat a female slave. "At every word them chillun missed," Harriet Robinson remembered, "she gave me a lick 'cross the head for it." Sarah Carpenter Colbert told her interviewer that her former mistress whipped slaves on a regular every-morning schedule; Hannah Plummer told how Caroline Manly, the daughter-in-law of North Carolina Governor Charles Manly, whipped her mother "most every day, and about anything, sometimes stripping her to her waist before beating her with a carriage whip." Jacob Branch's mother received a whipping every wash day.[11] Sometimes punishment depended simply on mood. Emma Johnson's mistress could show kindness when in "a good humor" and switch faces and moods just as easily: "When 'Old Harry' got in her, she was mean."[12]

In some cases, differences in character accounted for differences in women's resort to violence against slaves. Fannie Moore, born a slave in 1849 on the Moore plantation on the Tiger River in upstate Moore, South Carolina, answered to two mistresses, her master's wife and his mother, Granny Moore. She does not mention having ever been beaten by her mistress, but she described her master's mother as a "rip-jack," a woman for whom slaves were "jes like animals" and "didn't need nothin' to eat" and who seemed to take pleasure in mistreating them. "She whipped me many a time wif a cow hide," Moore stated. The mother-in-law's "rip-jack" character also emerged in the treatment of another woman, who she beat for resisting the advances of the overseer, and who he had already impregnated twice. When the slave woman would "not do what he ask he tell Granny Moore," who would then call "Aunt Cheney to de kitchen and make her take her clothes off den she beat her til she jes black an'

[9] Johnson, ed., *God Struck Me Dead*, quote is at p. 154; see also pp. 155 and 161.

[10] Maria White, *Mississippi Narratives*, Supplement Series 1, vol. 10, pt. 5, p. 2277; Austin Stewart, *Twenty-Two Years a Slave, and Forty Years a Freeman* (1856; reprint, New York: Negro Universities Press, 1968), p. 17.

[11] Harriet Robinson, *Oklahoma and Mississippi Narratives*, vol. 7, p. 271; Sarah Carpenter Colbert, *Alabama and Indiana Narratives*, vol. 6, p. 57; Lucretia Heyward, *South Carolina Narratives*, vol. 2, pt. 2, p. 279; Hannah Plummer, ibid., p. 180; Jacob Branch, *Texas Narratives*, vol. 4, pt. 1, p. 139.

[12] Emma Johnson, *Mississippi Narratives*, Supplement Series 1, vol. 8, pt. 3, p. 1153; Elizabeth Fox-Genovese, *Within the Plantation Household: Black and White Women in the Old South* (Chapel Hill: University of North Carolina Press, 1988), p. 135.

blue." Fannie Moore's overall judgment was that black people were treated no "more than effen dey was a dog."[13]

Mistresses's violence against slave women in the plantation household ran along a continuum: Bible-thumping threats of hell for disobedience, verbal abuse, pinches and slaps, severe beatings, burnings, and murder. Frederick Douglass described one victim as "pinched, kicked, cut and pecked to pieces," with "scars and blotches on her neck, head and shoulders."[14] The weapons mistresses took up against slaves ran the gamut from brooms, tongs, irons, shovels, and their hands to whatever was most readily available. Some mistresses did not leave the matter of choice of weapons to chance. The cowhide whip is ubiquitous in the slave narratives. It sat beside mistresses as they read to their children, knitted, or as they sat and rocked in their chairs doing nothing, as Frederick Douglass observed of "the psalm-singing Mrs. Hamilton," whose mistreatment of two slave women was common knowledge in the white community:

She used to sit in a large rocking chair near the middle of the room, with a heavy cowskin... and I speak within the truth when I say, that those girls seldom passed that chair, during the day, without a blow from that cowskin, either upon their bare arms or upon their shoulders. As they passed her, she would draw that cowskin and give them a blow, saying, '*move faster, you black jip!*' and, again, '*take that, you black jip!*' continuing, *if you don't move faster, I will give you more.*' Then the lady would go on, singing her sweet hymns, as though her *righteous* soul were singing for the holy realms of paradise.[15]

The cowhide whip, usually about three feet long, made from dried, untanned ox hide, was a weapon designed to cut the flesh and draw blood. Douglass described it "as hard as a piece of well-seasoned live oak" and "elastic and springy." The latter characteristic drew from its design: The whip was tapered from the part held by the hand to a point at the end. Douglass thought it was a more fearsome weapon than the more legendary cat-'o-nine tails. "It is a terrible instrument," he wrote, "and it is so handy, that the overseer can always have it on his person, and ready for use." And so the whip was for mistresses.[16] One mistress was reported to have beaten a female slave to death with one.[17]

Mistresses sometimes coupled physical violence with psychological violence. Slave children in the white household were introduced to these practices from an early age. The same hands, tongs, and shovels used in violence against adults were applied to children. Madison Jefferson said that his mistress pulled his hair

---

[13] Fannie Moore, *North Carolina Narratives*, vol. 15, pt. 2, pp. 128–37; quotes at pp. 128 and 131.

[14] Douglass, *My Bondage and My Freedom*, p. 150.

[15] Douglass, *My Bondage and My Freedom*, pp. 149–50; White, *Ar'n't I a Woman?*, p. 50.

[16] Douglass, *My Bondage and My Freedom*, p. 103. The cowhide whip was available in different colors: red, blue, and green.

[17] Henry Walton, *Mississippi Narratives*, Supplement Series 1, vol. 10, pt. 5, p. 2168.

so hard it came out and pinched his ears so hard that they bled. In addition to abusing enslaved children herself, she forced them to abuse each other. She had them "get a basin of water, and scrub each others faces with a corn cob . . . till they bled under the affliction." He thought she looked for excuses to find fault with their work and to beat them, and that she took voyeuristic pleasure in observing their pain. Some evidence also suggests that slaveholding women who beat their slaves and/or were beaten by their husbands, in turn, abused their own children. Eliza Bird's husband, a respected physician, beat her publicly in the streets. According to one account, local gossip held that their daughter had "the united temper of both parents," and was "withal . . . most wretchedly managed, sometimes whipped severely when her mother is in a passion, and then indulged in every whim as if to make up for the severity that had been used."[18]

Whatever form it took or instruments it involved, violence in the plantation household transgressed the idea of white female gentility. Mistresses's use of violence against slaves, often not the least bit shyly, underscored the fragility of the ideal even as southern patriarchy and the proslavery ideology ironically backed their right to do so. In fact, physical conflict seems to have occurred much more frequently between mistresses and slaves than between masters and slaves.[19] More than masters, mistresses seem to have ignored strictures governing slave management. At the same time, husbands and fathers often counseled restraint even as they turned a blind eye when mistresses ignored the counsel.[20] Slaves fought back, even knowing the price they would have to

---

[18] First quote is from John W. Blassingame, ed., *Slave Testimony: Two Centuries of Letters, Speeches, Interviews, and Autobiographies* (Baton Rouge: Louisiana State University Press, 1977), p. 218. Second quote is from Carol Bleser, ed., *Tokens of Affection: The Letters of a Planter's Daughter in the Old South* (Athens: University of Georgia Press, 1996), p. 108. Mistresses's abuse of enslaved children tempers the view that they played a central and positive role in the socialization of enslaved children. For this view, see White, *Ar'n't I a Woman?*, pp. 52–53, and Marli F. Weiner, *Mistresses and Slaves: Plantation Women in South Carolina, 1830–80* (Urbana: University of Illinois Press, 1998), p. 82. On the abuse of slave children, see also Painter, "Soul Murder," pp. 22–25.

[19] Eugene D. Genovese, *Roll, Jordan, Roll: The World the Slaves Made* (New York: Vintage Books, 1974), p. 333.

[20] A subject in need of study is the relationship between violence in the South and the widespread use of drugs like opium and its derivative, morphine, among elite women. Elite women and men readily and casually referred to the use of narcotics but rarely discussed drug addiction. Addiction, however, clearly wreaked havoc on the lives of some women and their families. Writing to his wife, Josiah Turner complained of the "deep mortification" her addiction to morphine caused him. Six years later the problem had apparently not diminished. Turner confessed to his wife's brother that it had made their home a place of "torture and torment" (Mary Moulton Barden, "Epilogue," in Catherine Ann Devereux Edmondston, *"Journal of a Secesh Lady": The Diary of Catherine Ann Devereux Edmondston*, ed. Beth G. Crabtree and James W. Patton [Raleigh: North Carolina Division of Archives and History and Department of Cultural Resources, 1979], p. 735). The Civil War created supply problems that were only partially alleviated by an increase in the acreage devoted to home-grown poppies. The Confederate government called on women and children to grow poppies as a patriotic duty for medicinal use on the battlefield. The effort was initially embraced enthusiastically, but very little opium was gathered and sent to Confederate doctors at the front (Parthenia A. Hague, *A Blockaded Family: Life in Southern Alabama During the Civil War* [Boston: Houghton,

pay. Peace accords were as fragile as the last dish broken or the most recent failure of a household slave to move fast enough. John Rudd's mother was one of many who returned her mistress's blows. It led to her being sold. With her child about to be sold, the slave Fannie fought her mistress, kicking and biting and tearing her clothes off. Silvia DuBois also fought her mistress.[21] Josie Jordan's mother and her mistress fought it out in the kitchen after the mistress had attempted to beat Jordan's mother with a broom for working too slowly.[22] Sophia Word was a young woman when she and her mistress tussled.[23]

The usual discussions of slave resistance and white female violence – day-to-day resistance in particular – cannot alone account for what happened between Sophia Word and her mistress or many of the other incidents recounted here. Day-to-day resistance, as Eugene Genovese notes, "generally implied accommodation and made no sense except on the assumption of an accepted status quo the norms of which, as perceived or defined by the slaves, had been violated."[24] It is possible that Sophia Word's mistress had on previous occasions tolerated Word's slowness in coming when called. It is also possible that she had used violence before and that Word simply decided she would not take a beating this time. These questions cannot be decided firmly from the available evidence but two things seem quite clear: Word did not hold her mistress in any esteem while her mistress did not feel hampered in her actions by notions of southern white womanliness. Neither did Jane Moore, a Kentucky mistress, who thought it a good idea to sneak up on one of her household slaves with a long whip hidden under her apron. She ended up fleeing, barely escaping a butcher knife thrown at her retreating back by the woman she had planned to whip.[25] The plantation household as a work site was always problematic.[26]

A kind of warring intimacy characterized many of the conflicts between mistresses and slave women in the household. The vision of a mistress dragging

Mifflin and Co., 1888], pp. 32–33; Mary Elizabeth Massey, *Ersatz in the Confederacy: Shortages and Substitutes on the Southern Homefront* [1952; reprint, Columbia: University of South Carolina Press, 1993], p. 121). For brief references to the problem of drug addiction among elite women, see Bleser, *Tokens of Affection*, p. 377; and William Alexander Percy, *Lanterns on the Levee: Recollections of a Planter's Son* (New York: Alfred A. Knopf, 1941), p. 9. By the late nineteenth century, storefront "treatment centers" for opium addiction operated in the South. The Nashville Healing Institute advertised a specialty in chronic cases, offering cures for opium and alcohol addiction and for other ailments such as rheumatism and neuralgia (advertisement for Nashville Healing Institute, *Confederate Veteran*, vol. 1, no. 9, September 1893, p. 287). Morphine was also used to treat slaves' illnesses, though the extent of its usage is unclear (see, for example, Bleser, ed., *Tokens of Affection*, March 14, 1838, p. 220).

[21] John Rudd, *Indiana Narratives*, vol. 6, pt. 2, p. 171; Mary Ellison, "Resistance to Oppression: Black Women's Response to Slavery in the United States." *Slavery and Abolition* 4 (May 1983): 57–59.

[22] Josie Jordan, *Oklahoma and Mississippi Narratives*, vol. 7, pt. 2, p. 161. Jordan's master stopped the fight but refused to further punish her mother, prompting his wife to send for her father and brothers to come and finish the job.

[23] Sophia Word, *Kentucky Narratives*, vol. 16, pt.1, pp. 66–67.

[24] Genovese, *Roll, Jordan, Roll*, p. 598.

[25] Rudd, *Indiana Narratives*, vol. 6, pt. 2, pp. 170–71.

[26] Painter, "Soul Murder," p. 22.

a slave woman into her house, or of a mistress and a household slave coming to blows in the mistress's kitchen, suggests one of the reasons we need not only to rethink relations between mistresses and slaves in the white household (and the image of mistresses as "ladies"), but also the very notion of that household as a space of domesticity apart from the public world of labor and labor disputes. The intimacy of working conditions between household slaves and mistresses gave a special cast to this workplace but did not make it less a place where work was done, and avoided, and goods produced. And the kind of everyday violence that took place bespoke the intimacy of those conditions – a mistress dragging a slave woman, a slave woman violently shaking her mistress, the biting and kicking and tussling – even as it bespoke the particular conditions of slavery. Slaveholders could hire out a troublesome slave, but there was no pay-packet to dock, and no firing except through sale.

Sometimes, to avoid such scenes, or because they found disciplining slaves unladylike, slaveholding women delegated the task to overseers, slave drivers, or male kin. Sallie Carder's mistress, whom Carder described as a "very mean" woman, "would make de overseer whip Negroes for looking too hard at er when talking to dem."[27] Going this route, however, did not always produce the results hoped for. When Thomas Jones attempted to punish a rebellious female household slave in his wife's absence, he failed miserably, a heavy beating notwithstanding. "Julie is the same still," he wrote his wife, "tho I do assure you that she has not wanted correction very often. I chear'd her with thirty lashes a Saturday last and as many more a Tuesday again and today I hear she's sick."[28]

During the Civil War, the option of resorting to male power was less available. One of the most frequently-voiced complaints then of slaveholding women who preferred not to do the whipping themselves was the difficulty of finding a man who could do it for them. With white men at the front and black men increasingly in a position to refuse such orders, they were less able to either delegate or order the work done by someone else. In the months immediately following the war, the problem remained. Alice Gaillard Palmer wanted very much to take a switch to one of her female employees, but as she had always found "the idea of a lady doing such a thing . . . repugnant . . . and no one would do it for you now," she was stuck with making idle threats.[29] Some mistresses, of course, neither beat their slaves nor delegated the task to others, rejecting the use of physical violence, sometimes using psychological tactics instead, or whipping, "as de las thing." A Wake County, North Carolina, mistress punished slaves variously by sending them to bed without supper, working them at

[27] Sallie Carder, *Oklahoma Narratives*, Supplement Series 1, vol. 12, p. 96; Narrative of Mr. Caulkins in Theodore Weld, *American Slavery As It Is*, pp. 13–24. Caulkins's testimony includes cases of young white women as well as mistresses ordering floggings.

[28] Quoted in Edmund S. Morgan, *American Slavery, American Freedom: The Ordeal of Colonial Virginia* (New York: W. W. Norton, 1975), p. 315.

[29] Alice Gaillard Palmer to Harriet R. Palmer, July 20, 1865, in *A World Turned Upside Down: The Palmers of South Santee, 1818–1881*, ed. Louis P. Towles (Columbia: University of South Carolina Press, 1996), p. 480.

night, or forcing them to memorize scripture and poems. But in the end, even if "once in a coon's moon," she used the whip.[30]

Overall, in narratives where slaves make explicit comparisons, mistresses are depicted as harder and crueler than masters. Mistresses emerge from these narratives not only as the principal actors in the violence that took place in the household, but as instigators inciting masters to violence. John Rudd was certain his mistress pressed his master to cruelties, always "rilin' him up."[31] Lucretia Heyward said that her master never whipped her but her mistress "cut my back w'en I don't do to suit her."[32]

Other slaves drew no such contrast between cruel masters and mistresses. According to Armaci Adams, they "was both hell cats." Yet, even in these mixed accounts, mistresses are named the more brutal and sadistic. Ria Sorrell's master whipped slaves, but Sorrell noted that he seemed to take no joy in it. Her mistress, on the other hand, was a "bad" person, "de pure debil," a woman who fed slaves as little as possible and "jist joyed whuppin' Negroes," especially when her husband was away. At such times, she "raised ole scratch wid de slaves."[33]

Bob Jones remembered his master, a small slaveholder, and his master's son favorably. But as to his mistress:

Mis Betsy was crabbed an' hard to git along wid. She whupped de servants what done de housework an' fussed so bad dat she moughtly nigh run us crazy. Hit wus her that sole my Aunt Sissy an' hit wus her what whipped my sister Mary so bad. Dar warn't but six of us but dem six run a race to see who can stay outen her sight.[34]

Melissa Williamson characterized her former mistress as a "hard" woman, calling forth an image of an unfeeling, callous, tough person. She recalled an incident in which her mistresses stripped an elderly slave woman (who was thought to be mentally ill) to her waist and beat her. "I neber thought that Mis' Mitchel wus hard till I seed her whup Aunt Pidea," Williamson commented. "Aunt Pidea wuz a good soul an' wuz good ter we youngins, an' we loved her."[35]

George King, selling prayers in depression-era Tulsa, Oklahoma, told his interviewer that he was born near Lexington, South Carolina, "on two hundred acres of hell, but the whitefolks called it Samuel Roll's plantation." He remembered it as a small place "but plenty room for that devil overseer to lay on the lash, and plenty room for the old she-devil Mistress to whip his mammy

[30] Valley Perry, *North Carolina Narratives*, vol. 15, pt. 2, p. 170.

[31] John Rudd, *Indiana Narratives*, vol. 6, pt. 2, p. 169.

[32] Lucretia Heyward, *South Carolina Narratives*, vol. 2, pt. 2, pp. 279–81.

[33] Charles L. Perdue, Jr., Thomas E. Barden, and Robert K. Phillips, eds. *Weevils in the Wheat: Interviews with Virginia Ex-Slaves* (Charlottesville: University Press of Virginia, 1976), p. 1; Ria Sorrell, *North Carolina Narratives*, vol. 15, pt. 2, pp. 300–301. On the brutality of masters, see, for example, Dave Lawson, *North Carolina Narratives*, vol. 15, p. 45.

[34] Bob Jones, *North Carolina Narratives*, vol. 15, pt. 2, p. 24.

[35] Melissa Williamson, *North Carolina Narratives*, vol. 15, pt. 2, pp. 411–12.

til' she was just a piece of living raw meat." His master "talked hard words"; his mistress whipped. Decades after the end of slavery, the senseless beating of his mother and the mistress's role in her torture remained with him:

They crossed her wrists and tied them with a stout cord. They made her bend over so that her arms was sticking back between her legs and fastened the arms with a stick so's she couldn't straighten up. He saw the Mistress pull his mammy's clothes over her head so's the lash could reach the skin. He saw the overseer lay on the whip with hide busting blows that left her laying, all a shiver, on the ground, like a wounded animal dying from the chase. He saw the Mistress walk away, laughing, while his Mammy screamed and groaned – the old Master standing there looking sad and wretched.[36]

The interviewer, seemingly undisturbed by the nature of the punishment, simply concluded that the mistress "was a great believer in the power of punishment."[37] For George King, however, his mistress's participation in the incident and her ability to "walk away, laughing" from the scene, prompted a different assessment. It fixed in his mind a portrait of southern white womanliness cropped of the metaphor of religiously sanctioned parental chastisement.

Slavery gave mistresses the power to be hard and cruel in punishing and humiliating slaves, and the prerogative to be indifferent. It was the cruelty of indifference that Lucinda Hall Shaw specifically recalled. Hall knew neither where she was born nor who her parents were. As a child she lived on a small farm belonging to Reuben and Sarah Humphries Hall along with three other slaves. Here she witnessed the fatal beating of a slave woman and the woman's burial on the spot where she had been tied to a post. She was then "jus' rolled" into a grave that "wuzn't nuthin but a hole in de groun." Decades later, the memory still gnawed at Shaw, for what happened next was, to her mind, as heinous as the beating. She recalled seeing something "shoveled in...dat I tho't I saw move." She immediately told her mistress who "tend lak she did't see nuthin'...she tol' me atterwards, dat de overseer whipped her so hard she birfed a baby."[38] It was the interviewer's superfluous conclusion that Lucinda Hall Shaw "cherishes absolutely no kindly feelings for her former masters and mistresses."[39]

Sally Brown's memories of slavery were defined by the beatings she took from her mistress (who used a cowhide whip) and her mistress's indifference on other counts. "That 'oman took delight in sellin' slaves," she stated.[40] William Moore remembered his master as "a turrible mean man." "I guess he is in hell," he concluded. On the other hand, his mistress was not only mean but "indifferent." Moore may have come to this conclusion after his mother was beaten "with a handsaw with the teeth to her back" by their master. His mother would later explain that "Marse Tom got mad at the cookin' and grabs her by the hair and drug her out the house and grabs the saw off the bench

[36] George G. King, *Oklahoma Narratives*, vol. 7, pp. 165–66.
[37] George G. King, *Oklahoma Narratives*, vol. 7, p. 166.
[38] Lucinda Hall Shaw, *Mississippi Narratives*, Supplement Series 1, vol. 10, pt. 5, p. 1927.
[39] Shaw, *Mississippi Narratives*, Supplement Series 1, vol. 10, pt. 5, p. 1925.
[40] Sally Brown, *Georgia Narratives*, Supplement Series 1, vol. 3, pt. 1, pp. 94–95.

tool and whips her." "She died," he stated, "with the marks in her, the teeth holes goin' crosswise her back." The mistress apparently neither protested nor intervened.[41] But when slave women and mistresses came to blows indoors or when masters dragged slave women out of their homes, the plantation household comes into clearer focus as an embattled workplace that extended to its outbuildings, lawns, and gardens.

A Very Special Case

Slave resistance sometimes arose in direct response to white women's abuse and in particular to the "nasty forms" it took.[42] The 1861 slave conspiracy at Second Creek, Mississippi, the record suggests, matured from just such circumstances. The testimony of the slaves called to explain why they had conspired to kill their owners is striking in this regard. The rebels had many grievances. The "whipping colored people would stop," for example. But one grievance stood out. The slave men stressed the abuse that their sisters, daughters, and wives had suffered at the hands of white women. The rebellion would rid their community of white women who "whips our children."[43] They referred repeatedly to the water torture of a young female slave who was beaten and had water thrown on her by a group of young white women. For "drowning and beating Wesley's sister," they testified, the young women deserved to be punished. This, the slaves offered, explained the decision of Wesley and his father to join the conspiracy to overthrow slavery. The participation of another slave, Paul, turned on his concern for his wife and his desire to see her freed from the heavy workload her mistress placed on her. "Mrs. D [Dunbar] kills up Paul's wife sewing," one of the slaves testified.[44] While the court seemed most interested in allegations that the conspirators planned to "take" white women as one of the spoils of the rebellion, the slaves themselves returned repeatedly to the subject of white women's violence.

The language the slaves used left little doubt about their view of the culture of white female violence. They emphasized the drowning, but they also stressed that this incident was just the latest in a series of provocations and abuses on

---

[41] William Moore, *Texas Narratives*, vol. 5, pt. 3, p. 134. Moore did not witness the beating, and it was some years after emancipation that his mother related the circumstances that had led to it. Up to that point, she had refused to talk about the incident.

[42] Quote is from Fox-Genovese, "To Be Worthy of God's Favor: Southern Women's Defense and Critique of Slavery," 32d Annual Fortenbaugh Memorial Lecture. Gettysburg College, 1993, p. 12.

[43] Winthrop D. Jordan, *Tumult and Silence at Second Creek: An Inquiry into a Civil War Slave Conspiracy* (Baton Rouge: Louisiana State University Press, 1993), pp. 164–65, 167, 201–2, 276, 279, 281, 294, and 298, quotes at pp. 295 and 281, respectively. See also Armstead L. Robinson, "In the Shadow of Old John Brown: Insurrection Anxiety and Confederate Mobilization, 1861–1863," *Journal of Negro History* 65 (Autumn, 1980): 287–88. The call for an end to beatings appears frequently in the slaves narratives. See, for example, William Moore Narrative, *Texas Narratives*, vol. 7, pt. 6, Supplement Series 2, p. 2770.

[44] Jordan, *Tumult and Silence at Second Creek*, pp. 164–65, 167 and 201, quotes at pp. 165 and 201.

the part of white women, constituting "a habitual pattern."[45] Winthrop Jordan interprets the drowning incident as "clearly a very special case," and argues that the slaves also saw it as such. The rules of slavery, written and unwritten, that shaped what slaveholders could and could not do, and how slaves could and could not respond, as Jordan rightly notes, were always in the process of being made and remade. The everyday give-and-take was part of the system, and taken for granted. Violations considered flagrant by either side always threatened the seeming placidity of day-to-day existence. Jordan believes that this explains the slaves' response to the incident. The "sheer egregiousness" of the drowning, he contends, explains why the men invoked it as justification for the planned rebellion, and why Wesley and Nelson Mosby, brother and father of the victim, joined the conspiracy. Thus, for Jordan, what the slaves probably found most disturbing was the source of the violence, that it came "at the hands of those who stood farthest from the core of authority and who thereby appeared to be taking especially unwarranted advantage of the system."

The "young ladies" who "drown and beat" Wesley's sister had blurred the customary lines of authority and devastated one of the best avenues for mutual trust and affection between slaves and members of the master class. Miss Mary was white, but she was also a woman and young. She had no call to abuse the young slave woman, and when "she poured water upon" her, she chose a method that conspicuously snapped the rules.[46]

From the evidence Jordan himself presents, however, the Mosby men and the other slaves who joined in the conspiracy seem to have actually made quite the opposite point. They saw the drowning incident as part of a "habitual pattern" of abuse by the white women. To them, it was not that the "'young ladies'... had blurred the customary lines of authority" but rather, that they had demonstrated their part ownership of this authority. Nothing in the available record suggests that the slaves were surprised by this violence at the hands of white females. The incident was egregious, though not because its perpetrators were women from whom slaves expected better, due to their sex, race, and age. Indeed, the slaves singled out "Miss Mary" because of the notorious reputation she had gained from previous incidents and because of her leading role in the abuse of the young girl in the incident at hand. Besides, they would have noticed, the women were not punished.[47] They got away with past and present offenses because they stood not just merely close to, but at the center of, authority and power. This incident reveals sufficient flexibility to accommodate women's impulses. And so far were they from historians' imagined world of women's influence as a surrogate for men's, that they also escaped the public opprobrium of their fellow white citizens.

---

[45] Jordan, *Tumult and Silence at Second Creek*, p. 201.
[46] Jordan, *Tumult and Silence at Second Creek*, p. 201.
[47] Jordan, "Testimony of Dick," *Tumult and Silence at Second Creek*, pp. 281 and 295.

The dichotomy of public versus private is a particularly problematic formulation for understanding plantation households or any domestic arena in which the work of the household is carried out by non-family members, whether the workers are slaves or labor for a wage. In feminist literature, the public/private distinction has come under increased scrutiny. But the terms of the debate remain beholden to some traditional conceptualizations of the notion of separate spheres in important respects. The transformation of private dwellings into private spaces, concealing what were once public activities, such as bathing, sexual activity, fighting, and so forth, is a key idea in this debate. These and other developments, notes Leonore Davidoff, "included an underlying assumption of more contractual, individualistic relations in public and a familial placing of social orders in private."[48]

Even as personal activities moved increasingly to the more private space of homes, those homes that employed servants, slave or free, remained open to the public scrutiny of the servants or slaves who worked within them. Slaves who labored in plantation households were witnesses to the private and personal activities of those they served. They witnessed the vomiting, sexual activity, sleeping, and fighting, and they cleaned up the mess these left behind. They washed the bodies of their masters and mistresses. Those who slept in the same room with their mistresses and masters – on the floor, in trundle-beds rolled out at night, or even in slaveholders' own beds – undoubtedly saw more than they wished to. What is more, they were often made to do these things while scantily clad themselves, often to the amazement and shock of northern visitors. This intimacy that so often shocked northern visitors and transplants helped to make what took place in the plantation household more public than private.[49] This matters for any attempt to understand the relations between black and white women within plantation households.

When mistresses abused slaves, they did so before a public audience that at the same time knew them intimately and even if they saw this audience as inferior. That alone could invite violence. Again, not to see this is to subscribe to the proslavery ideology that the enslaved and the enslavers constituted one family.

---

[48] Leonore Davidoff, "Gender and the 'Great Divide': Public and Private in British Gender History," *Journal of Women's History* 15 (Spring 2003): 13–15, quote at p. 15. For a concise summary and analysis of the growing body of literature on privacy and the transformation of the family, see Linda A. Pollack, "Living on the Stage of the World: The Concept of Privacy among the Elite of Early Modern England," in *Rethinking Social History: English Society 1570–1920 and Its Interpretation*, ed. Adrian Wilson (Manchester, UK: Manchester University Press, 1993). See also David Brion Davis, "The American Family and Boundaries in Historical Perspective," in Davis, *From Homicide to Slavery: Studies in American Culture* (New York: Oxford University Press, 1986).

[49] Genovese, *Roll, Jordan, Roll*, p. 336; Douglass, *My Bondage and My Freedom*, pp. 101 and 109. Important revisionist imperial histories draw our attention to the operation of power in places – from the plantation to the street and home – not traditionally seen as public spaces. See, for example, Tony Ballantyne and Antoinette Burton, eds., *Bodies in Contact: Rethinking Colonial Encounters in World History* (Durham, NC: Duke University Press, 2005), p. 6.

Despite proslavery ideology, which held that slaves were members, albeit inferior ones, of one family, black and white, this notion could not be sustained where relations of slavery existed. And mistresses's management of household slaves made the distinction clear. Even Winthrop Jordan, despite having concluded that the behavior of white women at Second Creek clearly represented "a special case," could not completely ignore the contrary evidence before him "of sadistically imaginative torture... perpetrated by white *women*."[50]

Not only was violence from the hands of mistresses often brutal and even sadistic, it was often disproportionate to the offense and, sometimes, manufactured in the absence of an offense. The outrageous nature of slavery itself encouraged provocations by slaves just as it encouraged violence by mistresses, as Ann Hardeman testified: "I lost control of my temper to-night Eliza provoked me very much – was insolent – & behaved very badly. I will try & regain my balance – anger is majestic – but makes *slaves* of weak minds." Hardeman says that this was not the first time Eliza had "behaved very badly."[51] She does not say whether it was the first time she had "lost control."

Following the insights of Michael Taussig's work in another region, the apparent disorder of Hardeman's incident conceals a disturbing yet fundamental order. "Behind the search for profits, the need to control labor, the need to assuage frustration, and so on," Taussig writes, "lay intricately construed, longstanding cultural logics of meaning – structures of feeling – whose basis lies in a symbolic world and not in one of rationalism." Although Hardeman's account uses the "rationalist" structure of Eliza's action and her reaction, Taussig's analysis offers the reminder that it was the nature of Hardeman's prerogative to leave room for a symbolic response to not-yet-committed "insolence." Not everyone in her position would have found it easy to resist the temptation to commit pre-emptive, or purely expressive, violence, of the kind that, in Taussig's words, constitutes "a ritual art form." Pointedly, he adds, "the danger lies with aestheticizing horror."[52]

The still widely-endorsed notion of the antebellum South as a civilized place courts precisely this danger. Defending that image two decades ago, historian William Scarborough wrote: "Just as the slaves exhibited certain common traits, so too did those who governed them. It is my contention that the class as a whole, especially at the highest levels, was permeated by a sense of honor, *noblesse oblige,* chivalry, justice, Christian compassion; in a word, the typical planter was a gentleman, a term which is ubiquitous in the correspondence of

---

[50] Jordan, *Tumult and Silence at Second Creek*, pp. 201–2, n.30. When he turned to discussing the motives of the rebels at Second Creek, Jordan drew the contradictory conclusion that such incidents were aberrations.

[51] Entry for November 23, 1859, "The Journal of Ann Lewis Hardeman, 1850–67," in Michael O'Brien, ed., *An Evening When Alone: Four Journals of Single Women in the South, 1827-67* (Charlottesville: University Press of Virginia, 1993), p. 288.

[52] Michael Taussig, "Culture of Terror – Space of Death: Roger Casement's Putumayo Report and the Explanation of Torture," in *Colonialism and Culture,* ed. Nicholas B. Dirks (Ann Arbor: University of Michigan Press, 1992), p. 139.

the period."[53] To accept the view slaveholders set down in their letters, is to imagine women's use of violence against slaves as "spontaneous, sui generis, and an abandonment of what are called 'the values of civilization.'" Far from it, Taussig argues; violence entailed instead "a deep history deriving power and meaning from those values."[54]

Like slaveholding men, slaveholding women acknowledged the integral role of violence in the mediation and maintenance of slavery. Beyond the compelling testimony of slaves and ex-slaves is the extraordinary record left by mistresses themselves. It is a record of the extraordinary recorded as ordinary, the ordinary language of power where "[e]xtreme acts of violence are depicted matter-of-factly because of their regularity."[55] Lucille McCorkle penned just such an account: "Business negligently done & much altogether neglected, some disobedience, much idleness, sullenness, slovenliness. ... Used the rod."[56] Lizzie Neblett's account of how she handled a slave stands out for its banality. "I haven't even dressed Kate [a teenager] but once since you left," she informed her husband in a letter during the Civil War, "& then only a few cuts." One finds no sense of equivocation in either account, no suggestion of anything unusual. Nor does either account suggest that the women found punishing slaves particularly disagreeable or necessarily viewed it as men's work. With her husband away serving the Confederate cause, Neblett allowed that she was simply "too troubled in mind to get stirred up enough to whip," that is, to the extent to which she was accustomed.[57]

There was a quality of ordinariness and a certain quality of casualness in the way mistresses talked about and meted out punishment. In rare moments of self-reflection, they recognized these qualities, and the recognition sometimes brought some of them up short. Sarah Morgan recorded one such moment. One day Morgan, her sister Miriam, and a friend, Anna Badger, were getting dressed. Badger, unable to find the "grease" for her hair, slapped her slave, who she apparently held responsible for the missing article of toiletry. Morgan

53 William K. Scarborough, "Slavery – The White Man's Burden," in *Perspectives and Irony in American History: Essays*, ed. Harry P. Owens (Jackson: University Press of Mississippi, 1976), p. 109. Scarborough revises this position in his latest work, *Masters of the Big House: Elite Slaveholders of the Mid-Nineteenth Century* (Baton Rouge: Louisiana State University Press, 2003), pp. 90–122. Here he writes, "Slaves in the antebellum South were oppressed; the wives and daughters of those who owned them were not" (p. 91).

54 Quotes are from Taussig, "Culture of Terror," p. 164.

55 Saidiya V. Hartman, *Scenes of Subjection: Terror, Slavery, and Self-Making in Nineteenth-Century America* (New York: Oxford, 1997).

56 As quoted in Anne Firor Scott, *The Southern Lady: From Pedestal to Politics, 1830–1930*, 25th Anniversary Ed. (1970; Charlottesville: University Press of Virginia, 1995), p. 37; see also Fox-Genovese, *Within the Plantation Household*, p. 136.

57 Neblett quoted in Drew Gilpin Faust, "'Trying to Do a Man's Business': Gender, Violence, and Slave Management in Civil War Texas," in Faust, *Southern Stories: Slaveholders in War and Peace* (Columbia: University of Missouri Press, 1992) p. 185. See also Drew Gilpin Faust, *Mothers of Invention: Women of the Slaveholding South in the American Civil War* (Chapel Hill: University of North Carolina Press, 1996), pp. 64–70.

described the transformation that afterwards occurred when the young women went downstairs to entertain their guest: "I looked in vain for any trace of the commotion which had disturbed the girls upstairs. Anna, smiling and simpering, looked the very personification of amiability as she prattled to Major Spratley.... And her hands reposed so innocently in her lap that I was inclined to believe she was not the girl who had so unnecessarily slapped her little maid before going down."[58]

The incident led Morgan to reflect more generally about the muddled ground on which the status of white women rested. She marveled at the seeming ease with which "amiable" elite women, including her sister Miriam, moved in and out of the costume of the "southern lady" and speculated briefly on the distance that separated black and white women. Having herself been the subject of some lesser abuse by her own sister that same day, from which the slave, Malvina, had helped to extricate her, Morgan thought that perhaps she and Malvina "should have sympathized." "Only we didn't," she wrote.[59]

Mistresses crossed and re-crossed the South's formally designated gender boundaries. They regularly contravened notions of white female gentility that undergird ideologies of race and class and southern domesticity, slipping in and out of the costume of the soft, gentle "southern lady." In doing so, they acted on their power (as when Malvina's mistress slapped her) and their powerlessness (the smiling and simpering before men) at one and the same time. And their slaves were (intolerable) witnesses to the moral nakedness in between. As Morgan confessed, Malvina was only too cognizant of the role playing, and understood too well the costume changes.

White women's participation in the elaboration of slaveholding culture and its attendant violence was, like white men's, always problematic. While the use of violence was a necessary part of the job of keeping people enslaved, violent mistresses undermined patriarchal authority. The resort by masters to violence exposed fundamental flaws in proslavery ideology. When mistresses exercised the power to be violent, those flaws appeared all the more glaring, highlighting the "troubling juxtaposition of the cruel mistress with the 'tender mother and agreeable companion.'"[60]

In admonishing daughters on proper etiquette, parents often used the occasion to provide instruction on the demeanor expected of slaveholding women in their relationships to slaves.[61] The colonial Virginia patriarch, Colonel Daniel Parke, gave this advice to his daughter Lucy Parke: "Mind your writing and everything else you have learnt, and do not learn to romp, but behave yourself soberly and like a gentlewoman. Mind reading, and carry yourself so that

---

[58] Sarah Morgan, *Sarah Morgan: The Civil War Diary of a Southern Woman*, ed. Charles East (New York: Simon and Schuster, 1991), Jan. 30, 1863, pp. 414–17, quote at p. 417.

[59] Morgan, *Sarah Morgan*, Jan. 30, 1863, p. 417.

[60] Quote is from Catherine Hall, *Civilising Subjects: Metropole and Colony in the English Imagination, 1830-1867* (Chicago: University of Chicago Press, 2002), p. 76.

[61] Clinton, *The Plantation Mistress*, pp. 96–97; Scott, *The Southern Lady*, pp. 4–21.

everybody may respect you. Be calm and obliging to all the servants, and when you speak, do it mildly, even to the poorest slave."[62] When she became the mistress of her own household, Lucy Parke ignored the advice.

Upon her marriage to William Byrd II, Lucy Parke Byrd dominated her household in the ways her father had cautioned against. She used the lash (and other instruments) frequently and brutally. Her husband's objections ultimately carried no more weight than her father's admonitions. He, like her father, objected to the more brutal punishments she inflicted on slaves, especially women. He chastised her for burning a slave with a hot iron and beating her with tongs. At other times, he kept his silence or sided with his wife. When she beat another woman for overstaying her leave to attend a wedding, and for her response when confronted about the matter, he seemed not much concerned.[63]

William Byrd generally tolerated his wife's violence, except when it was particularly brutal, and except when she "determined to show her authority before company." He was embarrassed when she beat slaves in the presence of guests. Lucy Byrd's "sadistic cruelty," writes David Fischer, "shocked even her husband, who was no humanitarian." It represented "a major breach of etiquette in Virginia where slaves were supposed to be beaten after the guests had gone home." By this standard, it was Lucy Byrd's disregard for the thin line that separated respectable and disreputable female behavior that brought disapproval, not the beatings, per se. To some extent, of course, her husband's concern reflected the general distaste on the part of the elite for "public" displays of emotion, considered evidence of a damning lack of self-control on the part of men as well as women.

Beyond that, the presence of guests opened the mistress's behavior to view by other white people – family, neighbors, friends, political and business acquaintances. William Byrd worried that his wife's actions contravened acceptable behavior, though with two minds in the matter. Yet his reaction was more coherent than might first appear. He condemned his wife's brutality and her use of the lash when he thought she acted out of mean spiritedness, or when she exercised her authority in the presence of guests, just as he would have condemned a man of his class for like behavior. He did not, however, deny "her authority" to beat slaves in the absence of guests when he thought she was justified. Her determination "to show her authority before company" breached prevailing conventions and undermined "her authority" among the slaves.

As the example of the Byrds reminds us, despite all manner of adjustment and rationalization, elite women's use of violence could but with difficulty be reconciled with dominant notions of white female delicacy and patriarchal authority conveyed in the letters and lectures of planters to their wives

---

[62] David Hackett Fischer, *Albion's Seed: Four British Folkways in America* (New York: Oxford University Press, 1989), p. 320.

[63] William Byrd, *The Secret Diary of William Byrd of Westover, 1709–1712*, ed. Louis B. Wright and Marion Tinling (Richmond, VA: Dietz Press, 1941), pp. 34–35, 205 and 494.

and daughters, and the admonitions of tutors and ministers. Slaveholders like William Byrd recognized the damage it did to master–slave relations and the breach it created in the plantation household's reputation and power structure that slaves could easily take advantage of. The slave Jane Minor condemned as hypocrisy the whole idea of a public/private dichotomy in the plantation household and exposed it after her own fashion. "Cousin Jane," a relative recalled, "use to wait til master have company in missus big parlor and when dey be in dar jes talking and lafing she goes in dar, pulls up her coat tail over her head, shows all she's got and say, 'Marse, is you gwine whip me? Here I is.'"[64]

When the mechanisms for encasing overt conflict within the plantation household shattered, mistresses neglected the most basic principles (promoted also in countless articles on slave management in planter journals and in planters' instructions to overseers) for using the lash. Savannah River rice planter Charles Manigault crafted explicit advice on the subject for his overseers. One "had best think carefully," about meting out punishment and "always keep in mind the important old plantation maxim – viz., 'Never threaten a Negro' or he will do as you & I would under such circumstances.... he will run."[65] The advice Reverend Charles Pettigrew gave his sons similarly called for restraint: "To manage *negroes* without the exercise of too much passion, is next to an impossibility.... I would therefore put you on guard, lest their provocations should on occasion transport you beyond the limits of decency and Christian morality."[66] Of course, even masters schooled in such principles often violated them or just plain rejected the precept that the threat rather than the actuality of punishment was a surer key to managing slaves.

Prescriptive literature that directly targeted mistresses sanctioned punishment from their hands but urged restraint. An article in the *Southern Planter* gave this advice to mistresses: "Never scold when a servant neglects his duty, but *always punish* him, no matter how mildly, for mild treatment is the best; severity hardens them. Be firm in this, that no neglect go unpunished. Never let a servant say to you, '*I forgot it.*' That sentence, so often used, is no excuse at all."[67] Notice that the article did not tell mistresses that punishing slaves was a male prerogative. It merely advised mild punishment, encouraging mistresses to believe that the work of managing slaves through the use of violence was not inconsistent with the job of being "ladies."

[64] Perdue, et al., *Weevils in the Wheat*, p. 238.

[65] Charles Manigault to James Haynes, March 1, 1847, in *Life and Labor on Argyle Island: Letters and Documents of a Savannah River Rice Plantation, 1833–1867*, ed. James M. Clifton (Savannah, GA: Beehive Press, 1978), p. 49.

[66] Kenneth M. Stampp, *The Peculiar Institution: Slavery in the Ante-Bellum South* (New York: Vintage Books, 1956), pp. 177–78.

[67] Ulrich B. Phillips, *American Negro Slavery: A Survey of the Supply, Employment and Control of Negro Labor as Determined by the Plantation Regime* (Baton Rouge: Louisiana State University Press, 1966), pp. 276–77; Cecelia, "Management of Servants," *Southern Planter* III (August 1843), p. 175, as quoted in Genovese, *Roll, Jordan, Roll*, pp. 334–35.

Most mistresses inevitably failed at some point to control their tempers. Some turned to prayer and expressed repentance, at least to God. After whipping a female slave, one mistress prayed "for government over my temper." Another, Lizzie Allman, beat a slave woman unconscious with a chair. Following a chastisement from her husband, who told her that she should be ashamed of herself, that if she could not control her temper she could not expect to control slaves, Allman prayed for forgiveness.[68] Mistresses appear to have had as much, if not more, difficulty as masters in following prescriptions that advised adjusting the number of lashes in proportion to the severity of the "offense," and controlling one's temper.[69]

Slavery made possible lives of privilege, comfort, and leisure for slaveholding women. It also made large demands of them – from managing households in which they were largely responsible for making inequality visible to the enslaved women with whom they shared intimacies and intimate quarters, to abiding the moral transgressions of their menfolk – that taxed their capacity to adhere in either demeanor or tongue to their society's mandates to delicacy. Ultimately, they proved no more capable of maintaining a posture of superiority and self-control before slaves than did slaveholding men. Their own subjection as the gentler sex may have made them less inclined to even make the attempt.[70] Observing the systems of management available to their husbands and fathers, mistresses might easily have thought they were more vulnerable to clashes with slaves.

All but the smallest slaveholders used systems of management for crop production – overseers or slave drivers – which allowed them to get cash crops produced, and maintain a certain distance from their slaves. Charles Manigault had one of the most insulating systems. Manigault's factor, for example, oversaw the purchase and sale of slaves and supplies, and hired, fired, and oversaw the overseers, thereby providing Manigault with several layers of protection and distance from the slaves. For elite men, the work of managing slaves was divided, parceled out to factors, overseers, drivers, and sons. This gave them an important advantage over mistresses. Slaveholding men might stroll, or invade, the slave quarters when they felt so inclined or ride out to check their fields, but those who had overseers and drivers were not required to do so every day. For slaveholding men, managing slaves was more apt to take place at a distance. Frederick Douglass captured the mechanism at work in the case of a young slave girl who walked twelve miles to report and show her bruised and bloodied body to her master, only to have him tell her that he supported the overseer's actions and believed she must have deserved the beating. He ordered

---

[68] As quoted in Stampp, *The Peculiar Institution*, p. 182; Elsie Rose, *Ohio Narratives*, vol. 5, pp. 438–39.

[69] Stampp, *The Peculiar Institution*, p. 175; Faust, "'Trying to Do a Man's Business,'" p. 175.

[70] On the importance of self-mastery and masculinity in colonial Virginia, see Kathleen M. Brown, *Good Wives, Nasty Wenches, and Anxious Patriarchs: Gender, Race, and Power in Colonial Virginia* (Chapel Hill: University of North Carolina Press, 1996). Brown does not address the implications for slaveholding women beyond indirect inference.

her to return to the plantation. To have done otherwise, "would have done away with the office of overseer, entirely; or in other words, it would convert the master himself into an overseer."[71]

Charles Manigault was an adept practitioner of male mastery. On one occasion, when his slaves went to him with complaints about a newly hired overseer, he labeled them "groundless," and accused the slaves of using them to gain advantage over the overseer. And he punished the slaves by selling for a "good deal of money" the small rice they were accustomed to having for their own use. He intended that it would serve as a lesson in how "they are favored by me in food & clothing." With that lesson still fresh in their minds the following year, he had the overseer convey a message reminding them of his paternal goodness and power. Ultimate ownership of the property in small rice that they believed theirs, was his: "Now I wish you to tell them that I can sell it & with half the money buy corn instead, & put thereby half the money in my pocket, that you wrote to me stating their good Conduct, & that I have decided to let them have all the small Rice again – on trial; & it depends entirely on them whether they shall have it in future or not."[72] It was an exquisitely measured dose of paternalistic domination applied from a distance. The slaves no doubt saw through it all: Allowing them the small rice in the future as a reward for "good conduct" was, in fact, an effort to ensure future "good conduct."

The distance that separated planters from intimate contact with their slaves was in other ways more often literal in comparison to that between mistresses and household slaves. Planters often spent months away from their plantations, and often from their town homes as well; their wives were much less mobile.[73] Charles Manigault owned several plantations and a house in Charleston. He spent months at a time in Europe. When absent from his planting operations, he guided and kept up with his business and slaves through frequent correspondence with his overseers. From Paris, he advised them on the management of unruly slaves and counseled them on which ones should be removed from the plantation, and which ones placed in solitary confinement in the Savannah jail and whipped. But brute force alone, he warned, would not "fix 'a bad disposed nigger.'" A few weeks in jail, followed by exposure to paternalism's softer side, was his preferred method. Following release from jail, he wrote, a slave should be told "that you will never dwell on old quarrels with

[71] Douglass, *My Bondage and My Freedom*, p. 83. Even in cases where masters supported the slaves and sometimes dismissed abusive overseers, the result was the same: The master remained above the fray. Drivers and overseers were, quite literally, the "men between" (Genovese, *Roll, Jordan, Roll*, pp. 34–61, 333, and 365–88). See also Weymouth T. Jordan, *Hugh Davis and his Alabama Plantation* (University: University of Alabama Press, 1948, p. 99). On the use of factors and overseers, see Charles Manigault to James Haynes, March 1, 1847, in *Life and Labor on Argyle Island*, ed. Clifton, p. 49, and other letters to and from Manigault and his son Louis, passim.

[72] Charles Manigault to James Haynes, January 1, 1847, in *Life and Labor on Argyle Island*, ed. Clifton, p. 45.

[73] See, for example, Drew Gilpin Faust, "Culture, Conflict and Community: The Meaning of Power on an Antebellum Plantation," *Journal of Social History* 14 (Autumn, 1980): 84.

him – that he has a clear track before him – & and all depends on himself.... Then give my Compliments to him & tell him that you wrote to me of
his conduct, & I say if he don't change for the better, I'll sell him to a slave
trader who will send him to New Orleans, where I have already sent several of
the gang for their misconduct, or for running away for no cause." Manigault
was ever ready to sell a rebellious field hand – male or female – but preferred
to do so surreptitiously to keep news of the business from getting to the slave
quarters before it was done. On hearing that a newly purchased female might
be trouble, he advised his son to "carry her off yourself while all the rest are
at work in the field."[74] It was paternalism at a safe but sure distance, and
practiced with a steady hand.[75]

By contrast, the work of mistresses was done at close quarters, on a daily
and intimate basis. In consequence, they were confronted with challenges from
slaves that often differed materially from those faced by their husbands, fathers,
and sons, and they faced them more often. The constancy and intimacy of
contact between enslaved women and mistresses gave a particular cast to their
relations.[76] In the kitchens, bedrooms, and parlors, where mistresses were
expected to rule, no parallel division of slave management offered the kinds of
buffers masters enjoyed through the employment of overseers and factors, and
the use of slave drivers.

Unlike European aristocrats, to whom they often compared themselves,
slaveholders generally did not hire butlers or white female managers, or use
slaves as household managers. Slave drivers and overseers stood between masters and field hands in a way that even the redoubtable "mammy," that most
improbable conduit for slave management, could not stand between mistresses
and other household slaves, and thereby reduce the occasions for conflict.[77]

---

74 Charles Manigault to James Haynes, 1st March 1847, in *Life and Labor on Argyle*, ed. Clifton,
quotes at pp. 50 and 179, respectively. Manigault's methods also included isolating slaves in a
room or space away from other slaves.

75 Men also learned self-control as a component of mastering hunting. The sport, writes historian
Nicholas Proctor, provided experience in "the effective use of violence" and served as an outlet
for mastery, even as it "reduced the potential for irrational volatility." (Nicholas W. Proctor,
Bathed in Blood: Hunting and Mastery in the Old South [Charlottesville: University Press of
Virginia, 2002], pp. 67–75, quotes at pp. 71 and 72).

76 Fox-Genovese, "To Be Worthy of God's Favor," p. 16; Painter, "Soul Murder," p. 22. An
important exception arises in the case of slave men such as ostlers, who were attached to the
plantation household under the authority of masters. Here the authority of masters was more
often announced in violence. See Douglass, *My Bondage and My Freedom*, pp. 112–15.

77 White, *Ar'n't I a Woman?*, pp. 46–49. In her study of Loudoun County, Virginia, Brenda
Stevenson notes a growing trend in the generally uncommon practice of hiring white servant
women to supervise slave women in the plantation household but that most of these appear to
have been temporary appointments. See Brenda E. Stevenson, *Life in Black and White: Family
and Community in the Slave South* (New York: Oxford University Press, 1996), p. 197. My
research turned up only a few such instances: see, Bleser, ed., *Tokens of Affection*, p. 311;
Sarah Morgan, *Sarah Morgan: The Civil War Diary*, Sept 6th [1863], p. 551; William T. Bain
Papers; and Cameron Family Papers. According to William Howard Russell, the wait staff at
Charleston's Mills House hotel was Irish and German (William Howard Russell, *My Diary*

Besides, mistresses had nothing comparable to small rice, a "right" established over decades of negotiations and considered inviolable, with which to bargain. A handed-down dress was hardly comparable.[78] Small slaveholding men faced problems similar to mistresses, in line with the greater frequency and intimacy of their contact with slaves. The interactions of Thomas Chaplin with his slaves, for example, show a master busying himself with the minutia of slave life and frequently jostling slaves about everything from their work habits to their personal relationships.[79]

Slaveholding women had daily contact with and direct managerial authority over slaves. Hiring persons specifically to manage their households, as planters used overseers and drivers to manage crops and field hands, would have relieved mistresses of many of the burdens of which they complained. It would have reduced the amount of direct contact with household slaves and, presumably, the number of confrontations. Such a solution, however, would have required a much more wider use of poor white women and unhinged, in the process, an important cornerstone of slaveholders' world. Elite women's class biases also stood in the way. Bias against the Irish, the group of European Americans most readily available for this work, was especially keen. One South Carolina mistress who employed an Irish orphan servant girl (who doubled as the family's cook) was unable even to see her as "white." After the death of the child's parents, she opposed her husband's suggestion that they adopt her along with her siblings. She "would not consent... as she did not think it well to have the children of another nationality" raised with her own.[80]

Mistresses could and often did call upon and rely on the authority of their husbands, brothers, and fathers for assistance in managing slaves, to help settle scores, real and imagined. Yet this resort to masculine authority carried its own drawbacks. It undercut their own claims to authority over slaves within the household, marking them as poor and inefficient managers of the domestic space.[81] The disabilities mistresses suffered as women made slaves' challenges to their authority appear all the more pronounced.

Though the power inherent in slave ownership gave white women the right to beat and otherwise abuse slaves, their gender subordination mattered nonetheless. There can be no question that white southern women understood clearly and without sentiment the peculiar ways of gender and race in the South, no question that they could hate their disabilities as women and the inequities

---

North and South [Boston: T. O. H. P. Burnham, 1863], pp. 112–13). On the use of white nurses, see White, *Ar'n't I a Woman?*, p. 54.

[78] Fox-Genovese, *Within the Plantation Household*, p. 141.

[79] Theodore, Rosengarten, *Tombee: Portrait of a Cotton Planter with the Plantation Journal of Thomas B. Chaplin (1822–1890)* (New York: William Morrow and Company, 1986). In contrast, Pierce Butler, with strong white management and drivers, did not (R. King, Jr., "On the Management of the Butler Estate," *Southern Agriculturalist* [December 1828]: 523–29).

[80] Nancy B. De Saussure, *Old Plantation Days: Being Recollections of Southern Life Before the Civil War* (New York: Duffield & Company, 1909).

[81] For an extended discussion of domestic space and southern domesticity, see Chapter 3.

they personally confronted, and no question that they could still believe in slavery. Gertrude Thomas, Mary Chaplin, and Marianne Palmer Gaillard, all members of powerful slaveholding families, and Lizzie Neblett, a small Texas slaveholder, demonstrated all of these characteristics. Neblett was exceptional in her candor, describing herself in a letter to her husband as "nothing but a poor contemptible piece of multiplying human flesh tied to the house by a crying young one, looked upon as belonging to a race of inferior beings."[82]

In the privacy of her diary, Gertrude Thomas chastised white men who failed to support their wives, who slept with black women, or kept white mistresses. She expressed her outrage at the public double standard that tolerated white men's sexual violations of black women, but not interracial marriage. It led her at one point to briefly entertain the notion that southern women were "all at heart abolitionists." But she quickly realized her error and revised the sentiment: To say that *"public opinion"* tolerated interracial sex was overly broad. Yet she refused to let go of the thought completely, satisfying herself with the declaration that slavery had a much more degrading effect upon white men and white children than upon black people. How else could she account for the 'white children of slavery' who lived in her midst? Her maid Lurany's child was "as white as any white child."[83]

These and other contradictions led Thomas to question whether Mary, the Savior's Mother, "possess[ed] no influence" upon God.[84] She read Harriet Beecher Stowe's *Uncle Tom's Cabin*, feminist literature, and a book about miscegenation but wanted most to believe that all was right with her world.[85] Divorcing herself from the privileges of membership in the master class was never an attractive enough idea, however. No matter the cost, she had no desire to work herself, and exemption from labor constituted one of her most treasured privileges. She retained her pride of class and remained convinced that black people were an inferior race.[86]

Mary Chaplin married into a wealthy slaveholding family but watched her husband's dissipation erode their wealth. Long before the Civil War, the

---

[82] Faust, "Trying to Do a Man's Business," p. 189; Faust, *Mothers of Invention*, p. 65. Lizzie Neblett's struggles reflected, in part, the particular circumstances of the Civil War.

[83] Virginia Ingraham Burr, ed., *The Secret Eye: The Journal of Ella Gertrude Thomas, 1848–1899* (Chapel Hill: University of North Carolina Press, 1990), January 2, 1859, quotes at pp. 168 and 167. See also the valuable introduction to this text by Nell Irvin Painter ("The Journal of Ella Gertrude Thomas: An Educated White Woman in the Eras of Slavery, War, and Reconstruction," p. 67, and Painter, "Soul Murder," pp. 37–39 and 68–79.

[84] Burr, ed., *The Secret Eye*, July 4, 1864, p. 226.

[85] Near the end of the war, Thomas was reading E. W. Warren's *Nellie Norton* (Ebenezer W. Warren, *Nellie Norton, or Southern Slavery and the Bible: A Scriptural Refutation of the Principal Arguments Upon Which the Abolitionists Rely, A Vindication of Southern Slavery from the Old and New Testaments* [Macon, GA: Burke, Boykin & Co., 1864]), a proslavery work she hoped would prove Stowe wrong (Burr, ed., *The Secret Eye*, September, 23, 1864, p. 239).

[86] Virginia Ingraham Burr argues to the contrary that in "matters of race" Thomas was "broad-minded and well ahead of her time." See "Epilogue," Burr, ed. *The Secret Eye*, pp. 450–51.

Chaplin family began its long descent into poverty, a circumstance that no doubt contributed to Mary Chaplin's growing depression and addiction to snuff and other habits so "unladylike" her husband could not bring himself, even in the pages of his diary, to name them all. However, between the scribbles of her husband, Mary Chaplin candidly inscribed her own failings, and returned the favor by noting his as well. She reminded him of his failures as a man: his inability to put sufficient food on the table or to ensure the financial resources needed to educate their children to elite standards.[87]

Marianne Palmer Gaillard, fearing that her husband's management of their affairs was leading to financial disaster, risked his censure by going behind his back to seek financial advice from her half-brother. By this point, the acute financial distress of her estate had made her desperate. "I have come to the conclusion," she wrote, "that I care not whether he approves or disapproves."[88] In her world, the open expression of such sentiments would have been considered scandalous. But even tucked away in the heart or mind, they undermined carefully scripted southern gender ideals. Mistresses had cause, beyond slave resistance, to wear lightly the garb of the southern lady.

Plantation mistresses did not have to be abolitionist-minded to deplore the seduction and rape of slave women by white men. They did not have to be feminists to resent the heavy costs in civic, financial, and social dependence that they bore. They would have had to be both, however, to alter the circumstances that made these abuses possible.[89] Nagging doubts about the morality of slavery could be bothersome but planter women like Ella Gertrude Thomas did not find them crippling. Thomas admitted: "I am not so philanthropic as to be willing voluntarily to give all we own for the sake of principle."[90] Alice Palmer might gripe about elite white men – "The Lords of Creation" – and the low opinion in which she believed they held all women, but she counted herself among the South's and slavery's staunchest defenders.[91] "Domination," as Fox-Genovese writes, "especially the abuse of male prerogative, inflicted misery and frustration upon many slaveholding women but did not tempt them into feminism, much less abolitionism.... their complaints rarely amounted to opposition to the system that guaranteed their privileged position as ladies."[92]

---

[87] *The Plantation Journal of Thomas B. Chaplin (1822–1890)* in Rosengarten, *Tombee: Portrait of a Cotton Planter*, pp. 452, 507–8, and 526.

[88] Marianne P. Gaillard to Edward G. Palmer, November 28, 1844 in *World Turned Upside Down*, ed. Towles, p. 97.

[89] See Elizabeth Fox-Genovese's discussion of this point in *Within the Plantation Household*, passim. Ella Gertrude Thomas's journal is an important record of planter women's struggles to juggle the constraints and privileges of slavery.

[90] Burr, ed., *The Secret Eye*, September 17, 1864, p. 236.

[91] Alice G. Palmer to Harriet R. Palmer, May 16, 1866 in *World Turned Upside Down*, ed. Towles, p. 513.

[92] Fox-Genovese, *Within the Plantation Household*, p. 30; Bertram Wyatt-Brown, *Southern Honor: Ethics and Behavior in the Old South* (New York: Oxford University Press, 1982), p. 226.

On the other side of that privileged position, black women stood exposed and pledged never to forget "de awlfulness of it."[93]

De Awfulness of It

In their old age, former slaves told their stories to interviewers, reciting over and again the most painful experiences. William Moore never forgot his mother's sawed-up back or, near Macon County, Georgia, Hanna Fambro that her mistress had beat her mother to death with a broomstick. For Lizzie Williams, eighty-eight years old when she was interviewed, slavery had meant having to compete with dogs at the children's trough at dinner time and watching her mother stand knee-deep in sleet and snow, washing clothes three days after giving birth.[94] Mary Armstrong recalled the death of her nine-month-old sister, beaten to death by their mistress because she was tired of hearing the baby cry. Henry Walton thought it important that the record show that his mother "was whipped to death with a cowhide" when he was just three or four years old; Mollie Kinsey said that her sister, "jes a small girl," was made to "go out and lay on a table and two or three white men would have in'ercourse with her befo' they'd let her git up."[95]

Memories of the injuries of enslavement stayed with black women, and their husbands and children into the twentieth century. Children born after emancipation were certainly not unaffected.[96] Dave Lawson was born long after emancipation – his mother was only six months old herself in 1865. He grew up, however, with the knowledge of slavery passed on to him by others who had been enslaved. From them he learned, when he was "ole enough to lissen," about Luzanne, whipped "kaze she burnt de biscuits," and from Aunt Becky, why his grandmother and grandfather were hanged, both at the "same

[93] Delia Garlic, *Alabama Narratives*, vol. 6, p. 129.

[94] William Moore, *Texas Narratives*, Supplement Series 2, vol. 7, pt. 6, pp. 2767–68, and William Moore, ibid., vol. 5, pt. 3, pp. 132–37; Hanna Fambro, *Ohio Narratives*, vol. 5, p. 333; Annie Hawkins, *Oklahoma Narratives*, vol. 7, p. 131; Lizzie Williams, *Mississippi Narratives*, Supplement Series 1, vol 10, pt. 5, pp. 2335–36.

[95] Mary Armstrong, *Texas Narratives*, vol. 4, pt. 1, p. 25; Henry Walton, *Mississippi Narratives*, Supplement Series 1, vol. 10, pt. 5, p. 2168; Mollie Kinsey, *Georgia Narratives*, Supplement Series 1, vol. 4, pt. 2, p. 373. The commitment of many ex-slaves to passing on the history of slavery, to sharing this history with their children and grandchildren, was resisted by some who made conscious decisions to suppress their stories in order to protect their children. Melissa Williamson stated that she did not talk to her children about slavery because she feared they would get too stirred up about it, not because she was ashamed (Melissa Williamson, *North Carolina Narratives*, vol. 15, pt. 2, p. 413). See also Weiner, *Mistresses and Slaves*, pp. 125–26.

[96] Norrece T. Jones, Jr., *Born a Child of Freedom, Yet a Slave: Mechanisms of Control and Strategies of Resistance in Antebellum South Carolina* (Hanover, NH and London: University Press of New England, 1990), pp. 7 and 57. Recent work on enslaved children also tempers this view. See Wilma King, *Stolen Childhood: Slave Youth in Nineteenth-Century America* (Bloomington: Indiana University Press, 1995), and Marie Jenkins Schwartz, *Born in Bondage: Growing Up Enslaved in the Antebellum South* (Cambridge, MA: Harvard University Press, 2000).

time an' from de same lim'" of an oak tree on a North Carolina plantation. The first time he heard the story he was unable to sleep for a week.[97]

Mandy Cooper left her story with her children. Like many parents, she found talking to her children about slavery difficult and put off doing so until they saw her back one day as she was bathing. She began to explain but the children "thought she was tellin' a big story," and "made fun of her." Angry and pained, Mandy Cooper taught her children a lesson both unorthodox and painful. She had them strip to the waist, and struck each with a whip severe enough to draw blood. She finished her story and her son conveyed it to posterity in the 1930s.[98]

For the first years of their lives most slave children were spared the back-breaking labor their parents endured.[99] But they endured experiences no less painful and in some ways worse: The sights and sounds of slavery were etched in their memories. For Ira Jones, it was the story of an aunt who died of lock-jaw after suffering a punishment that consisted of "having her hands placed on a barrel, palms down" into which "nails were then driven." His cousin, Eliza Hotchkiss, carried a deep scar across her chest all her life. Mattie Jenkins, enslaved on a small Georgia farm, recalled pins stuck through the tongues of slaves and tongues burned as forms of punishment. Rev. Wamble's mother died of a miscarriage after a severe beating in Monroe County, Mississippi. Born in 1860, John Smith spent only a few years in slavery, but it was sufficient time to appreciate slavery's destructive power. "De only time," he stated, "I saw anything in de slave situation dat made a big impression on my mind was when Marster Thomas tied my Aunt Anne Thomas to a peach tree and whupped her. I will never forget how she cried."[100]

Annie Tate learned that her grandmother had paid the ultimate price, committing suicide by throwing herself into the Neuse River in North Carolina when her husband was sold. She left behind a daughter, Tate's mother, then a child of eight or ten, and perhaps other children as well. Tate was only one year old when freedom came and thus had no direct memory of slavery; the story she told had been passed on to her by her mother long after emancipation.[101] Recalling slavery, black people remembered the "spectacle of public discipline" along with its geography and sensory attributes – the sight of dead

[97] Dave Lawson, *North Carolina Narratives*, vol. 15, pt. 2, pp. 44–50.

[98] Fred Cooper, *Indiana Narratives*, vol. 6, p. 61.

[99] This was certainly less true on small plantations and farms and less true, in general, in the less settled slave states. Elizabeth Smith, at the age of five, was responsible for spinning five cuts per day (Alex and Elizabeth Smith, *Indiana Narratives*, vol. 6, p. 183). Lulu Wilson's childhood experience was similar. As a child, she spun cloth, hoed, and milked ten cows a day (Wilson, *Texas Narratives*, vol. 5, pt. 4, pp. 190 and 193). Annie Hawkins worked in the field and in the plantation household (Annie Hawkins, *Oklahoma and Mississippi Narratives*, vol. 7, p. 131).

[100] Ira Jones, *Indiana Narratives*, vol. 5, pp. 99–100; Mattie Jenkins, *Indiana Narratives*, vol. 5, p. 95; Rev. Wamble, *Indiana Narratives*, vol. 6, p. 200; John Smith, *North Carolina Narratives*, vol. 15, pt. 2, p. 279.

[101] Annie Tate, *North Carolina Narratives*, vol. 15, pt. 2, pp. 333–34.

bodies floating in rivers, bleeding bodies hung from peach trees, the smell of burning flesh in plantation yards, the sounds of people in pain.[102]

Abuse sometimes galvanized entire slave communities in protest as in the case of Jane Moore. Moore was beaten frequently and eventually ran away along with her son, William, who had gone to her rescue during the latest beating. They hid out in the woods for several months, relying on Moore's daughters to bring them food and to dress the wounds on their mother's back. They stayed out until the daughters brought word that it was safe to return. This proved false, forcing them to again flee, barely escaping the mistress's attempt to capture William with a rope. The beating of Jane Moore and other slaves on this plantation ultimately moved the slave community to demand their safe return and an end to the beatings. Armed with shotguns taken from their master's house, they forced him to send the five men he had recruited to restore order on the plantation away.[103]

Memories of slavery resonated powerfully for Delia Garlic, who gave her testimony in 1937 when she was 100 years old. She recalled the speculators, the separation of families, the whippings, alcoholic masters and abusive mistresses, poor food and clothing, and the long hours of work. Each of these things she had personally experienced. "I could tell you 'bout it all day," she stated, "but even den you couldn't guess de awfulness of it. It's bad to belong to folks dat own you soul an' body."[104]

The historiography of American slavery tends to be squeamish about the inherent violence of the arrangements slavery required in the plantation house-hold, and the day-to-day manifestations of that violence. From that fact, the stories of slaves draw a peculiar ability to provoke shock and skepticism at the same time. But, taking a lesson from Michael Taussig's analysis, that need not be the case. Writing of the atrocities that surrounded the Putumayo rubber boom in Peru, Taussig argues:

While the immensity of the cruelty is beyond question, most of the evidence comes through stories. The meticulous historian would seize upon this fact as a challenge to winnow out truth from exaggeration or understatement. But the more basic implication,

---

[102] Unexplored here but central to the problems discussed is what Samuel Dennis terms "the role of the symbolic landscape in the constitution of southern social relations, particularly the "spectacle of public discipline" (Samuel F. Dennis, Jr., "Meaning and Materiality: The Racialized Landscape of Antebellum Georgia," paper in possession of author). See also Dell Upton, "White and Black Landscapes in Eighteenth Century Virginia," *Places* 2, no. 2 (1985): 59–72, and Mart A. Stewart, *"What Nature Suffers to Groe": Life, Labor, and Landscape on the Georgia Coast, 1680–1920* (Athens: University of Georgia Press, 1996).

[103] Jane Moore, *Texas Narratives*, vol. 5, pt. 3, pp. 134–37. The beating of slave women often mobilized slaves to take direct action against masters. In a similar case, slaves armed themselves and threatened to kill their master and mistress if they persisted in beating them. They singled out the beating of a woman (Blassingame, ed., *Slave Testimony*, p. 222.) See also, Jordan, *Tumult and Silence at Second Creek*, pp. 164–65, 201–2, and 279, quotes at pp. 298 and 295, respectively. On truancy as a form of resistance, see White, *Ar'n't I a Woman*, pp. 74–76, and Camp, *Enslaved Women and Everyday Resistance*, pp. 36–40.

[104] Delia Garlic, *Alabama Narratives*, vol. 6, pp. 129–32, quotes at pp. 129 and 131.

it seems to me, is that the narratives are in themselves *evidence* of the process whereby a culture of terror was created and sustained.[105]

The antebellum U.S. South was not Peru, but the culture of terror that arose respectively in southern slaveholding society and in the jungles of Peru rested on a similar logic. The narratives of ex-slaves (and slaveholders) are "evidence" of the process by which terror was created and sustained on southern plantations and mistresses's role in its production. Slaveholding women's exercise of power over slaves helped to define their place in the world of slavery. And this was not contradicted by their own vulnerability to violent acts committed by slaveholding fathers or husbands.

The scandal caused when Eliza Bird's husband "struck her down in the street," meaning to kill her, doubtless escaped neither the ears nor eyes of slaves nor, likely, the attempt of a drunken Georgia planter to "split" his wife's "head open" and kill her.[106] Lewis Wallace's master was an alcoholic. When intoxicated, Wallace recalled, he would "grab old Missus by de hair of her head an' drag her up an' down de long front gallery." A slave named Peggy witnessed Thomas Powell beat his wife with a horsewhip and tried to intervene.[107] Slaves talked about the mistress who died in childbirth along with her unborn child following a beating at the hands of her husband and noted that it was not the first time he had assaulted her and done so *publicly,* before their eyes. The last time, he had chased her around the house as he beat her with a whip.[108]

The battery mistresses faced from their husbands took numerous forms. One master "drove his wife to hide in terror in a swamp." Others paraded their "profligate sexuality."[109] Bun Eden's slaves knew that their mistress suffered from the knowledge that her husband had "his sweethearts 'mong his slave women." Savilla Burrell's master fathered several slave children. It was his "'lations wid de mothers of dese chillun," Burrell recalled, "what give so much grief to Mistress." The gossip of neighbors no less than slaves added to her grief.[110] Jacob Manson remembered a mistress who was reported to have shot her husband dead in self-defense following a quarrel about his relationship with a female slave:

Jimmie Shaw owned a purty gal nearly as white an he kept her. His wife caught 'im in a cabin in bed wid her. His wife said sumthin to him 'bout it an' he cussed his wife. She tole him she had caught him in de act. She went back to de great house an got a gun.

---

[105] Taussig, "Culture of Terror," pp. 148 and 150; Painter, "Soul Murder."

[106] Bleser, ed., *Tokens of Affection,* pp. 131 and 282; Ellison, "Resistance to Oppression," pp. 57–59.

[107] Lewis Wallace, *Mississippi Narratives,* Supplement Series 1, vol. 10, pt. 5, pp. 2165–66; Joan E. Cashin, ed., *Our Common Affairs: Texts from Women in the Old South* (Baltimore, MD: Johns Hopkins University Press, 1996), p. 208.

[108] Dave Lawson, *North Carolina Narratives,* vol. 15, pt. 2, pp. 44–48.

[109] Fox-Genovese, *Within the Plantation Household,* p. 9.

[110] Jacob Manson, *North Carolina Narratives,* vol. 15, pt. 2, pp. 97–99; Savilla Burrell, *South Carolina Narratives,* vol. 2, pt. 1, p. 150.

When de marster come in de great house she tole 'im he must leave de slave girls alone dat he belonged to her. He cussed her again an sed she would have to tend to her own dam business an' he would tend to his. Dey had a big fuss an den marster Shaw started towards her. She grabbed de gun an let him have it. She shot 'im dead in de hall. Dey had three chillun, two sons and one married daughter. Missus Shaw took her two sons an' left. De married daughter an her husband took charge of de place. Missus an her sons never come back as I knows of.[111]

Some mistresses even agreed upon marriage to "behave kindly" toward their husbands' enslaved children. It was a promise they could not easily keep.[112]

A commonplace among slaveholders was that slaves saw and heard too much, about which they "talk too much."[113] In these overheard conversations and by way of neighborhood gossip and their own witness, slaves indeed saw, heard, and talked about masters who, forgetful of patriarchal standards, neglected their families, and committed adultery and other forms of spousal abuse.[114] Caroline Taveau's marital troubles, for example, could hardly have escaped the notice of the family's slaves. Her husband's emotional and financial neglect, and his psychological abuse, are recurrent themes in letters she wrote to her son. Using the example of her husband's neglect and dissipation, she sought to point her son along a different path. "Your father," she wrote in one letter, "has been in town a whole fortnight, dissipating at the Races and Theatres; every day dining out so much that I could scarce see him but one evening we spent together." Several years later, her husband's neglect remained a sore topic: "Your father cannot rest unless he is doing something to torment and distract me." Her husband continued to spend a great deal of time away from home while she suffered: "I am so poor could not have spare a dollar," she wrote. In the "day of retribution coming for all who oppress and afflict God's children," her husband would regret having behaved so shamefully.[115] Yet, though her own suffering was palpable, Caroline Taveau did not think to include herself among the oppressors, nor her slaves among God's oppressed children.

Ultimately, mistresses found no shelter behind the curtains of the great house, not from slaves, not from the larger white public of which they were a part. Mary Culbreath was raped by the husband of one of her friends. The incident, remarkably, went to court, publicizing Culbreath's plight far beyond her home and neighborhood, where it had already caused great "excitement."

[111] Jacob Manson, *North Carolina Narratives*, vol. 15, pt. 2, p. 98.

[112] *Jelineau v. Jelineau*, 2 Dessausure 45, June 1801, in Helen Tunnicliff Catterall, ed., *Judicial Cases Concerning American Slavery and the Negro* (1926; reprint, New York: Negro University sities Press, 1968), p. 298.

[113] See Augustin L. Taveau to [Delphine Taveau], 7 October 1863, Augustin Louis Taveau Papers, DU.

[114] For additional examples, see Burr, ed., *The Secret Eye*, February 9, 1958, p. 160.

[115] Caroline Taveau to Master Augustin Taveau, March 6, 1839; ibid., January 8, 1843, Taveau Papers, DU. Taveau bribed her son to study the Bible with the promise of money. In the end, he turned out to be reprobate in the ways of his father.

Among those who took special notice were other white women in her community. Gertrude Thomas worried that the court might free the accused "to desolate the life of some other woman." Thomas's concern addressed the vulnerability of white women under supposed patriarchal protection. Culbreath's "insulted virtue," Thomas argued, required the defense of chivalrous men. The accused rapist, however, skipped town to avoid jail, leaving his wife and her friend, the rape victim, to face the consequences of his actions: the shame he had brought to two families and the embarrassed financial circumstance in which he left his wife and three children. A court levy against his already heavily mortgaged property left them further embarrassed and homeless.[116]

Mistresses turned out of their homes due to the fecklessness of their husbands, or who were victims of abuse, indeed may have kindled the greatest sympathy from slaves. But slaves also would have observed that they were not, as slaves were, without all protection or bereft of all civic capacity or rights. Despite the rule of patriarchy – and importantly because of it – white women found a judicial system that offered them some protection from errant husbands and, often enough, sympathetic judges willing to grant it. "A wife ill used, beaten and driven from her home by her husband, is entitled to the protection of the court, and will be allowed alimony, or the income of a settled property, for her maintenance until her husband received her home and treats her kindly," the Court of Chancery ruled in a case brought by Harriet Devall against her husband. The court heard testimony that Michael Devall "used vile and abusive language to her, struck her with a cane, brandished a sword above her head and threatened to take her life," and that he had, on another occasion, "Stood in the door with a pistol in his hand, and said, if she came in the house he would shoot her." The "extent of the abuse" Harriet Devall suffered, the court ruled, was compelling and "sufficient justification for [her] leaving the house." The court refused to be swayed by the testimony of a woman for the defense that Harriet Devall "had acted incontinently" or to allow into evidence testimony alleging the complainant's "lewd conduct . . . before marriage, as presumptive evidence of subsequent incontinence." Affirming the decision of the Abbeville District Court of South Carolina on appeal from Michael Devall, the Chancery Court awarded Harriet Devall alimony for as long as her husband refused to live with her.[117] Incontinence, defined as the inability to restrain one's sexual appetite, was a favored legal strategy in these kinds of suits.

In general, the courts claimed jurisdiction "to give relief, and to allow alimony to wives, in cases of improper severity by husbands." Jennet Prather took her husband to court on the grounds of "ill usage," which included being put out of their home in favor of an "adulteress" brought into their home by her husband. William Prather, like Michael Devall, sought to gain the court's

[116] Burr, ed., *The Secret Eye*, July 23, 1852, p. 111; March 30, 1856; p. 145. Quote is at p.145. See also, February 9, 1858, p. 160.

[117] *Harriet Devall, by her next friend, vs. Michael Devall and others*, Cases argued and Determined in the Court of Chancery of South Carolina (June 1809), pp. 78–81.

sympathy by throwing the charge of incontinence back at his wife. The court was not convinced and ordered him to pay alimony annually until he "would receive" her back into their home, and to treat her kindly. Jennet Prather's victory was, however, a partial one. She won alimony but lost custody of her three children, including an infant. In awarding custody of the older children to the father, the court reasoned that as there were no "allegations of extreme cruelty to the children" against him, it had no choice. The father, it intoned, "is the natural guardian invested by God and the law of the country," powers the court was "very cautious of interfering in the exercise of." Still, the court was troubled by its decision concerning the infant, which it feared was "treading new and dangerous grounds."[118]

Even though white women were generally required to make a clear case of "ill usage" on the part of their husbands, and "correct conduct" on their own part, in order to obtain alimony or access to their homes, the courts sought to ensure women's financial security even when they could not provide this kind of definitive evidence. This was especially true in cases involving the planter elite. But magistrates made it clear that they were not happy to see cases arising from the elite come before them. They were not above lecturing elite litigants on the impropriety of public airings of their domestic disputes. The court's position reflected its concern for the potential damage such cases could have on the stability of class and race relations. Unsavory behavior undermined elite power and authority, so the courts urged the elite to adjudicate in private charges of incontinence, adultery, or battery. Chancellor James emphasized in one case "how important it is for married persons to control their tempers." The significance of the case before him, extended, he wrote, to the "respectability of the parties litigant," and "the example it is to offer to the community."[119] In the community of slaves, the damage was most often already done. Patriarchy stood exposed in new ways. Yet sympathy for the plight of white women among slaves could still only be limited.

In the end, mistresses's use of violence manifested the regular demands and challenges of slaveholding. It drew upon the certain knowledge that they acted on their own rights. Although there might be rules about when, and before whom, they could exercise their power, not all mistresses felt obliged to follow them. The violence and humiliation that marked white women's treatment of enslaved women raised implacable barriers between them and tempered the very meaning of womanhood in the South. What did it mean to be a southern

---

[118] *Jennet Prather, by her next friend, vs. William Prather*, Report of Cases... in Court of Equity and in the Court of Appeals, 4 Dessausure 33 (S.C. 1809), pp. 33–44. For a different interpretation of the outcome of this case with respect to the disposition of the infant child, see Peter W. Bardaglio, *Reconstructing the Household: Families, Sex, & the Law in the Nineteenth Century South* (Chapel Hill: University of North Carolina Press, 1995), p. 90. In some cases, white women also received alimony in claims of incontinence against their husbands in relationships involving female slaves. See *Jelineau v. Jelineau*, 2 Dessausure 45 (S.C. June 1801).

[119] See, for example, Anonymous, Court of Chancery Cases, pp. 94–95. In this case, the social status of the plaintiff and defendant was raised specifically.

woman? How, out of the bramble of hate and terror, subjection and fear, did white and black women of the South construct and reconstruct their identities, their notions of what it meant to be female, their ideas about citizenship and freedom? For these endeavors, what did it mean that mistresses might have limited legal rights to divorce and could be beaten by masters, but that they could own slaves whom they could beat? Or, that enslaved women had hand-sawed-up backs or backs that looked like chokeberry trees?[120] The antebellum South was a world, ultimately, that neither white nor black women could easily abide. Enslaved women, Fox-Genovese writes, understood "that power was no abstraction: It wore a white male face."[121] Yet, it was also the case that the antebellum South was a place where power could wear a white female face. And that made the common vulnerability of black and white women to white male power distinctly different in operation and meaning. Slaves interpreted the abuse mistresses meted out as deliberate and calculated. But even if they thought it unpremeditated or "petulant," it is hard to imagine how they would come to the conclusion that white women were their allies or women to be emulated. A sobering verdict came in the case of *State v. Montgomery*. A husband and wife, master and mistress, were tried "for killing a slave by undue correction. The husband was acquitted, but the wife was convicted, and sentenced to pay the fine . . . $214.28."[122] As Frederick Douglass, who experienced violent and nonphysically violent mistresses, wrote: "To talk of *kindness* entering into the relation of slave and slaveholder is most absurd, wicked, and preposterous."[123]

---

[120] The chokeberry tree reference is from Toni Morrison, *Beloved* (New York: Signet 1991), pp. 20–21.

[121] Fox-Genovese, *Within the Plantation Household*, p. 190.

[122] *State v. Montgomery*, Cheves 120, February 1840, in *Judicial Cases Concerning American Slavery and the Negro*, ed. Catterall, p. 377.

[123] Douglass, *My Bondage and My Freedom*, p. 436.

3

Making "Better Girls"

Mistresses, Slave Women, and the Claims of Domesticity

My house is in order & my handmaidens wait upon me....

Catherine Edmondston, mistress

I will give you a full history of my belief of Darkey, to wit: I believe her disposition as to temper is as bad as any in the whole world. I believe she is as unfaithful as any I have ever been acquainted with.... I have tried and done all I could to get on with her, hoping that she would mend; but I have been disappointed in every instant. I can not hope for the better any longer.

Elisha Cain, overseer

How very domestic I am.

Gertrude Thomas, mistress

In *Gone With the Wind*, Margaret Mitchell has the fictional Gerald O'Hara understand that a plantation without a proper mistress was but a plantation in the making. O'Hara might accumulate land and slaves enough, but without "a thrifty and kind mistress, a good mother and devoted wife," Tara would never rise to the status of a great house and his ambitions to join the ranks of the planter elite, never succeed. A mistress meant order and efficiency: clean linen; polished furniture; timely meals; and an end generally to the disorder, sloth, and filth that governed his home without one.[1] But while O'Hara gets this point, Mitchell insists he misses another: That the work of efficiently-run households in fact required the unending attention and oversight of mistresses and the unending attention of slave women to the work on which depended mistresses's ability to fulfill those standards of order and efficiency. The stage is set for daily conflict on the home front, waged from bedrooms to out-houses and everywhere else in between; between enslaved women and mistresses, and mistresses and masters.

---

[1] Margaret Mitchell, *Gone With the Wind* (New York: Macmillan, 1936), pp. 53–54.

From the antebellum period into the twentieth century, the ideals of nineteenth-century domesticity proved to be as pervasive in the South as in the North, and mistresses were judged by their capacity to meet their evolving standards. How did these standards that guided the fictional O'Hara when "Tara cried out for a mistress," reflect actual relationships between mistresses and slaves? And what were the routine explanations when ideals (as is their wont) stood unattained or seemed unattainable? Scholars have been taken with that part of Mitchell's portrait that paints the work of mistresses as never-ending work, less so her unwitting portrait of slave women's intransigence and resistance to the plantation household – the dust that accumulated on the furniture, the dirty linen, and meals served late. Certainly, this is not the portrait Mitchell intended to paint, as it was not the portrait slaveholders preferred. For Mitchell and for slaveholders, slave women's inherent racial inferiority accounted for the disorder. This accounted for the fundamental flaws in their character, behavior that was unsuitable, and their failure to be "better girl[s]." In nonidiomatic terms, by this account, slave women simply failed to see their mistresses's needs as their own needs and sought within the confines of slavery to live their own lives. To get them to *be* slaves, Lizzie Bain Partin wrote from experience, "requires force."[2]

Enslaved women resisted the plantation household as an ideological construction and as a site of labor as they found themselves at the nexus of two interrelated but incongruous projects. The first was the maintenance of slavery; the second, the projection of the South along the path of western civilization. The call to domestic order highlighted white women's governance of the home and slave women, in ways similar to English and Irish servants, became projects of the western civilizing mission. Domestic life and civilized life were thus joined to the idea of nation.[3] This civilizing mission cast enslaved women as the antithesis of civilization, as a standard against which white women and their progress on the road to civilization would be measured. In the U.S. South, as elsewhere in western bourgeois culture by the mid-nineteenth century, order, management, and discipline became important touchstones of the meaning of civilization.

Historians have documented the transformation of elite women in the North and in England into zealous advocates of notions of domesticity.[4] The case of

---

[2] Lizzie Bain Partin to Mother [Mary Bain], January 6, 1857, Bain Papers, DU.

[3] For a discussion of this point on different ground, see Dipesh Chakrabarty, "The Difference – Deferral of a Colonial Modernity: Public Debates on Domesticity in British Bengal," in *Tensions of Empire: Colonial Culture in a Bourgeois World*, ed. Frederick Cooper and Ann Laura Stoler (Berkeley: University of California Press, 1997), pp. 374–76.

[4] See, for example, Kathryn Kish Sklar, *Catherine Beecher: A Study in American Domesticity* (New Haven: Yale University Press, 1973); Amanda Vickery, *The Gentleman's Daughter: Women's Lives in Georgian England* (New Haven & London: Yale University Press, 1998), p. 133; and Philip Ariès, "Introduction," in *A History of Private Life: Passions of the Renaissance*, vol. 9, ed. Roger Chartier (Cambridge, MA: Harvard University Press, 1989).

the South is more enigmatic. The transformation nowhere proceeded smoothly, but the effort to build and ground evolving notions of civilization and domesticity proved particularly problematic in the South. Here it had to grapple with different cultural, social, and material impediments. Northern and Western European models could only be reproduced on southern ground in aberrant form but southerners understood that they could not afford to ignore the call to domestic order. Mary Ann Mason's detailed manual for a "well-regulated household" was initially written "expressly for the benefit of residents of the Southern States, before emancipation."[5] As Mason pointedly noted, the making of a "well-regulated" southern household, because of slavery, required its own manual. Even when the vocabulary was similar to northern models, its application could not be. In the South, notions of domesticity camouflaged difficult labor relations and conflict within the plantation household. The plantation household was the principal site for the construction of southern white womanhood, making the place of black women within it critically important.

By the late antebellum period, the idea that black women were vessels of disorder and filth had become central to southern pro-slavery ideology and evolving notions of domesticity, more crucial to these concerns than all the vaunted notions about Jezebels and loyal mammies that came to occupy primacy of place in caricatures of black women in later years. In the aftermath of emancipation and Reconstruction, black women would again come to be considered obstructions to civilization as new campaigns aimed at the domestication of the white home arose in companion to larger colonial campaigns aimed at the domestication of the "uncivilized" world. Important historical antecedents to these campaigns lay in the slave South, and in the cross currents of proslavery ideology and English thought on the subject of mistresses, servants, and household economy.

The ideology of domesticity shared a common vocabulary across the Mason-Dixon line and across oceans, but marked differences distinguished how this vocabulary was translated and mobilized. To function and to meet the standards of domesticity, the plantation household required the labor of enslaved women – to beautify, clean, order, and thus civilize it. At the same time, it required negative representations of enslaved women and their labor – filthy, disordered – to deny them consideration as anything more than tools of the civilizing mission. But enslaved women did not become servants who could be counted on to support their mistresses's domestic ambitions and personal needs, and, thus, they could not be counted on to support the plantation household's civilizing mission. Like servants in England and New England, they refused to go happily along. So, for that matter, sometimes did mistresses. Impudence roiled elite households on both sides of the Atlantic.

---

[5] Mary Ann Mason, *The Young Housewife's Counsellor and Friend: Containing Directions in Every Department of Housekeeping including the Duties of Wife and Mother* (New York: E. J. Hale & Son, 1875), p. 5.

Obstinate, Self-Willed, Cross, and Dirty

In the diaries and letters of slaveholding women and men, enslaved women are seldom mentioned, but the exceptions are telling. Slaveholders wrote mainly about themselves. But the comparatively meager record they left on their slaves is rich on enslaved women in the plantation household. It is a record chronicling the efforts of mistresses and masters to organize the plantation household according to emerging ideas of domesticity, their own sense of power, and it is a record of slave women's resistance to these efforts and to slaveholders' sense of power. Masters and mistresses couched black women's resistance in the idiom of "backwardness," a more manageable language of personality type and disorder.[6]

By this inversion, slave women did not so much resist slavery as they resisted its supposed civilizing mission, no matter that slaveholders believed their status as slaves made them ineligible candidates for civilizing. This message was conveyed in mistresses's complaints about every aspect of the work slave women performed, and every aspect of the lives they lived or tried to live. It was present in mistresses' complaints that enslaved women failed, generally, to display sufficient dedication to either the white household, broadly speaking, or the particular needs of their owners, and in the complaint that they displayed insufficient gratitude. Mistresses and masters (and overseers) described slave women as lazier, filthier; more shiftless, slatternly, ignorant and impudent than slave men; more inclined to theft and lying; less easily managed; less trainable; and in a strategic low blow, less interested in their children and their responsibilities as mothers. By contrast, white women's labors were represented as the central operative mechanism of the plantation household: From the hands of white women, not those of black women, came whatever order and cleanliness there was in a world stained by black women's mere presence. They were the ones who, as Keziah Brevard put it, "raised" black children. By these inversions, black women's "behavior" accounted, too, for planter women's inability to maintain the self-control that southern propaganda and writings on domesticity bade them embrace. By this view, "racial traits," not slave women's resistance to the ideology of southern domesticity and to their enslavement, accounted for whatever disorder there was within the plantation household. Whatever the fallacies in these views, the resistance of household slaves did, in fact, mark the failure of southern domesticity.

Mistresses responded to this resistance by cajoling, scolding, hitting, and beating. In frustration, they claimed, they sometimes did the work of slaves themselves to set an example. Dismissing female slave resistance as a problem of behavior served to minimize fear of domestic slaves. If deep down they

---

[6] David Barry Gaspar has called attention to the disinclination of scholars to see "individual acts, attitudes, and thoughts" as forms of political resistance. See Gaspar, "Working the System: Antigua Slaves and Their Struggle to Live," *Slavery and Abolition: A Journal of Comparative Studies* 13 (December 1992): 131–55.

feared, the language of "behavior" offered a less disturbing framework for that fear than resistance. Here, after all, was baby's nurse, the whole family's cook, the maid near at hand at midnight. But embedded within the camouflaging language of disorder and behavior is the story of the damage unruly household slaves did to mistresses's worlds and the claims of southern domesticity. When mistresses beat and humiliated slaves, they betrayed the public point about slavery's good. When they or their husbands took slaves to court for stealing food, spoons with which to eat, or clothes to trade for food, the betrayals became a matter of public record.[7] The more comforting language of the civilizing mission concealed from public scrutiny the daily rumblings of dissatisfaction and resistance.

At the very least, black women's unambiguous rebuke of the plantation household at emancipation suggests the need to re-examine many of our assumptions about the plantation household and its operation and to explore slave women's resistance to it differently. The accusations against the child, Beckie, typify the rumblings and slaves' discontent that slaveholders characterized as behavioral problems. The response of her mistress illustrates the way in which mistresses transformed women's resistance into less threatening gestures. Beckie's mistress, Amelia Lines, faulted her for following "her own way of doing things," which included being perennially slow. Beckie gave particular trouble on ironing days when she appeared to her mistress especially "careless and stupid." Her mistress concluded that Beckie was simply *untrainable*, inherently incapable of meeting her mistress's specifications for good help despite the fact of her youth, which her mistress thought should make her amenable to good training. With a few months of training, Lines had once confidently predicted, "I can make her do my work just as I want it done." Beckie, instead, failed to do things her mistress's way. Moreover, she ran away. Yet, "bad as she is," Lines was willing to try Beckie once more if she were captured even though, she admitted, Beckie had never shown any appreciation for the lessons Lines taught her, or any intimation of a desire to please her mistress. But Lines had gone to "a great deal of trouble in teaching her" and to give up on her simply meant "going through the same trouble with a new servant." Besides, even Beckie was a more attractive solution than the one she now faced. "I find it very hard to be alone and do all the drudgery myself," Lines wrote.[8]

Like Lines, Tryphena Fox struggled to turn enslaved women into her ideal of what they should be. Like Lines, she found herself feeling outwitted and angry much of the time. "*[M]y temper is quite bad,*" she admitted. Fox and her

---

[7] See, for example, Spartanburg District Court of Magistrates and Freeholders (C2920), Case #82, January 15, 1847; Case #85, October 6, 1847; Case #27, April 18, 1839, among others. SCDAH. I want to thank Kathleen Hilliard for turning my attention to these records. Correspondence with author, June 24, 2003.

[8] Amelia Akehurst Lines, *To Raise Myself a Little: The Diaries and Letters of Jennie, a Georgia Teacher, 1851–1886*, ed. Thomas Dyer (Athens: University of Georgia Press, 1982), July 1, 1863, p. 203; February 14, 1863, p. 198; February 7, 1863; p. 197; July 24, 1863; July 26, 1863, p. 204, quotes at pp. 203–4.

husband hired and purchased slaves for their household, but whether purchased or hired, Fox never found one to suit her – just a "rabble of negroes & Creoles." At one point or another, she would describe them one and all as lazy, impudent, irresponsible, immoral, incorrigible, "slow & stupid," shirkers all. Mary, a slave Fox hired, harbored her runaway son in her room, where, Fox charged, she also kept a jug of whiskey. Further, Mary seemed never able to get a task completed in a timely fashion, or correctly. Fed up, Fox sent Mary back to her owner for retraining, and declared that she was happy to be rid of her.[9] When Mary returned a few months later, Fox was pleased. Mary seemed "hardly like the same servant." But the honeymoon did not last. Mary soon exhibited her old habits. She stole cream and butter. When Fox asked her to do anything, she took her time doing it and did it poorly. She refused to "do right," except "when she pleases," Fox wrote, "the better I treat her, the more impudent & lazy she grows."[10]

Of all the black women who labored in Fox's household, Susan, by Fox's account, proved the most unmanageable. She was the perennial slacker, a woman who was wont to deny herself neither pleasure nor leisure time. Fox owned Susan, but got no more work out of her than she did from Mary. Susan managed to avoid work for two weeks because of "a little sore on her finger." When Fox punished her, she ran away, but not before giving Fox "unheard of impudence." After Susan was captured, Fox sent her to her father-in-law's plantation for a month as punishment. Before the month was out, however, the burden of having to help care for Susan's three children, without Susan, led Fox to reconsider. Bringing Susan back would be *the worst of all evils.* "I know how it will be – if once she comes back," Fox wrote, "I shall have to put up with all sorts of laziness & impudence" and have "no peace." But ridding herself of the burden of Susan's children was apparently worth enduring the discord between herself and Susan. Fox brought Susan back but with the proviso that she would be hired out if she persisted in her old ways. It was an empty threat as Fox acknowledged. None of the threats made Susan any more accommodating to her slave status.[11] Within a few months, Susan inconvenienced Fox with the birth of another child, a "fine mulatto boy."[12]

In the meantime, Fox acquired a new servant, Elizabeth. Initially, Elizabeth worked "well & quietly & quickly," without Fox's constant oversight. But

[9] Wilma King, ed., *A Northern Woman in the Plantation South: Letters of Tryphena Blanche Holder Fox, 1856-1876* (Columbia: University of South Carolina Press, 1993), July 9, 1858, p. 73; January 4, 1857, p. 47; June 28, 1857, p. 56. Like Amelia Lines, Fox was born and raised in the North in humble circumstances. Both women, soon after moving to the South to take positions as tutors, quickly turned their ambitions to becoming mistresses. In Fox's case, marriage to a doctor whose sole income derived from his profession placed a huge strain on those ambitions. Yet the views they shared of slave women, and their treatment of them, resembled those of the most seasoned and wealthiest mistresses.

[10] King, ed., *A Northern Woman*, August 31, 1856, p. 62; November 1, 1857, pp. 64–65.

[11] King, ed., *A Northern Woman*, June 13, 1859, p. 89; November 17, 1859, p. 93, quotes at pp. 89 and 93.

[12] King, ed., *A Northern Woman*, March 17, 1860, p. 99. Fox gives no hint as to who the father of the child might be.

soon enough, the thirty-year-old Elizabeth was "slow" and "not very neat," no different from Susan. Breakfast dishes did not get washed before eleven o'clock. One day Fox complained that Elizabeth had done "nothing" since preparing the morning coffee except churn cream (making only a little butter), dress Fox's daughter, prepare a bath for Fox's baby, clean her master's and her mistress's rooms, sweep and dust the dining room, and eat her own breakfast. Fox once more declared her determination to rid herself of "hysterical" black women. After five years of relying on them to clean her house, Fox wrote: "I have found that I must give up my notions of a very nice & orderly house or scold & watch & oversee all the time, not only ruining my own mind & temper but making the servants really dissatisfied & the more careless from being looked after.... So [if] the house is passably decent I am going to let it go."[13]

Fox's own account of the work Elizabeth actually performed, in fact, bore no relationship to her description of Elizabeth's habits. Between 5:00 A.M. and 11:00 A.M., Elizabeth had, after all, made coffee and butter, cared for Fox's two children, cleaned three rooms, cooked her own breakfast, and washed dishes, hardly a study in shiftless behavior. For mistresses, however, this was not always the point. The contradictions endemic to slaveholding in the domestic sphere fueled mistresses's anger and rage against slaves (and sometimes against their own children). Fox felt keenly her inability to get slave women to view her interests as their own and took it as a reflection on her skills as manager of her household in line with the reigning ideology of domesticity. For a brief moment she harbored the notion that having a clock would bolster her efforts to bring system and order to her household. It made no difference. She resigned herself to keeping the clock merely to keep her company.[14] On the eve of the Civil War, Susan was again "beyond endurance," "*impudent & lazy & filthy*," and the enmity between the two women was clearly mutual. On this point Fox was as unambiguous as Susan:

Perhaps I do not treat her right – probably I do not for I do not like her & never did, & I *never shall*; it is not pleasant to live on the same place & in or as close proximity or as one is obliged to do with the cook & be all the time at enmity with her & feel angry, whether I say anything or not.[15]

When several months later Susan gave birth to another child, Fox was relieved; she would get a break as much as Susan. The "customary" four weeks Susan was allowed to recover was time she would take to rest her own nerves and gather her own strength. She looked anxiously to the end of the period

---

[13] King, ed., *A Northern Woman*, March 29, 1861, pp. 114–17; July 6, 1861, p. 125; August 8, 1861, pp. 128–29, quotes at pp. 115, 128, and 129.

[14] King, ed., *A Northern Woman*, January 1, 1860, p. 97. Other mistresses may have had better luck with the introduction of clock time. James Bolton, for example, remembered that his mistress taught the cook "to count the clock" (James Bolton, *Georgia Narratives*, Supplement Series 1, vol. 3, pt. 1, p. 87). On time consciousness in the South, see Mark M. Smith, *Mastered by the Clock: Slavery and Freedom in the American South* (Chapel Hill: University of North Carolina Press, 1997).

[15] King, ed., *A Northern Woman*, December 16, 1860, p. 107.

"when my authority must again commence," but took some consolation in the hope that she would "be pretty well rested by the time her month is up." Meanwhile, Maria, who Fox had devoted a year to training and on whom her husband had spent a fortune of $1500 to buy, "took a notion to *run away*."[16] Fox had tried to break Maria of her "fondness for *running out nights*," following which she slept in the next morning, by locking her in. She also whipped her, but it had not more effect than locked doors on Maria's behavior. Maria climbed out a window and despite an intensive hunt, remained at large for six months, harbored by a neighbor's carriage driver.[17]

And so it went on other plantations. Black women in the plantation household ran away and about.[18] Esther ran about and stole food so much that her mistress chained her up. On the same plantation, Priscilla was whipped for running away and a year later for "bad conduct."[19] Susan, as we have seen, took full advantage of her pregnancies to work less, thus disrupting her mistress's efforts at household and slave management. Even when Susan's newborn baby died, she did not get up from her bed to go back to work. Her mistress did not force the issue, but promised that at the end of the customary four weeks, Susan would be made to "go to work in downright good earnest." Maria Bryan similarly described her slave Caroline as "obstinate, self-willed, cross and dirty to a degree." Another of Bryan's slaves, Jenny, showed an equal disposition to obstinacy and a decided propensity to leave the house at night without permission.[20]

Despite the complaints of mistresses and the punishment they doled out, slave women persisted in working slowly, in stealing time to care for a sick child or tend to other family and personal needs, in seeking their own pleasure in life, and generally resisting confinement to the workplace of the plantation household.[21] Ideas about the different insurrectionary tendencies of men and women as a circumstance of gender played a part in how slaveholders framed slave women's "self-willed" resistance – i.e., women were less likely to run away

---

[16] King, ed., *A Northern Woman*, March 29, 1861, pp. 114–15. See also Wilma King, "The Mistress and Her Maids: White and Black Women in a Louisiana Household, 1858–1868," in *Discovering the Women in Slavery: Emancipating Perspectives on the American Past*, ed. Patricia Morton (Athens: University of Georgia Press, 1996), pp. 82–106.

[17] King, ed., *A Northern Woman*, March 29, 1861, p. 115; January 29, 1862, p. 133; and n.14, p. 133.

[18] On enslaved women's proclivity for truancy, see Deborah Gray White, *Ar'n't I a Woman?: Female Slaves in the Plantation South*, rev. ed. (New York: W. W. Norton, 1999), pp. 74–76; Stephanie M. H. Camp, *Closer to Freedom: Enslaved Women and Everyday Resistance in the Plantation South* (Chapel Hill: University of North Carolina Press, 2004), pp. 36–40.

[19] J. Carlyle Sitterson, "A Planter Family of the Old and New South," *Journal of Southern History*, 6 (August 1940): 349–350, quotes at pp. 350 and 349, respectively.

[20] King, ed., *A Northern Woman*, May 17, 1860, p. 100; Carol Bleser, ed., *Tokens of Affection: The Letters of a Planter's Daughter in the Old South* (Athens: University of Georgia Press, 1996), January 22, 1827, p. 31; May 29, 1833, p. 149; December 23, 1839, p. 275; December 24, 1840, p. 322, quote at p. 275.

[21] King, ed., *A Northern Woman*, January 1, 1860, p. 97; March 17, 1860, pp. 99–100. The "right" to time off for recuperation after the birth of a child was an important component of slave women's struggle to gain as much control as possible over their lives, and as much a product of negotiation as the "right" to small rice.

or rebel – but the introduction of notions of nineteenth-century domesticity also played a significant role. As trade brought new spices and foods to a growing middle class and the separation of commerce from the home took men away to counting houses and offices, two developments followed that were to have an impact on slavery in the plantation household. For one, the preparation of family meals took on new meaning and became more elaborate.[22] Secondly, the concept of frugality became more a part of the vocabulary of mistresses along with notions of discipline, order, and time management.

In the plantation household, the idea of domesticity meshed with the idea that women were less likely to revolt and the contradictory idea that resistance on the part of slave women was both harmless – a matter of temperament – and dangerous. These incompatible notions were made to meld via discourses that stripped insurrectionary intent or meaning from the forms of resistance in which slave women were most likely to engage. Like the vocabulary that would soon dominate the world of factories, the vocabulary of domesticity spoke of "production goals," "discipline," "routine," and "order." As it resonated in the South, it connoted personality and racial defects rather than intractable labor problems. As well, where notions of time and discipline were regarded in the North as a civilizing influence for the masses of new immigrants, in the South, the civilizing mission was for whites only. Disciplining slave women to the clock would contribute to the white South's civilizing mission for itself. Again, the vocabulary was familiar; the methods of conversion and the expected outcome diverged.

One hardly gets a sense of labor disputes in descriptions of slave women's resistance penned by mistresses such as this: working "by fits & starts – good three or four weeks & then so ugly & contrary that an angel could hardly keep mild & pleasant."[23] Even when mistresses placed such statements side-by-side with contrasting descriptions of their own labor as consistent and orderly, the dynamic is missing, as in this example from Fox. After having awakened the slaves at five o'clock to start the day, by seven o'clock breakfast still had not been served, which meant that the washing would, in turn, be pushed back.

Today it has been push, hurry, push, to get the washing anywhere near done & though it is four o clock [Susan] is just hanging out the colored clothes. The white things have been washed in *one* water and boiled – she has done nothing but wash since six o clock this morning, so you may know how slow she is – only Dr R – baby & myself to wash for.[24]

In this description, Susan is more obstinate and lazy than anything else.

[22] To accommodate the hours men now worked away from the home, the evening meal replaced the noon meal as the more substantial, and cookery books became a growth industry. But even as those books instructed women on how to prepare often elaborate and expensive new dishes, they emphasized frugality. The most famous of the nineteenth-century cookery books was *Mrs. Beeton's Book of Household Management* (Isabella Beeton, *Mrs. Beeton's Book of Household Management*, ed. Nicola Humble, abridged edition [1861; New York: Oxford University Press, 2000]). It sold over 60,000 copies in its first year of publication. By 1868, it had sold nearly 2 million copies. See also Vickery, *Gentleman's Daughter*, pp. 127–35.

[23] King, ed., *A Northern Woman*, July 9, 1858, p. 75.

[24] King, ed., *A Northern Woman*, July 9, 1858, p. 75.

Besides, it often did not matter even when slave women did the work demanded of them. The manner in which they did so angered mistresses because it left little doubt about black women's sense of violation. Sometimes, their simple presence was enough to vex mistresses. Whether in subtle or overt ways, they made the point that they hated the work, the workplace, and their enslavement, that they gave their labor neither voluntarily nor happily – sentiments that struck at the heart of slavery's rationalization and notions of southern white womanhood. The behavior mistresses characterized as "shiftless" allowed black women to claim greater control over their labor, decrease their workloads, take personal time, and mock pretensions to domesticity. The idea that a grown woman had to sneak out through a window to find some privacy was sufficient provocation for female slave resistance. Resistance of this sort did not break the back of slavery, but it made the job of maintaining slavery more difficult and was central to black women's sense of self and dignity.

Still, the making of race and gender ideologies in the American South relied heavily on images of "great, strong, fat" black women who lolled about while their mistresses worked dutifully and patiently to wrest their bad character and behavior out of them: "I had taught [Maria]," Tryphena Fox wrote, "after a great deal of pains & many an hour's hard work on my part, to sweep & dust & arrange a room nicely, to wash & iron fine clothes, particularly shirts, to cook cakes & custards & jellies & cut out & make quite a variety of garments." But instead of becoming the perfect, dependable, and neat servant, Maria slept when she should have been working, left the house at night, and left dirty dishes untouched.[25] Without their watchful eyes, mistresses knew, black women would "shirk" their "responsibilities." They would waste provisions and be, in general, improvident.[26]

By her own estimate, Mary Bain of North Carolina devoted years to the task of teaching Rose how to be a "good" slave. Rose refused the instruction and Bain sent her to the "hiring grounds" as punishment. Her owners consoled themselves in the belief that they had tried to teach her but she was simply incapable of learning. What they meant was that two years of trying several different arrangements and environments had not rid Rose of her seeming contempt for them or desire to live her own life. In 1857 they separated Rose from her mother, sending her to Virginia to cook and wash for their daughter, Lizzie Bain Partin. But Rose was as contemptuous of her new owners' claim to her being. Her removal to Virginia accomplished nothing. Lizzie Bain Partin reported "that, for except to nurse she is next to nobody.... for a month or more she has been the same old Rose." Partin's husband declared Rose "a hopeless case."[27]

[25] King, ed., *A Northern Woman*, March 29th 1861, pp. 114–15.
[26] King, ed., *A Northern Woman*, January 4, 1857, p. 47; September 14, 1860, p. 104.
[27] Lizzie Bain Partin to Mother [Mary Bain], January 6, 1857; Lizzie Bain Partin to Sister [Mollie Bain], February 16, 1858; Lizzie Bain Partin to Sister [Mollie Bain Bitting], February 3, 1859; Donald Bain to Sister [Mollie Bain Bitting], February 7, 1959, Bain Papers, DU.

The following year, Rose was hired out in the country.[28] With this move, her owners held out hope that she would "learn to be a better girl, if she can only be taught to do as she is directed she may make a valuable servant, she has had teaching enough to make her the best in the world, but it requires force and that of the strictest kind." Within months, however, desperate for someone to take care of her young daughter and unable to buy or hire another slave, Partin brought Rose back. She returned "worse than ever," indeed, "dreadful."[29]

The complaints of better-heeled southern mistresses were little different. Elizabeth Heyward Manigault, mistress of one of the South's largest and wealthiest slaveholdings, put up for a time with Mira, a slave she admitted she hated "like the devil." Her family agreed that Mira was "good for nothing but to milk a cow."[30] Gertrude Thomas spent years trying to turn Isabella, who she labeled a habitual thief, into a trusted slave. Declaring Isabella's habits incurable, Thomas gave up and sent her to the family's Burke plantation to work in the field. Isabella promptly ran away. After a few weeks of freedom, Isabella was captured and jailed and returned to Thomas sick with typhoid fever. When she was well enough, Thomas sent her back to Burke, deciding she should be "sold and a good steady woman bought in her place." Thomas never overtly cast Isabella's actions as a desire to live her own life. Instead, she framed it in terms of a refusal to be "a good house servant," who would not impose on her mistress's confidence and who would show proper gratitude. A little more than a year later, Isabella was once more on the run, staying out this time for several months before she was caught, again jailed, and sent to Burke.[31]

Despite her complaints about Isabella and the language in which she couched them, Thomas understood Isabella's actions as casting doubt on slavery's goodness, and on her own. Thomas was aware of the strange attachment she felt for Isabella. She thought that she could not live without her and felt something "amounting nearer to attachment than to any servant I have ever met with in my life." It was not the kind of human recognition Isabella sought.[32] Slave women's struggle for human recognition, visible in their attempts to bring dignity to their lives and create spaces of privacy, faced unceasing attack

[28] Lizzie Bain Partin to Sister [Mollie Bain], February 16, 1858, Bain Papers, DU.

[29] Lizzie Bain Partin to Sister [Mollie Bain], February 24, 1858; Lizzie Bain Partin to Sister [Mollie Bain Bitting], June 22, 1858; Lizzie Bain Partin to Sister [Mollie Bain Bitting], February 3, 1859; Donald Bain to Sister [Mollie Bain Bitting], February 7, 1859, Bain Papers, DU.

[30] Louis Manigault to Charles Manigault, December 28, 1854, in *Life and Labor on Argyle Island: Letters and Documents of a Savannah River Rice Plantation, 1833–1867*, ed. James M. Clifton (Savannah, GA: Beehive Press, 1978), p. 192.

[31] Virginia Ingraham Burr, ed., *The Secret Eye: The Journal of Ella Gertrude Thomas, 1848–1889* (Chapel Hill: University of North Carolina Press, 1990), August 19, 1855, p. 133; November 1857, pp. 157–58; January 13, 1859, p. 170. Isabella was eventually sold.

[32] Burr, ed., *The Secret Eye*, November 1867, p. 158. For a different assessment of the ideology of domesticity and mistresses's behavior toward enslaved women, see Marli F. Weiner, *Mistresses and Slaves: Plantation Women in South Carolina, 1830–80* (Urbana: University of Illinois Press, 1998), pp. 74–75.

from mistresses. Descriptions of them as "impudent & lazy" and "filthy"[33] seem deliberately invoked to support the contrasting image of the plantation mistress as weak and fragile, yet tireless in her efforts to manage her household and teach black women the niceties of domesticity. Conflict was inevitable as slave ownership encouraged mistresses to see their actions as benevolent, rather than violent. Gertrude Thomas's attachment to Isabella is understandable in this light. Like English gentlewomen, she clung to Isabella "with a pathetic sense of her own vulnerability." When one of Englishwoman Elizabeth Shackleford's servants ran away "without leaving a word to any person," Shackleford saw it as the ingratitude of "an Impudent Dirty Slut." At other times she dismissed her servants as "saucy dirty & Ungovernable" and "vulgar."[34]

Like English servants, black women resented the intimacies and humiliations of household service. But race and their slave status set black women apart. British servants might well be ungovernable, but by the mid-nineteenth century, as Susan Thorne writes, "the shift to more incorporationist strategies of social control with respect to the working classes" in British society fostered the view that the working class was part of "a kindred nationality."[35] Black people in the South found no similar consideration and would continue to be imagined as alien, both in their civic capacity and in their relationship to humankind. White southerners held fast to the notion that they resided in the midst of a savage people who could never be brought to the level of civilized behavior, but who could reduce the civilized to savagery.

White southerners measured themselves partly in the distance that separated them from enslaved (and free) black people. Southern white women were expected to measure that distance in their gentility and in certain habits – order, punctuality, and frugality. Black women represented the obverse of all these things, which is why mistresses could rail about the inefficiency of slaves even when they in fact completed their work. So ingrained were the symbols of difference that slaveholding women often voiced their sense of disorder and failure in the idioms of disorder used to describe slave women and poor white women. Managing slaves and a household, Sarah Gayle had become "'large, roughened almost toothless, *smoking* and *chewing!'* – the scolding manager of

[33] King, ed., *A Northern Woman*, December 16, 1860, p. 107; March 29, 1861, p. 114. These descriptions ill fit the idealized image of "mammy." Even Fox's description of Susan as "a great, strong, fat thing" bears little resemblance connotatively to "mammy," of large stature, but soft, nurturing bosom. Indeed, in age, size, and other physical attributes, "mammies" may have more closely approximated the young girl who served as William Alexander Percy's nurse than the image made famous by the film *Gone With the Wind*. Percy wrote: "Southerners like to make clear, especially to Northerners, that every respectable white baby had a black mammy, who, one is to infer, was fat and elderly and bandannaed.... Nain was sixteen, divinely café-au-lait." Chiefly, Percy added, acknowledging his violations of the child, "I remember her bosom. It was soft and warm" (William Alexander Percy, *Lanterns on the Levee: Recollections of a Planter's Son* [New York: Knopf, 1941], p. 26).

[34] Vickery, *Gentleman's Daughter*, quotes at pp. 145 and 142, respectively.

[35] Susan Thorne, *Congregational Missions and the Making of an Imperial Culture in Nineteenth-Century England* (Stanford, CA: Stanford University Press, 1999), p. 169.

the family of four children." Gayle chronicled similar changes in her sister-in-law, Ann, whose "complexion has lost its whiteness and polish, her teeth are much gone – her beautiful black hair which used to curl over her shoulders when she threw it down, is now thin, and can no longer be call'd an ornament."[36]

Trying to run a small household with too few slaves to suit her taste, and these refusing to accommodate her wishes, left Tryphena Fox changed physically and emotionally. Fox described the woman she had become as "dark or as a *mulatress*, crass & ugly." She looked like a "scare-crow" and had become "almost *black*." In these rare moments of self-reflection, Fox considered how strikingly different her life was from the romanticized life of the fabled plantation mistress.[37] She rationalized the state of her own life this way: Living in a slave society in a household among enslaved women could turn white women into the dark and uncivilized, and make them violent. In general, slaveholding women did not acknowledge their own complicity in the uncivilized state of the plantation household. Nor did they assess the matter analytically as a question of power. Keziah Brevard was rare in this regard. Brevard confronted and named the slaves in her home who made her life a living hell, and she acknowledged her own contribution to that hell.[38]

The idea that slavery greatly complicated the task of creating a civilized home, especially one run by a "scolding manager" or a profligate wife or mistress, had deep roots in American thought. Long before women's journals, advances in household machinery, and the rationalization of household work as "domestic science" urged women's surrender to scientific household management, the urge had become imbedded in the discourse of American civilization. Orderly households came increasingly to mean efficient households run by prudent women. Efforts to tie women's behavior and manners to the ordering of the household and its dependents surfaced in colonial-era writings. In the early eighteenth century, New Jersey Quaker John Hepburn lashed out against slavery and its inherent evils, including the immoral uses to which slavery's ill-gotten profits were put. Hepburn charged his fellow Quakers with the sin of accumulating money, and for wicked purposes, to:

Keep their Wives idle (Jezebel-like) to paint their Faces, and *Puff*, and *powder their hair*, and to bring up their Sons and Daughters in *Idleness* and *Wantonness*, and in all manner of *Pride* and *Prodigality*, in *decking* and *adorning* the Carkases with pufft and powdered Hair, with *Ruffles* and *Top-knots*, *Ribbands* and *Lace*, and *Gay Clothing* and what not.[39]

36 Elizabeth Fox-Genovese, *Within the Plantation Household: Black and White Women of the Old South* (Chapel Hill: University of North Carolina Press, 1988), p. 4.

37 King, ed., *A Northern Woman*, June 28, 1861, p. 120; June 28, 1857, p. 55.

38 John Hammond Moore, ed., *A Plantation Mistress on the Eve of the Civil War: The Diary of Keziah Goodwyn Hopkins Brevard, 1860–1861* (Columbia: University of South Carolina Press, 1993). See, for example, her entry of January 30, 1862, p. 83. Hereafter cited as Brevard, *Diary*.

39 As quoted in C. Duncan Rice, *The Rise and Fall of Black Slavery* (Baton Rouge: Louisiana State University Press, 1975), p. 192.

For nineteenth-century feminist and abolitionist Lydia Maria Child, the problem was more mundane. Dedicating her book, *The American Frugal Housewife*, to "Those Who Are Not Ashamed of Economy," Child offered it as a moral and economically principled guide to the proper management of domestic economy. Mixing advice on marriage with recipes for frugal household management, the book opened with a declaration that would have delighted early twentieth-century rationalizers of assembly line production: "The true economy of housekeeping is simply the art of gathering up all the fragments, so that nothing be lost. I mean fragments of *time*, as well as materials." Tying slaveholding women's obligation to proper household management to the health of the republic and the health of the republic to the proper "*domestic education*" of women, she warned against the dangers of extravagance in all forms and among all classes, though her primary concern was the reformation of the poor.[40]

Mary Ann Mason, to the contrary, was concerned expressly with slaveholders, with providing "advice respecting the management of slaves," which, she wrote, might "appear unsuitable in some degree for those who are nonresidents."[41] Northern women who moved to the South recognized the difference explicitly. In letters to her family in the North, Tryphena Fox was constantly trying to rationalize her dependence on slaves. Things were different in the South, she stressed, and, thus, her unending complaints about the trying time black women gave her. She expressed concern, however, that her family and "those ranting abolitionists" would not understand, that they might misconstrue her complaints as evidence that she had "turned out to be a Southern monster," and, so, beseeched her mother not to share her communications on the subject.[42]

Amelia Lines also often found herself explaining to her northern family why she could not do her own housework. Like Fox, she came from a workingclass family. In the South, both women argued, no white woman of any standing, nor who hoped to have any, did her own housework. Both were willing to tolerate servants who resisted them at every turn and to pay more than the market price for them if the choice was to have none at all. To do without a black servant, *in the South*, was not an option. The only option was to return to the North. "I want to go *home*," Lines whined at one point, "where people can live independent of Negro help."[43]

---

[40] Mrs. [Maria] Child, *The American Frugal Housewife*, 12th ed. (1833; reprint, Bedford, MA: Applewood Books, N.D.), passim; for quotes see, respectively, pp. 1, 4, 91, and 92.

[41] Mason, *Young Housewife's Counsellor*, p. vi.

[42] King, ed., *A Northern Woman*, August 31, 1856, p. 61.

[43] Lines, *To Raise Myself a Little*, February 7, 1863, p. 197. After the war, Lines, and her husband and daughter went to visit her family in the North. She found that she did "not like these Yankee people," especially workingclass northern women like those in her own family. She criticized them as "great workers" who "think the greatest virtue in a woman's character is to be able to do a great amount of hard drudgery." While no disgrace in some sense, she nonetheless

Not only, mistresses believed, could they not live without "Negro help," neither could they practice "true economy," if doing so meant living without extravagance. Women of the South's ruling class defined themselves in part by their consumption of luxury goods, from household furnishings to clothing. Wealthy planter women adorned themselves and their homes with expensive kid gloves, French calico, black silk, organdy, embroidered handkerchiefs, damask napkins, and French towels. Fashion reviews from Europe were closely watched and followed.[44] Yet, there remained in the South, as in the North, though with vastly different consequences, a sense that the pursuit of worldly trappings undermined the larger task of building the republic and sustaining republican mothers. Slaveholding men generally abided such extravagance, though not without criticism.[45]

By the late antebellum period, the call to domestic economy linked to a call for the education of white women in domestic affairs sounded a constant refrain in the letters and journals of planter men and sermons from the pulpit. By this, most southern white men did not mean that mistresses needed to learn how to cook and clean, but that they needed education in the proper management of the home – from managing their own domestic habits to managing the time and work habits of their slaves. The *Southern Cultivator* earnestly warned young white women to "cease to act like fools. Don't take a pride in saying you never did housework – never made a bed." The eminent Virginia planter and reformer, John Hartwell Cocke, wrote approvingly of a relative in New Orleans who was "plane [sic] in her tastes & domestic in her habits." He contrasted her to certain New Orleans Creole women who aspired to nothing "above a certain style of dress & jewelry," and were "too lazy to comb their own heads but employ professional hair dressers."[46]

---

believed it demonstrated a lack of "cultivation and refinement when one does kitchen drudgery for the pleasure of it as many seem to here." She expressed astonishment that her widowed sister-in-law who ran a boarding house, prepared her own Christmas dinner in order to allow her Irish servant to have the day off, a burden a southern housekeeper would not think of taking on. (Lines, *To Raise Myself a Little*, Jennie [Amelia Lines] to Maria [Anna Maria Akehurst], Sept. 1865, pp. 217–18, [1865], p. 220; see also Sept. 1 [1871], p. 245.)

44 See, for example, Account for Mrs. Joseph E. Davis with Miguel & Jamison, Joseph Davis Family Papers, Misc. Correspondence, Box 2, Folder, 26, MDAH. The first year of the Civil War saw little reduction in the spending habits of Eliza and Varina Davis, who spent on average $143 per month between January 1861 and February 1862. Perhaps reflecting the impact of the war, the last six months of 1862 witnessed a precipitous drop in their spending to an average of only $6.70 per month. Two years after the war, part of the 1861 charges remained on the factor's books. See Miguel & Jamison to Joseph E. Davis, Esq., November 1867, Joseph E. Davis Family Papers, Misc. Correspondence, MDAH.

45 Fox-Genovese, *Within the Plantation Household*, p. 212.

46 As quoted in White, *Ar'n't I a Woman?*, p. 57; see also, pp. 55–61; Clement Eaton, *The Mind of the Old South*, rev. ed. (Baton Rouge: Louisiana State University Press, 1967), p. 33. On the role of evangelical ministers in this discussion, see Christie Anne Farnham, *The Education of the Southern Belle: Higher Education and Student Socialization in the Antebellum South* (New York: New York University Press, 1994), Chapter 7.

Daniel Call certainly expected more from his daughter, Anne, though he was repeatedly disappointed. Anne Call married well into the prominent and wealthy Cameron family of North Carolina, but continued to rely heavily on her father's purse. Her lack of habits of economy irritated and angered her father, who received her many requests for money increasingly "with grief and astonishment." On one occasion, he sent her two thousand dollars along with a very strong note of disapproval: "Will not pay any debt which you already have contracted or may hereafter contract." Over and again, he advised her to practice restraint, "for it will be, in vain to expect further relief from me."[47] Within the year, however, Call was going over the same ground. "I live from necessity, with the utmost frugality," he wrote, "whereas you, I think, incur a great many unnecessary expenses. Among the rest, the frequent trips of your children to Virginia is burthensome to you; for, to say nothing of charges on the road, the additional clothing must be heavy." Call continued to send money in small amounts, though he sometimes balked and refused to help her. "I am so sorry for your difficulties," he wrote curtly in one letter, "but I cannot relieve them." To his grandchildren, he conveyed the same message. Sending twelve dollars to Anne's daughter, Mary, he cautioned her that it was money "which I can illy share."[48]

The sentiments of men like Call were vividly captured in a popular sketch penned by Augustus Baldwin Longstreet in 1835, an essay entitled "The 'Charming Creature' as a Wife." The essay is rather like an instructional manual presented in the form of a parable. It is a lesson in the art of choosing a wife, a moral tale of the dangers of choosing badly, and a treatise on the false education of women. It is, simultaneously, a guide to the proper management of southern households. In its latter guise, it is a parable about the importance of controlling household slaves and the threat that inefficient management posed to southern civilization, slavery, and white households."[49]

[47] Dan Call to Nancy [Mrs. Anne Cameron], February 14, 1831, Folder 1, Box 1, Sarah R. Cameron Papers, SHC. Call was also paying tuition, room, and other expenses for his grandson's college education.

[48] Daniel Call to Nancy [Mrs. Anne Cameron], September 3, 1831, Folder 1, Box 1, Sarah R. Cameron Papers, SHC.

[49] The essay appears in A. [Augustus] B. [Baldwin] Longstreet, *Georgia Scenes: Characters, Incidents, &c, in the First Half Century of the Republic* (1835; reprint, New York: Sagamore Press, 1957) and was first published in the Augusta *Sentinel* during Longstreet's tenure as editor. Longstreet, a native of Augusta and a Yale graduate, practiced law in Georgia prior to becoming a Methodist preacher and, besides, in 1829, president of the newly established Emory College. He also served as president of the University of Mississippi (1848–1856) and president of The University of South Carolina (1858–1861). His brother was Confederate General James Longstreet. The sketch could well have been loosely based on the lives of some of his acquaintances. It bears a resemblance to aspects of the life of Gertrude Clanton Thomas, who Longstreet knew well. Longstreet and his wife attended slave weddings and religious meetings at the Thomas plantation. (Richard Gray, *Writing the South: Ideas of an American Region* [Cambridge: Cambridge University Press, 1986], pp. 69–74; Anne Firor Scott, *The Southern Lady: From Pedestal to Politics, 1830–1930*, 25th Anniversary Ed. [1970; Charlottesville: University Press of Virginia, 1995), pp. 5 and 58–59. Most histories of the work focus on Longstreet

In Longstreet's sketch, George Baldwin is the son of a "plain, practical, sensible farmer" father and a "pious, but not austere; cheerful, but not light; generous, but not prodigal; economical, but not close; hospitable, but not extravagant" mother. His mother is the quintessential domestic manager.

To have heard her converse, you would have supposed she did nothing but read; to have looked through the departments of her household, you would have supposed she never read. Everything which lay within her province bore the impress of her hand or acknowledged her supervision. *Order, neatness, and cleanliness* prevailed everywhere. All provisions were given out with her own hands, and she could tell precisely the quantity of each article that it would require serving a given number of persons, without stint or wasteful profusion. In *the statistics of domestic economy* she was perfectly versed. She would tell you with astonishing accuracy, how many pounds of cured bacon you might expect from a given weight of fresh pork; how many quarts of cream a given quantity of milk would yield; how much butter to so much cream; how much of each article it would take to serve so many persons a month or a year.... when a given quantity of provisions of any kind would be exhausted.... *And yet she scolded less and whipped less than any mistress of a family I ever saw.* The reason is obvious. Everything under her care went on with *perfect system.* To each servant was allotted his or her respective duties, and to each was assigned the time in which those duties were to be performed.... Her children were permitted to give no orders to servants but through her, until they reached the age at which they were capable of regulating their orders by her rules.[50] (Emphasis added.)

Following his graduation from Princeton, the fictional George Baldwin returns to Georgia and opens a law practice. It is his fate to meet, be charmed by – though not without some apprehension – and engage to marry the "Charming Creature," Evelina Caroline Smith, who has recently returned home from a course of study in the North. Her parents, a wealthy but crude and uneducated merchant and a mother unskilled in domestic economy and slave management, are the exact opposites of Baldwin's. As the courtship proceeds, Baldwin keeps his parents informed of its progress. His letters, however, are not reassuring, leaving his mother to worry about her future daughter-in-law's capacity to *"practice"* "the value of industry, economy." She warns her son to not trust his fiancé's words, but to pay strict attention to her "habits of life." "Golden sentiments are to be picked up anywhere. In this age they are upon the lips of everybody; but we do not find that they exert as great an influence upon the morals of society or as they did in the infancy of our Republic, when they were less talked up." She warns him to be on his guard against "sentiments from the lips of *'a lady possessing strong personal attractions.'*"[51]

as a Southern humorist and the scenes in which he negatively depicts the lives of poor white southerners (see, for example, Eaton, *The Mind of the Old South*, pp. 132–34; R. S. Cotterill, *The Old South* [Glendale, CA: Arthur H. Clark Co., 1937], pp. 307–08; William B. Hesseltine, *A History of the South, 1607–1936* (New York: Prentice-Hall, 1936).

[50] Longstreet, *Georgia Scenes*, pp. 78–79.

[51] Longstreet, *Georgia Scenes*, p. 83.

The course of the engagement does not bode well. Baldwin himself becomes increasingly alert to his fiancé's faults: her indifference to his work, her demands for his constant attention and companionship. He is "more tortured by her unabated thirst for balls and parties of pleasure."[52] He marries her nonetheless. A post-wedding trip to introduce the bride to his parents proves disastrous and summons up his suppressed fears and his parents' warnings. His wife turns up her nose at the simple folks to whom she is introduced. Her "habits," in turn, confirm for them that he has chosen badly. "Her irregular hours of retiring and rising, her dilatoriness in attending her meals, her continual complaints of indisposition, deranged all the regulations of the family and begat such confusion, that even the elder Mrs. Baldwin occasionally lost her equanimity."[53]

Still, Baldwin remains hopeful. Cutting short their visit, the newlyweds return to their new home, a wedding present from the bride's father. Perhaps in an effort to convince himself that he had not made a horrible mistake, the groom lays out his hopes for their new life together and his ambitions for his wife. It is his hope that she, like his mother, will establish system and order in their home, regularize her time and efforts, and rise early to "regulate your servants with system; see that they perform their duties in the proper way and the proper time; let all provisions go through your hands; and devote your spare time to reading valuable works, painting, music, or any other improving employment or innocent recreation."

The story of the "Charming Wife" is the story of the destruction of a home and a marriage. The new Mrs. Baldwin protests the implementation of the regimen her husband desires. The couple's first evening in their new home begins less than propitiously, and when the slaves enter the picture, the source of the household's coming destruction is made plain. The cook requests the keys from her mistress to prepare supper and her mistress simply hands them over, telling her to "try and have everything very nice." When her husband reprimands her for allowing the cook such unsupervised access to the food supplies, Mrs. Baldwin retorts that she follows the rules established in the household in which she was raised. Her mother had always operated in this fashion. To do otherwise would provoke the cook's anger and indicate a lack of trust. It was not the response her husband had hoped for.

The couple's first meal at home – supervised neither in the planning nor execution stage – was, unsurprisingly, a complete failure. There was not much to it by elite southern standards, and that much, badly prepared. Mrs. Baldwin sees no point in confronting the cook. Breakfast the next morning is no improvement. For the first weeks of his marriage the groom "bore in silence, but in anger, [the slaves'] idleness, their insolence, and the disgusting familiarities with his wife." Sneaking to the kitchen at night, he watches from a hiding place as the slaves entertain company with his food. When at the end of three weeks the cupboards are bare, he is furious, but his wife sees nothing amiss.

[52] Longstreet, *Georgia Scenes*, p. 88.
[53] Longstreet, *Georgia Scenes*, pp. 90–94.

The final straw comes on the occasion of the couple's first important dinner, where they are to host a meal for Mr. Baldwin's colleagues who are in town for the meeting of the Superior Court. Baldwin's public and private reputations are at stake. Not trusting his wife to make the necessary arrangements, he does the shopping himself and personally gives instructions to the slaves. For added insurance, he attempts to succor them with good cheer and the promise of presents. "Time," he emphasizes, is of great importance because his colleagues would have only an hour and a half between sessions. Yet, despite his preparations, the supper is a disaster. It is served nearly an hour late and in the worst possible state. Dishes are half-cooked, some meats raw, and the presentation defies any semblance of good taste or order. In the kitchen, he rages at the women, calling one an "infernal heifer." The slaves, however, appear nonplused and blame his rushing them for the sorry state of affairs. He apologizes to the guests but his wife appears not in the least affected by what has happened.[54]

Despite one last attempt at repair, the ruin of the Baldwin household was now complete. Evelina Baldwin lost the struggle against her "nature" and her husband surrendered to the bottle, "a warning to mothers against bringing up their daughters to be 'CHARMING CREATURES.'" And not least, "charming creatures" who rather than run their households with authority, allowed household slaves to rule them; and when things went badly, sought sympathy and support from the slaves. The "beautiful cottage scene" that George Baldwin had envisioned for his married life had turned instead into a nightmare of inefficiency, unregulated slaves, and an undomesticated wife.

In this story, Evelina Caroline Smith is the victim of mis-education, and thus a threat to the South's domestic order. She is a victim of her slaves, who manipulate her into believing that being a "Charming Creature" is a charming thing, and that being shooed out of her kitchen by the slave cook to her proper place – a place where she does nothing – is a charming thing. The result, Longstreet argues, is a "Charming Creature" who is the epitome of the uncivilized: dull, lazy, disorganized, a creature of "irregular" hours who delights mostly in the vanities of costume and flattery, and falls to the level of her slaves. In the end, her failure as a wife and domestic manager precipitates her husband's failure as patriarch. He loses his job as an attorney and his manhood, and dies an alcoholic. His public failure (bankruptcy and alcoholism), the sketch emphasizes, derived from the private failure of his home, the foundation of his public presence.

At first glance, Longstreet's portrait seems perhaps a bit affected, the characters a bit exaggerated. Yet the story was clearly meant to be a serious comment on the dangers to southern domestic order of unregulated households. It spoke to the ways in which the cultivation of the creed of the "southern lady" existed uneasily with the notion of women as the bearers of domestic tranquility. The

---

[54] Longstreet, *Georgia Scenes*, p. 96. It is perhaps not a coincidence that the destroyer of domestic is given the name Evelina, which recalls the Biblical story of Eve.

inevitable tension no doubt increased mistresses's sense of inferiority and lack of accomplishment. The southern belle and the southern mistress could be at once revered and the brunt of criticism.[55]

Low country South Carolina planter Thomas Chaplin painted a rather unpleasant picture of his own "charming wife." What could be more injurious to a man, he asked himself, "than that his wife should be a victim to… demoralizing and injurious habit?" Chaplin did not name all of the habits to which he referred. Some, he declared, were unmentionable. He explained neither how or why his wife had come to have such habits nor why he considered her a "victim" in the situation. He was certain, though, that his wife's behavior was destroying their home. Her habits, he wrote, "entirely destroy all social and domestic enjoyments & comforts and prevent all chances of prosperity."[56] Mary Chaplin took some exception to this characterization from a man known for his spendthrift ways, who expected her to be uncomplaining even when she had nothing at times to eat but bacon and hominy. His management of their affairs had led to a sheriff's sale of their property, the pinnacle of public disgrace, and, she believed, without any assistance from her. Thomas Chaplin acknowledged his own follies and financial failures, but this did not temper his conviction that his wife and her half-sister, Sophia, who lived with them (and whom he married after Mary's death), failed to live up to reigning standards of domesticity.

Chaplin remained convinced that his wife's actions were in large measure responsible for the damage to his "public" reputation. He attributed his inability to live up to southern patriarchal standards to her deficiencies as a southern lady. These glaringly undermined his ability to act his part. Like the wife of Longstreet's satire, Mary Chaplin's habits, at least from the perspective of her husband, were destructive of his happiness, prosperity, and public reputation. Although Mary Chaplin and her half-sister often denied themselves food when the pantry was low in order that Thomas Chaplin and the children might eat, Chaplin believed they did not economize enough. When a shortage of hauling carts interrupted work in the fields, he blamed their extravagance. Instead of having two carts to haul manure, he had only one because they had commandeered the second cart to haul firewood for the separate fireplaces they maintained in their bedrooms. Chaplin saw this as unwarranted extravagance when they could save resources and free up a cart by sharing

---

[55] Tally Simpson to Caroline Virginia Taliaferro Miller, June 1, 1863 in *"Far, Far From Home": The Wartime Letters of Dick and Tally Simpson, Third South Carolina Volunteers*, ed. Guy R. Everson and Edward H. Simpson, Jr. (New York: Oxford University Press, 1994), p. 238; see also Simpson to Miller, March 6, 1862, p. 200, and Simpson to Anna Tallulah Simpson, August 9, 1863, p. 272.

[56] Theodore Rosengarten, *Tombee: Portrait of a Cotton Planter with the Plantation Journal of Thomas B. Chaplin (1822–1890)* (New York: William Morrow & Company, Inc., 1986), October 24, 1850, November 5, 1850, pp. 506–7. References to the journal hereafter cited as Chaplin, *Journal*.

a fire in the hall. They acted like town girls, he fumed, rather than planter women.[57]

This acting like town girls included his wife's failure to rise early and establish a routine for herself and their household and take charge of the slaves. Instead, she took her breakfast in bed, only making her appearance "Sometime between 11 A.M. & 1 P.M.," and only "*sometimes* took her place at the dinner table." On these occasions, she immediately returned to her chamber for an hour or two to indulge in habits her husband found disgusting: There she lay in bed filling her mouth with snuff, "when, if per chance a little of the saliva escaped down her throat, a fit of vomiting is invariably the consequence, then farewell to the small quantity of nourishment her sedentary habit allowed her to take at dinner." She remained in her room until dusk when she might take a walk. Sometimes she took tea with him, but more often had it sent to her room where she went not to retire to bed but to "put *snuff in her mouth*, take a *novel* & lie on her back till twelve or one o'clock at night, unless, perchance, she enacts the vomiting scene over again & thereby loses her *tea*.... there to remain till the late hours previously mentioned, the next day, to live the same routine of life over & again, each succeeding day, not to mention one or two *other* items."[58]

While his wife suffered, Chaplin vented his rage on the household slaves, "those that eat & do nothing in the world for me." Mainly women, they included a seamstress, washer, cook, nurse, dairy person, gardener, a slave in charge of the hogs, three assigned to general duties, two other women and eight children whose jobs he did not note, likely because he did not know what they were, and a man who, Chaplin did say, did nothing. He calculated that he had thirty heads to feed and only nine to "make feed for them." With more slaves "about the yard" than working in the fields, he tried to get his wife to transfer some of the house slaves to field labor. She refused. "[I]t appears," he wrote, "that not one of those about the house & yard can be done without."[59]

Like Longstreet's fictional George Baldwin, Chaplin believed that his wife was too much in the power of her slaves. He wrote off a wedding supper she gave for two of the house slaves as "tomfoolery," believing it demonstrated a lack of proper control over the slaves and encouraged the women to view themselves as "ladies of quality." He was especially critical of his wife's seamstress, Mary. To his annoyance, Mary (whom he variously referred to as "Black

---

[57] Chaplin, *Journal*, February 6, 1849, pp. 452–53. Returning to his journal in the years after the Civil War, Chaplin made this notation in the margins of the passage: "Alas, it was too true." Yet he also recognized, as he had at the time, his wife's frustration at his inability to provide the kind of life she had anticipated when they married. In an amendment to his journal long after Mary Chaplin's death, he wrote: "Oh God, what a woman was lost. What a mind – sunk in despair & grief & disappointment" (ibid., November 5, 1850, p. 508). There is no indication, however, that Chaplin amended his judgment of her domestic habits.

[58] Chaplin, *Journal*, November 5, 1850, pp. 507–08.

[59] Chaplin, *Journal*, February 18, 1850, p. 488.

lady Mary," "her Ladyship," or "old Moveum") demanded her own separate cart and other accommodations for their annual move between their winter and summer homes.[60] Chaplin's rants may have appeared mostly unintelligible to his wife. The strength of the myth of the southern lady could blinker its contradictions. Southern women who fit the image of Longstreet's "Charming Wife" did not always recognize themselves as such. Amelia Lines, for example, read Longstreet's work but claimed to see no relation to her own life. It was an "amazing" work, she wrote, but "neither instructive nor interesting."[61]

Still, it seems that more often than not, slaveholding women tried to maintain at least the fiction of domesticity. And some clearly took to heart Mary Ann Mason's advice to "Waste not, want not," require slaves to rise early, and set an example in this department themselves. And, no doubt, as well, her cautions against the use of violence. "The eye of a kind but firm mistress," she wrote, "is the great inspiration to produce efficiency and regularity in her subordinates." But this advice came with a warning against cooks with dispositions to "obstinacy or self-will," which may have encouraged the very violence she counseled against.[62] In encouraging mistresses to take pride in doling out – sometimes by the teaspoon – ingredients for cooks to prepare meals, the call to domesticity fit neatly with the characterization of these cooks as untrustworthy, and more. "Economy," wrote Mary Boykin Chestnut of her mother-in-law, "is one of her cherished virtues." She ran her household like a "well-oiled clock." Nancy De Saussure recalled her mother as the very picture of domestic efficiency. The manager of twenty-five household slaves, she "made a pretty picture in her quaint gown carrying a basket of keys on her arm."[63] Control, even symbolic, of the keys to smokehouses, corn cribs, and other stores of supplies constituted for many mistresses, the very essence of adherence to the ideology of domestic authority, the most "obvious emblem of female domestic authority."[64]

In doling out supplies, or cutting out and overseeing the construction of slave clothing, plantation mistresses paid homage to the philosophy to which Longstreet and others would have them aspire. Some set great store in their "executive ability." Setting up housekeeping for the first time, Lizzie Bain Partin found the perfect cook, "a nice old woman.... just what I wanted, one that I can depend on to take care of the baby in my absence, and in everything or as far or as I wish." She assured her mother, however, that she remained in control. Though the cook was just what she wanted, Partin did

[60] Chaplin, *Journal*, December 26, 1849; May 28, 1850, pp. 481 and 499.

[61] Lines, *To Raise Myself a Little*, February 26, 1857, pp. 49–50.

[62] Mason, *Young Housewife's Counsellor*, pp. 10, 11, and 17; quotes at pp. 11 and 17. C. Vann Woodward, ed., *Mary Chesnut's Civil War* (New Haven, CT: Yale University Press, 1981), September 24, 1861, p. 202.

[63] Woodward, ed., *Mary Chesnut's Civil War*, September 24, 1861, p. 202; Fox-Genovese, *Within the Plantation Household*, p. 115; Nancy B. De Saussure, *Old Plantation Days: Being Recollections of Southern Life Before the Civil War* (New York: Duffield & Company, 1909), p. 38.

[64] Vickery, *The Gentleman's Daughter*, p. 142.

not place full confidence in her. "Of course I keep the keys," she emphasized.[65] This diversion was not apt to give mistresses more than a superficial sense of "executive ability" especially when set beside the fact that their slaves seemed not the least impressed. Mistresses like Partin who made an effort to bend to the rules of domesticity only made more conspicuous those who did not.

Sarah Gayle's slaves gave her "sour looks" and "surly language." They laughed at her to her face. Comparing her situation to her parents', who seemed to rule more perfectly by a "uniform and strict," but not tyrannical, system of management, Gayle could only appear incompetent.[66] But such comparisons were not necessarily unproblematic. Sarah Morgan, for example, thought her sister, Miriam, similarly competent. Miriam, she wrote, "presides with grace and dignity" over the household slaves. By contrast, Morgan wrote:

I have no talent that way; I could not receive the complaints of each servant with civility, and promise instant redress to each, complacently. The cook says if the wet nurse has milk in her tea at lunch, she will have it too; the washerwoman and nursery maid insist on having all the privileges of the cook; dining room servants object to washing dishes, so appoint Tiche to her place; mother objects to the abuse of furniture while cleaning up, and nursery maid objects to being interfered with by her, and so it goes. Miriam keeps her temper, preserves peace, quells disputes, holds the keys, and is recognized as Supreme Head by children and servants.[67]

But what Morgan saw as graceful and dignified leadership, Longstreet would have considered a serious breach of the principle that mistresses should strictly control the slaves in their households. "Complacently" allowing slaves to dicker and complain about their duties, to demand milk in their tea, or object to washing dishes when their job was to serve in the dining room, suggested not command and order, but weakness and chaos.

For some mistresses, the domestic ideal was both a fanciful notion and one to take seriously. Gertrude Thomas often boasted of her efforts to economize. On one occasion she took a fifty-cent piece of muslin fabric to her seamstress and requested to have the dress cut out and basted only. She would finish it off as part of her endeavor "to be economical," as well as to overcome her distaste for sewing in general.[68] Though she never became an accomplished manager of the domestic space and generally failed in her efforts to economize – even when faced with the threat of losing her home, she was willing to spend a small fortune to rent a townhouse belonging to her mother's estate – from an early age, Thomas delighted in the idea. In the summer of 1852, in the months before her marriage, she wrote triumphantly of rising "early" and gathering

[65] Lizzie Bain Partin to Mother [Mary Bain], January 6, 1857, Bain Papers, DU. Lizzie Bain, like Fox and Lines, was not born to great wealth, and her marriage, too, failed to lift her into the planter elite.

[66] Fox-Genovese, *Within the Plantation* Household, p. 23.

[67] Sarah Morgan, *Sarah Morgan: The Civil War Diary of a Southern Woman*, ed. Charles East (New York: Simon & Schuster, 1991), May 30 [1863], pp. 500–501.

[68] Burr, ed., *The Secret Eye*, June 13, 1852, p. 108.

vegetables from the garden for dinner: "How very domestic I am!" Thomas wrote with the innocence of youth certainly, but also with a sense of what her society expected of her. The next day, "commenced my duties of housekeeping which I have assumed by giving out supper."[69]

Like other women of her class, Gertrude Thomas found comfort in the language of domestic bliss and its symbolic display (donning her bonnet to gather plums and pears). Even when she could not gather herself to a "regular" discipline of slave management, or "prudent economy," she knew what was expected of her. She knew this, not instinctively, but through the homilies that echoed from the pulpit, the press, and the home. Yet she had no illusions as to her own fulfillment of the ideal. She was not the hard-working, efficient manager of the plantation household's domestic space and she would not have thought to call her work "difficult, demanding, frustrating, and above all never-ending."[70]

The ideal Gertrude Thomas and other mistresses fell short of, not the reality they dealt with, has long captured the historical imagination. A source frequently cited in support of the argument that mistresses faced unceasing labor and responsibilities (and, thus, the argument that they were in many respects little more than slaves themselves) is the following section from the journal of South Carolinian Meta Morris Grimball:

A Plantation life is a very active one. This morning I got up late having been disturbed in the night, hurried down to have something arranged for breakfast, Ham & eggs.... wrote a letter to Charles... had prayers, got the boys off to town. Had work cut out, gave orders about dinner, had the horse feed fixed in hot water, and the box filled with cork; went to see about the carpenters working at the negro houses.... these carpenters Mr. Grimball told me he wished me to see about every day, & now I have to cut out the flannel jackets.[71]

Even the most casual review of the work Grimball did this day shows it to be far too little to mount so large an argument. Granting the most generous allowances, on this day Grimball probably put in no more than one and a half to two hours of "work," and that consisted in directing the labor of slaves. She ended the day writing in her journal. Yet from this record, one scholar concludes: "The round of obligations that absorbed women's days was long, varied, and arduous."[72] Plantation mistresses did not put in eight-hour days or work from sun-up to sun-down, despite the hyperbolical nature of their complaints. They mainly directed the work of household slaves. This could, of

---

[69] Burr, ed., *The Secret Eye*, April 11 [10] 1855, p. 121; April 25, 1855, p. 125. Mistresses had no illusions that the work they performed paid the bills. Thomas, for example, expressed sorrow for her cousin, Mary Ann Cooper, and an acquaintance, Sarah Blalock, who had to sew for the bread they ate. (Burr, ed., *The Secret Eye*, March 30, 1856, p. 145.)

[70] The quote is from Scott, *The Southern Lady*, p. 36.

[71] Meta Morris Grimball Diary, December 29, 1869, SHC.

[72] Weiner, *Mistresses and Slaves*, p. 25. See also White, *Ar'n't I a Woman?*, p. 51. As Anne Scott does point out, Grimball said nothing about the fact that she had time enough to keep a diary (Scott, *The Southern Lady*, p. 32).

course, be time consuming, but that is another matter entirely. Grimball's own language – "had something arranged for breakfast," "gave orders for dinner," "had work cut out" – bespeaks not toil, but authority and command. Mistresses enjoyed large amounts of leisure time for reading, letter- and journal-writing, annual trips to the springs and summer homes, and, for the very wealthiest, the requisite Northern and European tours. But hyperbole perhaps is unsurprising when the expectation of many young women was that their adult lives would square with the storied lives of their youthful fantasies, an expectation that resisted all manner of evidence to the contrary passing before them in the lives of their mothers.[73]

The transition from carefree belle to plantation mistress was difficult, and it could be traumatic.[74] Sarah Morgan's father was a small slaveholder (their urban household contained eight slaves in 1860), but his professional income provided for a relatively affluent life. Yet Morgan was not insensitive to the difficulties of this transition or to the dissipation that she saw in the lives of young women on the cusp of that transition:

I see so many dear, sweet little women in the world, who slept their early youth away and eat [*sic*] sugar plums; who passed through the ordeal of boarding schools, certainly no wiser, perhaps worse than when they entered; who spent the days of their childhood as they did their money – on useless objects, taking no account of either... women who lounge through life, between sofa and the rocking chair with dear little dimpled hands that are never raised except to brush a fly away... many such I see.[75]

A writer in the *Southern Literary Messenger* used even stronger language, calling southern belles so many "hundreds and thousands of... gay, simple, fluttering insects dignified with the name of fashionable belles – born and reared in the lap of luxury, – reposing in moral and intellectual sloth, and quaffing the delicious but fatal poison of adulation."[76]

As mistresses, elite women encountered lives much different from those they had as young women. Running a household was a job for which most had no training and that many would never master. When forced to take on household work during and after the Civil War, they rebelled. "The realities of my life and the situations in which I have been placed," wrote South Carolinian Susan Middletown, "have been so strangely different from what my character and the

---

73 Clinton, *The Plantation Mistress: Woman's World in the Old South* (New York: Pantheon, 1982), pp. 16–35; Fox-Genovese, *Within the Plantation Household*, pp. 100–45.

74 According to ex-slave Savilla Burrell, belles also faced competition from more experienced widows. After the death of his first wife, Burrell's master married a widow whom Burrell believed won his heart because "widows.... done had 'sperience wid mens and wraps dem 'round their little finger and git dem under their thumb fore the mens knows what gwine on. Young gals have a poor chance against a young widow like Miss Mary Ann was." Burrell went on to state that Miss Mary Ann had her own troubles with the master after she married him, stemming from the fact that he had children by several slave women (Savilla Burrell, *South Carolina Narratives*, vol. 2, pt. 1, p. 149).

75 Morgan, *Sarah Morgan*, p. 83.

76 As quoted in Fox-Genovese, *Within the Plantation Household*, p. 209.

early promise of my life would have led me to expect. Anxiety, responsibility, and independence of thought or action are what are peculiarly abhorrent to my nature, and what nevertheless has so often been required of me."[77]

Mistresses most frequently staked their claim to being overburdened on the matter of the labor associated with clothing and feeding slaves: the production and distribution of clothing and the distribution of food allotments. They did so even though in the matter of clothing their part consisted mainly in directing the work of slave women. Indeed, if one did not know that slaves generally received two distributions of clothing per year, that masters also distributed slave clothing, or that turning the cloth into the scanty clothing slaves wore was work delegated to slave women, one might easily get the impression that this work engaged the labor of mistresses constantly the entire year. The idea, nevertheless, represented an important symbolic component of the ideology of southern white female domesticity, serving as evidence of the mistresses's practice of economy and of slave women's domestic incapacity. Harriet Martineau observed that on many plantations, "the ladies make it their business to cut all the clothes for the negroes. . . . The slave women cannot be taught, it is said, to cut out even their scanty and unshapely garments economically." The resulting "ugly, scanty, dingy dresses," Martineau concluded, were "more hideous" than anything she knew of. She believed a better result would be gained by allowing slaves to clothe themselves. "There would be nothing to lose on the score of beauty, and probably much gained. . . . But it is universally said that they cannot learn."[78]

Despite its invocation of accomplished domesticity, white women's control of the household's keys was much less than it seemed in other respects as well. This much vaunted exercise of power was checked in part by masters' patriarchal authority. Compared to English "gentlewomen," plantation mistresses were much less involved in one of the most important aspects of domestic management, keeping household accounts. There is little evidence that they engaged fully "the proper Business of Woman," in keeping detailed records of household expenses or ordering supplies prior to the Civil War.[79] This task typically fell to masters, factors, and overseers. Charles Manigault, for example, ran his Argyle Island plantation with a firm hand in matters of

---

[77] As quoted in Jean E. Friedman, *The Enclosed Garden: Women and Community in the Evangelical South, 1830–1900* (Chapel Hill: University of North Carolina Press, 1985), p. 98. See also Scott, *The Southern Lady*, pp. 1–15.

[78] Harriet Martineau, *Society in America*, vol. 1 (1837; reprint, New York: AMS Press, Inc., 1966), p. 302. By the late antebellum period, many of the largest plantation owners found it more economical to buy ready-made clothes for slaves, especially for enslaved men. Friedman, *The Enclosed Garden*, pp. 24 and 26–32; White, *Ar'n't I a Woman?*, pp. 122–23.

[79] Quote is from Vickery, *The Gentleman's Daughter*, p. 127. A few examples of exceptions to this trend can be found at Scott, *The Southern Lady*, p. 32, and Nancy D. Bercaw, *Gendered Freedoms: Race, Rights, and the Politics of Household in the Delta, 1861–1875* (Gainesville: University Press of Florida, 2003), p. 51.

plantation economy, taking charge of ordering shoes for his slaves; cloth for slave clothing; and ready-made jackets, trousers, flannel shirts, and caps for male slaves. He determined what kind of cloth was ordered, and when it was distributed.[80] More often than masters, mistresses provisioned slave weddings, passed down old clothing, and attended slave births and illness. These activities, however, did not secure to them ties of loyalty or sympathy from female slaves, nor ties of intimacy of the kind that denote friendship.[81]

It was in the nature of slavery that mistresses and masters had obligations to fulfill. These obligations were not all different or gendered. Masters and mistresses, alike, nursed sick slaves, doled out supplies, and passed on old clothing. From the slaves' point of view, it made little difference which of them carried out these responsibilities. On the same day that Gertrude Thomas went to the plantation to distribute flour, her husband arrived to give out blankets and shoes. When Elizabeth Palmer Porcher distributed shoes and clothes to her family's slaves, she did so as a representative, not subordinate functionary, of the Palmer household.[82] Distribution of rations and clothing were practical matters designed to protect slaveholders' investments while demonstrating and coalescing their power over slaves.[83] In that latter guise, they constituted a ritual, "the social lubricant of gestures," E. P. Thompson terms it, announcing the authority of mistress as well as master.[84] Only the calculated return in deference slaveholders hoped for did not materialize.

The plantation mistress's chronicle of her domestic work can be understood as an idiom for a particular kind of domesticity, one intimately linked to the idea of the home as a critical agent of "southern civilization," with mistresses charged with managing the domestic space. U. B. Phillips got part of the matter right when he described the master and mistress as the plantation's "double head." He erred, though, in his explanation of what this meant, as his description of the mistress's part makes clear. This "mother of a romping

---

[80] Manigault remained in charge even when out of the country. From Paris in 1846, he sent precise and detailed instructions to his overseer, James Haynes, and his factors, Mathiessen & Company. See Charles Manigault, "Plantation Journal," December, 1843; Charles Manigault to James Haynes, August 15, 1846; Charles Manigault to Mathiessen and Company, September 15, 1846; Charles Manigault to James Haynes, November 1, 1846; James Haynes to Charles Manigault, December 7, 1846, in *Life and Labor on Argyle Island*, ed. Clifton, pp. 8, 38, 39, and 41.

[81] For a different interpretation, see, for example, Weiner, *Mistresses and Slaves*, pp. 74–75 and 79–82.

[82] Philip E. Porcher to Elizabeth Palmer Porcher, December 10, 1859, in *A World Turned Upside Down: The Palmers of South Santee, 1818–1881*, ed. Louis P. Towles (Columbia: University of South Carolina Press, 1996), p. 254.

[83] See Eugene D. Genovese's cogent analyses of this point (*Roll, Jordan, Roll*, pp. 3–7) and E. P. Thompson, *Customs in Common* (London: Merlin Press, 1991), pp. 42–49; Philip E. Porcher to Elizabeth Palmer Porcher, December 10, 1859, in *A World Turned Upside Down*, ed. Towles, p. 254.

[84] Thompson, *Customs in Common*, p. 46.

brood of her own and over-mother of the pickaninny throng, was a chatelaine of the whole establishment. Working with a never-flagging constancy, she carried the indoor keys, directed the household routine and the various domestic industries, served as head nurse for the sick, and taught morals by precept and example. Her hours were long, her diversions few, her voice quiet, her influence firm. Her presence made the plantation a home; her absence would have made it a factory."[85]

Catherine Edmondston, for one, understood the matter quite differently. Like most mistresses, she complained about slaves' work habits and the tediousness of having to oversee their labor to get things done as she wanted them done. But she had no illusions that the work she did in any way compared to the work slaves performed. On one occasion, for example, she put several slaves to work preparing meat and flour for the plantation. This was not a task she customarily performed. If it had been, she would have likely given instructions and left the slaves to perform the appointed tasks. It was not only an unusual job for her, but, moreover, took place in the second year of the Civil War and she stayed to oversee their labor out of concern that without her "bodily presence" the slaves would steal the meat and flour. Still, it was a "tiresome" business, this "waiting on them" to finish. So, she wrote:

I sat down in the store room and sent for my book, "Literature du Midi," & when Charles came upon me I had a hearty laugh at myself and the situation in which he caught me: Harry pounding the flour into the Barrels with a heavy pestle, Dolly & Vinyard with a pot of boiling water & all the sides [of meat] spread out on the grass, peeping into, scalding & examining them, whilst further on Angeline with a cauldron like the witches in Macbeth, which with "double double, toil & trouble" she was making "boil & bubble," whilst Mistress sat composedly on the step, deep in the Chansons & Tensons of Troubadours & Trouvareres, occasionally lending an eye or an admonition to each. Such is life, such is Southern Life. What would an English lady have thought of my situation & occupation? Would the ridiculous or the sympathetic have predominated as she looked at me? And yet I was in happy unconsciousness of exciting either. The occupation was not distasteful to me, for it was a necessary & ordinary duty, & I enjoyed my book none the less for my surroundings.[86]

Edmondston seems not to have questioned what her slaves might have thought of her "situation & occupation," relaxed and reading literature while they worked, particularly the women she delighted in calling her "handmaidens."

Enslaved women could take no delight in Edmondston's fanciful position. Their struggle was to dismantle the system that allowed her to watch them

[85] Ulrich B. Phillips, *American Negro Slavery: A Survey of the Supply, Employment and Control of Negro Labor as Determined by the Plantation Regime* (1918; reprint, New York: Knopf, 1966), p. 323.

[86] Catherine Ann Devereux Edmondston, *"Journal of a Secesh Lady": The Diary of Catherine Ann Devereux Edmondston*, ed. Beth G. Crabtree and James W. Patton (Raleigh: North Carolina Division of Archives and History and Department of Cultural Resources, 1979), August 13, 1862, p. 235.

work in a state of "happy unconsciousness." This struggle against southern white domesticity meant working to bring dignity to their lives where they could. That dignity was displayed in their preparations for death, in their attempts to maintain love relationships and protect their children, and in their day-to-day struggles to restructure and lessen their workloads. In working slowly, using impudent language, and in myriad other ways, they impeached the ideology of white female supremacy. In the process, they carved out small spaces of autonomy and prepared the foundation for the struggle against the restoration of the plantation household after the Civil War. The oppositional culture they built during slavery had radical implications for the free society to be built.[87]

The Civil War would widen the spaces for black women to act and speak more openly, to make claims, and represent themselves. Their actions, words, claims, and self-representations linked past to present. They carried into the war an understanding of the meaning of freedom born of the struggle for it, in gestures that spanned the range of what is termed day-to-day resistance or, as James C. Scott's famous coinage has it, "weapons of the weak," and went beyond these.[88] Too often, however, these gestures are dismissed as impotent weapons that more often denigrated than helped those who stooped to use them. This happens when scholars insist, especially, that slave women, in staking their ground on such lowly terrain (with the high and moral terrain being revolt explicitly geared to the overthrow of slavery), thereby demonstrated and confirmed their own inherent impotence. Day-to-day resistance constituted the principal weapon of slave women against the plantation household. This has worked against them in the historical record. Because of the nature of the weapons they took up against slavery, they have come to be ranked in historical scholarship as the least troublesome of slave property; and the tools they took up, as weapons raised in frustration, not resistance.[89]

In burying slave women's resistance in the gendered language of domesticity, slaveholders discounted it. Resistance could thus be construed, by turn, as a management problem and as incontrovertible evidence that black women were "by nature" savage and uncivilized. Though hardly a solution to the problem of slave women's resistance, this strategy masked and inverted it. It made resistance tolerable while at the same time summoning its reality in support of the ideology of white women's racial superiority. Slave emancipation in the

---

[87] White, *Ar'n't I a Woman?*, pp. 161–90. See also Elsa Barkley Brown, "Negotiating Community and Freedom: African American Political Life in the Transition from Slavery to Freedom, *Public Culture* 7 (Fall 1994), and Julie Saville, *The Work of Reconstruction: From Slave to Wage Laborer in South Carolina, 1860–1870* (Cambridge: Cambridge University Press, 1994).

[88] James C. Scott, *Weapons of the Weak: Everyday Forms of Peasant Resistance* (New Haven, CT: Yale University Press, 1985).

[89] For recent work that has begun to shift this paradigm, see, for example, White, *Ar'n't I a Woman?*, rev. ed., pp. 70–74. See also Eric Hobsbawm, *Revolutionaries* (1973; reprint, New York: Free Press, 2001), pp. 256–60.

American South would be accompanied by the rise of a new dialogue that took its cue from the antebellum critique of black women, and worked to mask and erase black women's continued resistance to the ideology of white southern domesticity, even as it masked the fear that white women themselves had, to borrow from Catherine Hall, "lost their domestic skills."[90]

The slaves' emancipation would not change Amelia Lines's belief that the drudgery of housework was the sphere of black women, or her view of herself as a bearer of civilization to ultimately untrainable black women. She could not imagine Caroline, the free black woman she hired, any differently from the black women she had owned or rented during slavery. Caroline's ironing did not suit; to get her to a satisfactory level took "a good deal of talking, showing, and some ironing on my part." Patience and constant oversight, Lines hoped, would one day make Caroline a worthy servant. Neither approach had the desired affect. Caroline refused to "take interest enough" in getting the washing done in a timely fashion or to manage the stove so that it worked. She seemed interested only when Lines did much of the work herself.[91]

Caroline's opposition to the demands Lines placed on her drew on patterns of resistance black women had honed during slavery. By pretending that she was incapable of managing certain things, Caroline kept Lines on her feet as long as she was on hers. Lines's annoyance returned: "I have showed her and told her so much too. I lost my patience with her to-day (sic) perhaps that will improve her will or memory which is ever at fault." It took Lines about two weeks longer to admit defeat: She could not make Caroline interested in her household, and so she fired her. Lines seemed finally convinced that she would not get the deference she wanted and needed from black women. She would just have to put up with their lack of interest in her. It was the price she would have to pay to avoid becoming a "kitchen drudge" herself. It was worth it to her to "be annoyed with filthy, indolent impertinent servants" than to do such drudgery herself.[92] Such thinking continued well into the twentieth century as white women continued to construe black women's resistance as a problem of character rather than of politics.

A reassessment of elite women opens the way to a re-examination and fuller understanding of the cult of the southern lady and of the history of black and white women in slavery and freedom. There is general agreement among scholars that the Civil War constituted a "radical disjuncture" in the lives of planter women, that it created "an environment in which southern white women could not feign weakness, could not shrink from the public gaze, and could not assume the presence of protection that was supposedly their right." This is true in that the war forced white women to assume responsibilities

---

[90] Catherine Hall, *Civilising Subjects: Metropole and Colony in the English Imagination, 1830–1867* (Chicago: University of Chicago Press, 2002), p. 185.

[91] Lines, *To Raise Myself a Little*, [Oct.] 19, [1871], p. 250; [Oct.] 24 [1871], p. 252; [Oct.] 29 [1871], p. 253.

[92] Lines, *To Raise Myself a Little*, [Oct.] 29 [1871], p. 253; [Nov.] 3 [1871], p. 253.

previously shouldered by male members of their households, overseers, and slaves.[93] With men away at war, they managed plantations and supervised larger numbers of slaves. They experienced poverty and larger numbers of recalcitrant slaves. Many had their first experience in working for a living. Some turned to political protest, "rioting" in the streets for bread or addressing letters to public officials detailing their destitution and perceived injustices.[94]

In many respects, however, white women were prepared to shoulder the adversities of war. They were not, importantly, inexperienced at managing slaves in the domestic sphere. The war brought abrupt and often severe changes, but it did not make for as radical a disjuncture as is often supposed. In the context of war, plantation mistresses's notoriously feigned weaknesses succumbed to new realities. Among slaves – in the slave quarters, the plantation yard, and the plantation household – it had always lain exposed. If southern households were to be governed by order, women held the operational keys, but the cultural ground of slavery had made southern white women, theoretically, ineligible candidates for work, while making work essential to their status.[95] Slave women saw and rejected the notion of mistresses as fragile flowers in the ways that were imaginable to them.

What was imaginable to slave women has not always seemed imaginable to historians. Historical manuscripts make most clear those forms of resistance that masters and overseers were most culturally attuned to: running away, rebellions, and conspiracies to rebel. Unsurprisingly, slave women do not figure prominently in discussions of resistance. Black women's resistance was "insubordination," and in the historiography, it is considered the most individualist and, thus, the most insignificant kind of resistance. This is often explained by way of slave women's inferior knowledge of geography (which is, in turn, explained by the gendered division of plantation labor and the greater opportunities this gave slave men to have planter-sanctioned authority to be moved about) and by slave women's greater sense of parental duty (again explained by gender).[96] These explanations are as problematic as the analytical frameworks often invoked to support them for understanding how slave

---

[93] See, for example, George C. Rable, *Civil Wars: Women and the Crisis of Southern Nationalism* (Urbana: University of Illinois Press, 1989), p. 35.

[94] See Rable, *Civil Wars*, and Drew Gilpin Faust, *Mothers of Invention: Women of the Slaveholding South in the American Civil War* (Chapel Hill: University of North Carolina Press, 1996).

[95] For a discussion of the theoretical and practical inconsistencies of the ideology of womanhood in the South as they affected the lives of yeoman women, see Stephanie McCurry, *Masters of Small Worlds: Yeoman Households, Gender Relations, and Political Culture of the Antebellum South Carolina Low Country* (New York: Oxford University Press, 1995); McCurry, "The Politics of Yeoman Households in South Carolina," in *Divided Houses: Gender and the Civil War*, ed. Catherine Clinton and Nina Silber (New York: Oxford University Press, 1992), pp. 22–41; and "Producing Dependence: Women, Work, and Yeoman Households in Low-Country South Carolina," in *Neither Lady nor Slave: Working Women in the Old South*, ed. Susanna Delfino and Michael Gillespie (Chapel Hill: University of North Carolina Press, 2002), pp. 55–71.

[96] See, for example, Camp, *Closer to Freedom*, pp. 28–34.

women experienced slavery and how those experiences shaped their responses to their enslavement, and later, the Civil War and emancipation.

Though to a more limited extent than enslaved men, enslaved women had numerous occasions to be off the plantation and thus to gain a wider knowledge of geography. Some made the annual pilgrimages with their owners to vacation spots and summer homes and traveled on less ambitious occasions with mistresses on shopping trips as personal servants, nurses, and wet nurses. It was not uncommon for women to be sent on errands to neighboring plantations. Enslaved women on the Clanton and Thomas plantations in Georgia regularly moved about between their owners' plantations on plantation business and to visit extended kin and friends, and also between the plantations and the city of Augusta. "Abroad" marriages gave them additional reasons to travel beyond the boundaries of the plantations. Women who were hired out annually would have become familiar with local and sometimes regional geography. Susan, a North Carolina slave, for example, was hired out to fourteen different slaveholders over the course of nineteen years.[97] Women also traveled to market to vend their goods, and slave women who worked in hotels had access to knowledge unavailable on plantations.

Close examination of idiomatic usages brings into focus the ways in which slaveholders disguised the resistance of slave women. Such idioms as "harder to manage," "good for nothing," and "dirty," in the context of nineteenth-century ideals of domesticity raised other questions and conveyed specific messages. Could women who could neither be managed nor manage time be women? Could "dirty" women and poor mothers ever be civilized? Slaveholders answered no on all counts. Rendered childlike and irresponsible, slave women could also not be serious contenders for the status of rebels. Such thinking intellectually contained the threat of rebellious women. Slaveholders worked hard at refusing to see enslaved women as rebellious, sometimes finding sustenance in that part of the ideology of separate spheres that held that only men could be warriors. At the same time, slaveholders were not much given to respecting traditional views about the capacities of men and women where African Americans were concerned. Why they were inclined to do so in the matter of resistance is an important question.

Gender notions about warfare doubly affected "the prevailing pattern of who would be charged by whites with concerted rebelliousness, and formed a defining framework that affected black women in thousands of daily interactions with slaveholders, as well as with each other and black men."[98] By and large, slave women would not be charged with "concerted rebelliousness,"

---

[97] Thomas Carroll Account Book, Financial Papers, 1847–67, Thomas Carroll Papers, DU.

[98] Winthrop Jordan, *Tumult and Silence at Second Creek: An Inquiry into a Civil War Conspiracy* (Baton Rouge: Lousiana State University Press, 1993), p. 175. See also Eugene D. Genovese, *From Rebellion to Revolution: Afro-American Slave Revolts in the Making of the Modern World* (Baton Rouge: Louisiana State University Press, 1979), and Herbert Aptheker, *American Negro Slave Revolts* (New York: Columbia University Press, 1943).

despite the thousands of incidents of rebelliousness traceable to their hands. Slaveholders' gender expectations, however, answer the question only in part. In cloaking female slave resistance in the language of domesticity and uncivilized disorder (or silence), slaveholders put gender ideas to the task of deflating the claims female slaves raised against them. In marvelous irony, they masked their expectation that slave women would revolt in the language of domesticity. The seeming theoretical inconsistency was offset here, as it was in other areas, by the threat of greater anarchy. The slave girl who hung herself in the smokehouse where she had been remanded as punishment defied the claims of her owners at last after at least two unsuccessful attempts to run away.[99]

By 1861, generations of women, black and white, had shared in the making – and continuous remaking – of the world of slavery. In the small spaces of great houses and slave cabins where they made their lives, and in their speech and actions, they had participated in the ongoing debate about what it meant to be free or enslaved, male or female, black or white, to have the power to freely act on one's behalf or not. It had led the slave Sylvia's mistress to believe that Sylvia hated a white face, despite all she had done for her. It had allowed Sylvia's mistress to see others of her slaves as "miserable creatures." By miserable, she explained, she meant "self-willed."[100] It had often led to violence. "De blacks and de whites," stated ex-slave Mary Grandberry, "would have terr'bles' battles sometimes."[101] The "terr'bles' battles" were not only those of storied history like Nat Turner's, but also those fought daily within the plantation household and throughout its extended domain. The Civil War witnessed an escalation in both the rancor and the violence in the South as white southerners pledged allegiance to the perpetuation of slavery, and the enslaved pledged to undo it entirely.

Emancipation fundamentally rearranged the lives of all southerners. The question of what that arrangement would look like beyond the new legality that barred ownership in human beings took center stage in the struggle that followed. The legal end of slavery was but the moment to begin determining freedom's meaning on the ground. Whatever emancipation failed to accomplish, it plowed up the ground of slavery, paternalism, and racism. In its furrows black women planted the seeds for free lives based on their understanding of why freedom mattered. Slave women's resistance within the plantation household is the least acknowledged component of the larger struggle of slaves for survival and dignity. It is central, however, to understanding the struggles of slave women in the South's cotton, rice, sugar, and tobacco fields after emancipation. Just as it was central to the making of slavery, the plantation household was central to its unmaking. Whether slaves left white homes or

---

[99] James R. Lyons to [William Renwick], April 4, 1854, William Renwick Papers, 1850–69, SHC.
[100] Brevard, *Diary*, February 13, 1861; February 7, 1861, quotes at pp. 88 and 89.
[101] Mary Ella Grandberry, *Alabama Narratives*, vol. 6, p. 161.

stayed put and gave aid from the inside, they contributed to its unmaking. We might want to rethink, however, the tendency to term the wartime phase of this process "defection." Defection means the "conscious abandonment of duty, as to a person, cause, or doctrine." People cannot abandon what they have not claimed.

4

"Nothing But Deception in Them"

The War Within

To the credit of the colored people be it said that during the Civil War, when on plantation after plantation the mansions were occupied only by wives and daughters, not a disloyal act or word ever occurred.

Mary Norcott Bryan, ex-mistress

Liddy has run off to the Yankees.

Sarah Morgan, mistress

... it has been my constant desire to make my negroes happy & I am every now and then awakened to the fact that they *hate* me ... it is nothing on earth but that I am *white* & own slaves.

Keziah Goodwyn Hopkins Brevard, mistress

The Negro women marched off in their mistresses' dresses.

Kate Stone, mistress

In 1861, Betsey Witherspoon of Society Hill, South Carolina, was murdered "by her own people. Her negroes." The news of Witherspoon's death left her "neighborhood in a ferment," in a state of shock that this woman, "a saint on this earth," "so good – so kind," a mistress who had "indulged and spoiled" her household slaves "until they were like spoiled children," had come to such an end. This they said even as they simultaneously noted that Witherspoon's "pampered" slaves were "indolent and "insubordinate." Her cousin, Mary Boykin Chesnut, began to consider whether she herself should be afraid, though she had "never thought of being afraid of negroes" before. Chesnut turned first to proslavery ideology. After all, "I had never injured any of them," she wrote in her journal, so "Why should they want to hurt me?" But she quickly reconsidered that position. Perhaps she rethought the definition of injury, for she added: "Somehow today, I feel that the ground is cut away from under my feet. Why should they treat me any better than they have done Cousin Betsey Witherspoon?"[1]

Chesnut knew not only that she might herself be murdered, but that the chance she might suffer her cousin's fate had greatly increased with the outbreak of war. In this state of mind, she received an unwelcome reinforcement of the point from Betsey, her sister Kate Miller Williams's slave. As Chesnut and Williams sat mulling over Witherspoon's death and their own fate, Betsey entered the room dragging a mattress behind her. She had come, she informed them, to guard her mistress. In *"these times,"* she explained matter-of-factly, "you ought not to stay in a room by yourself." Williams, however, was not totally comforted by Betsey's offer of protection. "For the life of me," Chesnut recalls her sister saying, "I cannot make up my mind. Does she mean to take care of me – or murder me?"[2] Even the usually confident Chesnut appeared flummoxed:

We know Betsey well. Has she soul enough to swear by? She is a great stout, jolly, irresponsible, unreliable, pleasant-tempered, bad-behaved woman with ever so many good points. Among others, she is so clever she can do anything. And she never loses her temper but she has no moral sense whatever.[3]

Whether she noticed or not, Chesnut's description of Betsey tellingly echoed the white community's description of Betsey Witherspoon's slaves. Betsey might be stout and gay, but she was also unreliable and immoral. If she had no moral sense, what was to stop her? Williams went to bed with Betsey in her room. Later, perhaps rattled by the similarity, she got up and moved to the more certain safety of her sister's company. Betsey, she must have concluded, did *not* have soul enough to swear by. In Chesnut's room, the sisters sat up all night in fear. Were Betsey's hands, the hands of a "jolly.... pleasant-tempered" but "bad-behaved" slave woman, any different from the black hands that belonged to Mary Witherspoon's "indulged" but "insubordinate" slaves? They were all slaves' hands. And Chesnut and Williams, like Witherspoon, were mistresses.

---

[1] C. Vann Woodward, ed., *Mary Chesnut's Civil War* (New Haven, CT: Yale University Press, 1981), quotes at pp. 198–99; C. Vann Woodward and Elisabeth Muhlenfeld, eds., *The Private Mary Chesnut: The Unpublished Civil War Diaries* (New York: Oxford University Press, 1984), p. 164. In her 1880s revised manuscript based on her wartime journals, Chesnut added that Witherspoon was smothered and had bruises on her face, arms, and legs, indicating she had fought her attackers. See Woodward, ed., *Mary Chesnut's Civil War*, September 19, 21, and 24, 1861, pp. 195–99; Woodward and Muhlenfeld, eds., *The Private Mary Chesnut*, September 27, 1861, p. 164, September 21, 1861, p. 162. For a critical analysis of the wartime and postwar manuscripts, see Thavolia Glymph, "African American Women in the Literary Imagination of Mary Boykin Chesnut," in *Slavery, Secession, Southern History*, ed. Louis Ferleger and Robert Paquette (Charlottesville: University Press of Virginia, 1999), pp. 140–59. See also Drew Gilpin Faust, *Mothers of Invention: Women of the Slaveholding South in the American Civil War* (Chapel Hill: University of North Carolina Press, 1996), pp. 54–57; Eugene D. Genovese, *Roll, Jordan, Roll: The World the Slaves Made* (New York: Vintage, 1974), pp. 363–65.

[2] Woodward, ed., *Mary Chesnut's Civil War*, September 21, 1861, p. 199.

[3] Woodward, ed., *Mary Chesnut's Civil War*, September 21, 1861, p. 199.

"I sleep & wake with the horrid vision before my eyes of those vile black hands smothering her," Chesnut would write.[4]

In concluding that Betsey's actions revealed an awareness of their vulnerability that she might decide to take advantage of, Williams and Chesnut acknowledged the loss of any confidence they might have had in Betsey.[5] They acknowledged the increased threat slavery posed for their lives. Before the war, slaves could be "pampered" and "insolent." It was, after all, consistent with proslavery ideology. The "pampered" part suggested how well they were treated; the "insolent" part, their alleged inherently uncivilized condition. "Insolent" also submerged the evidence of discontent on the part of slaves that might contradict claims of pampering, bad character, rudeness, or ingratitude. Within the context of proslavery ideology, both adjectives conveyed a kind of harmlessness and slaveholders gained the threat of a more ominous meaning. The Civil War forced a reconsideration of this perspective. Slaveholders could no longer afford to delude themselves. They had no choice but to acknowledge that their lives might depend on reading "insolence" more carefully and taking it more seriously.

Mary Chesnut's oft-cited account of Witherspoon's death suggests some of the ways in which the Civil War changed everything. In its bright glare, the public character of the plantation household stood fully exposed. Conflicts between mistresses and slaves multiplied as slaves became more determined to be free and live fuller lives. At first, mistresses and masters sought refuge in idioms that had comforted them in the past as rationalizations for black people's response to their enslavement. These comforting idioms quickly wore thin and the language gradually changed, sometimes, no doubt, imperceptibly. By 1865, mistresses were calling black women's resistance what it was. The self-assertions of slaves they had once had the luxury of judging humorous or harmless, or attributing to race, no longer appeared even superficially innocent or manageable. It became less easy to make the old associations and dangerous to believe them. The juxtaposition, "proud and high-tempered, but intelligent and trustworthy," no longer made sense or did so in new ways. Chesnut's description of Betsey as at once jolly and pleasant-tempered, irresponsible, unreliable, badbehaved, and immoral is a knot of contradictions, a linguistic discourse that no longer suited in the midst of war. Slaveholders had learned with certainty by the end of the Civil War just how badly they had misjudged black people. Their initial expectation that slaves would willingly defend the plantation household was dashed by the contrary actions of slaves clearly eager to seize their freedom. The shock was most often registered by planter women faced with the "betrayal" of their household slaves. The Civil War laid bare the core

---

[4] Woodward, ed., *Mary Chesnut's Civil War*, September 21, 1861, pp. 198–99; Woodward and Muhlenfeld, eds., *The Private Mary Chestnut*, September 27, 1861, p. 164.

[5] Woodward, ed., *Mary Chesnut's Civil War*, September 21, 1861, p. 199. Also on the minds of Chesnut and her sister were the recent murders of Dr. William J. Keitt and a Mrs. Cunningham. See Woodward, ed., *Mary Chesnut's Civil War*, October 7, 1861, p. 211; Woodward and Muhlenfeld, eds., *The Private Mary Chestnut*, October 18, 1861, p. 181.

antagonisms within the plantation household and stripped it of its veneer of privacy, respectability, and gentility. By the end of the war, slavery's hurts and damages, its injuries that Chesnut could barely imagine, were plainly visible.

Ungovernable People

Domestic slaves have come down in history to us as fairly uncomplicated people who did their job, knew their place, and, after slavery, remembered the plantation mistress and her household fondly.[6] This received understanding does not explain why or how, and long before the power of masters was eclipsed by military defeat, the power of mistresses had been as much undone by domestic slaves as by war. Granted, few mistresses were murdered by their slaves and there was no general uprising, but even so, household slaves expanded their repertoire of tools of resistance and became more firmly committed to the destruction of the plantation household. The upheavals incident to war, from the mobilization of armies to the task of putting the southern economy on a war footing, gave household slaves vital aid. They found more room and capacity to act on their desires for freedom, privacy, mobility, and respect. Mistresses and planter homes, as symbolic and physical manifestations of slavery's injuries, were obstacles to the realization of these desires just as masters and acres of cash crops were for field hands. By the time Sherman's army conquered the Southeast, enslaved women had through their own actions done much to challenge the power of mistresses, setting the stage for the postwar struggle and the long journey to free homes. The contesting ideologies of the North and South gave them reason to believe that Northern victory would confirm their actions. Pressures the war placed on relationships between mistresses and masters created additional opportunities for black women to press their freedom, even as the risks of doing so multiplied in old and new ways.

Household slaves were the first to make trouble. In late June 1861, Kate Stone recorded evidence of the first round: "The house servants have been giving a lot of trouble lately – lazy and disobedient. Will have to send one or two to the field and replace them from the quarters if they do not settle down. I suppose the excitement in the air has affected them. The field hands go on without trouble."[7] The first battle at Bull Run had taken place the week

---

[6] For arguments that complicate this notion, especially in regard to "mammy," see, for example, Genovese, *Roll, Jordan Roll*, pp. 327–65; Deborah Gray White, *Ar'n't I a Woman? Female Slaves in the Plantation South*, rev. ed. (New York: W. W. Norton, 1999), pp. 46–49; George C. Rable, *Civil Wars: Women and the Crisis of Southern Nationalism* (Urbana: University of Illinois Press, 1989), pp. 34 and 116–20.

[7] Kate Stone, *Brokenburn: The Journal of Kate Stone, 1861–1868*, ed. John Q. Anderson (Baton Rouge: Louisiana State University Press, 1995), pp. 33, 35, and 37. Stone believed the slaves had expected some great event to take place on July 4th. For an elaboration of this phenomenon, see Steven Hahn, "'Extravagant Expectations' of Freedom: Rumour, Political Struggle, and the Christmas Insurrection of 1865 in the American South," *Past and Present* 157 (November 1997): 122–58.

before. This and Confederate military mobilization helped to produce what Stone called the "excitement in the air" that slaves understood as a signal that their freedom was in the offing.

The departure of masters for war added to the drama as slaveholders used the occasion to validate their sovereignty and to create the impression that theirs was a righteous cause. They called slaves together to announce the departure of a master or a son and to express their expectation that the slaves would show their loyalty by supporting the Southern cause. The coming war, Alabama planter John Gaillard had stated, would be "sanguinary and merciless" and the South "must do battle not only for their civil and political rights but for their property, their lives, and their domestic households."[8]

As they prepared to leave for war, masters reminded slaves of the ties that joined slavery and white womanhood; that in going to war for slavery, they went to war for the honor of white women as well as nation. They asked slaves to protect white women and white homes, as well as to cook, make beds, and produce goods in support of the Confederacy. The political consciousness of slaves was no doubt sharpened with each reminder, and their interest in the war, heightened. From the moment that the first rumors of war began to circulate and filter into slave communities, slaves, without any assistance from their masters, linked the South's decision to fight for slavery to the place white women occupied in southern society. Their analysis drew on their own experience. Former slave Isaac Stier put the matter in a broad yet precise context. Stier's understanding of the war's origins does not adhere to the facts precisely but is a splendid piece of anecdotal evidence on the subject. According to Stier, Jefferson Davis's "mulish" disposition led him to refuse a proffer of peace from President Lincoln that had included a pledge to protect slavery where it already existed. Instead, Davis "flew into a huff an swore dat afore he'd let his wife and daughter dabble their purty white hands in dish water en wash tubs he'd fight till ebbery gun en sword in de country wuz gone."[9] Stier's analysis could only come from slaves' own experience.

Like many masters, Gertrude Thomas's husband declared a holiday in honor of his impending departure. Slaves, accustomed to planter displays of mastery, often performed their part. When the time came on the Thomas plantation, the slaves "appeared very much affected. Aunt Patience burst into tears

---

[8] Thomas Gaillard to John S. Palmer, May 4, 1861, in *A World Turned Upside Down: The Palmers of South Santee, 1818–1881*, ed. Louis P. Towles (Columbia: University of South Carolina Press, 1996), p. 305.

[9] Isaac Stier, *Mississippi Narratives*, Supplement Series 1, vol. 10, pt. 5, p. 2055. Several versions of Stier's reading of the cause of the war circulated in slave communities throughout the South, coming to reside in the testimonies of ex-slaves in the twentieth century. Stier himself went to the front in the garb of a body servant and returned in the uniform of the U.S. Army. As a soldier, he saw people live and die in the worst circumstances. He recalled the horrors of death on the battlefield, of white and black civilians reduced to eating cats, dogs, horses, and mules, and to drinking sweat squeezed from blankets during the seize of Vicksburg. Over the decades that followed, the death and suffering remained linked in his mind to the pledge white men had made going off to war, to fight for their domestic households, white women, and slavery.

and sobbed bitterly." A few weeks later Thomas overheard the slaves singing and praying. One offered a prayer for her and the absent master. When they turned to singing "Hallelujah praise ye the Lord," she pretended not to understand that it was a prayer for their freedom. But before long Thomas could not avoid understanding. Gradually, incrementally, she lost nearly every one of her household slaves. By the end of May 1865, all but two had taken their freedom.[10]

Slaves began leaving at the commencement of the war and mistresses began immediately to grapple with what the flight of household slaves meant for their lives. For mistresses, the war's meaning took shape as much in the decisions of slave women to seek their own freedom as in the victories and losses on the battlefield. The plantation household became a critical site of wartime slave rebellion, forcing mistresses to confront their own self-deception. Betty Maury seesawed between old idioms and a new awareness in the early spring of 1862, when her slaves began "going off in great numbers" and those who remained refused any longer to acknowledge the dominion she claimed over them. They were "beginning to be very independent and impudent."[11]

The war crystallized Keziah Brevard's thinking about the people she owned. She did not change her opinion that "the vast body" of slaves was "little above brutes." Of this she was convinced. "*I believe it*," she wrote emphatically. Still, she confessed puzzlement about what they thought of *her*. It is hardly imaginable that her slaves were oblivious to the contempt in which she held them, and altogether unimaginable that she could have prevented her feelings about them from influencing her treatment of them. Still, only now, with war on the horizon, did she seriously contemplate what they must think of someone who held such a low opinion of them. The most relevant question became where she fit in *their* world. Her conclusion: All of them – those she believed she knew well from intimate association and the larger number of the some 200 she owned but knew less well – put her in the mind to "dwell on insurrections." "We know not," she wrote, "what moment we may be hacked to death in the most cruel manner by our slaves."[12]

Moreover, Brevard believed the slaves most capable of revolting and most likely to hack her to death were those she knew best, and from intimate association. But even they were "strange creatures." "I cannot tell whether they have any good feeling for their owners or not," she wrote, "sometimes I think they

---

[10] Virginia Ingraham Burr, ed., *The Secret Eye: The Journal of Ella Gertrude Thomas, 1848–1889* (Chapel Hill: University of North Carolina Press, 1990), July [30], 1861, pp. 190 and 194; May 29, 1865, p. 272.

[11] Betty Herndon Maury, *The Civil War Diary of Betty Herndon Maury (June 3, 1861–February 18, 1863)*, ed. Robert A. Hodge (Fredericksburg, VA: Privately Published, 1985), April 25, 1862, p. 52.

[12] Keziah Goodwyn Hopkins Brevard, *A Plantation Mistress on the Eve of the Civil War: The Diary of Keziah Goodwyn Brevard, 1860-1861*, ed. John Hammond Moore (Columbia: University of South Carolina Press, 1993), February 28, 1861; November 28, 1860; April 4, 1861, quotes at pp. 95, 54, and 110. Hereafter cited as Brevard, *Diary*.

have – then I think their (sic) is nothing but deception in them – I am heartily tired of managing them."[13] Some she could "scarce ever get a civil word from no matter how kind & indulgent to them" despite, she wrote, "all I have done for them." The slaves in her home, she continued, "seem at times to hate me as though I had satan's principles in me ... I am now & then awakened to the fact that they *hate me*."[14] Given her own hatred of them, their hatred of her ultimately could not have really been surprising. It was just that the reality stood out much more clearly in the glare of war. She now thought more clearly, and took their opinion of her as seriously as she took hers of them.

The Civil War forced mistresses to look at slave women subject to their personal dominion differently, to reconsider the meaning of previous experiences. By her own account, Brevard was nearly constantly at odds and in confrontation with the black women who labored in her home. More than any of them, Sylvia, who she had "ever disliked," epitomized for her all that was wrong, not with slavery but with the enslaved. So much did Sylvia occupy her thoughts that she sometimes wrote in her diary as though Sylvia was at that very moment standing before her and being addressed directly by her. In one entry, as she contemplated the possibility that she might die before the Confederacy won its independence, Brevard considered Sylvia's future in the event of such an occurrence: "Sylvia, I hope no relative I have will keep you about them," she wrote, "nothing on this earth can change your heart – it is a *bad one*." Resuming a more traditional narrative voice, she added: "The truth is, Sylvia *hates* a white face – I firmly believe this from the conduct of her whole life."[15]

Sylvia, it turns out, was a child. Perhaps, Sylvia's age made her resistance all the much more unsettling to Brevard, her "bad" heart that much harder to reconcile with Brevard's sense of her charge as mistress. In fact, Brevard felt her authority besieged by the conduct of Sylvia's entire family. Sylvia's sisters, Tama, Mack, and Maria, were no more governable despite the fact that *she* had "raised" all four of them. All of them gave her "impudence unmeasured." They "dislike me & never care to look at me," she wrote. Brevard blamed their parents, Jim and Dolly, both of whom, like their daughters, she considered incorrigible, impudent, ungrateful, and impossible to live with. She hated Dolly's rebellious spirit, her taste for fashionable clothes, her pride, her "stubborn as an ox" ways, "the example" she set for Sylvia and her other daughters and the entire slave community. All of this made Dolly, in Brevard's eyes, "a miserable woman." Jim's *"daring impudence"* equally unsettled her. "I wish their hearts could be changed," she wrote. By the example of their own conduct, she understood, they gave their daughters license to disrespect her and treat her with contempt. From "Mamy or Dady on," they gave her nothing but trouble, "every one" of them, "just as impudent as they desired to be."[16]

---

[13] Brevard, *Diary*, January 26, 1861, pp. 81–82.
[14] Brevard, *Diary*, January 30, 1862; February 3, 1861, pp. 83 and 86.
[15] Brevard, *Diary*, February 3, 1861; January 30, 1861, quotes at pp. 87 and 83, respectively.
[16] Brevard, *Diary*, February 3, 1861; February 13, 1861; February 7, 1861; February 9, 1861; January 26, 1861, quotes at pp. 87, 89, 88, 81, 88–90, 88, 88, 89, 89, 88, 88, 89, 88, and

It did not occur to Brevard even to attempt squaring her conviction that Dolly and Jim had raised such "impudent" children with her own sense of herself as the girls' parent, the one who had "raised" them. In usurping that role, she sometimes whipped them, but "whipping did very little good." Nor did "good treatment," which "made them think themselves better than white people." They were simply "ungovernable." In the end, she concluded, "I know I treat *them* far better than they treat me . . . but they care nothing for me – self is all." "My God!! My God!! – save us from the wars within."[17]

As George Rable writes, postwar reminiscences by white southerners give the impression that there was no war within.[18] Quite to the contrary, those accounts held that slaves who had been inefficient and impudent before the war could not be otherwise, for their racial nature decreed it. But by those same accounts, their racial nature had the opposite effect in the midst of war. Now, slaves who had been inefficient and impudent turned to embrace their enslavement. That alleged embrace stands exhibited in reports of "loyalty," a far cry from Brevard's "wars within" and yet readily recognizable as the opposite extreme of one and the same continuum. What the "slave loyalty" of southerners' reminiscences actually meant remains a largely unexamined question. Historians have been understandably quite skittish about the subject, in general reacting to the racist historiography of another time with silence or fervent denunciations. Neither is satisfactory. The decision of a slave to stand side by side with an owner during the war or to stay put after the war, it would seem, had little to do with the concept of loyalty as it is typically understood in our everyday usage. Its complexities and ambiguities of meaning to those who fought or lived through the Civil War must be teased out.

Even so, what slaves and ex-slaves said about slaveholders, and the renderings by slaveholders of what they said, are not as ambiguous as scholars often suggest. Lee Ann Whites argues that southern white women, as members of the dominant class, were "frequently ignorant of the manner in which their identities are defined and sustained by their relations with the non-dominant," while slaves, "without such obfuscating privilege are more fully cognizant of the ways in which they actually construct others." Whites, however, does not believe that slaves' greater awareness led to the formation of radical political sensibilities. Rather, "this very knowledge demands a kind of responsibility,

---

81, respectively. Brevard also accused the family of using their strength in numbers to force other "small families" "to succumb to them." "No other servant in this yard but *Jim or one of his family would have risked such an insult to me* – Jim is an impudent negro – & every servant knuckles to him – if they do not – his family will put them down," she wrote after an incident in which Jim countermanded her instructions to another slave. Jim and Dolly's family also occupied larger than usual slave quarters, a three-room cabin divided into a sitting room and two bedrooms. A similar situation existed at Brevard's Cabin Branch plantation where two other families, "old Dick's & Old Jacob's descendants" ruled. (Quotes at January 26, 1861, p. 81; February 7, 1861, p. 88; March 18, 1861, p. 100, respectively.)

[17] Brevard, *Diary*, February 13, 1861; February 7, 1861; January 30, 1861, quotes at pp. 89, 90, 88, and 83, respectively.

[18] Rable, *Civil Wars*, pp. 116–20.

what might be described as a 'loyalty' even to those who dominate and exploit them." Citing with approval Booker T. Washington's argument that slaves were loyal during the war and his contention that it reflected the slave community's commitment to values that disloyalty betrayed, Whites maintains that when masters left for war and placed the protection of white women in the hands of slaves, "the slave community chose not to violate this trust." To do otherwise "would entail an abdication of one's self-respect and sense of humanity," she writes.[19] The actions of slaves and ex-slaves hardly demonstrate that they held to such a self-defeating philosophy. They rather reveal a political sensibility in which disloyalty, if it can even be called that, was understood as the key to exploiting the war's possibilities for their freedom, with the understanding that planter women, no less than planter men, were their enemies.

Postwar reminiscences paint a story few white people experienced during the war itself. The contemporaneous stories were more like Susan B. Jervay's and Kate Stone's. Jervay found herself startled by the least noise, her "head being full of negroes and yankees."[20] For Kate Stone, fear of "lawless Yankee soldiers" took a back seat to the more pressing fears arising from closer quarters. "We would be practically helpless should the Negroes rise, since there are so few men left at home," she wrote. The "fear of the negroes should they rise against us," was ever present.[21] Slaveholders acknowledged the existence of spies in their midst. They used words like treachery, treason, and defection to describe slaves' wartime resistance, words that suggest abandonment of duty and that have meaning only in the context of some form of a prior existing trust or allegiance. Every slave was a "possible spy," even mammy. "Father says we must not trust mammy too far," wrote Eliza Andrews. Some worried that "every servant who answers the bell will shoot them thro the heart."[22]

The longer the war lasted, the more mistresses feared for their safety in the midst of slaves, the more they feared that their homes would be burned down over their very heads or in their absence, and that they would be murdered

---

[19] Lee Ann Whites, *The Civil War as a Crisis in Gender: Augusta, Georgia, 1860–1890* (Athens: University of Georgia Press, 1995), pp. 6–7. For a more complicated analysis, see Rable, *Civil Wars*, pp. 116–20, and Faust, *Mothers of Invention*, pp. 60–61.

[20] Susan B. Jervay, *Diaries of 65*, [Feb. 21], 65, p. 4 in *Two Diaries: from Middle St. John's Berkeley, South Carolina, February–May, 1865: Journals Kept by Miss Susan B. Jervay and Miss Charlotte St. J. Ravenel, at Northhampton and Poshee Plantations, and Reminiscences of Mrs. (Waring) Henagan, with Contemporary Reports from Federal Officials* (1921; reprint, St. John's Island, SC: St. John's Hunting Club, 1994). Hereafter referred to as Jervay, *Diaries of 65*.

[21] Stone, *Brokenburn*, September 5, 1864, p. 298; Maury, *Civil War Diary*, April 25, 1862, p. 52; Faust, *Mothers of Invention*, pp. 56–61; Gary Gallagher, *The Confederate War: How Popular Will, Nationalism, and Military Strategy Could Not Stave Off Defeat* (Cambridge, MA: Harvard University Press, 1997), pp. 148–50; Steven V. Ash, *When the Yankees Came: Conflict and Chaos in the Occupied South, 1861–1865* (Chapel Hill: University of North Carolina Press, 1995).

[22] Eliza Andrews, *The War-Time Journal of a Georgia Girl, 1864–1865* (New York: D. Appleton & Co., 1908), p. 355; Sarah Strong Baxter Hampton to her father, December 22, 1860, SCL.

outright. Even from the safety of the North, Mary Duncan was certain that her family's slaves would leave and equally convinced that before doing so, they would burn the family's plantation.[23] Rachel Pearsall's cook told her before her face that she intended "to burn her up."[24] One Georgia mistress narrowly escaped death after being shoved into a fire by a slave woman. Her life was spared only because the "negro taking fire... had to let go of her mistress to extinguish herself."[25] In the last months of the war, a group of slaves led by a woman and her son burned to the ground planter homes in Pineville, South Carolina.[26]

The torching and destruction of planter homes was sometimes but not always random violence. One stated goal was to make them uninhabitable, to prevent mistresses from ever returning and occupying them. As one mistress made her way back to her plantation, a slave woman she had trusted sent word that she should keep moving.[27] With the defeat of the Confederacy in sight in late March 1865, slaves at Cherry Grove plantation in South Carolina begged Union soldiers to burn the great house to keep their mistress, Catherine Marion Palmer, from returning. Louisa, the slave of a Georgia state legislator, wanted Sherman's troops to burn her master's newly built home, explaining, "It *ought* to be burned," because it was linked to "so much devilment... whipping niggers most to death to make 'em work to pay for it."[28] The burning continued for months after the war ended. At Richfield plantation in South Carolina, former slaves torched the big house in January 1866 after being ordered off the plantation for refusing to sign contracts.[29]

In the making of freedom, the destruction of slavery and the destruction of planter homes were of a piece. "The burning, slashing and punishment," writes Charles Royster, "were inseparable from the freedom – a single memory." Slaves linked the two explicitly. Savilla Burrell remembered claiming her freedom when the Yankees arrived and "burnt de big house, stables, barns, [and] gin house." Sherman's Georgia and South Carolina campaigns helped to forge this single memory. An ex-slave who followed Sherman's troops into

[23] Mary Duncan to Edwin Stanton, May 30, 1863 [L-98]. See also Mary Duncan to Adjutant General Lorenzo Thomas, in Ira Berlin, Joseph P. Reidy, and Leslie S. Rowland, eds., *Freedom: A Documentary History of Emancipation, 1861–1867*, ser. II, *The Black Military Experience* (Cambridge: Cambridge University Press, 1982), pp. 146–48.

[24] Mathew Page Andrews, comp., *The Women of the South in War Times* (Baltimore, MD: Norman, Remington Co., 1920), p. 241.

[25] Faust, *Mothers of Invention*, pp. 56–62, quote at p. 58.

[26] Pineville was a summer resort village for low country planters. Ravenel Papers, 30–80–101, SCHS; J. Russell Cross, *Historic Ramblin's through Berkeley County* (Columbia, SC: R. L. Bryan Co., 1985), pp. 194–97; Maxwell Clayton Orvin, *Historic Berkeley County, 1671–1900* (Charleston, SC: Comprint, 1973), pp. 142 and 157.

[27] Elizabeth P. Porcher to Philip E. Porcher, March 23, 1865, in *A World Turned Upside Down*, ed. Towles, p. 452.

[28] Quoted in Charles Royster, *The Destructive War: William Tecumseh Sherman, Stonewall Jackson, and the Americans* (New York: Knopf, 1991), p. 344.

[29] Richard N. Côté, *Mary's World: Love, War, and Family Ties in Nineteenth Century Charleston* (Mt. Pleasant, SC: Corinthian Books, 2001), p. 263.

Atlanta from a nearby Georgia plantation described the burning of Atlanta as a "grand sight." The "people of the South needed some such a dose as that – they needed to learn that war is a serious thing – no boys play at all, nor fooling. And Sherman seemed to be the man for that kind of teaching," another ex-slave explained.[30] At Newberry, South Carolina, as rumors of the Emancipation Proclamation circulated in 1863, it "did not affect us," a former slave recalled. "We work on, til Sherman come and burn and slash his way through the state in de spring of 1865. I just reckon I member dat freedom to de end of my life." They then gathered at his grandmother's cabin to hear her speak the words that they were indeed free.[31]

Union soldiers, however, sometimes disappointed. Slaves took note of those who openly sympathized with slaveholders. Belle Garland Myers Caruthers (she insisted that the interviewer record her full name) believed she had every reason to assume that the U.S. soldiers who arrived at the plantation where she was enslaved would burn the place. Instead, the officer sat on the big house porch relaxing and chatting with her mistress. He listened politely as the mistress spoke with pride of her "six sons in the Southern Army" and stated that she wished she had sixty to give. Caruthers understood her mistress's proslavery stance but was baffled by the Union officer's response that he "admired her patriotism." The officer went on to grant her mistress's request for a guard and received a good meal in return. "On account of that," Caruthers stated, "our house was not burned when all the others in the neighborhood were."[32] For the most part, however, slaves witnessed increasingly more antislavery activism on the part of Union soldiers, including a greater willingness to torch plantation homes, mills, rice, and other property, particularly in the last months of the war.[33] By the end, more and more mistresses, like Caruthers's, were calling on the enemy without to protect them from the enemy within. Requests for Union military details soared in the closing months of the war.

[30] Royster, *The Destructive War*, pp. 345–46; Savilla Burrell, *South Carolina Narratives*, vol. 2, pt. 1, p. 151; Alfred Sligh, *South Carolina Narratives*, vol. 3, pt. 4, pp. 92-93; "The Story of a Contraband," *Minnesota Narratives*, Supplement Series 1, vol. 1, p. 127. In the process, Sherman became an unlikely hero. Black people, Royster writes, "were the first celebrators of his fame." Certainly, many black people did not celebrate Sherman. Sherman's well-known antipathy to black people and his adoption of policies that led to the death of many who tried to follow his army to freedom fostered a different assessment.

[31] Alfred Sligh, *South Carolina Narratives*, vol. 3, pt. 4, pp. 92–93.

[32] Belle Garland Myers Caruthers, *Mississippi Narratives*, Supplement Series 1, vol. 7, pt. 2, p. 366. Caruthers was about 18 years old when the war ended. White Union soldiers were sometimes as eager as slaves to see planter homes burnt, and sometimes that work was done by Confederate soldiers. As he watched the burning of houses torched by Confederate troops on St. John's Island, one Union soldier described it as "a splendid sight" (Charles B. Fox, *Record of the Service of the Fifty-Fifth Regiment of Massachusetts Volunteer Infantry* [1868; reprint, Freeport, NY: Books for Libraries Press, 1971], p. 32). Hereafter cited as Fox, *Record of the 55th*.

[33] At Fripp plantation in South Carolina, for example, houses used by Confederate soldiers as lookouts were ordered burned in early January 1865. See Fox, *Record of the 55th*, pp. 47 and 63.

Overall, the capacity of black people to wreak vengeance on planters and their households took on a new gravity. As Augustin Taveau tried to communicate to his wife, they now lived in a different world. When he sent her arsenic to combat a rat infestation, he included detailed instructions on its use and storage. He emphasized that she must put it "out of *sight* and harm's way," normal precautions for handling poison. But Taveau obviously had slaves in mind when he added: "Do not let any one know anything of it, mix it in your room, and if you have not the opportunity of taking it to the store room unseen, *lock it up in a draw* (sic) untill (sic) you have the chance. For heaven's sake remember it is poison."[34]

Slaves did not rise up en masse, as in the common usage of the phrase, but they did rise up. They began as the secession movement gathered steam, ascribing to the coming conflict meanings relevant to the lives they hoped to gain. Jane, called to account for throwing a chair at another slave woman, arrived at the meeting with a carving knife in her hands and showing no sign of contrition. Once the interview was over, she left for the nearby Union camp at Desota, Mississippi. "We would not have been surprised," Kate Stone wrote, "to have her slip up and stick any of us in the back." Following the incident, Stone carried a five-shooter around with her, only later discovering that it was not loaded. Some mistresses took to carrying revolvers in their belts. Others prepared make-shift bombs or made plans to learn how to load and shoot.[35]

Enslaved women decided at the outset of the Civil War that the conflict concerned them directly even if at first they were unsure what this meant precisely or how it would turn out. On the strength of this belief, they risked their lives by refusing to minister to the needs of their mistresses and by fleeing to Union lines. But it was not just a matter of getting away but also, getting through. Slave patrols, Confederate soldiers, and deserters on the roads posed one kind of danger; weather and geography, others. Winter travel meant braving cold weather and icy roads. Summer travel brought its own risks. Slaves might spend days or weeks in the woods with little food before reaching Union lines. Sloughs, bayous, and rivers were year-round obstacles. We will never know the number of slaves who died in the effort. Jane, who with her children had left the Stone household hoping to make it to the Union camp at Desota, was one of many who did not make it. Two weeks after she left, it was reported that mother and children had drowned crossing a break. "A short space of freedom for them," Kate Stone commented dryly.[36]

Judai White understood clearly the implications of her decision to leave with her daughters Maria and Hannah as soon as she heard talk of freedom. She had been forced to witness her children suffer beatings and other abuse

---

[34] [Augustin] Taveau to [Delphine Taveau], October 13, 1863, Augustin Louis Taveau Papers, DU.

[35] Kate Stone, *Brokenburn*, March 2, 1863, pp. 171–72; Faust, *Mothers of Invention*, pp. 54–56; Catherine Clinton, *Tara Revisited: Women, War, & the Plantation Legend* (New York: Abbeville Press, 1995), pp. 118–19.

[36] Fox, *Record of the 55th*, p. 47; Stone, *Brokenburn*, March 2, 1863; March 17, 1863, pp. 171 and 180, quote at p. 180.

from her mistress, witnessed her mistress order another woman whipped, and been forced to spin cotton thread from which to make clothing for Confederate soldiers. When she took her leave, "Old Miss was in bed with a young baby." As her daughter Maria later recalled, "None of us didn't so much as go near her to say good-bye, cause none of us didn't care if we never seed her again."[37]

Over the course of the war, thousands of mistresses would wake to find themselves left to cook their own meals, make their own beds and do their own laundry. One plantation lost 75 slaves, including field hands and domestic slaves, one night in early March 1863. "The ladies had to get up and get breakfast."[38] Emma LeConte was thirteen when the war began. It robbed her of the expectation that her teenage years would be spent in luxury and enjoyment. Instead, she found, "No pleasure, no enjoyment – nothing but rigid economy and hard work – nothing but the stern realities of life." The war was not yet quite over and emancipation not yet formally decreed, but LeConte saw the end in February 1865. By that point her family's slaves had declared their freedom. She wrote resignedly: "They are free however at present and we ask as little as possible of them.... If Jane offers to clean up our room, all very well – if not, we do it ourselves." LeConte and her family moved into one room of the house. It was all that she could "manage to keep neat and clean" by herself and her "first experience in work of this kind."[39]

Realities of this sort weakened rhetorical calls for Confederate women to stand tall and together in sacrifice. LeConte's seeming nonchalance was but a fig leaf for she neither welcomed nor celebrated her newfound independence. Five months after having declared that she and her family could manage quite nicely whether Jane, "a great nuisance" at any rate, helped or not, she was forced to acknowledge that Jane's actual "leaving so unexpectedly caused us some inconvenience."[40] Yet, neither financial disaster nor military losses led mistresses to seriously consider taking on domestic work long term as the price of liberty. But that so much of the inconvenience came from the hands of slaves with whom they were most intimate made the losses appear all the more cruel. Still, it can hardly be said that mistresses "shouldered with dignity" the "sacrifices" they were called to make. With "slaves running off to Lincolnland and bare pantries," dignity was often in even shorter supply than slaves.[41]

Some slaves took temporary leaves and threats to make them "pay for it" no longer carried the same authority. Sometimes, leaving involved, as it had during slavery, just getting away for a moment of freedom, a few hours to

[37] Maria White, *Mississippi Narratives*, Supplement Series 1, vol. 10, pt. 5, pp. 2277–81, quote at p. 2280.
[38] Stone, *Brokenburn*, March 3, 1863; March 5, 1863, pp. 173, 176, quote at p. 173. See also Faust, *Mothers of Invention*, pp. 74–78; Rable, *Civil Wars*, pp. 116–20.
[39] Emma LeConte Diary, January 28, 1865; June 27, 1865, SHC.
[40] LeConte Diary, January 28, 1865; June 27, 1865, SHC. On the erosion of white women's patriotism and, for some, an initial ebullience about doing their own housework, see Rable, *Civil Wars*, p. 256, and Faust, *Mothers of Invention*, pp. 6–7, 74–79, and 238–44.
[41] Quotes are from Clinton, *Tara Revisited*, p. 122.

visit a child, or spouse, or boyfriend. Lucy, for example, ran away the morning of July 2, 1861 but was back by dinner time. Her return, however, did not mean victory for her mistress. It did not end Lucy's quest for freedom, a quest slaveholders put down as slaves' demoralization.[42] Some mistresses, hoping to stem the tide and get a minimal amount of work done, lightened slave women's workload only to be forcefully reminded that while the gesture might win them a temporary reprieve, it was not the freedom black women sought. Riah, or "Madame Riah" as her master derisively called her, took full advantage of the chaos and promise of freedom, running away for periods of time and returning each time secure in the knowledge that each absence would result in a reduction of her workload. She was secure, that is, in the knowledge that her labor, no matter how grudgingly given, was of value to her owners. Even though given "so little to do" each time she returned, she continued to place her own happiness before that of her owners.[43] Beating and ill-treating female slaves, mistresses also learned, worked less and less.[44] Susanna Clay resorted to "'moral suasion' to get slave women to do their duty," which generally got her nowhere. Not only did they not see meeting her needs as a matter of ethical behavior, they no longer saw any need to meet them at all, and said so. "We cannot expect any authority. I beg ours to do what little is done," a defeated Clay declared.[45]

The harder white women pushed, the less slave women worked and the more they claimed personal time and space and authority over themselves and their families. When, with Union forces closing in, Emmeline Trott's mistress prepared to flee to Alabama, Trott made her claim, refusing to allow her mistress to take one of her sons along. This she could not have done before the war. Trott's husband, the carriage driver, ordered to drive the white family to Alabama, instead stole a horse and escaped to Union lines. Emmeline Trott had helped her mistress hide valuables from Union soldiers. She was not willing to sacrifice her freedom or her son's for her mistress's sake.[46] In the wake of the departure of masters and mistresses, slave women like Trott began their own

---

[42] Stone, *Brokenburn*, July 2, 1861, p. 35. Lucy would later be found plotting against her mistress and roundly abusing her name (ibid., May 22, 1863, p. 209).

[43] Augustin L. Taveau to [Delphine Taveau], August 1, 1863; August 5, 1863; September 6, 1863; Taveau Papers, DU. Quote is from August 5, 1863 letter.

[44] Historians tend to see slaveholding women's use of violence as a troubling wartime development occasioned by the demands of war which forced white women to take on larger roles in plantation management. "Disciplining subordinates – be they children or slaves," notes Drew Faust, "had been the ultimate responsibility of white male heads of households in the prewar South." By contrast, she adds, during the war "women were called upon to maintain a system founded in an assertiveness and a violence they could not fully embrace" (Faust, *Mothers of Invention*, pp. 132, 134).

[45] Quoted in H. E. Sterkx, *Partners in Rebellion: Alabama Women in the Civil War* (Rutherford, NJ: Farleigh Dickinson Press, 1970), p. 132.

[46] Emmeline Trott, *Mississippi Narratives*, Supplement Series 1, vol. 10, pt. 5, p. 2130. Similarly, all but two of the slaves in Kate Stone's family refused to be refugeed (Stone, *Brokenburn*, p. 203).

journey to freedom. Like Trott, the vast majority of slave women would make freedom on the ground where they stood in 1861.

Some slave women were left behind by owners in flight. Others refused to flee with their owners or to attempt flight at all. These women stayed put for a thousand reasons. Sometimes, extended family ties made leaving more difficult; sometimes, the distance to safety within Union lines was too great; sometimes, they were simply too old or ill to travel. For some, the decision to remain where they were was based on the simplest of calculations. The flight of their mistresses and masters cleared the way for them to claim freedom where they stood. When owners fled, slaves had less reason to. Some refused to be refugeed, hiding as their masters made preparations to retreat or, like Trott's husband, ran away. At other times, owners left hurriedly with plans to return for the slaves. Whatever the immediate determining circumstance, life on plantations without masters or mistresses allowed many slaves their first experience in freedom, and their first opportunity to place their own imprint on its making.

Under these circumstances, often slaves' first act after the departure of slave-holders was the physical destruction of planter homes. Slaves did not torch or destroy fields or store houses as they did in other slave societies, but they burned and destroyed plantation houses and the material accoutrements of planter power that graced them. What they did not destroy, they sometimes commandeered and carried away to their cabins.[47] At White Hall and Buck Hall plantations, with the encouragement of Union soldiers, slaves stripped the big house of its furnishings.[48] More than one mistress learned that their beds were "all in the quarters." With the approach of Union forces in late spring 1863, Kate Stone and her family and many of their neighbors abandoned their plantations, becoming refugees for the duration of the war. The slaves they were forced to leave behind took what they had left, which was most of their possessions. "Our house is stripped of furniture, carpets, books, piano, and everything else, the carriage, the buggy, harness, and everything of that kind," Stone learned. Her family lost likenesses and "all their fine and pretty things." One slave family had moved into her mother's room. At the time, Stone, her mother, sister, her sister's nurse, and her aunt were refugees, all living in one small room, sharing one bed covered with dirty linen, and

---

[47] In other slave societies like Saint Domingue and Jamaica, different dynamics made the torching of fields or storehouses as much a part of the destruction of slavery as the torching of great houses. While slaves in the U.S. South did not burn fields, they no doubt experienced some satisfaction when cane and cotton crops were burned by slaveholders, or by Confederate military forces to prevent their falling into Union hands. With Union forces threatening Vicksburg, for instance, planters set fire to thousands of bales of cotton. The smoke from the burning cotton darkened the sky from Memphis to New Orleans. To the slaves, the smoldering bales provided additional evidence of the disintegration of the Confederacy. (Stone, *Brokenburn*, May 9, 1862; May 10, 1863, pp. 100–101 and 103).

[48] Diary of Harriet Palmer, March 7, 1865, in *A World Turned Upside Down*, ed. Towles, p. 437; Mary Duncan to Edwin Stanton, May 30, 1863 [L-98]; Edward Ball, *Slaves in the Family* (New York: Farrar, Strauss, and Giroux, 1998), p. 76.

taking meals of "sassafras tea, coarse cornbread, and fat bacon." In language identical to LeConte's, Stone wrote, these were "the stern realities of life."[49]

The flight of mistresses and masters thus had immediate benefits for slaves who remained behind. Many for the first time in their lives came into possession of beds, spoons, forks, crockery, and plates, and clothes that did not scratch the skin. They ate openly from formerly forbidden larders that were the product of their labor. Some had their first taste of milk, cream, butter, and coffee. Gardens left flush with vegetables, and yards, pens, and barns with pigs, chickens, and cows became theirs to enjoy. One slave carried away woolen homespun, two bed quilts; one sheet; clothing; and two dishes for his wife. Mary and Salindes took crockery ware, bed clothing, and clothes from the home of Mrs. E. M. Burkett.[50]

These transfers of property from the big house to slave cabins dramatize the meagerness of black people's lives as slaves. Spoons and plates replace communal troughs and tin cups. The impoverishment of slave life had always forced slaves to help furnish themselves and take more than mistresses and masters allowed. The majority of the cases (some 75 percent) heard by the Spartanburg District Court of Magistrates and Freeholders between 1824 and 1865 involved theft. Slaves brought before the court were accused of stealing everything from corn meal, wheat, and bacon to a wash pot and spoons, revealing the long history of want and slaveholders' neglect. Spoons were apparently much sought after. Seven women and two men were accused of stealing them. As ex-slave Levi Ashley explained, slaveholders had "spoons an' forks" with which to eat, while the slaves "had to eat wid mussel shells fer spoons."[51]

In the privacy of their own homes, away from the prying eyes of mistresses and freed from the labor they demanded, slaves who remained behind began to forge new lives with the tools at hand. Amanda Stone had fled with her children on the approach of the Union army. When she sent her son back to Louisiana to retrieve slaves she had left behind, she knew they would not be eager to leave, and therefore requested an escort of Confederate troops to accompany him. On arriving, the men hid in the canebrake, a fodder loft, and under Lucy's cabin, waiting for daylight to surround the cabins. What they heard and saw while waiting validated Amanda Stone's cautionary measures.

.... while hiding under Lucy's house they saw her sitting there with Maria before a most comfortable fire drinking the most fragrant coffee. They were abusing Mamma, calling her that Woman and talking exultantly of capering around in her clothes and

---

[49] Stone, *Brokenburn*, April 21, 1863; April 27, 1863; May 22, 1863, pp. 193, 202–3, and 210, quotes at pp. 193, 203, and 210.

[50] Clarendon County Freeholders & Magistrates Court Records, 1863-65, December 3, 1863; February 15, 1865, SCDAH; Stone, *Brokenburn*, May 22, 1863, p. 210; Sallie Brock Putnam, *Richmond During the War: Four Years of Personal Observation* (1867; reprint, Lincoln: University of Nebraska Press, 1996), pp. 264–66.

[51] Spartanburg District Court of Magistrates and Freeholders, Reel C920, SCDAH. For the theft of spoons, see Case #82, among others. For similar cases, see Pendleton/Anderson District Magistrates and Freeholders Court Records, SCDAH; Levi Ashley, *Mississippi Narratives*, Supplement Series 1, vol. 6, pt. 1, p. 79.

taking her place as mistress and heaping scorn on her. Capt. Smith said that he never heard a lady get such a tongue-lashing and that Lucy abused the whole family in round terms.[52]

They Say They are Free

The vast majority of slaves who remained on farms and plantations, however, did not get to experience the pleasures of absentee ownership. Masters might be away but not mistresses. Over the course of the war, these slaves endured the war's greatest privations. They were made to work harder while receiving less in the way of food and clothing. Adequate medical care, a luxury on the battlefield, became almost nonexistent on the home front. Elderly slaves suffered perhaps the greatest neglect.[53] The call for white women's patriotic support through spinning, knitting, and sewing for Confederate soldiers meant additional work for slave women. Much of the outfitting of Confederate soldiers that was done on plantations and farms ultimately fell to them, and sometimes to slave men as well. Nancy Johnson recalled with bitterness having "to work hard for the rebels." "I was nearly frostbitten," she testified, because "my old Missus made me weave to make clothes for the soldiers till 12 o'clock at night." Slaves had their own families to care for, and that burden shifted massively to black women as a growing number of black men enlisted in the U.S. military, adding to losses already borne due to the conscription of slave men as laborers for the Confederacy and the Union. Others, taken to the front by masters as body servants, sometimes took flight from there, but not always to return to their families.[54]

Yet, whatever the circumstances that made flight unrealizable, slave women who could not get away did not cease their "miserable" ways. Attempts to rationalize their behavior, their indifference to the needs of mistresses and masters, by resort to the language of impudence or savagery, were now clearly

---

[52] Stone, *Brokenburn*, May 22, 1863, p. 209. Like other refugee slaveholders, Amanda Stone had placed some of her slaves at the salt works near Winfield, Louisiana (see pp. 170, 194, and 204–5).

[53] Roberta Manson, *North Carolina Narratives*, vol. 15, pt. 2, pp. 102–3. By the last months of the war, starving conditions were a major cause of slave flight from plantations. See, for example, L. H. Card to P. C. Cameron, January 12, 1865, Cameron Family Papers, SHC.

[54] Testimony of Nancy Johnson, March 22, 1873, Southern Claims Commission in Ira Berlin, Barbara J. Fields, Thavolia Glymph, Joseph P. Reidy, and Leslie S. Rowland, eds., *Freedom: A Documentary History of Emancipation, 1861–1867*, ser. 1., vol. 1, *The Destruction of Slavery* (Cambridge: Cambridge University Press, 1985), p. 151. Increasingly, too, the labor of slave women provided food for the table and brought in the cash crops that allowed large slavehold-ers to continue to import and consume luxuries despite the Confederate government's criticism of this trade. By 1864, illicit traffic with the enemy was so extensive that some Confederate officials called for lifting restrictions on trade with the enemy. U.S. Government, *The War of the Rebellion: A Compilation of the Official Records of the Union and Confederate Armies* (Washington, DC: Government Printing Office, 1900), ser. 1, vol. 32, pt. 2, pp. 568–69. Hereafter cited as *OR*. Slave narratives are especially valuable sources for documenting slave women's work making clothing and other necessaries for Confederate soldiers. See, for example, Henry Gibbs, *Mississippi Narratives*, Supplement Series 1, vol. 8, pt. 3, p. 5.

self-deluding. Conspiracies and actual resistance made slaveholders rethink how they talked about and categorized slave resistance. Not only were slaves ready to initiate actions that would assist the Union armies and free themselves personally, they expected big things from the Union army. Even if they themselves did nothing themselves, the Yankees would "make the South shit behind their asses."[55] In the plantation household, the voices of dissent made themselves heard and understood.

While some slaves made furtive plans to run away, sneaking away in the night, many no longer tried to hide their desire and determination to be free. They tossed aside the use of coded speech. They spoke openly of freedom, calling for an end to the brutalities associated with slavery, especially violence against women. The conspiracy at Second Creek, Mississippi, and the uprising that led to the death of Betsey Witherspoon at Society Hill, South Carolina, were both launched with the rallying cry, "There will be no whipping here tomorrow."[56] Enslaved women increasingly refused to work. Dolly had "ever been a miserable woman" in the eyes of her mistress. "Now she sits & does nothing," Brevard wrote.[57] Moreover, household slaves increasingly broadcast their designs to leave. "We hear that our three are going soon," Betty Maury wrote. Some gave the news to their owners directly. "Jane left us yesterday, having only informed mother the day before of her intended departure," wrote Emma LeConte.[58] Mistresses saw sufficient impudence in these advance warnings but they also recognized something new in the way black people talked.

Even Keziah Brevard detected a difference in the demeanor of black people. "I think," she wrote, "a desperate state of affairs exists at the South – our negroes are far more knowing than many will acknowledge. The children even. I had a little negro girl about the house to say to me the other day – 'twas a sin for big like them to say sir to Mass Thomas & Mass Whitfield & little ones like them (T. & W. – a babe & a little boy) – now if black children have this talk what are we to expect from grown negroes – this same little girl has told me how my negroes hated white folks & how they talked about *me*." Brevard was an experienced observer of slaves' self-regard, but even she seemed shocked by this. It would seem, given her previous encounters with Sylvia, that nothing Sylvia did or said could unsettle her. But she was clearly rattled by Sylvia's assessment of her neighbor and friend, Dr. Duncan Ray. According

---

[55] Quote at Winthrop D. Jordan, *Tumult and Silence at Second Creek: An Inquiry into a Civil War Slave Conspiracy* (Baton Rouge: Louisiana State University Press, 1993), p. 274; Woodward and Muhlenfeld, eds., *The Private Mary Chesnut*, October 9, 1861, pp. 174–75.

[56] The call for an end to beatings was a common feature of slave rebellions throughout the Atlantic world. It was raised, for example, by the slaves at Demerara in 1823, who called specifically for an end to "the flogging of females" (Emília Viotti da Costa, *Crowns of Glory, Tears of Blood: the Demerara Slave Rebellion of 1823* [New York: Oxford University Press, 1994], pp. 216 and 220).

[57] Brevard, *Diary*, February 13, 1861, p. 90.

[58] Sterkx, *Partners in Rebellion*, p. 133; LeConte Diary, January 28, 1865; June 27, 1865, SHC; Maury, *Civil War Diary*, April 25, 1862, p. 52.

to Sylvia: "*Dr Ray was no body, no how.*" Brevard wrote: "This is the way negroes talk in these days. These were her very words."[59] Similarly, another mistress wrote in a seeming state of shock: "The negroes are worse than free, they say they *are* free."[60]

Some mistresses settled for self-delusion, calling on old, worn, and unreliable management tools, acting just as they had before the war. Maria White's master was away serving in the Confederate army, but this fact seemingly had no effect upon her mistress's behavior. She was a "fractious lady" before the war and remained so. She "would whack me over the head with whatever she had in her hand," White recalled. "I slept on the floor by the baby's crib. When she called me to get up if I didn't hear her, she would throw a glass of water in my face no matter how cold the weather was."[61]

Others tried to adapt to the changed realities. A heightened sense of vulnerability propelled some mistresses to try to take charge by means of heightened aggression. Emily Dashiell Perkins made the decision to meet any sign of slave resistance with force. Perkins applauded her victory over a slave woman she had "just got thru humbling" for speaking impudently to her daughter and refusing to provide an explanation. Taking up what she thought was a shovel (fortunately for the slave, it was a broom), she beat her repeatedly. She then had the woman brought to her room and tied up, whereupon she knocked her down and "laid it on" until the woman "promised she never would speak impudently or be otherwise than perfectly obedient to me." Perkins justified the violence as necessary to maintain order on her plantation and throughout the region. In beating the woman, she said, she acted on behalf of the entire white community in the countryside around Murfreesboro, Tennessee, where the slaves were in "perfect rebellion" and "no one in the country dares correct them." If others followed her example, she reasoned, the black rebellion would end. Perkins took particular satisfaction in the fact that the woman she had beaten had a reputation for being self-willed: "It has been thought *no one could whip her.*"[62]

For some mistresses, the war provided justification for habits of violence they had before the war. Harriet Robinson remembered her mistress, Julia Sims, as a "mean" woman whose taste for violence went undiminished during the war. "Miss Julie whipped me every day in the mawning," Robinson stated. "During the war she beat us so terrible. She say, 'Your master's out fighting and losing blood trying to save you from them Yankees, so you can get your'n here. Miss Julie would take me by my ears and butt my head against the wall. She wanted to whip my mammy, but old Master told her, naw sir. When his

[59] Brevard, *Diary*, April 4, 1861; February 22, 1861, pp. 110–11 and 93, respectively.

[60] As quoted in Sterkx, *Partners in Rebellion*, p. 132.

[61] Maria White, *Mississippi Narratives*, Supplement Series 1, vol. 10, pt. 5, pp. 2277–81, quote at p. 2277.

[62] Emily Dashiell Perkins to Belle Edmondson, February 22, 1864, in *A Lost Heroine of the Confederacy: The Diaries and Letters of Belle Edmondson*, ed. William and Loretta Galbraith (Jackson: University Press of Mississippi, 1990), pp. 192–93.

father done give my mammy to Master Sam, he told him not to beat her, and iffen he got to whar he jest had to, jest bring her back and place her in his yard from whar he got her."[63]

Determined, however, to do violence to Robinson's mother and further violence to Harriet, even with Union forces camped nearby, but fearing her husband would stop her, Sims had her brother whip Harriet and her mother, directing him to "give Miss Harriet...a free whipping." Sims's husband was furious when he found out and called his wife and brother-in-law "infernal sons o' bitches" for attempting such a thing with "300 Yankees camped out here and iffen they knowed you'd whipped this nigger the way you done done, they'd kill all us."[64] Julia Sims's husband tolerated her violent behavior in most cases. This time he drew the line, not for the sake of the "family" slaves but for fear of his own family's safety.

As the war seemed increasingly unwinnable, mistresses took their revenge and released their stress where they could – on slave women and children. When Anna Williamson openly admired the uniform of Union soldiers and "brass buttons so pretty on the blue suits," which made the "men pretty" in her eyes, her mistress slapped her until her "eye was red" for the offense.[65] Union commanders also reported mistresses's "barbarous and inhumane treatment" of slave women.[66]

With husbands, fathers, and sons away, some white women, however, were more hesitant to use their power to punish slaves. Sarah Fay sought advice from her husband on how she should handle Cynthia. His answer, that she should "sell or swap her" as she wished, was doubtless not very helpful. They both agreed that Cynthia was trifling. Cynthia's trifling behavior consisted of a steadfast refusal to either work or bear children. Edwin Fay wrote that he had learned from his body servant that Cynthia used abortifacients. Previous threats to get her to have children had failed, but Fay held out the hope that they might still. He told his wife to convey to her as forcefully as she could that her refusal to bear children was unacceptable, that, "If she does not have children, I will not keep her for the work she does herself." Cynthia persisted in her refusal to bear children and to work despite renewed threats to sell her.[67]

---

[63] Harriet Robinson, *Oklahoma and Mississippi Narratives*, vol. 7, pp. 271 and 274. Robinson and her father belonged to different owners. She described his mistress as a "good" woman.

[64] Harriett Robinson, *Oklahoma and Mississippi Narratives*, vol. 7, p. 274.

[65] Anna Williamson, *Arkansas Narratives*, vol. 11, pt. 7, p. 194. See also Charles Joyner, "The World of the Plantation Slaves," in *Before Freedom Came: African American Life in the Antebellum South*, ed. Edward D. C. Campbell, Jr. with Kim Rice (Charlottesville: University Press of Virginia, 1991), pp. 55–91.

[66] Acting Lieut. Commander Selim E. Woodworth to Commander D. D. Porter, July 1, 1862, Squadron Letters, LR, vol. 209, Ser. 30, M89.

[67] Edwin Fay to Sarah Fay, June 4, 1863, in *This Infernal War: The Confederate Letters of Sgt. Edwin H. Fay*, ed. Bell Irwin Wiley (Austin: University of Texas Press, 1958), pp. 279–80. Cynthia's work habits and her refusal to bear children continued to be a sore topic. Several months later, Fay inquired whether there were yet "prospects of an increase in her family?" See letters of August 3, 1863 and February 5, 1865, pp. 311 and 424.

To Triumph or Perish as a People

From the start of the war in 1861, as slaveholders' rhetoric linked the military battlefield and the homefront as twin elements of the struggle for southern independence, the homilies to domesticity took on new urgency. Slaveholding and non-slaveholding women – though with vastly different resources – were called upon to be mistress and master, ladies and working women. In the absence of men, they were called to manage households and fields and to take on the kinds of work that war places disproportionately on females, from "manning" the home fires and keeping up home front morale to caring for the sick and mourning the dead. Warriors could be their best only if their mothers and wives took up their part with clear-headed attention to duty and economy and without complaint.

At first, white women responded eagerly, forming sewing and knitting clubs, organizing for hospital relief, and bolstering each other up in support of the cause. The fight was theirs no less than that of their men folk. "It involves," Mary Chesnut wrote, "our liberty, but, what is greater (if to freemen anything can be), existence itself." Chesnut minced no words about slavery's centrality to southern society or the absolute requirement that it be defended even "should it cost every drop of blood and every cent of property.... There would be to us but one alternative, – to triumph or perish as a people." "This Southern Confederacy," she wrote at the outset, "must be supported now by calm determination and cool brains."[68]

With the official pronouncement of South Carolina's decision to secede from the Union just days away, South Carolinian Leonora Sims declared herself "a regular fire eater," and looked forward to the "halo of glory" that awaited an independent South. A year later, her confidence remained unshaken. For independence from the North, she declared her willingness to exchange her privileged social status for poverty.[69] The enthusiasm of white women in Charleston at the start of the conflict convinced planter John Palmer that "if a regiment of ladies were ordered to assemble at the court house and armed that they would do it without any pretense or fuss."[70] Among elite southern women there were initially few dissenting voices. At least, few were willing to voice publicly the sentiment expressed by Sarah Morgan. "It is a rope of sand this Confederacy founded on the doctrine of Secession and will not last many years – not five," she wrote. But even Morgan's was a qualified dissent. "I don't believe in Secession," she wrote, "but I do in Liberty."[71]

For some white women, mounting casualties and sacrifices only deepened their commitment to the "glorious cause." They declared their eagerness to do more, from turning draperies into dresses, bandages, and blankets, to wearing

---

[68] Woodward, ed., *Mary Chesnut's Civil War*, February 18, 1861, p. 3
[69] Leonora Sims to Harriet R. Palmer, December 10, 1860; Leonora Sims to Harriet R. Palmer, December 9, 1861, in *A World Turned Upside Down*, ed. Towles, pp. 278 and 317–18.
[70] Harriet R. Palmer Journal, January 11th [1861], Palmer Family Papers, SCL.
[71] Sarah Morgan, *Sarah Morgan: The Civil War Diary of a Southern Woman*, ed. Charles East (New York: Simon & Schuster, 1991), May 14, 1862, p. 74.

homespun clothing and learning to weave. "Pa is having a loom made," Mary
W. Milling wrote proudly to her husband in 1863, "and then I am going to
learn to put cloth in and weave it. – I spun a little last summer."[72] Mary Legge
longed for an end to the dreadful war but not if it meant a "hasty peace patched
up" between the North and South that would leave white southerners attached
to the North as they had been before the war. For "now that we are free," she
wrote, "I trust, never again to be in bondage to such a people." As the loss
of loved ones and dear friends grew, she was certain there must be a day of
"retribution."[73]

Sarah Morgan had at first criticized southern white women's displays of
defiance, considering them unladylike. While she continued to pray for recon-
ciliation, she was not immune herself from the overheated rhetoric that she had
previously criticized. Gen. Nathaniel Banks' order of April 27, 1863 requiring residents of Baton Rouge to register as enemies of the United States or to
leave the city "had roused the Devil.... We women will tear you to pieces yet!
Don't care that I smuggled in a dozen letters! Wish I had had more!" When
her mother seemed ready to give up after Lee's defeat at Gettysburg, Morgan
lectured her for being insufficiently patriotic. She, by contrast, was ready to
"die shouting Lice and Confederates for ever!" Rather than give up, or register
as enemies, "all gathered together, we should light our own funeral pyre, and
old men, brave soldiers, fair women and tender children should all perish in the
bright flames we would send up to Heaven as a memorial to our toil, sorrow,
and suffering."[74]

With the end of the war just a few months away, and hopes for a negotiated
peace for independence dead, Mary Audubon declared that there was "nothing
now to do but to fight it out." She would put white women everywhere short of
the battlefield in order to free up more men to fight. Some white women were
ready to take up arms, to die on the battlefield. "Why does not the President
call out the women?" asked Emma LeConte. Even after Lee surrendered his
army, LeConte was unwilling to let go. "We would go and fight too," she
wrote, "we would better all die together."[75]

Here was great rhetoric and, for some white women, a sincere expression of
their commitment to the Confederate cause. But LeConte's was not a unani-
mous sentiment nor necessarily, even for those who expressed it, an unambiguous one. As Drew Faust argues, for a great many white women, expressions of
dissent, discontent, and resentment at the burdens of war and its management
by men were increasingly common and problematic. As they were made more
and more responsible for maintaining soldier morale and for "garrisoning a

---

[72] Mary W. Milling to [Dr. James S. Milling], November 20th, 1863, James S. Milling Papers,
   SHC. Several months later, Milling informed her husband that the slaves were making progress
   learning to spin without cards (ibid, February 16, 1864).
[73] Mary Legge to Harriet R. Palmer, July 17, 1861, in *A World Turned Upside Down*, ed. Towles,
   p. 305.
[74] Morgan, *Civil War Diary*, April 30 [1863]; May 30 [1863], pp. 492 and 519–20.
[75] Mary R. Audubon to [Mildred Cameron], February 12, 1865, Cameron Papers, SHC; LeConte
   Diary, April 20, 1865, SHC.

second front," dissent had mounted.[76] Men had led the South, Dolly Sumner Hunt cried, "into this, perhaps the greatest error of the age." For Confederate leader Robert Toombes's comment that he "would drink every drop of blood [the North] will shed," she had only contempt. "Ah blinded men," she wrote, "Rivers deep & strong have been shed & where are we now? A ruined subjugated people."[77]

Elite women lashed out at incompetent generals and political leaders and bemoaned their personal plight, and sometimes did so in the same breath in which they claimed to hold the southern cause sacrosanct. Gertrude Thomas considered herself a proud white southerner yet she literally cheered her husband's decision to resign from the Confederate army. That his decision rested upon a rather slim point of honor – the promotion of others over him – given the stakes involved, did not seem to bother her. Nor did Sherman's threatened occupation of Atlanta change her mind. "Am I willing to give my husband to gain Atlanta for the Confederacy?" she wrote. Her answer: "No, No, No, a thousand times No!"[78]

While some elite women gloried in official appeals linking patriotism, home front morale, and the production of clothing and food for soldiers, others flatly rejected such appeals. When a friend of Susan Blackford's proudly informed her that his daughter was weaving flannel, "that the sound of the loom [was] far sweeter to him than that of the piano," Blackford was not impressed. "I do not object to Fanny's doing the weaving," she wrote her husband, "but I think he ought to regret the necessity of her doing so, for it is very hard work."[79] Mistresses were attracted and repulsed, often simultaneously, by the need to take on greater responsibility in support of the war. Throughout it all, they retained their racism, and hung on to their sense of class power and belief that black women existed to serve them, even when the realities before their eyes merited a different conclusion.

In 1862, Amelia Lines hired sixteen-year-old Matilda for four dollars a month, a price she considered "cheap for a grown woman." To Lines, the teenager was a woman despite her age. She intended to work her like a grown woman whether she was one or not. "She is large enough and strong enough to do everything, and I mean she shall if I keep her," Lines wrote. Matilda saw their relationship differently. Lines was soon enough calling her a "mope" and cooking her own meals, no doubt just as Matilda intended: "As too (sic) cooking I do not let her poke over my victuals (sic). We have eaten our share of negro filth.... I do despise the race." She despised black women especially

76 Faust, *Mothers of Invention*, pp. 53–79, 121–35, quote at p. 54.

77 Christine Jacobson Carter, ed., *The Diary of Dolly Hunt Burge, 1848–1879* (Athens: University of Georgia Press, 1997), April 29, 1865, p. 171.

78 Burr, ed., *The Secret Eye*, September [late] 1862, p. 209; October 21, 1864, p. 240, quote at p. 240; Faust, *Mothers of Invention*, pp. 240–43.

79 Susan B. [Blackford] to [Charles Blackford], November 18, 1861 in *Letters from Lee's Army or Memoirs of Life in and Out of the Army in Virginia during the War Between the States*, comp. Susan Leigh Blackford (1947; reprint, New York: A. S. Barnes & Co., 1962), p. 59; Faust, *Mothers of Invention*, pp. 46–48.

because they cared more for themselves than they cared for her. In her words: "I think it is a pity, they cant (sic) be made to feel a little of the care which oppress white people [in] these hard times."[80]

Like many Northern women who made homes in the South, Lines took on the ambitions and thinking of a plantation mistress. That she could afford few of the luxuries associated with elite planter life did not deter her. But no matter how many or how few slaves she had at her disposal, and no matter that, ultimately, their resistance forced her to do much of her own housework, she liked the very look of a household with slaves fully as much as the actual labor black women performed. Domestic servants – at least one – were a necessity despite her husband's small income, which was made smaller still by the straitened economic conditions of wartime. Hiring out her wash and keeping a house servant were absolutely vital accoutrements. Otherwise, she wrote, "I could never look nice myself, keep my baby or house clean." Besides, her husband did not want her "to do kitchen drudgery in this country – says he will break up house keeping if I insist on doing without help."[81]

Like Tryphena Fox, Lines blamed southern conditions, not her aspirations. Of course, she insisted, should she ever return to the North, she would do all her housework herself as others there did. She ruled out hiring white servants because it would be too expensive. She would have to fix up a bed for a white servant and dress her better, which she did not have to do for black women. So, she concluded, "it is best for me to have a negro."[82] With the signs and sounds of freedom all around them, black women had less incentive than ever to pretend even to "feel a little" a white woman's problems. Like Matilda and her replacement, they were more likely to leave mistresses to their own cares and rejoice in the knowledge that their leaving multiplied those problems immeasurably.

Mistresses who were small slaveholders and native to the South fared no better. Barely literate, Charlotte Rowell pleaded for help in a letter to North Carolina Governor Zebulon B. Vance. Describing herself as "a old widow lady that has a grat many servants and other property and has no person to attend to enny bisness at tall for me," she requested the release of her overseer from military duty. She, otherwise, had no one "to at tend to bisness for me and to pertect my servants." Alone, except for two daughters, her "property

---

[80] [Amelia Lines] to [Anna Maria Lines Akehurst], April 30, 1862; [Summer 1862], in Amelia Akehurst Lines, *To Raise Myself a Little: The Diaries and Letters of Jennie, a Georgia Teacher, 1851–1886*, ed. Thomas Dyer (Athens: University of Georgia Press, 1982), quotes at pp. 188 and 192–93. For some mistresses, little distinguished a black child from a grown woman. One month Kate Stone was referring to one of her slaves as "Little Annie." Within a few weeks, "Little Annie" had become "Annie, our woman," now nurse, maid, and washer (Stone, *Brokenburn*, April 24, 1863; May 23, 1863, pp. 193 and 211.)

[81] Lines to Akehurst, December 2, 1862, in Lines, *To Raise Myself a Little*, p. 193.

[82] Lines to Akehurst, December 2, 1862, in Lines, *To Raise Myself a Little*, p. 193. Determined to have black help, Lines hired another woman who soon took the same path to freedom (ibid., February 11, 1864, pp. 204–5 and 211).

has ben goin to destruction."[83] Addie Harris pleaded similarly to Alabama Governor John Shorter for relief. She and her sister were both trying to manage plantations and slaves who were already "very near free" without husbands or any other white man. She had sought help from her neighbors, but "they will not come," she wrote.[84] In 1863, the Confederate Congress attempted to address such concerns by tacking on to the act repealing the most infamous and protested exemption clauses of the October 1862 conscription act, a provision that allowed an exemption for "the police and management of slaves . . . one person on each farm or plantation, the sole property of a minor, a person of unsound mind, a *femme sole* or belonging to a soldier in Confederate military service containing twenty or more slaves."[85]

Mistresses, whether poor or wealthy, were further disadvantaged in being called on – the first time for most – to be "the boss of things" generally. Responsibility for managing field hands in addition to their customary authority over household slaves presented, for most, unprecedented authority.[86] The complaints of white women and their calls for help reflected this new circumstance as efforts to extend their authority to field hands met firm resistance. Jane Brasfield complained that under her control, the slaves were "pretty much at the mercy of their own will." Mary Pugh's slaves worked indifferently: She could only threaten them with unspecified consequences on their master's return, which she prayed would be soon. White women admitted the drawbacks that came from inexperience in managing plantations and a lack of confidence.[87] Nancy Bercaw finds planter women experienced in keeping books, and knowledgeable about crops and work cycles in the Mississippi Delta. Yet, even they, she argues, felt "unqualified to act" in the context of war due to the "fundamentally different relationship" they had to slave society

---

[83] Frontis W. Johnson, ed., *The Papers of Zebulon Baird Vance* (Raleigh, NC: State Department of Archives and History, 1963), p. 389. Hereafter cited as Vance, *Papers*.

[84] As quoted in Armstead L. Robinson, "In the Shadow of Old John Brown: Insurrection Anxiety and Confederate Mobilization, 1861–1863," *Journal of Negro History* 65 (Autumn, 1980): 292–93. See also Armstead L. Robinson, *Bitter Fruits of Bondage: The Demise and the Collapse of the Confederacy, 1861–1865* (Charlottesville: University Press of Virginia, 2005).

[85] OR, Series 4, vol. 2, pp. 690–91. The 1862 law exempted one white male for every twenty slaves on a farm or plantation, or on two or more plantations within five miles of each other, the latter to address the concerns of small slaveholders. To further counter criticism that the 1862 act favored the wealthiest slaveholders, the 1863 act of repeal required a payment of $500 for each exemption and permitted presidential exemptions in areas short of slave labor sufficient to produce grain.

[86] Quote is from Maria White, *Mississippi Narratives*, Supplement Series 1, vol. 10, pt. 5, p. 2276. Mistresses had sometimes been given wide authority over plantation affairs in the absence of their husbands, including power over overseers. The overseer, James Haynes, for example, was fired by the mistress of the plantation during her husband's absence over, he thought, complaints from the slaves. See James M. Clifton, ed., *Life and Labor on Argyle Island: Letters and Documents of a Savannah River Rice Plantation, 1833–1867* (Savannah, GA: Beehive Press, 1978), pp. 46–47.

[87] Sterkx, *Partners in Rebellion*, pp. 133–34, quote at p. 133; Rable, *Civil Wars*, pp. 114–18, quote at p. 115; Faust, *Mothers of Invention*, pp. 62–74.

in comparison to masters, and their gendered understanding of the household. Lacking "agency," then, they were incapable of handling their new responsibilities precisely because those responsibilities took them outside the boundaries of the household. Thus, even these frontier women, who were accomplished in understanding crops, cultivation, and bookkeeping, had seldom interacted with field hands. Moving out to the fields or into the world represented a severe, unmanageable disruption of their identity as elite white women. Planter-class women found themselves unable (and perhaps unwilling) to master a slave labor force of field hands.[88]

Historians have tended to explain the difficulties mistresses faced during the Civil War as a symptom of their general inexperience in managing slaves (though this was certainly not the case within the household) and as a product of gendered rules of conduct. Bercaw insists that the confinement of mistresses to the household, narrowly defined, in addition to their status as women, meant that while masters enjoyed the "community resources necessary to maintain the coercive structure of slavery," mistresses did not.[89] This argument assumes that coercive structures must necessarily rest on publicly- or state-sanctioned institutions as well as on the brute physical strength of men. It rests, in the final analysis, on the view that slave resistance to wartime management by mistresses was grounded in their sex. Slaves by this view simply rejected the idea of being directed by women. Some, influenced by gender ideals dominant in the white community, clearly did. At the same time, field hands could resent and resist mistresses for the same reasons they resented and resisted masters, who were themselves not immune to the problems of wartime slave resistance.

The evidence lends itself more to an interpretation that centers on white women's status as slaveholder, not simply on their predicament as helpless females. More than anything else, it was often the role and status of manager, in and of itself, that provoked the backlash, not the sex of the managers. The resistance mistresses faced from field hands drew on slaves' perception, increasingly salient in wartime, that the division between the big house and the fields was often arbitrary and superficial. This North Carolinian Catherine Edmondston proved when she moved outside of her household to manage slaves in a task normally supervised by her husband in 1862. She complained that the slaves were less attentive to their work in her husband's absence.[90] But Edmondston's functioning as a wartime manager has sometimes been exaggerated by historians, making much of her stop one day to look after her husband's cotton, then drawing an unwarranted conclusion about slaves'

[88] Nancy D. Bercaw, *Gendered Freedom: Race, Rights, and the Politics of Household in the Delta, 1861–1875* (Gainesville: University Press of Florida, 2003), pp. 51–67, quotes at pp. 60, 53, and 54, respectively. On the problem of demoralization among white women occasioned by this new role, see Faust, *Mothers of Invention*, pp. 72–74, and 78.

[89] Bercaw, *Gendered Freedoms*, p. 65.

[90] Beth G. Crabtree and James W. Patton, eds., *"Journal of a Secesh Lady": The Diary of Catherine Ann Devereux Edmondston* (Raleigh, NC: North Carolina Division of Archives and History and Department of Cultural Resources, 1979), August 13, 1862, p. 235. Hereafter cited as Edmondston, *Diary*.

supposed adherence to slaveholders' gender ideals.[91] We cannot necessarily count, as "management," such intermittent visitations from the big house as hers. The point, though, is that even if we did follow precedent and regard them as management, we would assume too much if we then attributed slaves' resistance to wartime management by white women exclusively to slaves' supposed affinity to slaveholders' gender ideals. Especially in the context of the Civil War, slaves stood ready to deny anyone who stood between them and freedom, whatever their gender. And mistresses had long before the war demonstrated where they stood.

The part the mistress had played as "co-master" before the war had important repercussions for white women's attempts to extend their authority to the fields.[92] Even though most field hands had not suffered as directly as household slaves at the hands of mistresses, the great house – whether big or small – was a sore and visible manifestation of their exploitation. Resistance to white women derived from a hatred of their position as slaveholders whose leisure, luxuries, and power derived from the work of slaves who understood that their value as chattel property upheld the plantation household in countless ways.

The rituals of power extended from the big house to the fields and from birth to death, uniting field and great house. Slaves were expendable and exchangeable for cash, eligible to be "sold ter dress young missus for her weddin." Harriet Robinson recalled another ritual that united slaves and slaveholders across the divide of field and plantation household: "Whenever white folks had a baby born all de old niggers had to come thoo the room and the master would be over hind the bed and he'd say, 'here's a new little mistress or master you got to work for.' You had to say, 'Yessuh Master' and bow real low or the overseer would crack you."[93] By means of such rituals, the ties between the big house and the fields of cash crops, between master and mistress, were constantly imprinted and reinforced, as they were as well by work routines.

Not only was the division between slaves who labored in plantation households and those who labored in the field breached by ties of kinship and friendship, but also seasonal work patterns and holiday customs. When they had days off such as Christmas, household slaves headed directly for the quarters for parties and other celebrations. In addition, women field hands were put to work on household tasks, especially such seasonal tasks as making lard and sausages. Or they might be called to the great house to fill in for a slave who was ill.[94] During the war, field hands and household slaves ran away together,

---

[91] Edmondston, *Diary*, August 20, 1862, p. 239.

[92] Quote is from Ball, *Slaves in the Family*, p. 19.

[93] Ben Johnson, *North Carolina Narratives*, vol. 15, pt. 2, p. 9; Bob Jones, *North Carolina Narratives*, vol. 15, pt. 2, p. 24; Harriet Robinson, *Oklahoma and Mississippi Narratives*, vol. 7, pt. 1, pp. 270–71. Narratives such as these belie the view that slave men were less critical of white women than black women. For the latter view, see Brenda Stevenson, *Life in Black and White: Family and Community in the Slave South* (New York: Oxford University Press, 1996).

[94] Stone, *Brokenburn*, January 6, 1682; January 16, 1862, pp. 77 and 78; Edmondston, *Diary*, August 28, 1862, p. 243. Amanda Stone paid female field hands when they helped with household chores.

destroyed plantation homes together, and generally plotted together to put emancipation on the war's agenda.

The War Will Bring You Out

White men's criticism of white women worked to help undermine mistresses's authority in the great house, and beyond. The disintegration of the plantation household was, in important respects, unwittingly abetted by masters. As slaves asserted their independence, white men's criticism of mistresses's management of affairs on the home front helped to render the plantation household a parody of domesticity. Letters from husbands, sons, and fathers from the front inevitably expressed love and encouragement. They also constitute a perhaps unparalleled elaboration by southern white men of southern patriarchy. The war clarified patriarchal ideals and exposed the tensions within them in new ways.

Confederate soldiers expecting Confederate women to take charge in their absence, roundly criticized those who, in their judgment, failed. All the while, they demanded more and more from them. After the war, there was glowing praise for white women's wartime contributions, patriotism, and stoicism. Though such praise was also an important part of the wartime discourse, it was, arguably, more than matched by withering criticism of white women's management of their households and slaves in their husbands' absence. In the estimation of many men, they failed their duty as the wives, mothers, and sisters of soldiers.

Criticism of white women's capacity for household management and economy, long a staple of the discourse on white manhood as much as womanhood, took on an increasingly strident tone. It was present in the letters requesting care packages, despite growing shortages on the home front. It was there in the demands for more attention, sympathy, and a greater show of morale; and there in the insistence that white women demonstrate greater independence and, simultaneously, show evidence of their dependent status. Husbands, sons, and fathers wrote home seeking greater evidence of concern for the dangers they faced, and for their needs, desires, and ambitions. They wanted more letters from home, more and better-supplied care packages, and sometimes help getting released from military service.

Over the course of two years, in the hundreds of letters he wrote home, Confederate Sgt. Edwin S. Fay rarely missed an opportunity to let his wife know how negligent of his welfare he considered her. He wanted out of the army and in his judgment, she was putting forth a less than energetic effort to help get him mustered out. "I must come home on some ground," he wrote on one of the many occasions he addressed the matter, "and you *must prepare the way*. Can you do it?" He was determined to find a way to get out of military service and needed her help to manufacture an excuse the military would buy. Even when his wife was sick, and when she had just given birth, he complained that she was not holding up her part of the bargain of their marriage. When illness compelled Sarah Fay to wean one of their sons earlier than she had planned, he was unsympathetic, to put it kindly. "I sucked until I was five years old," he scolded her, "and he might have done the same."[95]

Confederate men chastised their wives for not working hard enough and thus shirking their duty to home and nation. One of the more damning charges held them responsible for desertions, a charge that tended to ignore the class dimensions of the problem and even the self-interested desires of many men themselves. Following the execution of four Confederate soldiers from his unit convicted of desertion, North Carolinian James A. Graham wrote his mother that a widely held opinion among the soldiers was that the men were "caused to desert by letters from home" and it was not an isolated case. Low morale on the home front had caused others to falter. "Many a poor soldier has met with the same disgraceful death from the same cause, he wrote. "I wish the people at home would keep in as good spirits and as good condition as the soldiers in the army do." A year later, neither the problem nor his view of it had changed. "Most of the desertions" were still "caused by letters from home. If the people at home would only write cheering letters to their friends instead of counseling them to commit this base crime, everything would go on so much better with us." In a bit of irony, Graham's sister-in-law, believing her husband had done his share of fighting, was urging him to apply for a surgeon's position before he found himself in another battle and dead.[96]

At the same time, Graham's letters almost unfailingly included requests for provisions and clothing. He gave no sign that he saw any relationship between the demands soldiers placed on the home front, their criticisms, and the low morale on the home front. Nor did he seem to comprehend how his life as a soldier differed from those of the men who typically filled the ranks of deserters. His letters document an extravagant and privileged soldiers' life: money, tailored uniforms, coffee, blankets, food – nothing was beyond his needs or his wants. With just a few months in uniform under his belt, he began what would become a constant stream of requests. He urgently needed a cook, a slave to take care of his horse, and "a servant to wait on my room." If his mother could not spare one, he would have no choice but to hire one. Unlike most in the ranks, Graham, like other wealthy Confederate soldiers, was able to take advantage of the services of private couriers, entrepreneurs who made a specialty out of traffic between the home and war fronts. For Christmas 1864, he expected a courier to bring him "a turkey, some chickens, butter, vegetables, sorghum, apples, a big cake, some 'slapjacks,' a pound or two of sugar, a few eggs, and two or three bottles of brandy."[97]

95 Edwin H. Fay to Sarah Fay, October 18, 1862; May 13, 1865; July 26, 1863, in Wiley, ed., *This Infernal War*, pp. 173, 306, and 455, quotes at pp. 173 and 306.

96 H. M. Wagstaff, ed., *The James A. Graham Papers, 1861–1884* (Chapel Hill: University of North Carolina Press, 1928); James A. Graham to Mother [Mrs. W. A. Graham], February 1, 1864; ibid, March 8, 1865, pp. 178 and 211. See also pp. 169 and 198–99. Charles Ramsdell, *Behind the Lines in the Southern Confederacy* (Baton Rouge: Louisiana State University Press, 1944), pp. 28–30; Faust, *Mothers of Invention*, pp. 240–43.

97 Wagstaff, ed., *Graham Papers*, pp. 111, 158, 167, 175, 177, 182, 186, 199, 200, and 202, quotes at James A. Graham to Mother, January 24, 1862, p. 111, and ibid., December 3, 1864, p. 200.

Augustin Taveau, although also no model of the southern patriarchal ideal, similarly expected much from home, including that his wife should be a model of ideal southern white womanhood. Taveau had enlisted reluctantly and belatedly in the Confederate Army and, from the first, had worked hard to keep from being attached to a unit likely to end up on the killing fields of Virginia, where the chances of dying in battle were for him too high. Ensconced in a cushy position in Charleston, he bragged to his wife of his "fortunate escape from the doom of going to Virginia with a musket on my shoulder in the ranks as a common soldier," as he had "no desire to bury [his] carcass in that fatal State." At the same time, he continued to be a disappointing husband. Over the course of his enlistment, he kept up a steady barrage of complaints in letters to his wife. Little Delphine Taveau did pleased him. He complained of the smallest things. A hat cover she sent was too large or the stitching on cuffs she made for him displeased him as they were "*not* very neat." The pattern she used to make his collars was all wrong. "Do not make anymore of that pattern," he groused, "I do not like them."[98] Taveau's boorish behavior was unrelenting despite his occasional professions of affection and sympathy for his wife's condition. "Poor Girl," he wrote on one occasion, "how I pity you up there all by yourself to fight out all these difficulties alone. The War will bring you out and make you independent."[99] More commonly, he insulted and demeaned her.

Like many men of his class, Taveau expressed annoyance at his wife's dependence on him, insisting that she learn to be more independent and then berated her efforts to do so. He expected her to rise to the occasion as he ladled out advice on everything from how to plant cabbage, collards, carrots, and beets, to purchasing molasses. He told her how to determine which acreage to have plowed for the wheat crop. He even advised her on how to use sugar.[100] And in the most emphatic manner, he conveyed his lack of trust in her judgment when it came to managing her personal affairs. His complaints, though, suggest that he was less concerned for how her ill-management might affect her welfare than its potential to embarrass him among his peers.[101] When his wife allowed the owner of the house where she boarded to place a loom on her piazza, he took it as a personal insult to his manhood:

Oh my God! Have I not always told you that I was afraid, whenever the occasion occurred, you would not know how to take care of yourself; and here it is already! You are in a *false position* and have not a moment to lose in correcting it. Have the loom, in his absence, taken downstairs immediately. . . . For God's sake pick up a little *character*, and know your *rights*, and protect yourself. . . . Remember that it is a duty you owe

---

[98] Augustin L. Taveau to Delphine Taveau, June 9, 1864. On his "escape" from service in Virginia, see also letters to his wife dated March 26, 1864, March 31, 1864, and April 29, 1864, Taveau Papers, DU.

[99] Augustin L. Taveau to Delphine Taveau, October 3, 1863, Taveau Papers, DU.

[100] Augustin L. Taveau to Delphine Taveau, June 1863; October 3, 1863; October 13, 1863, Taveau Papers, DU. See also Faust, *Mothers of Invention*, p. 123.

[101] See, for example, Augustin L. Taveau to Delphine Taveau, November 2, 1865, Taveau Papers, DU.

to your husband to endeavor to let him feel confident that you will, in all things, act *discreetly*, and take care of your rights under *any circumstances*, otherwise I shall be miserable. Had you reflected on the matter, you would, at once have seen what a *false position* it was going to put you in, and avoided it.[102]

On this and other occasions, he implied that she was stupid. Sometimes he was blunt. She was incapable of reflecting or thinking, even "a little."[103]

In criticizing his wife's lack of independence, Taveau would have had to dismiss the contrary evidence before him. He had, after all, made it her responsibility to find suitable lodging for herself and their children, placing her in the embarrassing situation for a woman of her class of having to go before the public to seek her own housing, even though it was one many Confederate women increasingly faced. And, he never placed her needs before his own. She should consider herself fortunate that he was close by, and that she did not have to earn her own living when women of much higher status from the ranks of the wealthiest planters had been forced to take jobs. "Did you know," he wrote, "that Mrs. Huger and Mrs. Manigault have been obliged to become Confederate clippers in Columbia in order to support themselves. So much for military glory – had I smothered all the better feeling on my nature, and neglected the welfare of you and my children, and sought after military distinction; I, too may have become a Hero, and *you* and my children might ere have been reduced to want." When an acquaintance was killed in battle, Taveau reminded his wife that it was "poor satisfaction" to the wife of the dead soldier, "the glory he has won."[104]

In fact, Taveau's own household was in considerable disarray and his family "reduced to want," in no small part due to his neglect. His geographical proximity to his wife had not made her life easier. Prior to enlisting, he sold their house, leaving his family to take lodging as boarders. He also sold several of their slaves but refused to permit his wife to have use of Caesar, whom he took to camp with him. He needed Caesar and it was "impossible to spare" him.[105] When his wife's personal slave, Betty, became pregnant, Taveau was angry about the resulting inconvenience for his wife but not sufficiently bothered to let her have Caesar.[106]

A final irony perhaps was that Taveau's enlistment made his wife even more dependent on her family in Boston for financial support than previously, and they increasingly balked at giving it. More than once they suggested that she learn to economize and that her husband find a way to support her. Taveau, meanwhile, belittled her and them. He accused her relatives of being "selfish."

---

[102] Augustin L. Taveau to Delphine Taveau, June 2, 1864, Taveau Papers, DU.

[103] Augustin L. Taveau to Delphine Taveau, October 3, 1863, Taveau Papers, DU.

[104] Augustin L. Taveau to Delphine Taveau, May 24, 1864; see also letter dated May 17, 1864, Taveau Papers, DU.

[105] William Whaley to Augustine Taveau, February 10, 1864; Augustin Taveau to Delphine Taveau, March 26, 1864; June 16 1864, Taveau Papers, DU. Taveau purchased a female slave, Mary, and her daughter in February 1864 for $4000 (Bill of Sale, February 22, 1864).

[106] Augustin Taveau to Delphine Taveau, May 17, 1864, Taveau Papers, DU.

"Could you have fancied," he wrote, "how much sympathy your folks had for you; could you have persuaded yourself to believe, in the present undisguised position they assume, how perfectly indifferent they could be to you and yours in misfortune.... And these are the kind of people who presume to whine and complain that you *sew* too much – that you *work* too much – that you ought to have *servants* to do all these things for you... such canting yankee hypocrisy." This, after his wife's family had contributed thousands of dollars to the support of his household.[107] No doubt it was their suggestion that she learn to economize and that her husband find a way to support her that angered him. The Taveau's dependence on Delphine's relatives continued long after the war. By the 1870s, her family had run out of patience. Delphine Taveau continued to plead with them to send money and to rescue her husband's financial situation. Her brother's frank advice, finally, was that Mr. Taveau should declare bankruptcy and "in the meanwhile choose an economical place of abode" while "seeking employment in a way compatible with his desires & ability."[108]

Criticism of white women also came from the highest level of the Confederate government. Confederate President Jefferson Davis castigated Confederate women who contributed to the "gloom" on the home front, particularly in the aftermath of military reversals. It was unjustified and bad for morale, he lectured them. White women needed to "show as much fortitude as we are entitled to expect from those who display such conspicuous gallantry in the field." He applauded the "loyalty and true-heartedness of the women of the land" who endured losses and pain without complaint.[109]

The women Davis applauded were chiefly planter women, and those, he chided, chiefly the wives of poor and small slaveholding soldiers who as early as the summer of 1861 began making their way to Confederate camps seeking discharges for their husbands. As elite women took on the dress of the poor as patriotic expression, poor white women who did not have draperies to turn into dresses in the first place and for whom homespun clothing was already, so to speak, patriotic, began calling for an end to the war or, at least, the return of their own sons and husbands. From the beginning, they understood their more exposed position even when they supported the war. The crisis escalated in the ensuing years as three factors converged: food shortages, fear of slave insurrection, and growing class conflict among white southerners. As Armstead Robinson argued, before the war slaveholders "made slavery pay while simultaneously enmeshing poorer whites in an egalitarian ideology of white dominance, an ideology which compelled nonslaveholders to assist in maintaining control

---

[107] Augustin Taveau to Delphine Taveau, October 13, 1865; November 2, 1865, Taveau Papers, DU. Indeed, the financial support of his wife's family in Boston kept the Taveaus from the poor house on more than one occasion. In the spring of 1864, Delphine Taveau's brother, Richard Sprague, sent $13,000–$14,000 (Groning to Mrs. Augustus (sic) L. Taveau, May 2, 1864).

[108] Augustin Taveau to Delphine Taveau, May 17, 1864; May 20, 1864; Delphine Taveau to Victoria Sprague, April 9, 1872; Richard Sprague to Delphine Taveau, June 4, 1872, Taveau Papers. DU.

[109] Jefferson Davis to Hon. J. M. Howry, August 27, 1863, OR, Series 2, vol. 4, p. 766.

over the slaves.... The war situation changed all this by forcing the slave-holders to violate their own norms in ways that deeply offended poorer whites."[110] By 1865, poor white people's support for the war had become, for many, unsustainable. Jamina A. Thomas, who described herself as "oald and nervous," pleaded for help. Her only son had volunteered at the outset "to fite for his country." A recently enlisted son-in-law had died from the "forteague of the battles around Richmond," leaving six children behind. And, her daughters being "of delicate constitution," were useless to her.[111]

The flight of slaves to Union lines and their impressment by the Confederate government left poor white southerners embittered, afraid, and more conscious than ever of their subordinate status. "If the Slaveholders, being men of means," an ally and southern politician wrote, "fly upon the approach of danger, & leave the poorer classes who are unable to move, & the families of soldiers in the Army, exposed not only to the enemy but to the gangs of run away slaves, it will produce a state of things & of feeling much to be dreaded."[112] All along, appeals from Confederate officials had been designed to put the home front on a war footing, to appeal to non-slaveholding as well as elite white southerners, though neither group needed to be reminded of the threat from the South's "domestic institution."

When racism was no longer sufficient to deflect attention from poverty and political inequality, poor white people were forced to confront the massive inequities of slave society. Small slaveholding women left alone to manage one or two slaves, and perhaps already more prone to the use of violence against slaves, may have become even more likely to abuse slaves. Lulu Wilson testified that her mistress was "meaner than the devil all the time. Seems like she just hates us worser than ever. She said blobber mouf nigers done cause a war."[113]

Despite the problems they faced on the home front, Confederate women generally accepted that wartime deprivations, wartime slave resistance, even obstinate men folk, were but "the price in part of our liberty."[114] Yet, no mat-ter how it was couched – as patriotism or love of family – and no matter the

[110] Robinson, "In the Shadow of Old John Brown," quote at p. 282. See also Robinson, *Bitter Fruits of Bondage*; Ramsdell, *Behind the Lines in the Southern Confederacy*; Georgia Lee Tatum, *Disloyalty in the Confederacy* (Chapel Hill: University of North Carolina Press, 1934); Albert B. Moore, *Conscription and Conflict in the Confederacy* (New York: Macmillan Co., 1924); Bessie Martin, *Desertion of Alabama Troops from the Confederate Army* (New York: Columbia University Press, 1932); Charles H. Wesley, *Collapse of the Confederacy* (Washington, DC: Associated Publishers, 1937). On the class dimensions of homespun, see Faust, *Mothers of Invention*, p. 46; Rable, *Civil Wars*, pp. 6–7.

[111] Jamina A. Thomas to [Governor Zebulon Vance], November 29, 1862, Vance, *Papers*, pp. 410–11, quotes at p. 411.

[112] John Pool to [Gov. Zebulon Vance], September 18, 1862, Vance, *Papers*, p. 199. As a member of the N.C. State Senate, Pool had strongly opposed secession and remained a Union supporter. Despite his well-known political position, he was re-elected to the State Senate in 1864, where he worked to find a peaceful solution to the conflict.

[113] Robinson, "In the Shadow of Old John Brown," pp. 289–91; Lulu Wilson, *Texas Narratives*, vol. 1, pt. 9, p. 4196.

[114] Diary of Nancy Emerson (1862–1864). http://etext.lib.virginia.edu/etcbin/toc ... diaries&tag+ public&part=25&division=div1.

delight many white women voiced in their new roles, one significant ideological tension was never far from the surface. Southern white women understood that they were being asked to do both the work of slaves and the work of men, and therefore to incur a double loss of status. Those losses took on even more meaning when, in the disintegration of slavery and white hegemony in the last days of the war, mistresses learned poignant lessons in the ways of the least powerful.

Long experience with the negotiation of power had given slaves, especially household slaves, a particular vantage point and expertise in the discursive position of the powerless. They had learned when to speak and the limits of acceptable speech and posture. They knew the cost of "impudence" and other violations of the norms, customs, and laws governing relations between slaves and owners. Much is made (and celebrated) in scholarly and popular writings of Confederate women's defiance of Union soldiers, to which is attributed the sparing of many homes from destruction. Perhaps many more were saved by the lessons the enslaved gave mistresses on the politics of language, posture, and subordination, a complex politics that has often been viewed simplistically as slaves' "loyalty."

The scene on the Kirkland plantation in South Carolina upon the arrival of Union soldiers cautions against such simplifications. Even Mary Chesnut, who recorded it, seemed oblivious to its ironies. This is the advice the slave Monroe gave his mistress: "Monroe, their negro manservant, told her to stand up and keep her children in her arms. She stood against the wall, with her baby in her arms and the other two as closely pressed against her knees as they could get." Meanwhile, "Mammy Selina and Lizzie stood grimly on each side of their young Missis and her children. For four mortal hours the soldiers surged through this room. Sometimes they were roughly jostled against the wall. Mammy and Lizzie were staunch supporters, and the Yankee soldiers reviled the negro women for their foolishness in standing by their cruel owners. And they taunted Mary with being glad of the protection of her poor, ill-used slaves. Monroe had one leg bandaged and pretended to be lame so that he might not be enlisted as a soldier." A reluctant soldier Monroe might have been, but he was not unaware of the profound changes the war had ushered in as underscored by the scene taking place before him. He further counseled Mary Kirkland: "Don't answer 'em back, Miss Mary. Let them say what they want to. Don't answer them back. Don't give them a chance to say you are impident to 'em."[115] It was sage advice grounded in the realities of the enslaved. From an unaccustomed place, "Miss Mary" gained new insight into the ways and defects of hegemony.

Mary Kirkland was not only forced to stand by and watch the desecration of her home but also to endure the desecration of her status and have these realities translated to her by her slaves. Standing against the wall clutching her

---

[115] Woodward, ed., *Mary Chesnut's Civil War*, May 7, 1865, p. 802. One black soldier is said to have put the matter more bluntly, commanding a mistress to "stop your jaw" (Stone, *Brokenburn*, p. 196). No doubt, such advice coming from a black soldier was even more disconcerting.

baby while her other two children clutched her body, gave her the posture of slave women who had clung to their children, and their children to them, in the face of sales and other violations of home and spirit. Even her "loyal" slaves, Selina and Lizzie, who would have taken note of her posture of powerlessness, were doubtless not the fools the Union soldiers took them to be. Flanking their mistress, they stood less as protectors of the old order than as symbols of the new. No less than the advice Monroe gave, the circumstances that put them in the position of their mistress's protector announced in unmistakable terms the ongoing transformation of the plantation household and its residents.

Blinded by their own sense of power, mistresses often missed the transgressions and transformations before their very eyes. Writing about a similar encounter between a mistress and Union soldiers, Catherine Edmondston, like Mary Chesnut, focused on what she took to be slaves' "loyalty" rather than transgression and transformation. Edmondston noted with pride that her slaves and most of those belonging to her brother had "remained true." She singled out Adelaide for special commendation, seemingly oblivious to the irony in Adelaide's "loyalty." When Union soldiers arrived at her brother's plantation, Adelaide "would go to her Mistress & young mistresses & beg them to excuse her & then beseech them to bear all and to keep their tongues in 'their heads before these devils' if they wanted a single shingle left over them." Like Monroe, Adelaide instructed her mistresses in the ways of the least powerful. "I hears 'em, honey," she said referring to the soldiers, "I hears what they say & I knows what they will do if you give them any excuse. Be civil to them."[116]

Adelaide's owners may have interpreted her advice on the ways of power as evidence of "loyalty," but slaves clearly saw the matter differently. The former slave Margaret Thornton put it this way: "White folks hated the Yankees like pizen but dey had ter put up wid deer sass jist de same. De also had to put up wid de stealing' of dere property what hey had made dere slaves work an' make."[117] Slavery demanded submission of the tongue no less than the body and mind, and while slaves never renounced their right to speak their minds, they understood the cost and often willingly paid it as the price of their dignity and humanity. Now, in marvelous irony, they tutored mistresses on the price of impudence. It was also the case that by war's end, slaves had learned that while civility might protect mistresses from the wrath of northern soldiers, it would not necessarily protect them when their ideas of a revolution collided with those of the Union soldiers who had come to stem a revolution, not make one.

In sum, the Civil War was a defining moment in the transformation of the plantation household. Household slaves discovered new openings through which to claim personal time or to flee the household entirely. Whether they left or stayed put during the war, they obliged their mistresses to take on the work of slaves. If, during slavery, the "big house often resembled a battle ground," and was "akin to a psychological battleground," it became one during the Civil

[116] Edmondston, *Diary*, May 8, 1865, pp. 710–11.
[117] Margaret Thornton, *North Carolina Narratives*, vol. 15, pt. 2, p. 354.

War.[118] A clear trajectory connected slaves' antebellum experience of the plantation household and their actions against it and on their own behalf during the war. Slaves who did not flee were as important to the transformation as those who did, adding immensely to the stresses that culminated in the plantation household's wartime disintegration. From inside, they aided and abetted the war's assault on the plantation household, helping to ensure that it was increasingly unmanageable and, long before the war's end, unrecognizable by its old terms. The requirements of war gave vital aid to the struggle, providing unprecedented opportunities for resistance to the notion of "one family, black and white" with mistresses as matriarchal heads.

By the end of the Civil War, the vast majority of southern women, irrespective of race or class, had come to know the meaning of war – dead, maimed, or lost loved ones; diminished food supplies and starvation; loss of property and homes; scantily clad bodies; and fear. They had come to understand the meaning of General Sherman's dictum as put to the residents of Memphis in 1862: "We must bear this in mind, that however peaceful things look, we are really *at war.*"[119] Those who had disproportionately suffered hunger, rape, murder, or other brutalities knew this best. Yet, even where the wartime experiences of southern women were broadly similar, they could be starkly dissimilar in impact and meaning depending on their race, class, or status as citizen or slave.

The death of a husband at the front, for example, did not translate into similar reckonings for black and white women or for planter women and white women less well-placed socially or economically. Up to the last months of the war, well-placed white women were more likely to know where a loved one had died and how; they were more likely to be able to send a male relative or slave to retrieve the body and to know whether a son or husband or brother had died a "Good Death," or had with him in his last hours a letter from home or a picture of a beloved family member. White women were more likely to have a formal opportunity to grieve.[120]

Most white women could also take comfort in knowing that their male kin knew their whereabouts and how they were faring. Black soldiers had fewer

---

[118] First quote is from Genovese, *Roll, Jordan, Roll,* p. 361; second quote is from White, *Ar'n't I a Woman?,* p. 16.

[119] William T. Sherman, *Memoirs of William T. Sherman,* 2nd ed., 2 vols. (1875; reprint, New York: D. Appleton and Co., 1931), I: 306.

[120] See, for example, Frederick A. Porcher to wife [Emma], June 13, 1864, and December 6, 1864, Frederick A. Porcher Papers, SCHS; Isaac Perkins to Isaac B. Youngman, August 28, 1862, Isaac B. Youngman Papers, DU. On the meaning of a "Good Death" and the importance of "dying declarations" and condolence letters, see Drew Gilpin Faust, "The Civil War Soldier and the Art of Dying," *Journal of Southern History* 67 (February 2001): 3–38. Slaveholding women continued to adhere where they could to rituals of mourning such as dressing in black. The shortage of black cloth increasingly forced many to forego this aspect of mourning. Many, refugeed far from home or dealing with the daily struggles of wartime, increasingly had "no time to mourn." As early as 1863, news from the front became harder to obtain. In addition, many of the most recent enlistees were young men who had not yet had adult likenesses made (Stone, *Brokenburn,* April 10, 1863; November 13, 1863, pp. 187–88, and 258).

opportunities to communicate with their families and were further circumscribed by illiteracy and the dangers posed by attempts to communicate with
families still enslaved, so they nearly always went into battle not knowing if
their families were alive or how they were faring. As James Trotter reported,
they had much more reason to "[grow] blue and disheartened."[121]

Whether rich or poor, white women did not suffer from the knowledge that
their husbands, fathers, or brothers had been butchered on the field of battle
like the black soldiers in South Carolina who were decapitated by Confederate
troops or those at Petersburg whose tongues the rebels cut out. White women
did not see their children stolen and carried off to the North "on speculation
probably to Barnum," to be placed in a circus because they could whistle and
sing.[122] Notwithstanding the criticism they endured from husbands, sons, and
brothers and even the Confederate government for insufficient attention to
their womanly duties, white women's contributions to the war had not gone
unnoted or without praise. Although southern black women worked to relieve
the suffering of black refugees, cared for wounded soldiers, sewed flags and
clothing for black soldiers, and put food on the table, their work went largely
unnoticed by the nation whose citizens they fought to become.[123]

But as the war tumbled to a conclusion, it brought down with it – at least
for a time – the quite substantial divisions between southern women by race
and class, freedom and unfreedom, citizenship and statelessness. Black women
became free, legally entitled like their former mistresses to the lesser freedoms
of female citizenship. But the smallness of those freedoms did not make them
inconsequential. They included civic capacities and everyday norms of respect.
This is what Katie Rowe believed. Freedom, Rowe stated simply but powerfully, meant a world where there would be "nobody cussing fire to my black
heart."[124] In the end, history proved her wrong, but that diminishes neither the
work she and other black women attempted, nor the successes they had, even
if only for a moment.

The very nature of slavery had made white and black women cognizant of the
ways in which their identities were intertwined, how the status of each defined

---

[121] James M. Trotter to Edward W. Kinsley, June 2, 1864, Edward W. Kinsley Papers, DU.

[122] Spencer Drayton to Edward W. Kinsley, August 17, 1864; Gen. Edward Augustus Wild to
Edward W. Kinsley, July 28, 1863, quote at Gen. Edward Augustus Wild to Edward W.
Kinsley, July 28, 1863, Kinsley Papers, DU. At New Bern, North Carolina, recruiting officers
reported that the news from Petersburg had greatly dampened enthusiasm for black enlistment.
Joseph E. Williams, a man General Wild described as a "swindler ... and an audacious and
scheming one," was accused of taking the child. Williams was one of many shady characters
who populated contraband camps and Union occupied territories like New Bern. Wild ordered
him evicted from the area.

[123] These activities remain largely invisible in Civil War historiography. An important exception is
Ella Forbes, *African American Women During the Civil War* (New York: Garland Pub., Inc.,
1998). On the work of black women in New Bern, North Carolina, see the letters of Mary
Ann Starkey to Edward Kinsley, Kinsley Papers, DU. Starkey led the Colored Women's Union
Relief Association of New Bern, North Carolina.

[124] Katie Rowe, *Oklahoma Narratives*, vol. 7, pt. 1, p. 284.

the other. But freedom elaborated the extent to which white women's sense of identity, of who they were and could become, was invested in and riveted to (socially, psychologically, and economically) the existence of a subordinated race of women. Black women's sense of who they were and could become was not similarly dependent on white women's. This point mistresses were more and more forced to concede as war and emancipation gave encouragement to black women to speak their minds and act more forthrightly.

The "disloyalty" of household slaves during and after the war was the subject of such widespread comment and so widely castigated, and despite its contradiction with the popular motif of slaves' loyalty, precisely because white southerners understood its implications for southern white identity. With emancipation in sight, white women bent to the task of redrawing class and race lines within their spheres of influence. They denied, pushed back, and ridiculed black women's bid for citizenship, autonomy, and personal dignity, and, most of all, black women's assertions of freedom. Emancipation threatened and challenged white southerners' understanding of what constituted a civilized world. The withdrawal or rearrangement of black women's labor within planter homes formed part of the contest that ensued; and it ultimately marked a critical moment in the transformation of southern homes, reared on enslaved labor, to free homes. "Home" thus remained political even as it became free, and as mistresses, like black women, became free.

For enslaved women, freedom would bring a new audience of soldiers and officers of the United States military forces, northern missionaries, planters, teachers, congressional committees on investigative missions, and Freedmen's Bureau agents to developments in the South. The new participants, together with former slaves would construct and leave different and unprecedented archival trails. While neither freedom nor the presence of northerners guaranteed former slave women a more sympathetic audience, they did help to enlarge the spaces in which black women could more openly and freely explore the meaning of womanhood and their place in the new political economy as well as in civic life. New public and private venues – public streets, Freedmen's Bureau offices, churches, and organizations freed from the oversight of slaveholders, and the homes of black people – were places to talk about the kind of work they wished to do and how and where they could enact freedom's promises. Among these was the transformation of domestic work.

For white women, the slaves' emancipation brought unprecedented trials. Early in the war, Kate Stone wrote: "In proportion as we have been a race of haughty, indolent, and waited-on people, so now we are ready to do away with all forms and work and wait on ourselves." "I have a strong presentment," she wrote a year later, "that we shall yet lose all that we have and be compelled to labor with our hands for our daily bread."[125] Her prediction came true for many former mistresses. Ultimately, however, none were prepared to willingly

[125] Stone, *Brokenburn*, May 22, 1862; September 9, 1863, pp. 110 and 243.

give up the labor of black women, especially over the long haul. Some were not even prepared to acknowledge emancipation. Catherine Edmondston was appalled to learn in late May 1865 that some slaveholders, her brother and father included, planned to announce to black people that they were free. "I could not understand it," she wrote, "it seemed inexplicable to me & suicidal in the last degree." She was relieved to find that they had not done so, that they had only told the slaves that it was "*said*" that they were free. Her trials were not over, however. Hearing that northern soldiers were having "nightly balls & that the *Yankee officers* dance with *the Negro women!*" filled her with disgust.[126] Of course, she thought that her own former slaves were "terribly dejected" about their "unsolicited gift of freedom" even though even as she wrote, they apparently were making plans to leave and her seamstresses were already refusing to sew for her. Despite her fantasies that black people would starve and come to no good end without masters and mistresses, Edmondston in the end was faced with this: "At present all is as gloomy as can well be, at home present domestic discomfort & dismal anticipations of still greater evils to come."[127]

Black and white women carried into freedom vastly different expectations. They arrived with vastly different gender experiences and a history of labor relations that had fostered mutual antagonism. The notion that a "common gender experience and a degree of mutual understanding" united black and white women during slavery across the divide of freedom and unfreedom, of citizenship and statelessness, can only rest ultimately on uncritical acceptance of a huge assumption: that a gentle and noble white womanhood had once existed in fact, together with a cult of domesticity to which enslaved and free women mutually ascribed. If accepted without the scrutiny it merits, that assumption leads readily to the idea that freed women viewed struggles for justice as "mostly . . . irrelevant." They then come into view as apolitical beings, while their efforts to reorder southern society after the war become less visible.[128] Such an outcome is entirely possible if the flesh-and-blood power mistresses once wielded stands outside the analysis.

Freedom was made in spaces where women dominated, as much in the plantation household as in the cotton, rice, sugar, and tobacco fields. As freed and becoming-free domestic servants denounced the political and social conventions of the past – some tentatively, others forcefully – they placed on the Reconstruction agenda the transformation of the plantation household and the making of new and free homes, black and white, and of new women, black and white. In freedom, black women pursued citizenship, their claim to femaleness, fair wages, land ownership, and their right to private lives. Perhaps most of all, they claimed the right to determine for themselves what all of this meant.

---

[126] Edmondston, *Diary*, May 8, 1865, pp. 709–11, quotes at pp. 709 and 711.

[127] Edmondston, *Diary*, May 13, 1865; June 26, 1865, pp. 711–13.

[128] Marli F. Weiner, *Mistresses and Slaves: Plantation Women in South Carolina, 1830–1880* (Urbana: University of Illinois Press, 1998), p. 232.

The making of free homes and free women was not unconnected to those struggles that are generally taken to represent the larger project of Reconstruction. Just as slave labor within the plantation household was an integral part of the larger ideological and practical work of slavery, slave labor within the plantation household was inextricably linked to the work that took place in the fields, the larger political culture with which that work was entwined, and to the understandings white and black women had about themselves and their place in the world.[129] As symbols of slavery's good, mistresses, "exotic" and "doll-like" in the words of W. E. B. DuBois, thereby came to stand, from the perspective of slaves, as symbols of their enslavement.[130] In turn, the transformation of the plantation household – that space where the ideology of southern white womanhood was constructed and reproduced through the labor and denigration of black women – came to be viewed by slaves as central to the redefinition of freedom, citizenship, and womanhood.

Emancipation promised a remarkable transformation in the lives of southern women and posed one of the most important tests of freedom. It bears remembering that slavery was "more than a legal relationship; it had social and psychological dimensions that did not disappear with the passage of a law or a constitutional amendment."[131] The social and psychological dimensions shadowed efforts to reconstruct the plantation household on the basis of free labor just as they did plantation agriculture. The antebellum social arrangements of the densely gendered and racialized world of the plantation household proved equally resistant to adjustment. Here, some of the most determined and significant struggles to create new social arrangements took place.

---

[129] On the centrality of the household to southern society, see, among others, Elizabeth Fox-Genovese, *Within the Plantation Household: Black and White Women of the Old South* (Chapel Hill: University of North Carolina Press, 1988).

[130] The quotes are from W. E. B. Dubois, *Black Reconstruction in America, 1860–1880* (1935; reprint, New York: Atheneum, 1973), pp. 34–35.

[131] Harold D. Woodman, "The Reconstruction of the Cotton Plantation in the New South," in *Essays on the Postbellum Southern Economy*, ed. Thavolia Glymph and John Kusma (College Station: Texas A&M University Press, 1985), p. 106.

5

Out of the House of Bondage

A Sundering of Ties, 1865–1866

Sacrificed for *nothing*!

Emma Le Conte, ex-mistress

It was the fourth day of June in 1865 I begins to live...

Katie Rowe, ex-slave

The word *home* has died upon my lips.

Mary Jones, ex-mistress

... the conduct of the Negro in the late crisis of our affairs, convinced me that we have all been laboring under a delusion. Good masters and bad masters, all alike, shared the same fate – the sea of Revolution confounded good and evil.... I believed for a season that these people were content, happy, and attached to their master. I have lived to change all these opinions.

Augustin L. Taveau, ex-master

At the end of March 1865, with the war closing in, a group of female slaves left their chores to take a ride in their mistress's carriage. When they returned, their mistress whipped one of them, Laurie, and sent her away with instructions never to return to the yard. Two days later, Laurie, her mother, and her sister took four oxen and an ox cart, piled their belongings into the cart, and left. A party sent after them found them still on the road, dumped their belongings from the cart, and left the women where they stood.[1] The path to freedom was never straightforward, but freedwomen were determined to take it. Laurie no longer had to put up with beatings from her mistress. Her mother no longer had to witness them silently or impotently. On this, their first venture into freedom, they lost the few possessions they claimed from years of toil, but they were free. And they carried into freedom concrete ideas about what freedom must entail.

---

[1] Diary of Harriet Palmer, March 30, 1865, in *A World Turned Upside Down: The Palmers of South Santee, 1818–1881*, ed. Louis P. Towles (Columbia: University of South Carolina Press, 1996), p. 454.

As they set about the task of "setting up for themselves," making new homes and spaces for new selves, black women drew on residual ideas about what it meant to live freely and new ones that arose *sua sponte*. Nancy Johnson's case is emblematic. When her former master asked her to stay, she declined, saying that she wanted to be free just like the other black people who were leaving. She left but soon returned, only to have her initial instincts about why it was necessary to leave confirmed. The terms her mistress dictated as the conditions on which she would be allowed to return were impossible to accept. "I went away & then came back & my old Missus asked me if I came back to behave myself & do her work & I told her no that I came back to do my own work," she recalled. The following day, she stated, "my Mistress came out again & asked me if I came back to work for her like a *'nigger'* – I told her no that I was free & she said be off then & called me a stinking bitch."[2]

This was probably not the first time Mrs. David Baggs had spit out vulgar words or that Johnson had resisted some aspect of the work assigned to her. Now, however, Johnson and her former mistress stood in a new relationship. Her former mistress no longer had control over Johnson's "whole life," a reality that transformed Johnson's insubordination and her former mistress's verbal abuse into new things. Under certain conditions, in E. P. Thompson's insightful remark, the insubordination of the poor is "an inconvenience," but not a "menace."[3] The power and hegemony of the slaveholding class had permitted slaveholders the luxury of viewing regularized slave resistance as merely "an inconvenience." With that hegemony closed off after 1865, black people's insubordination appeared increasingly as a "menace." Certainly, Johnson's former owners could only see her statement when she returned, "I went to my own house," in that light.[4]

In the first few months after the war, former slaves in every corner of the South made similar claims, ideologically framing the battles to come. From the vantage point of 1865, freedpeople measured planter women's stake in southern society by the power they had wielded as mistresses, by the enthusiasm with which they had supported the Civil War, and by their determined loyalty to the ideals of the Old South and the Confederacy. When white women dressed in muslin long after the economic need to do so had diminished, or

---

[2] Testimony of Nancy Johnson [22 March 1873], claim of Boson Johnson, Liberty Co., GA case files. Approved Claims, ser. 732. Southern Claims Commission, 3d Auditor, RG 217, in Ira Berlin, Barbara J. Fields, Thavolia Glymph, Joseph P. Reidy, and Leslie S. Rowland, eds., *Freedom: A Documentary History of Emancipation, 1862–1867*, ser. 1., vol. 1, *The Destruction of Slavery* (Cambridge: Cambridge University Press, 1985), p. 151. Johnson stayed on and worked for a while weaving for her former mistress, but quit weaving after she was repeatedly denied wages. She continued to live on the place and sometimes did small, odd jobs for her former mistress, for which she received in payment, a "meal of victuals."

[3] E. P. Thompson, "Patrician Society, Plebian Culture," *Journal of Social History* 7 (Summer 1974): 382–405, and the expanded version of this essay in E. P. Thompson, *Customs in Common* (London: Merlin Press, 1991), pp. 16–96.

[4] Testimony of Nancy Johnson, [22 March 1873], in Berlin et al., eds., p. 151.

in Confederate grey long after Confederate armies had been vanquished, they stood as potent and visible symbols of the ideological threat to freedom. In 1866, the Confederate stockings that continued to afford Mary Rowland "a vast deal of pleasure" and the rest of her Confederate attire, were reminders of what was still at stake, and so, too, her declaration: "I am Confederate all over & ever mean to be." But the Confederacy and its ideals were no longer viable.[5] In the end, therefore, the attire marked and symbolized white women's defeat more than the defiance they intended. It had a motive but no practical purpose. It was meant to exact deference, and in this it failed. Black women were equally determined to wipe away race and class privileges grounded in their unfreedom.

Purty White Hands

For the first time in their lives, elite women performed household tasks formerly delegated to enslaved women. For the first time, they entered the marketplace as employers of free labor – of washers, cooks, cleaning maids, and nurses. Nothing had prepared them for these roles, not even those with experience in hiring slave domestic help. Even then, masters had been mainly responsible for hiring slaves. R. S. Russel, for example, spent several weeks before the war searching for a wet nurse: "a healthy + suitable negro woman to suckle my little boys."[6] Most slaveholders in need of a wet nurse, however, had to look no further than the slave quarters. The antebellum market for slave hires to work in domestic capacities was small, so few white women would have gained experience in it even had the markets, as male-dominated public spaces, not been off-limits to them. In any event, hiring slave labor was a vastly different task from hiring free labor.

In the last month of her pregnancy, this realization hit Lizzie Roper as she began making preparations to hire a nurse, something she would not have had to worry about before the war. Roper called on a friend for help in securing the services of Mary Jones, a black woman known to be an experienced nurse. Matters she would have previously taken for granted, she now had to consider. Would Jones be available at the time she expected to give birth? If so, how much would she charge? Roper could no longer assume the availability of a slave woman to help her. Nor did she any longer have the option of ignoring market considerations. Forced to become an employer of free labor, Roper, unsurprisingly, objected to the entire process. It was "provoking to be dependent upon these miserable free negroes," she wrote.[7]

[5] Mary Rowland to Mrs. Paul Cameron, January 20, 1866, Cameron Papers, SHC.

[6] Keith C. Barton, "'Good Cooks and Washers': Slave Hiring, Domestic Labor, and the Market in Bourbon County, Kentucky," *Journal of American History* 84 (September 1997): 440–41.

[7] Lizzie Roper to Mrs. Mordecai, August 21, 1865, Cameron Papers, SHC. The nurse Lizzie Roper sought to hire was clearly neither "miserable" nor in desperate need of employment. See A.K.C. [Annie K. Collins] to Aunt Milly [Mildred C. Cameron], August 14, 1865, Cameron Papers, SHC.

The final months of the war and the first year of freedom saw desperate attempts by former mistresses to salvage something of their prewar status in the face of the steady erosion of slavery. It was easy to turn to fantasy, to look back and see tranquility and elegance, or to look back and imagine, as Susan Dabney Smedes did, that emancipation had liberated only white people. "Who can wonder," Smedes wrote in 1887, "that we longed for a lifting of the incubus and that in the family of Thomas Dabney the first feeling, when the war ended, was of joy that one dreaded responsibility, at least, was removed." Dabney's fantastical remembrance of slavery as an evil spirit and oppressive nightmare that slaveholders had been forced to suffer, and "joy" at its destruction doubtless hardly recommended itself to her father. For two years after the lifting of the incubus, Dabney's aged father did the family's laundry "to spare his daughters."[8]

Susan Leigh Blackford also looked to the past for consolation, to a time when "there was a charm, a grace, an elegance in the Virginia hospitality of those days which have no equal."[9] Others, like Mary Jones of Georgia, were sure that the hand of God would ultimately uphold the side of the planter class. She believed the defeat of the Confederacy would indeed constitute evidence of God's "sore judgment" upon her people, now "desolate and smitten." But she clung to the hope of a merciful God, who, when he "hath sufficiently chastised and humbled us as individuals and as a nation in wrath, He will remember mercy, and that we shall be purged and purified...to His honor and His glory." The purging and purification that Mary Jones envisioned and prayed for would end not in slavery's destruction but in its reformation and reconstitution. Her faith, though shaken, took strength from her belief that ultimately God's favor remained with white people. In the end, she believed, white people would be purified and black people would by divine providence cease to exist. This made her happy: "The *workings* of Providence in reference to the African race are truly wonderful. The scourge falls with peculiar weight upon them: with their emancipation must come their extermination."[10]

Black people saw the hand of God working differently. Ex-slave Sallie Paul was confident that "God set de slaves free." Paul dismissed rumors that the credit for emancipation belonged to President Lincoln, for "Lincoln couldn't do no more den what God give de power to do." Lincoln "was just de one what present de speech. It was revealed to him en God was de one dat stepped in en fight de battle." Indeed, Paul's analysis echoed Lincoln's own in the aftermath of the qualified Union victory at Antietam. It was not the sort of victory

---

[8] Susan Dabney Smedes, *Memorials of a Southern Planter*, ed. Fletcher M. Green (New York: Knopf, 1965), pp. 180 and 223–25, quotes at pp. 180 and 223.

[9] [Journal], [May 1863], Susan Leigh Blackford, comp., *Letters from Lee's Army or Memoirs of Life In and Out of the Army in Virginia During the War Between the States* (1947; reprint, New York: A. S. Barnes & Company, 1962), p. 174.

[10] Mary Jones Journal, 11 January 1865, in *The Children of Pride: The True Story of Georgia and the Civil War*, ed. Robert Manson Myers (New Haven, CT: Yale University Press, 1972), p. 1244.

Lincoln said he "should have liked best," but it satisfied the terms of the covenant he had made with God: If Lee's army were driven from Maryland, he would issue the Emancipation Proclamation.[11] It was not a covenant, however, that recommended itself on the ground of the pure abolitionism black people advocated. In the waning days of the Confederacy, the Reverend W. B. Allen was asked by his master's family to pray for the Southern armies, "to pray to God to hold the Northern armies back." He told them "straight from the shoulder that I could not pray along these lines. I told them flat-footedly that, while I loved them and would do any reasonable praying for them, I could not pray against my conscience; that I not only wanted to be free but I wanted to see all the Negroes freed!" Where Mary Jones believed emancipation to be God's scourge, a sign of his displeasure more with black people than slaveholders, black people found a different sign in the transpiring events. Allen told his master's family that God "was using the Yankees to scourge the slaveholders."[12]

As Mary Jones penned her sentiments, the Confederacy was entering the last three months of its existence. Over the coming months, she and other mistresses would become, in the words of her daughter-in-law, Eva Jones, "chained witnesses" to transformations they could hardly have imagined four years before. Black women who had remained in planter homes during the war now packed to go. Mistresses were helpless but to "only look on and draw inferences and note occurrences." Eva Jones called it "a most unprecedented robbery." In her household, the robbery took form in July 1865, when Adeline, Grace, and Polly became the first of her slaves "to assume freedom," leaving "without bidding any of us an affectionate adieu." They would be followed by others, and leaders of the movement emerged. None of her former slaves, Jones admitted, had "done more to keep the servants away than Sue." In leaving, black women claimed their freedom and independence. Patience, Jones wrote, had "designs [for] setting up for herself."[13] James A. Graham put the phenomena in almost identical shorthand: "Two of Aunt Violet's have left," he wrote his mother, "one of them hiring herself to a Jew and the other setting up for herself."[14] To him, as to Jones, the very idea seemed preposterous.

Looking back on the months preceding the fall of Richmond from the vantage point of the 1880s, Mary Chesnut remembered them simply as "confused." With the slaves of her friends and acquaintances abandoning plantation households all around her, she took little pride in the "loyalty" of her own. The

---

[11] Sallie Paul, *South Carolina Narratives*, vol. 3, pt. 3, p. 247; James McPherson, *Battle Cry of Freedom: The Civil War Era* (New York: Oxford University Press, 1988), p. 557.

[12] Rev. W. B. Allen, *Georgia Narratives*, Supplement Series 1, vol. 3, pt. 1, pp. 19–20.

[13] Eva Jones to Mary Jones, June 13, 1865, p. 1274; ibid., July 14, 1865, p. 1280; Mary Jones to Mary S. Mallard, January 17, 1866, p. 1319, in *Children of Pride*, ed. Myers. Adeline and Grace, who left Eva Jones's household without so much as a proper goodbye, found gainful employment in Savannah, Adeline as a cook and Grace as an independent seamstress.

[14] James A. Graham to mother, May 20, 1865, in *James A. Graham Papers, 1861–1864*, ed. H. M. Wagstaff (Chapel Hill: University of North Carolina Press, 1928), p. 214.

defeat of other women of her class, she recognized, was hers as well. Chesnut's confusion had varied sources: from the sight of Confederate soldiers moving in the wrong direction, away from the battlefield in Virginia, to her belief that the white women she knew personally had too often shown less than sterling patriotism. But it was the behavior of black women that was for her so poignant: "The Martins left Columbia the Friday before I did. And their mammy, the negro woman who had nursed them, refused to go with them. That daunted me."[15]

Soon, however, the departures of black women who had belonged to people she knew and loved ceased to trouble Chesnut in the hard way they had initially. They became such a regular part of her world that they ceased to daunt her. Her writing on the subject remained dramatic but increasingly less emotionally engaged: "The black ball is in motion. Mrs. DeSaussure's cook shook the dust off her feet and departed from her kitchen today, free, she said. The washer woman is packing to go."[16] For most former mistresses, however, the departure of household slaves was paralyzing. They could barely write, talk, or think about anything but their domestic troubles. "These times," Eva Jones wrote, "try men's souls – and women's too!"[17]

Without Provocation or Warning

The assumption of freedom by domestic slaves shook white households in the spring of 1865 and into the fall, winter, and spring of 1866, cutting to the quick of southern fantasies of devoted domestic servants. Harriet Palmer's early youth had prepared her to one day become a mistress. But the clouds of war in January 1861 forced a different assessment of her future prospects. As she began the task of making a pair of drawers for herself, she wrote, "I would like to know how to make every article of my clothing for one of these days I may have it all to do with my own hands."[18] That day came. By the start of the Civil War, Gertrude Thomas had experienced life as a belle, a mistress, a wife, and a mother. In the ways of domestic work, however, she was as much a novice as the much younger Harriet Palmer. Short of help in 1865, Thomas helped a servant wipe dishes, "a thing," she wrote, that "I never remember to have done more than once or twice in my life."[19]

[15] C. Vann Woodward, ed., *Mary Chesnut's Civil War* (New Haven, CT: Yale University Press, 1981), February 16, 1865, p. 715.

[16] Woodward, ed., *Mary Chesnut's Civil War*, June 4, 1865, p. 823; C. Vann Woodward and Elisabeth Muhlenfeld, eds., *The Private Mary Chesnut: The Unpublished Civil War Diaries* (New York: Oxford University Press, 1984), p. 257.

[17] Eva B. Jones to Mary Jones, July 14, 1865, p. 1280, in *Children of Pride*, ed. Myers, p. 1280.

[18] Harriet Palmer Journal, January 11, [1861], Harriet Palmer Journal, SCL. See also *A World Turned Upside Down*, ed. Towles, p. 285; James W. Garner, *Reconstruction in Mississippi* (Baton Rouge: Louisiana State University Press, 1968), pp. 122–23.

[19] Virginia Ingraham Burr, ed., *The Secret Eye: The Journal of Ella Gertrude Thomas, 1848–1889* (Chapel Hill: University of North Carolina Press, 1990), May 29, 1865, p. 272.

Catherine Edmondston professed shock that her maid, Fanny, after tenderly nursing her "in a most devoted & affectionate manner" through a recent illness and even weeping over her, left when she "was scarce able to walk without assistance . . . with provocation or warning . . . in the night, and that too without the slightest notice." "She actually left," Edmondston wrote, "without bidding me good bye."[20] Young Rebecca Cameron of North Carolina rejoiced to hear that an aunt still retained a servant in June 1865. In her own family, none remained. The Camerons were further shocked that, with the exception of one family, none of the hundreds of field hands "expressed any interest to come to us at all." Slaveholders continued to refer to the loss of domestic servants as defection and abandonment of duty. How else could they imagine it? It was shameful behavior, Elizabeth Porcher wrote, resulting in so many of her friends and relatives having "to wash and cook" for themselves.[21]

In late May of 1865, Gertrude Thomas chronicled a succession of departures and trials of all sorts. The ironing piled up with flies swarming all over it as Nancy, the ironer, took to her bed saying she was too sick to iron. The next morning, Thomas caught her walking out the gate with her two children. "She had expected to leave with flying colors," Thomas wrote, "but was compelled to tell a falsehood for she replied 'I will be back directly.' I knew at once that she was taking 'french leave' and was not surprised when I went into her room sometime afterward to find that all her things had been removed. I was again engaged in housework most of the morning." Her mother's servants were also leaving.[22] For her part, Tryphena Fox had "the pleasure of going over to the kitchen (across the yard) & cooking my own breakfast & bringing it out to the house myself" when yet another black woman in her employ left.[23] Eva Jones was trying to get used to sewing, which came "very hard to [her] unused fingers." Trying at the same time to find a nurse for her four-year-old stepdaughter, she took some consolation in the fact that the child was growing "so fast I will *almost* be able to attend to her myself."[24] A Mississippi mistress, bereft of slaves, "did the washing for six weeks, came near ruining myself for life as I was too delicately raised for such hard work." In South Carolina,

[20] Catherine Ann Devereux Edmondston, "*Journal of a Secesh Lady*": The Diary of Catherine Ann Devereux Edmondston, ed. Beth G. Crabtree and James W. Patton (Raleigh: North Carolina Division of Archives and History and Department of Cultural Resources, 1979), October 1, 1865, p. 717.

[21] Rebecca [Cameron] to [Mildred C. Cameron], June 2, 1865, Cameron Papers, SCH; Elizabeth P. Porcher to [Philip E. Porcher], March 23, 1865, in A World Turned Upside Down, ed. Towles, p. 450. Porcher's own household would suffer the same fate. On the misuse of words like treason, treachery and defection, see Chapter 4.

[22] Burr, ed., *The Secret Eye*, May 29, 1865, pp. 272–74, quote at p. 273.

[23] Wilma King, ed., A Northern Woman in the Plantation South: Letters of Tryphena Blanche Holder Fox, 1856-1876 (Columbia: University of South Carolina Press, 1993), September 10, 1865, p. 158.

[24] Eva B. Jones to Mary Jones, July 14, 1865 in Children of Pride, ed. Myers, quotes at pp. 1280 and 1281, respectively.

Mrs. Ben Rutledge, with her children reduced to eating mush, wished she had learned at least to make bread.[25]

Here, in the Jones family's view, was the "unprecedented robbery" that struck at the core of white southern society, especially planter life and identity, and that signaled the destruction of the old order. The Rev. John Jones described the "emancipation trials" in these terms: "The dark, dissolving, disquieting wave of emancipation has broke over this sequestered region. I have been marking its approach for months and watching its influence on our own people. It has been like the iceberg, withering and deadening the best sensibilities of master and servant, and fast sundering the domestic ties of years."[26] As his daughter and son-in-law struck out for Mississippi at the end of 1865, Paul C. Cameron's anguish was palpable. "I find it hard to reconcile myself to this state of things," he wrote, "& nothing but the *necessity* which I felt was upon us could have obtained my consent." Cameron had complete faith in his son-in-law's ability but none in the "broken reed" of free labor, which had already appeared in his own household. He felt little joy at the approach of Christmas: "We have killed some of our pork – and will have food to eat if we shall have anyone to *cook* it."[27]

A generally astute observer of her world, Mary Jones traced, with no little irony and in excruciating detail, the assault she felt on her sense of place in the world when black women departed from her household. One day the former slave Susan was there. By nightfall she was gone. For some two weeks, Jones tracked the movements of two other former slaves, Sue and her daughter, Elizabeth, as they sought a life of freedom. She kept herself apprised of where they went and for whom they worked, as if expecting their "extermination" at any moment. Sue's ability to find work for herself and her daughter "beating rice and grinding and washing" tested Jones's religious faith and her racist beliefs. She could not fathom why Sue would remove Elizabeth from her employment, cutting rice, only to hire out to work for someone else. After all, by her

---

[25] Armstead L. Robinson, "'Worser dan Jeff Davis': The Coming of Free Labor During the Civil War, 1861–1865," in *Essays on the Postbellum Southern Economy*, ed. Thavolia Glymph and John J. Kushma (College Station: Texas A&M University Press, 1985), pp. 36–37; Woodward, ed., *Mary Chesnut's Civil War*, February 19, 1865, p. 723; second quote at Woodward and Muhlenfeld, eds., *The Private Mary Chesnut*, February 18, 1865, p. 232. On postwar disputes in the household, see also Leon Litwack, *Been in the Storm So Long: The Aftermath of Slavery* (New York: Vintage, 1979), pp. 347–51; Drew Gilpin Faust, *Mothers of Invention: Women of the Slaveholding South in the American Civil War* (Chapel Hill: University of North Carolina Press, 1996), pp. 74–79; George C. Rable, *Civil Wars: Women and the Crisis of Southern Nationalism* (Urbana and Chicago: University of Illinois Press, 1989), pp. 240–64; Leslie A. Schwalm, *A Hard Fight for We: Women's Transition from Slavery to Freedom in South Carolina* (Urbana: University of Illinois Press, 1997), pp. 207–11; and Marli F. Weiner, *Mistresses and Slaves: Plantation Women in South Carolina, 1830–1860* (Urbana: University of Illinois Press, 1998), pp. 185–206, among others.

[26] Rev. John Jones to Mary Jones, August 21, 1865, in *Children of Pride*, ed. Myers, quotes at pp. 1293 and 1292, respectively.

[27] Paul C. Cameron to Mrs. M. B. Mordecai, December 22, 1865, Cameron Papers, SHC.

reckoning, they owed their very lives to her. She had cared for them, labored to supply their wants, and "expended everything I had upon their support, directly or indirectly; and this is their return." No matter. Jones predicted that Sue would soon enough come to "feel the loss of her comfortable home."[28]

That Sue considered Jones's home neither comfortable nor her home did not cross Jones's mind. Nor did it occur to her that Sue might understand the matter of who had supported whom differently. Jones discerned no contradiction in the evidence of Sue's effort to earn a living and her own description of Sue and her daughter as "walking about at large" without a sense of purpose. She never stopped to consider these contradictions, obvious to a reader today, because they did not exist for her. That for her there was but one "home" for black people made for the final irony. Susan and her daughter no longer belonged to Mary Jones, nor were they employed by her. Without them, it was her world, her home, that was shattered and gone. "The word *home* had died upon my lips," she wrote.[29]

The Women are the Controlling Spirits

Under Dutch colonial rule, Ann Laura Stoler argues, "domestic and familial intimacies were critical political sites in themselves where racial affiliations were worked out."[30] This was also true in the American South. The geography of the plantation household was a landscape of black and white women "in contact."[31] The resulting intimacies fostered sentiment and personal attachment, but these of necessity canted toward falsehood. This reality helps to make Mary Jones's collapse comprehensible. Even though their status had depended upon the work of slave women, former mistresses did not believe their former slaves capable of working – or surviving – without them or their direction. Emancipation brought that stark contradiction into full view. Jones's tortured confession attempts to surmount it.

Former mistresses understood that the making of free black homes threatened the reconstruction of white homes as privileged social, political, and economic spaces. They also saw the destruction of the white home as the destruction of the black one as well. From their perspective, the two were one and the same. The black family was an *invention*, their own, and it existed at

---

[28] Mary Jones to Charles C. Jones, Jr., June 26, 1865, p. 1275; Mary Jones to Mary S. Mallard, November 7, 1865, p. 1303; Mary Jones to Mary S. Mallard, November 17, 1865, p. 1308 in *Children of Pride*, ed. Myers, quotes at p. 1303.

[29] Mary Jones to Charles C. Jones, Jr., June 26, 1865, in *Children of Pride*, ed. Myers, p. 1275.

[30] Ann Laura Stoler, *Carnal Knowledge and Imperial Power: Race and the Intimate in Colonial Rule* (Berkeley: University of California Press, 2002), p. 310.

[31] See Tony Ballantyne and Antoinette Burton, *Bodies in Contact: Rethinking Colonial Encounters in World History* (Durham, NC: Duke University Press, 2005); Nell Irvin Painter, "Soul Murder: Toward a Fully Loaded Cost Accounting," in Nell Irvin Painter, *Southern History Across the Color Line* (Chapel Hill: University of North Carolina Press, 2002). My interpretation, however, differs in key respects from Painter's and Weiner's (Weiner, *Mistresses and Slaves*, pp. 74–76).

their will.[32] Independent of white will and direction, it would cease to exist, and former slaveholders stood ready to lay the blame for that expected outcome at the feet of black women. Watching the departure of their former slaves, Charles C. Jones was certain that "The women are the controlling spirits."[33]

In freedom, the self-will that black women had demonstrated while enslaved had room to blossom. Grace Elmore determined to give up on Cynthia, finally admitting that "her will is too strong, and she loved her own way too much." Elmore had a much harder time, however, recognizing the same traits in "Old Mary," who, when told she was free, "expressed quiet satisfaction." Two days later, the "hypocrite" was gone, "leaving the poor baby without a nurse." Elmore's plan for revenge was ample evidence of why "Old Mary" left.[34]

I feel so provoked, of course one cannot expect total sacrifice of self, but certainly there should be some consideration of others. Old Mary is off of my books for any kindness or consideration I may be able to show her in after years. I would not turn on my heel to help her, a more pampered indulged old woman one could find no where, she has done nothing but fold her hands over her fat self for years, till little Grace came, and then she was made nurse. If she supposes she is to live on our place, she is much mistaken, and when I see her, I shall tell her in Mother's name to go, we have no use for her on the place and she can go. I think a marked difference should be shown between those who act in a thoughtful and affectionate manner, and those who show no thought or care for you.[35]

Of course, Mary was already gone.

While former mistresses blamed black women for the disorder that racked their domestic lives, they sometimes cast black men as co-conspirators. When Fanny, her "loyal" maid, decided to leave, Catherine Edmondston ascribed the decision to the underhandedness of Fanny's husband. She accused him of enticing Fanny away, luring her with the promise that he would take care of her so that she would have no other responsibility than to attend to their sick child. Joe "promised that if she would go with him she should do naught but tend it whilst he would support her in idleness." Fanny "at length" "succombed (sic)" and went "off into the unknown future with only him to depend on."[36] Here, for her, was the only explanation she could imagine for Fanny's desire to have her own life. When black women took care of white children, it was

---

[32] Herbert G. Gutman dismantled this notion in scholarly circles over a quarter of a century ago. See Gutman, *The Black Family in Slavery and Freedom, 1750–1925* (New York: Pantheon, 1976). New work in the field, however, has challenged Gutman's thesis, questioning the extent to which black families in slavery were able to surmount the barriers slavery erected in building and sustaining strong family relationships.

[33] Charles C. Jones, Jr. to Mary Jones, November 26, 1865, in *Children of Pride*, ed. Myers, p. 1308.

[34] Grace Elmore Diary, March 15, 1865, SHC.

[35] Grace Elmore Diary, May 30, 1865, SHC.

[36] Edmondston, *Diary*, October 1, 1865, p. 717. In this interpretation, black women are duped by their husbands or fathers to desert the place in southern society white southerners would have them occupy.

a job. When they cared for their own, former mistresses saw not work but "idleness."

Throughout the spring, summer, and fall of 1865 and into 1866, cooks, seamstresses, waiters, bed warmers, washers, ironers, fanners, chambermaids, and scullions in every corner of the South left or made preparations to leave. Rumors circulated from household to household. In homes not yet struck, former mistresses watched warily for signs of discontent or imminent departures, fearing the day when they would join the ranks of those already reduced to being their own chambermaids, or nurses for their own children. Visiting a female relative at the beginning of 1866, Mary Jones "found her on the eve of a domestic January revolution" with one of her servants gone and another preparing to leave.[37]

Homes not yet struck stood in constant danger of being so. Subtle and not-so-subtle changes in the behavior of freedwomen were catalogued and weighed for their meaning. Esther Simons Palmer, mistress of Balls Dam plantation, recorded her observations of Peggy: "I knew for weeks before she left that she was going. Her countenance changed, and she did nothing, not even darning stockings. Every week I expect to hear Lucy say she too is going."[38] Gertrude Thomas's slaves, in her view, ever a cheerful lot, appeared more cheerful than ever after learning they were free. Thomas noted the change in Tamah, who just days before had declined to wash some clothes, citing a prolapsed uterus as the reason. Yet there she now was, lively as could be and sewing a pair of pants for her own son.[39] As the mistress kept watching, a sense of betrayal overshadowed her comprehension of Tamah's medical problem. The fact that sewing would not worsen Tamah's condition, but that washing might, seemed more or less immaterial to Thomas at that moment. What riveted her attention was Tamah's liveliness, which Thomas took as a sign that she had "either decided to go or the prospect of being paid has put her in a very good humour." The next morning Thomas rose to find herself without a cook, Tamah having departed the night before."[40]

Tamah was neither the first nor the last of Thomas's slaves to leave. Betsy, sent on her usual errand to pick up the Augusta *Chronicle*, did not return. Thomas discovered her clothes missing. She learned that Sarah, Betsy's mother (a woman she described as having the "wiles of a Delilah" and "dishonest"), had hatched "a concerted plan" to get Betsy to Augusta where Sarah now lived.[41] Although Betsy's leaving inconvenienced and angered Thomas, she worked hard to make a show of not caring. She would not let the other black women in her employ think any of it affected her. According to her calculation,

37 Paul C. Cameron to Mrs. M. B. Mordecai, December 22, 1865, Cameron Papers, SHC; Mary Jones to Mary Mallard, January 2, 1867, in *Children of Pride*, ed. Myers, p. 1365.

38 Esther Simon Palmer to Elizabeth Palmer Porcher, March 11, 1866, in *World Turned Upside Down*, ed. Towles, p. 503.

39 Burr, ed., *The Secret Eye*, May 2, 1865, p. 267.

40 Burr, ed., *The Secret Eye*, May [17], 1865, p. 268.

41 Burr, ed., *The Secret Eye*, May 27, 1865, quotes at pp. 270, 268, and 267, respectively.

a show of indifference would rob them of their expectation of an "expression of surprise or sorrow" on her part.[42]

But to herself, Thomas was forced to acknowledge loss of power and authority, and indeed self-confidence. That inner distress inclined her to overlook the fact that Sarah was Betsy's mother. Instead, she held fast to the idea that Sarah's motive in taking Betsy was to exact revenge for a past grievance. It so happened that Sarah, a newly purchased slave, had been with Thomas for less than a year when she left. In that short period, Sarah had not only washed and ironed but also been placed in charge of the yard. Then trouble struck. She was accused of stealing meat and sent to the plantation as punishment.[43] Quite possibly, in addition to claiming her daughter, Sarah really was seeking revenge (if that she had been falsely accused, for instance). Another possibility is that for Thomas, as for other former mistresses, effective self-determination by former slaves merely looked and felt like revenge.

What is certain is that the new *"whole life"* of black women, to invoke E. P. Thompson's phrase, was a rebuke to former mistresses. As free women, they gained not only parental rights, but also the right to no longer be shuttled from place to place at a mistress's discretion. When the former mistress of a young slaved named Phillis asked her how she felt about freedom, she said she "could complain of nothing," but added in the same breath that she looked forward to freedom. She had heard it said that freedom was "a sweet thing to be able to do as she chose, to sit and do nothing if she desired, or to go out as she likes, and ask nobody's permission."[44]

When Sarah left Gertrude Thomas's household, and removed her child, she denied Thomas the role of "over-mother," and stripped away her power to determine Betsy's future. Thomas thought Betsy "a bright quick child" who, properly raised in a white family, "would have become a good servant." Raised by her mother, Thomas continued, Betsy would "run wild in the street."[45] In that duel between women, Sarah's moves were at once bold and hesitant. She did not, after all, confront Thomas directly either in assuming her own freedom or in taking her daughter. That she resorted to surreptitious devices to get her child was in some sense an acknowledgement of the still provisional nature of freedom in the spring of 1865.

Whether they took themselves and their children off in the darkness of night or in the full brightness of day, black women did not claim their freedom lightly. Leaving took courage. Some left not knowing what their next move

---

[42] Burr, ed., *The Secret Eye*, May [17], 1865, p. 268.

[43] Burr, ed., *The Secret Eye*, May 27, 1865, p. 270.

[44] Grace Elmore Diary, May 24, 1865, SHC. By the end of June 1865, all of Elmore's former household slaves had departed (see entry for June 15, 1865).

[45] Burr, ed., *The Secret Eye*, May 27, 1865, p. 270. Sarah's beauty also disturbed Thomas. She believed Sarah had used her charms to seduce the plantation driver to assist her in getting Betsy and herself away. The driver, she wrote, "had left an ugly faithful black wife in Burke to follow the more attractive face of Sarah who is a good looking mulatto or brown complected woman," only to have her leave him for her husband once she got to Augusta.

would be. But whether or not they planned their departures carefully, black women often entered unknown territory. The next job might offer no better promise of the freedom that they hoped for than the job they left. The wartime problems with stragglers from both armies had diminished but remained a concern. Those who left unannounced at night sometimes had to leave behind children and what few meager material possessions they owned. They knew they might never see their children again, and that their former owners would likely rebuff any effort to retrieve personal belongings or children. Returning to claim anyone or anything also entailed the risk that they might come to personal harm. Some called on Union soldiers to escort them back to retrieve property and children, in the process further provoking the wrath of their former mistresses.

Former slaves returning in the company of Union soldiers were a powerful symbol of a world turned upside down. Mary Luke Clanton accused a Union soldier who accompanied Nancy when she returned for her property in late May 1865 of depriving her of her right to manage black people. Clanton and her daughter Gertrude Thomas believed that Nancy, the most "impertinent" of all their former slaves, brought the Union soldier along for show, to "awe" them.[46]

Nancy did indeed make a point about the changed social relations of the South. Returning in the company of a U.S. soldier also suggested that she had reason to fear returning alone. Whether she sought to "awe" her former mistress with the presence of a greater power, feared harm to herself, or feared difficulty in securing her property, in going back as she did, she embraced her newfound, if still provisional, rights as a citizen. In secreting her child Betsy away, Sarah, too, became part of the "wave of emancipation." By taking her daughter out of slavery, she made freedom a concrete reality for them both, and enlisted her daughter in its making.[47] Betsy's memory of freedom's arrival no doubt was forever entwined with the memory of the struggle her mother waged to free her.

Compelled to Bargain and Haggle

In slavery, black women and mistresses argued and fought over the terms under which enslaved women labored and white women supervised them. By 1861, that struggle had resulted in some rationalization of domestic labor in plantation households with discrete tasks and individual slaves assigned to particular

---

[46] Burr, ed., *The Secret Eye*, May 29, 1865, quotes at pp. 273 and 274, respectively. Weiner, *Mistresses and Slaves*, p. 188.

[47] Allen F. Isaacman, "Peasants and Rural Protest in Africa," in *Confronting Historical Paradigms: Peasants, Labor, and the Capitalist World System in Africa and Latin America*, ed. Frederick Cooper et al. (Madison: University of Wisconsin Press, 1993), pp. 205–317. Isaacman's cogent analysis of the political culture of African peasants provides useful insights for the study of the political culture of former slaves in the American South.

tasks. Beyond the image and work of plantation cooks and nurses, this division of labor has not always been easily discernable to scholars. But as former slave Mattie Stenston recalled, field hands, cooks, maids, servers, spinners, and weavers each had "his or her own job."[48] Privileges were sometimes attached to these jobs. To the uninitiated, and indeed sometimes to those raised in its midst, the labor specialization and attached privileges could seem bewildering. Sarah Morgan, for example, seemed mystified by the bargaining power of household slaves.[49]

The "rights" household slaves claimed had their grounding in many of the same factors that fueled rights claims among field hands, such as a reduction in the labor demands placed on them. Northern visitors often alluded to the problem but could not put it in the language of labor rationalization, in part because it could look so much like the opposite. A bed unmade could be taken as slaves' slovenliness though it might be that the bed maker was sick that day. The complaints of mistresses about the way slave women worked, about insubordination, irregular work habits, general indiscipline, and so forth, in reality cloaked transformations in household labor. The same held true for masters' complaints about white women's irregular management of the home. Those transformations included the systematization of tasks and workloads. And they were the result of ongoing negotiation.

Once free, black women who had labored in planters' homes – like slaves who labored in the South's cotton, rice, sugar, and tobacco fields – drew on a long tradition of struggle and negotiation. In some ways, the particularity of the struggle within the plantation household gave former household slaves an advantage over field hands in postwar negotiations and over their former mistresses as well. Women slaves employed in the household had already begun the process of rationalizing their labor, sometimes largely unknown to their mistresses. By contrast, masters and overseers kept records – how much labor to an acre of rice, how much time to a task of hoeing, etc. – that made them better equipped to navigate in the free labor economy. Mistresses had no such paper trail to guide them in marking labor to time. Because they had done the actual work, freedwomen had the advantage of knowing, or being able to better estimate, how much time it took to perform a particular task.

What constituted a day's labor or a fair wage for nurses, cooks, or washers? In answering, black women brought their own sense of the value of their labor based on their experience as slaves. How much time had they actually spent malingering or in other ways undermining the system's capacity to exploit them? They drew on experience to determine how much work or how many

---

[48] Mattie Stentson, *Mississippi Narratives*, Supplement Series 1, vol. 10, pt. 5, p. 2037. See also Chapter 1. Leslie A. Schwalm sees the breakdown of household chores into separate tasks as a postwar development (Schwalm, *Hard Fight for We*, pp. 209–10). See also Tera W. Hunter, *To 'Joy My Freedom: Southern Black Women's Lives and Labor after the Civil War* (Cambridge, MA: Harvard University Press, 1997), pp. 27–28.

[49] Sarah Morgan, *Sarah Morgan: The Civil War Diary of a Southern Woman*, ed. Charles East (New York: Simon and Schuster, 1991), May 30, 1863, p. 501.

hours constituted a task or a day's work. Washerwomen and ironers who as slaves had insisted that it took a day's labor to perform a certain amount of work, might as free workers calculate their time differently. Time marked as a slave was not the same as time marked as a free worker. Former mistresses learned how little they knew about slaves' time. They learned they were far less well equipped to make such calculations, and it was a shocking revelation. But despite their compromised position, they had to go forward, not least because the black women they were trying to keep or hire were ready to negotiate. Black women took as the baseline for wartime and postwar labor negotiations where things had stood in 1861.

The specialization of labor in the antebellum plantation household is typically examined simply as evidence of slaveholders' ostentatiousness: Slaves, like English china, conveyed household wealth and standing in the community; the greater the number of slaves on display, the greater the household's reputed wealth and reputation. Slaveholders themselves were generally eager to give this impression, though masters (more commonly than mistresses) often complained of having more slaves about the house than needed. Few mistresses could match Mary Cox Chesnut's sixty to seventy domestic slaves and the corresponding array of discrete specializations; but all had to deal with a more mundane reality: the rationalization of housework as the outcome of continuous dispute and negotiation. In freedom, black women fought to maintain the separation of tasks that had characterized prewar forms of domestic labor.

Cooks hired to cook and washers to wash rebuffed attempts to turn them into all-purpose servants, to put "something more" on the table than had been agreed to. Cooks whose work took no more than two to three hours a day refused to perform additional work when they had completed the work they had been contracted to do. They would get no extra pay for it.[50] This attitude left former mistresses perplexed and angry, whether they managed to hire servants to work in their homes or were forced to put out their work.[51] Testifying before the Senate Committee on Labor and Capital in 1883, a number of white witnesses held that former slaves could not be trusted to honor a contract, and that the South's labor problems stemmed from that supposed fact. When it was the turn of Rev. E. P. Holmes to testify, he rejected that reasoning, and quite bluntly: "An employer hires a colored person to cook. Now, when I am hired to cook I want to cook. I don't want to go and clean up the house and do a lot

---

[50] Testimony of Mrs. George Ward, U.S. Government, *Report of the Committee of the Senate Upon the Relations between Labor and Capital and Testimony Taken by the Committee*, 5 vols. (Washington, DC: Government Printing Office, 1885), IV: 315; hereafter cited as *Senate Committee Report*; Hunter, *To 'Joy My Freedom*, pp. 26–28; Schwalm, *Hard Fight for We*, pp. 209–11; Weiner, *Mistresses and Slaves*, pp. 196–203.

[51] See, for example, the Testimony of Mr. Frederick A. Eustis before the American Freedman's Inquiry Commission [June 1863], LR, ser. 12, RG 94, in Ira Berlin, Thavolia Glymph, Steven Miller, Joseph P. Reidy, Leslie S. Roland, and Julie Saville, eds., *Freedom: A Documentary History of Emancipation, 1861–1867*, ser. 1, vol. 3, *The Wartime Genesis of Free Labor: The Lower South* (Cambridge: Cambridge University Press, 1990), pp. 246 and 248.

of other things; and if, after I have been cooking for a month or so, you want me to clean up house also, why I won't do it."[52]

Former mistresses resisted this understanding of wage relations. Meanwhile, domestic servants kept pushing for personal autonomy, improved working conditions, and a voice in determining the terms of their work. They fought off efforts to increase individual workloads amidst a dwindling domestic labor supply. They worked to establish, formalize, and regularize standard rates of pay, and demanded formal written contracts.[53] Turning to the judicial system, they sued former mistresses for unpaid wages, a step that one observer branded "a most unwarrantable procedure."[54] Struggles to bring the terms of wage relations to household work accelerated throughout the fall and early winter of 1865. As former mistresses began to acknowledge, black women were "fast learning the Northern way of hiring by the week," and getting paid by the week, or else "they would not come back at all."[55]

Over time black women workers organized and systematized this struggle. They built support groups – informal and formal combinations – in defense of their freedom and the associated right to refuse to work for abusive or miserly employers. White women employers labeled these organizations subversive, and declared them a contributing factor in the shortage of domestic labor. As Mrs. George Ward told the Senate Committee, "there is a society organized among them to look after and provide for the wants of those who are out of a job," organizations with "funny" names that made black women "perfectly independent and relieves them from all fear of being discharged, because when they are discharged they go right straight to some of these 'sisters.'" She mentioned the Immaculate Doves, the Sisteren, the Beloved Disciples, and "others with all kinds of curious names within their church organizations." Other white women employers may have followed Ward's inclination to belittle these organizations with "funny" or "curious" names, but they took seriously the threat such organizations represented.[56]

Black women also adopted less formal designs against the symbolic and material standing of white homes. Gossip did important work. Reputedly, "very troublesome servants to keep," black women could be still more troublesome after they left. Their gossiping, in particular, was a source of great annoyance to their erstwhile employers. As one white woman employer admitted, "one of the chief grievances of white ladies since the war has been the

[52] Testimony of Rev. E. P. Holmes, *Senate Committee Report*, IV: 609.

[53] On contracts, see, for example, Mary Jones to Charles C. Jones, Jr., August 18, 1865, in *Children of Pride*, ed. Myers, p. 1291; Eric Foner, *Reconstruction: America's Unfinished Revolution, 1863–1877* (New York: Harper and Row, 1988), p. 136; Daniel E. Sutherland, "A Special Kind of Problem: The Response of Household Slaves and Their Masters to Freedom," *Southern Studies* 20 (Summer 1981): 158–162.

[54] Charles C. Jones, Jr. to Mary Jones, July 28, 1865, in *Children of Pride*, ed. Myers, p. 1284.

[55] Ward Testimony, *Senate Committee Report*, IV: 315.

[56] Ward Testimony, *Senate Committee Report*, IV: 315 and 343–44; Hunter, *To 'Joy My Freedom*, pp. 70–73.

way in which house servants who leave them and hire to others gossip about them or slander them to their new employers."[57] Gossip, by definition, transmits rumors or talk of an intimate nature. It makes the home more public and exposes the good and bad that take place there. Through gossip, black women transmitted information about their employers, the working conditions in white homes, and the personal and intimate lives of the families in which they worked. Gossip about white women's character as human beings circulated far and wide and gave black women seeking employment critical information. Freedom gave black women the right to move around, and that new mobility enabled them to carry such information further abroad than before. Of course, domestic servants' gossip had many generations of antecedents in slaves' gossip about their owners. With emancipation, the white home was no longer a space veiled by the lack of mobility that slavery imposed. This made its public attributes more visible and the white home more vulnerable as white women's efforts to silence black women's gossip testify.[58]

As important as the freedom to leave the plantation household and to organize against abusive employers was, only a minority of black women could ultimately command the resources necessary to stage permanent strikes against white households. The challenge, then, was to transform white households and their personnel. Washerwomen sometimes transformed both by doing their work at home, thereby eliminating constant oversight by their employers. This adjustment allowed for critical readjustments in employer–employee relations, along with giving black women greater autonomy over their personal and work lives.[59] It pushed forward other kinds of transformations in

[57] South Carolinian, "South Carolina Society," *The Atlantic Monthly* 39 (June 1877): 675. On gossip and workingclass women's culture, see Melanie Tebbutt, "Women's Talk? Gossip and 'Women's Words' in Working Class Communities, 1880–1939," in *Workers' Worlds: Cultures and Communities in Manchester and Salford, 1880–1939*, ed. Andrew Davies and Steven Fielding (Manchester, UK: Manchester University Press, 1992), pp. 49–73. White women employers tried to combat the problem of gossip through organizations established to find solutions to the "servant question" generally. The Domestic Efficiency Association movement served this purpose. On the Domestic Efficiency Association and kindred organizations, see the Epilogue.

[58] White women did not object, however, when black women gossiped to them about the lives of black people. (See, for example, Eliza Frances Andrews, *The War-Time Journal of a Georgia Girl, 1864–1865*, ed. Spencer Bidwell King, Jr. [Macon, GA: Ardivan Press, 1966], p. 320). For two excellent examinations of the power of gossip and the work it does in making homes witnessed, see Carolyn Steedman, *Landscape for a Good Woman: A Story of Two Lives* (New Brunswick, NJ: Rutgers University Press, 1987), and Elizabeth Madox Roberts, *The Time of Man* (1926; reprint, New York: Viking Press, 1963), pp. 150–51. See also the Introduction and Chapter 7.

[59] Margaret Stockman Dickson, *Vocational Guidance for Girls* (Chicago: Rand McNally & Co., 1919); David M. Katzman, *Seven Days a Week: Women and Domestic Service in Industrializing America* (New York: Oxford University Press, 1978); Judith Rollins, *Between Women: Domestics and their Employers* (Philadelphia: Temple University Press, 1985); Elizabeth Clark-Lewis, *Living In, Living Out: African American Domestics in Washington, D.C., 1910–1940* (Washington, DC: Smithsonian Institution Press, 1994); Susan Tucker, *Telling Memories: Domestic Workers and their Employers in the Segregated South* (New York: Schocken Books, 1988); Hunter, *To 'Joy My Freedom*.

domestic work. One of the most important was a gradual systematization of pay rates for domestic labor. Another was the systematization of tasked work.

Like all of her encounters with free labor, Gertrude Thomas's experience with domestic task-work ended badly. In the spring of 1865, she hired a washer, agreeing to pay her thirty cents a day, admitting that she "had no idea what was considered a task in washing." Still, she made the effort to sort her wash into what she thought was a day's work or washing task. Her sense of the matter led her to make her children's clothes a priority and to exclude some of the laundry – the bigger pieces like tablecloths, sheets, and counterpanes. Her instincts were based on her experience as a mistress, but she learned that these were poor measures at best. The shock came when she discovered that the woman she hired had completed the work by noon. Thinking herself cheated, Thomas tried to add additional clothes to the task but the washer waved her off. Perhaps not wanting to offend, she muted her objection, saying simply that she was tired. In the end, Thomas got a few additional items washed but only by threatening to withhold the woman's pay. She had no intention, Thomas told the woman, to engage "a woman to wash for me by the day and she stops by dinner time, if you suppose I intend paying for the days (sic) work you are very much mistaken."[60] With this declaration, Thomas confirmed her ignorance about a day's work. After all, it was she who had sorted the laundry according to what she thought was a day's work.

The disjuncture between the light from the past that guided former mistresses and that which guided black women appeared to both groups as a gaping hole. It explains why Thomas could complain about the work of a washer who, in fact, had worked steadily through the morning. Thomas had no quarrel with the quality of her work. A problem arose only when she discovered that the job could be done in less time than she thought it would take, or in less time than she was accustomed to having it done by enslaved women. It irked her that she had miscalculated and underestimated, and while there was still more washing that needed to be done. Even though, in the end, Thomas got more of the wash done, she did so at a cost. She got the extra laundry washed for no extra money, but she lost a washer. The woman she coerced into doing extra work for free did not return.

Thomas's predicament was not unique. Most former mistresses had little idea how much time it took to do a week's laundry or clean a room. Esther Palmer also made this discovery and also to her embarrassment. Fearing that she was about to lose Lucy, a valued washer, who informed her that "she could not do all the washing alone," as "it would break her down," Palmer agreed to hire someone to assist Lucy two days a week. She suspected, however, that Lucy's complaint was a ploy, a cover for Lucy's desire to quit the job entirely. Lucy

[60] Burr, ed., *The Secret Eye*, May 27, 1865, p. 272; see also Nell Irvin Painter, "The Journal of Ella Gertrude Thomas: An Educated White Woman in the Eras of Slavery, War, and Reconstruction," in *The Secret Eye*, ed. Burr, pp. 51–52.

found an assistant – even at the lowly rate of a peck of corn for the two days' work Palmer offered – but Palmer discovered that she had nonetheless been outwitted, though not in the way she had anticipated. It turned out, to her chagrin, that Lucy had not only saved her back but with the help of an assistant was able to finish the job in much less time. "She brings the clothes in Thursday evening," Palmer complained, "and has Friday and Saturday for herself, which I think is not right. She ought to employ someone herself if she wants two days."[61] By Palmer's calculations, her wash should occupy Lucy, even with help, six days a week, which doubtless made little sense to Lucy.

Negotiations between employers and women hired as cooks revealed similar disagreements. As mistresses, white women had taken delight in being shooed out of the kitchen by black women and taken it as evidence of their superiority. Had they stayed, they might have been better prepared to make the transition to a wage economy.[62] With fewer servants available, the resources to pay them scarcer still, and irreconcilable notions about the meaning of freedom, clashes between women employers and their employees were inevitable. Former mistresses were accustomed to having servants on demand, even if it meant having several on demand at once, which always left some standing by. Given their unfamiliarity with hiring and managing free labor, and their resistance to the implications of free labor ideology for household labor, the most basic requirements of mobilizing and managing a free labor force appeared unintelligible, inconvenient, and even sinister.

Bargaining with free black women was different from bargaining with slave women. Just as importantly, it felt different. Even when a mistress gave in to the refusal of a slave cook to making beds, she could still keep calm in the knowledge that the woman remained her slave. Not so, however, if the same woman made the same refusal after slavery was over. "It seems humiliating," Eliza Andrews wrote, "to be compelled to bargain and haggle with our own former servants about wages."[63] But her only choice was to do the work herself. She might attempt to leverage the old terms of power, and the mandatory courtesies that came with them, but that strategy often led to disappointment, with the rebuff sometimes emerging from unexpected places. Gertrude Thomas learned this lesson over and over again, though apparently the lessons seemed never to quite take. Milly, her daughter's nurse, sneered at Thomas' offer to pay her in old clothing and a silver quarter every Saturday night, then left without a word.[64]

[61] Esther Simon Palmer to Elizabeth P. Porcher, March 11, 1866, in *World Turned Upside Down*, ed. Towles, p. 503; Marli F. Weiner, *A Heritage of Woe: The Civil War Diary of Grace Brown Elmore, 1861–1868* (Athens: University of Georgia Press, 1997), p. 121.

[62] On the kitchen as a contested site, see Mary Titus, "The Dining Room Door Swings Both Ways: Food, Race, and Domestic Space in the Nineteenth-Century South," in *Haunted Bodies: Gender and Southern Texts*, ed. Anne Goodwyn Jones and Susan V. Donaldson (Charlottesville: University Press of Virginia, 1997), pp. 245–47.

[63] Andrews, *War-Time Journal of a Georgia Girl*, p. 319.

[64] Burr, ed., *The Secret Eye*, May 27, 1865, p. 271.

Desperate to hire help, Thomas was thankful when Leah, an elderly black woman with cooking experience, applied for the position. Yet, with so many white women having trouble finding and keeping a staff, Thomas had to wonder how she could be so favored as to have someone actually apply for the job. She was curious enough to ask Leah to account for her availability. Whether she was convinced by Leah's explanation is not clear – Leah said that she had been dismissed by her former mistress to find her own employment – but it suited Thomas just fine. She now had a fine cook regardless of the reason for her availability. She hired Leah immediately and marveled at her good fortune when she was treated to the best biscuits and plum pies she had ever tasted. Thomas's husband, however, was more skeptical of Leah's story, suspecting that she had simply walked away from her former owners because she wanted to. Before he would sanction his wife's decision to hire Leah, he demanded that she secure a note from her previous owners confirming her account of the matter. But Leah, a free woman, was finished with passes. She left promising to get the note but did not return. "I told Mr Thomas," Gertrude Thomas wrote, "that I did not know but what we are fighting shadows." In demanding that Leah, in effect, produce "free papers," Thomas realized that they had "sacrificed a good deal to principle." They had "lost an opportunity to get an excellent cook at $5 per month," and she doubted that Leah's former owners would benefit from their standing on principle, such as it was.[65]

Leah, on the other hand, lost a job but experienced some of the fullness of freedom's promise. Believing that as a free person she had the right to seek work without the "permission" of her former owners, she acted in conformity to the principles of northern free labor ideology. In accordance with a now routine policy, some employers required potential employees to provide references from former employers. Character, reliability, temper, and the like, mattered as much as qualifications for the specific job in these references. In the pre-modern and the industrial world of the late nineteenth century, letters of introduction had analogous functions among the elite, but common or casual laborers were not yet required to provide job references as they moved from one unskilled position to the next. This development came early to former slaves. It could not, however, even begin to approach its meaning elsewhere.

In the early twentieth century, employers of domestic labor sought to arrest black women's mobility by creating such organizations as the Domestic Efficiency Association. Members agreed to only hire women who could give evidence of having given a week's notice to their previous employer, to require "a full reference." They were encouraged not to "tempt" servants from each other by, for example, offering higher wages. They were also instructed on how to handle the problem of gossip.[66]

---

[65] Burr, ed., *The Secret Eye*, May 29, 1865, p. 273.

[66] This now common process has important roots in domestic labor. Important precursors to the system that evolved in the United States were the networks of patronage and recommendations used by Englishwomen at least as early as the eighteenth century.

Former slaves resisted the notion that they should have the approval of former slaveholders to seek employment with someone else. The collusion of mistresses in the effort to control the market in domestic labor, and to protect themselves from each other's avarice, had the similar effect of hindering mobility. Agreements between mistresses not to hire each other's former slaves or particular black people could fall apart in the face of the competition for domestic servants. As a practical matter, they were problematic. Still, they doubtless had some effect. Such tactics may have influenced some former slaves to explain their availability for employment, for example, as Leah did. On the same day that Leah sought employment with Gertrude Thomas, Thomas hired a woman as temporary help to wash and iron. The woman represented herself as the former slave of a master whose plantation was destroyed by General W. T. Sherman. As a result, she said, her master had instructed some of his former slaves to find whatever work they could until a crop was planted. (Such strategies, of course, allowed planters to rid themselves of the problem of feeding extra hands during the less labor intensive seasons.) Thomas, however, did not believe the woman's account as her husband had not believed Leah's. She may have been right. Perhaps the woman understood that her best strategy was to give the impression that her mobility and unemployment had been forced upon her, and was not the independence that employers dreaded and despised.

But, already by the fall of 1865, and in spite of employers' resistance, the regularization of rates for the various components of domestic work, such as piece and tasking rates for washing, had begun to take shape. The development signaled both the movement by black women out of live-in arrangements and the dynamism of labor negotiations over workload and compensation. Left with only one elderly servant in her home by October 1865, Elizabeth Porcher was forced to put out her washing. She discovered that this was not as simple a matter as it appeared. First, Porcher learned that she would have to pay market rates. The going rate in her neighborhood was $1.25 for six dozen pieces. In addition, she would be responsible for supplying the wood, soap, and starch. It was an early sign of the extent of labor organizing among black women to set rates for the hire of their labor and to diminish the overall rate at which they could be exploited. Porcher was appalled at what she considered an excessively high rate, but the option of doing the laundry herself was even more unattractive.[67]

The dilemma Porcher faced points to another important development initiated by black women, the separation of washing into discrete tasks with associated costs that thereby reduced the overhead costs to black women and the number of hours the job entailed. The business of washing required soap, starch (and the ingredients to make them), water, and wood for the fires to heat the water. Like Porcher, other employers were increasingly asked to furnish the

[67] Elizabeth P. Porcher to Hattie [Harriet R. Palmer], October 25, 1865, in *World Turned Upside Down*, ed. Towles, p. 488.

wood, soap, and starch, and to pay for the labor required to get the water from springs or wells to the wash pots.[68] As mistresses, white women had taken pride in holding the keys to storage rooms to prevent the theft of household supplies like soap. In an ironic twist, they now found themselves, as employers, still measuring out starch and soap. Only now they did so at the behest of their former slaves.[69]

Such transformations highlighted the difference between slave labor and free labor and the expectations black women carried into freedom. Like field hands, household slaves had tasked their work, even if less formally, and even where their mistresses were unaware. The pattern was most evident, of course, on large plantations where household work was extremely specialized, but the evidence indicates that even on small holdings, slave women had come to a similar reckoning about their labor. As slaves, black women had no incentive to do in four hours what they could get by with doing in eight. Freedom and a wage changed that.

Propositions to Hire Themselves

Although reconstruction of the plantation household's domestic center directly involved only a minority of former slaves, it had immediate and long-term significance for the resolution of larger questions of political and social change. The same issues and concerns that drove former slaves to demand changes in the organization of agricultural labor resonated with domestic workers. A. B. Jones, manager of the Cameron plantation in Alabama, rejoiced that no major disturbance had surfaced during the Christmas season of 1865 but still worried because people on his plantation had shown no inclination to sign a contract for the coming year. "They all expect," he wrote, "that the Yankees will do something for them, that will materially better their condition – Christmas was the time at which they thought this revelation was to be made to them – having been disappointed in this, they begin to talk more rationally, & in a few days from this time they will I think have all made their contracts & go steadily to work." The Camerons found that the expectation of better conditions was not confined to field hands. The Camerons had only one servant in mid-October 1865. "My wife will I fear not hold out very much longer under such domestic trials – she is very much changed in her life & labor," Paul C. Cameron wrote.[70] Their domestic servants were holding out, intent upon securing better terms. At the end of December 1865, they presented "propositions to hire themselves for another year."[71] Demands by domestic workers for written contracts became

---

[68] Although this question requires additional research, the effort of freedwomen to separate the tasks of washing, making soap, and carrying water for the wash, in particular, probably also drew on work patterns established during slavery. The use of children to carry water from springs or wells is well-documented. For example, see Chapter 6.

[69] Burr, ed., *The Secret Eye*, December 5, 1870, pp. 344–45.

[70] Paul C. Cameron to [?], October 11, 1865, Cameron Papers, SHC.

[71] A. B. Jones to Paul C. Cameron, December 30, 1865, Cameron Papers, SHC.

increasingly common. In August 1865, Mary Jones noted that she had "made a written contract with Flora to remain with me until the end of the year," and other white women she knew had done the same.[72]

Frustrated by their experience with tasked domestic work and with mothers who removed their children from white homes or demanded that they be paid if they worked, some white women thought they might try to circumvent the power of freedwomen by ridding themselves of the need to rely on them at all. Desperate for help, some former mistresses and young white women establishing households for the first time placed their hope in the ranks of workingclass white women, though this ultimately proved illusory.[73] Gertrude Thomas scouted the Irish neighborhood of Dublin in Augusta, Georgia, for a white woman to cook for her. She also turned to the local orphans' asylum to secure a female white child. The beauty of it lay in the child's orphan status: She would "have no outside influence exerted upon her" by a mother or father.[74] By this time, all but two of Thomas's former house slaves had departed; only Patsey and Frank, a small boy remained. Servants she had secured on loan from relatives or hired had gone as well, leaving her to wipe her own breakfast dishes, perform other household chores, and to try her luck again in the open market, this time in hopes of hiring an ironer.[75]

In North Carolina, the Cameron family had apparently been unable to come to terms with the women holding out for a contract.[76] Depressed by their failure to find a cook to hire, the Camerons were momentarily seduced by the fantasy of white servants in the hope of having "a more settled order of things, in household matters." "I think it likely," Paul Cameron wrote to his sister in Raleigh, "that by Monday night we shall not have a servant on our lot with the exception of Ann King, who has spent the last three days in bed." He appealed to his sister, "Do you know of a pretty cook to be had!"[77]

Ironically, the disorder that continued to plague the Cameron household was attributable in part to Ann King, a white servant, who apparently left shortly after spending those three days in bed. In January 1866, the Camerons tried to woo her back from Raleigh, where she had taken employment at a hotel. But King's bargaining position, like that of black women, had improved with emancipation. She sent word that she was willing to return under certain conditions, "upon the same terms but she could not do as much as she did

---

[72] Mary Jones to Charles C. Jones, Jr., August 18, 1865 in *Children of Pride*, ed. Myers, p. 1291; Noralee Frankel, *Freedom's Women: Black Women and Families in Civil War Era Mississippi* (Bloomington: Indiana University Press, 1999), p. 62.

[73] Charles Manigault to Louis Manigault, April 30, 1865, in *Life and Labor*, ed. Clifton, p. 353. See also Jane Turner Censer, *The Reconstruction of White Southern Womanhood, 1865–1895* (Baton Rouge: Louisiana State University Press, 2003), pp. 69–71.

[74] Burr, ed., *The Secret Eye*, May 27, 1865, pp. 271–73; quote is at p. 272. Thomas makes no further reference to the child. It is possible that the arrangement did not work out or that the child was claimed by her stepmother. Hunter, *To 'Joy My Freedom*, pp. 36–37.

[75] Burr, ed., *The Secret Eye*, May 29, 1865, pp. 272–74.

[76] Paul C. Cameron to [?], October 11, 1865, Cameron Papers, SHC.

[77] Paul C. Cameron to Mrs. M. B. Mordecai, December 22, 1865, Cameron Papers, SHC.

before." Her pay would stay the same. The Camerons responded immediately, accepting her "proposition to take charge of the dining room & basement," and have "all the washing up & fixing of lamps &c . . . under her charge." They agreed that she would "have nothing to do with the parlor." Then they did not hear from her. Even though King had been less than an ideal servant, and even though the terms she set called for a significant reduction in her overall responsibilities, the Camerons engaged relatives in Raleigh to find her "and find out whether she is coming." In the meantime, the one black servant who remained had apparently decided that she, alone, could not and should not do the work of several people. Rebecca Cameron described her as "so very inefficient that the housework devolves almost entirely on us." Yet, as despairing as they were, the Camerons wished to avoid giving King the impression that they were "too anxious for her return."[78]

In Raleigh, Paul Cameron's brother-in-law, George W. Mordecai, tracked down King and delivered Cameron's message. King's position was unchanged. "She says she is willing to return to Hillsboro for the same wages," Mordecai wrote, "but with the understanding that she is only to attend to the dining room & superintend the cooking & shall not be required to clean up any other part of the house." Mordecai was not optimistic. Despite what she said, he did not think she was "very anxious to go back." He was willing to speak to her again, he wrote, but thought the Camerons should forget about her and move on. Indeed, Mordecai's own personal experience led him to conclude that white domestic servants were not the answer. "These girls are not much more reliable than the darkies," he wrote, "our girl has been sick & absent herself nearly all this week & is still absent."[79]

The use of white women as domestic servants in the homes of other white women contravened and compromised southern racial ideology as Ann King doubtless reasoned. While she might be poor, working as a hotel maid must have seemed preferable to working as the house maid of other white people, especially at tasks deemed fit only for black women. This reasoning is evident in her insistence that she would not cook or clean *any* part of the house. Even in the parlor, her responsibility would only be to "superintend" the cleaning. Yet, despite the compromises to racial ideology that the employment of white women as domestic servants in the South entailed, former slaveholders were ready to risk them. Whatever the cost to ideology or purse, the risk seemed worthwhile if it meant that they could get domestic help that would not run away or talk back. It would take many more lessons in class, labor, and race relations, however, for them to realize that the human beasts of burden they sought did not exist.

A Florida man boasted that he and his wife had taken "a girl about 18 as ignorant and poor as any cornfield negro, but respectable and willing to do any work to support herself and mother and 6 children," and had transformed

---

[78] [Rebecca Cameron] to Mrs. George W. Mordecai, January 23, 1866, Cameron Papers, SHC.
[79] George W. Mordecai to [Paul C. Cameron], January 27, 1866, Cameron Papers, SHC.

her into a servant "much better than any negro." His boast said more about the woman's dire poverty than her willingness to work for them.[80] Generally, white women domestic servants demanded better beds and clothing than were typically given to black women, along with other accommodations and amenities. Amelia Lines rejected the opportunity to secure a white servant because she would have to "fix up a bed for a white girl" and spend more on clothing. Besides, former slaveholders found that white servants resented and rejected the expected display of "familial" intimacies. Grace Elmore was confident that a white servant would never exhibit the "tender affection" expected of black women. When she at last hired an Irish woman, she called the experience "a sore trial," and eventually fired the woman for refusing to clear cob webs from the hallway.[81] A yeoman woman who apprenticed her daughter to a former mistress removed the child upon learning that the employer had renamed her, as one would a slave, and dressed her in homespun (while attiring her own children in calico), a fabric with distinctly racial and servile connotations.[82]

As early as 1865, Tryphena Fox had talked about trying to find white servants – "a white man with a wife & no children who will come & live with us & do the work – some Irishman or Dutchman." Two years later, she managed to hire an English couple, but they, too, proved unwilling to meet her demands.[83] She kept trying. In 1868, despite her disappointing experience with the English couple, she talked of placing an advertisement in a New Orleans newspaper for a white servant woman. She would come to conclude, like George Mordecai, that white servants were no "more reliable than the darkies."[84]

Efforts to mobilize poor white women for domestic service also had to overcome poor white women's resentment of elite women. At Laurel Hill plantation in South Carolina, as the war wound to a close, poor white women stripped the place of cotton, corn, and fodder. Harriet R. Palmer learned as well that "some of the [poor white] women [were] saying before the negroes that they were very glad now we would have to cook and wash pots. Also that we would often pass them on the road riding in our carriages and would not even speak to them. Now they were equal to us."[85] It is significant that these poor white women chose to make their declaration before an audience of black people, people they could be assured their judgment of southern elite women.

[80] Litwack, *Been in the Storm So Long*, pp. 351–54, quote at p. 351.
[81] [Amelia Lines to Anna Maria Akehurst], December 2, 1862, in Lines, *To Raise Myself a Little*, p. 193; Grace Elmore Diary, December 9, 1861; [Summer] 1865, SHC.
[82] Fox-Genovese, *Within the Plantation Household*, p. 224.
[83] King, ed., *A Northern Woman*, undated letter enclosed with September 10, 1865; Feb. 10, [1870], pp. 158 and 241, quote at p. 158.
[84] King, ed., *A Northern Woman*, October 9, 1868, p. 228.
[85] Harriet R. Palmer Journal, March 12, 1865, in *World Turned Upside Down*, ed. Towles, p. 440.

In the end, some white households found short-term relief, but the effort to find white women who would work like slaves in the homes of other white women failed as signally as the parallel attempt by planters to replace black field hands with white and Asian immigrant workers after the war. Poor white women with their own politics showed no more enthusiasm than black women for domestic labor in the homes of the southern white elite.

For the most part, former mistresses continued to place their faith in black women. Taking a page from antebellum strategies, they sometimes returned to the language of paternalism – avoiding the language of resistance or labor organizing – to explain black women's demands for change in household labor, especially in the back-breaking labor of washing. To former mistresses, freed-women's complaints about the heavy labor that washing required smacked only of insolence. Where they did not just quit, black women resorted to various strategies to force changes, some of longstanding utility. Accompanying her former mistress, Alice Palmer, on a visit to Palmer's parents, Hagar finally extricated herself from doing the wash by doing it poorly.

On Monday when I gave her the clothes and told her to go and wash with Maum Liddie, she said she was not strong enough to do my washing. . . . I asked her what had I brought her for. I told her before I left home that she was to do my washing and wait on me. Said she could bring water and help fix the rooms but she could not do my washing because she did not have the strength. She pretends she can't even help to throw the mattress off to beat up the feather bed. She is positively not worth the corn she eats. Would have been better off if I had come without a servant for she is only a bother to me. I often feel like giving her a switching.[86]

Alice Palmer finally gave up. "I have sent Hagar back," she wrote. "She is of little use to me. All she does is clean out my room. She has been here a month and can't or won't wash even a towel fit to look at." Hagar, a child, was now free to rejoin her mother and besides, perhaps not to have to subsist on a diet of corn.[87]

No matter what form it took, black women's resistance to white women's efforts to reconstruct the plantation household on its antebellum model was invariably termed "impudence" or "insolence." Much of it was probably just that, as in Marianne's response to her employer's request to fetch a towel. "You can go and bring it yourself." Her employer slapped her for saying so, but Marianne was free, so she quit.[88] Freedom included the right to simply ignore white women, as Alice Palmer observed. "Have you ever noticed," she wrote,

[86] Alice G. Palmer to Harriet R. Palmer, July 20, 1865, in *World Turned Upside Down*, ed. Towles, pp. 479–80.

[87] Alice G. Palmer to Harriet R. Palmer, August 7, 1865 in *World Turned Upside Down*, ed. Towles, p. 484. The letters of Tryphena Fox document conflict over the job of washing. Like most white women, Fox relented and put her wash out. Only on one occasion during the period from 1865 to 1868 did she find someone to work as an all-purpose maid, to do her wash, and cook and clean (King, ed., *A Northern Woman*, pp. 145, 174, 207, 227, 230, and 238).

[88] Alice G. Palmer to Harriet R. Palmer, August 2, 1865, in *World Turned Upside Down*, ed. Towles, p. 483.

"with the negroes at home that when you call they will never answer. Everybody up here finds it a sign of their freedom. Heard one of them say, 'My Mis don't like it because I won't answer, but I ain't got no call to answer now.'"[89] Former slaveholders continued to use such responses to support the argument that black people were uncivilized, and the inscriptions of white female purity that traveled with it. The "careless dirty ways & impudent replies" of black women continued to serve as ideological counterpoints to white "ladies," as evidence, white women insisted, of the work they continued to undertake to train uncivilized black women.[90] Re-inscriptions of white female purity highlighted white women's racism: White women declared black women uncivilized for refusing to do the kind of work they themselves found objectionable and so tried their best to avoid doing.

"Paternalism," E. P. Thompson writes, "is nearly always backward looking."[91] The tight market for household help did not dissuade former mistresses from their mission to find the kind of black servant they imagined they had once owned. They wanted a "good one," a black woman who would stand in awe of them, and wash, cook, and clean for them with a smile and a grateful attitude, a black woman who would understand that black women were best constituted for the kind of work they were expected to do. It was not, Tryphena Fox maintained disingenuously, that white women like her were lazy. Rather, they suffered a constitutional "inability" to do back-breaking labor. They were too fragile. After cooking breakfast and making two beds, she was "completely tired out." "It is of no use trying to look like a lady when you are doing work in a *nigger* kitchen."[92] For a brief moment, Fox's life was repaired. Her maid, Milly, who had been out ill returned and everything was again "straight & nice." Fox could now go "up in my little sitting-room (where I belong, I'm thinking) looking & feeling quite decent." Her pleasure was increased with a new addition to her domestic staff, a twelve-year-old black girl apprenticed to her husband for five years and to whom, therefore, they did not have to pay wages. It was, as always, a brief respite. Fox would soon be hoping to "live some day where either one can control or command labor, or where it is the fashion for ladies to do their own work." She perhaps had in mind her native New England, where her indigent mother took in boarders and her sister worked for a living, first at the Berkshire Hotel and then the Pontoosuc Mill.[93]

The transformation of the plantation household speeded up in the years between 1866 and 1870 as freedwomen who had stayed put in 1865 moved on. Yet white women seemed to have learned little. Many responded as they had at freedom's first arrival – with a sense of betrayal. They continued to

---

[89] Alice G. Palmer to Harriet R. Palmer, September 19, 1865, in *World Turned Upside Down*, ed. Towles, p. 485.

[90] King, ed., *A Northern Woman*, [October 1866], p. 201.

[91] Thompson, *Customs in Common*, p. 23.

[92] King, ed., *A Northern Woman*, October 3, 1866, p. 200.

[93] King, ed., *A Northern Woman*, [October 1866], October 2, 1868, pp. 201, 227. On her family's plight, see pp. 153, 197, and 217–18.

study subtle and not-so-subtle changes in the "countenance" of black women for signs of their intentions. They still refused to recognize the claims of black women to personal freedom or to family ties, or to understand that the needs of white families were not their primary concern. Naturally, therefore, in the eyes of former mistresses, the reasons black women gave for leaving lacked even the bedrock of plausibility to which judgments of truth and falsehood are secondary. It is no wonder that many women simply left, giving no reason at all.

When Kate gave Mary Jones notice of her intent to quit, saying she was going to start a new life with her husband, Jones tried to persuade her to stay. Jones seemed incapable of treating Kate's notice as a normal aspect of employer – employee relations. She could frame her reference to it only in the language of paternalism. It was the same device she had resorted to when her field hands called a work stoppage, citing their dissatisfaction with the contract they had signed. Jones informed them that she considered the "outbreak" a great personal insult, for she "had considered them friends and treated them as such, giving them gallons of clabber every week and syrup once a week, with rice and extra dinners; but that now they were only laborers under contract, and only the law would rule between us."[94] The freedpeople responded to her interpretation of their relationship, and its material basis, by leaving.

Like most former mistresses, Jones never mastered the legalistic pose of a disinterested employer. Instead, she ridiculed the decision of black women to quit working for her. "Cook Kate," she wrote, "wants to be relieved of the heavy burden of cooking for two and wait on her husband. Lucy sighs and groans." She made light of Sue's "pretensions" and regarded with contempt the aspirations of other women she had once owned. To her daughter Mary, she wrote: "I heard an amusing conversation between Cook Kate and [Flora]! They are looking forward to gold watches and chains, bracelets, and *blue veils* and silk dresses!"[95] In fact, Jones was not amused. Neither were her contemporaries.

From the perspective of white women, the idea of black women dressing up like white women could only seem ridiculous. Kate Stone probably did not think twice when she commented: "I never saw a woman before without a ribbon."[96] Stone was referring in particular to her revulsion at the physical appearance and living conditions of the poor white people she encountered as a refugee in Texas. Still, the comment is revealing as much for its racism as for its class bias. In the end, the mocking words of white women were intended to help brace the crumbling ideology of white womanhood. But that laughter at black women's expense subsided, for in freedom black women were determined to

[94] Mary Jones to Mary Mallard, January 2, 1867, in *Children of Pride*, ed. Myers, p. 1365; for quoted passage, see Mary Jones to Charles C. Jones, Jr., May 28, 1866, p. 1341.

[95] Mary Jones to Mary S. Mallard, November 17, 1865, in *Children of Pride*, ed. Myers, p. 1308.

[96] Kate Stone, *Brokenburn: The Journal of Kate Stone, 1861–1881*, ed. John Q. Anderson (Baton Rouge: Louisiana State University Press, 1972), p. 359.

answer only to themselves, and to celebrate the world of women turned upside down. The Rev. John Jones, trying to convince a former slave to remain, blamed the man's refusal on "his stupid wife," who would "not listen to any counsel on the subject." Jones counseled his half-sister, Mary, that any who left should not be allowed to return "unless they gave unmistakable evidence of repentance."[97] Repentance, he said, a word foreign to the vocabulary of a free labor economy.[98]

The brief experience of the former slave Peggy is instructive. Peggy left her former owners in August 1866, hired out her sons and "tried to live to herself." By early November 1866, she was dead of consumption. Louisa Robarts, her former mistress, paid the burial cost, complaining (or perhaps bragging) all the while. She took two of Peggy's sons back to her home while two remained hired out. Robarts could not, however, bring herself to commend Peggy's effort at independence, at establishing a life of her own. To Robarts, the situation had concluded as expected, in failure.[99] The record does not detail what Peggy's life was like in the short time she lived "to herself" surrounded by her four sons, but it was the only period of her life that she lived as a free person. That must have counted as something for which she felt no need to repent.

Former mistresses resisted black women's efforts to teach them that they could and should learn to take care of their own homes and lives, and that doing so would make them better human beings. In the spring of 1865, Lizzie Jones's husband was still in the army while she was mired in poverty and virtually deserted by her kin. "I would be distressed," she wrote to a cousin she had asked for help, "to think my dear cousin was deprived of any of her comforts in her helpless condition.... I sometimes think perhaps some of my relatives would not care about owning the connection if they could see how I am living now, in a little log cabin on the side of the main road only one room and no window in it." Yet, even in the poverty of living in a windowless, one-room log cabin, Jones was still trying to hold on to her servants. They, too, eventually deserted her.[100]

Although black and white women chose different paths, those paths only led them back to each other, to a single road. On that road, they renewed their struggle, white women to reclaim black women's labor and their former privileges; and black women, to claim their freedom. "It seems strange that we can journey now where we please," wrote Kate Stone in late May 1865.[101] There was a certain irony in this observation, and a new reality that she may

---

[97] Rev. John Jones to Mary Jones, October 31, 1865, in *Children of Pride*, ed. Myers, pp. 1302–3.

[98] On the transition to a free labor economy, see, among others, Eric Foner, *Reconstruction*, pp. 77–175, and Harold D. Woodman, "The Reconstruction of the Cotton Plantation in the New South," in *Essays on the Postbellum Southern Economy*, ed. Thavolia Glymph and John J. Kushma (College Station: Texas A&M University Press, 1985), pp. 95–119.

[99] Louisa J. Roberts to Mary Jones, November 28, 1866, in *Children of Pride*, ed. Myers, p. 1361.

[100] Lizzie [Jones] to [Mildred Mordecai], March 6, 1865, Cameron Papers, SHC.

[101] Stone, *Brokenburn*, May 27, 1865, p. 347.

have perceived only subconsciously. Stone had in mind the end to wartime hostilities that had made travel for white women dangerous, limiting their mobility. But the end of the Civil War held the promise that the limits on black women's mobility would fall away, so that they, too, could journey where they pleased.

Black people, no matter their gender, fought efforts to reestablish white supremacy. They fought individually and collectively, as families and as communities, and the efforts of black men and women were joined. If it is nevertheless worth investigating the particular part endured and played by women, the reason is plain enough. In the arrangements former masters and mistresses hoped for in the postwar world, the subjugation of black women – as workers and as women – was as important as the defeat of black men's political rights. In leaving white homes and in demanding reduced hours and a reorganization of household work, black women accomplished part of the interconnected work of claiming their freedom and, in consequence, reconstructing notions of southern womanhood. They forced white women to take on previously unthinkable tasks, and to re-think their place in southern society. Some white women managed a semblance of the former dispensation, and some did not. In late 1865, A. Beaufort Sims could exult in the fact that her family still had servants when so many of her friends were "doing their own work." She had no plans and no desire to join this latest "attempt for independence."[102] Ann Pope, on the other hand, had no choice. "I live in dirt, eat and sleep in it," she wrote. Mary Jones hoped that freedom would lead to the extermination of black people if she could not have them at her disposal when she wished. Ann Pope had her own genocidal fantasy: "I want the power of annihilation," she wrote.[103] In the coming years, these fantasies receded, but others remained.

---

[102] A. Beaufort Sims to Harriet R. Palmer, November 3, 1865, in *World Turned Upside Down*, ed. Towles, p. 490.

[103] Ann J. Pope to Rosa Biddle, 1865, Samuel Simpson Biddle Papers, DU.

6

"A Makeshift Kind of Life"

Free Women and Free Homes

I think I was very foolish last month to make up beds and wash soiled dishes. I began seriously to think that it was in very bad taste to have three meals in one day and wondered at the rapidity with which my homely but necessary duties followed each other and if I had dessert, or the plates were changed, seriously considered the subject in a new light, as so many more dishes to wash.

Gertrude Thomas, employer

Celestine *left suddenly* taking Rosella with her without any provocation from me or *notification* to me.

Tryphena Fox, employer

Mrs. Wms has engaged Anna for a cook.... She used to be about us when we lived at Gravel Hill and was a very good woman, but they have all changed so she may not be worth much now.

Sarah Palmer Williams, employer

Cretia is the comfort – animal comfort – of my every day life.

Mary Pringle, employer

"I have such a nice servant in Katy," Elizabeth Porcher wrote to her sister in 1866. "She is a nice washer and a good cook and has a little girl of Annie's size who helps a good deal and I am to give her $8. I really hope I am at last comfortably fixed. I never have to show her anything hardly and she is so humble and civil."[1] In the coming years, Porcher would see that prospect dissipate bit by bit. She would see her share of poverty and servants not so "nice" or "humble." The labor troubles of 1865–66 marked a beginning, not an end, to strife within the plantation household. Over the coming decades, the plantation household would be thoroughly transformed. Elizabeth Porcher's

---

[1] Elizabeth Porcher Palmer to Harriett R. Palmer, August 6, 1866, in *A World Turned Upside Down: The Palmers of South Santee, 1818–1881*, ed. Louis P. Towles (Columbia: University of South Carolina Press, 1996), p. 528.

experience exemplifies that transformation. Although economic problems and political turmoil certainly were influential, the resistance of black women to a restoration of the plantation household's prewar labor relations played a notable role in its postwar reconstitution.

From 1866 through the 1880s, tasked work remained a visible hallmark of the strategies black women employed to institute free labor relations in domestic employment. This chapter explores the connections between tasked work, black and white women's part-time employment, and their efforts to build free homes. Taking on jobs by the task and working part-time as day or casual labor allowed household servants precious time for their own domestic production and moved white women employers toward a new order in labor relations in the domestic sphere. For a time, the pedestal of white womanhood was cracked. Former mistresses worked, and black women suffered far less violence than previously.[2]

Part-time and tasked domestic work gave black women the flexibility to live larger lives. They could decide to devote a part of their labor to their families' crops, to work at home for themselves and their families, or simply to have more time to themselves. Their struggle to put planter homes and planter women on free ground and to build their own free homes and lives widened after the first year of freedom. Freedwomen continued to give priority to securing the right to manage their own time and to establish fair rates for their labor. In the process, they forced former mistresses to accommodations that were previously unimaginable. None of the new arrangements appeared magically or inevitably. Women who left plantation households had reasons enough, but, for most, there was hardly any clarity about what shape the future would take. When Leah appeared on Thomas's doorstep to apply for a job as cook, she took as big a step into the unknown as Thomas did in advertising the position. Women with children would have been deeply torn, not knowing how they would feed or house them with or without the help of a husband. Still, it must have been tremendously liberating to leave without saying goodbye, to leave ironing that needed to be done and meals uncooked, to walk away in a mistress's gown, to confiscate her bed, or to return for one's child or property in the company of U.S. soldiers. None of these things, however, could in and of themselves translate into a free home or life with its own security, autonomy, and privacy. This, black women would have thought about in the midst of savoring the liberating moments of freedom.

Regardless of the place or circumstance in which freedwomen found themselves, the practical work of figuring out what they must do to have the kind of life they thought freedom promised took time, and was worked out by trial and error. How many wash jobs would it take to put food on the table, buy a setting hen, or a new dress? How many days' work in someone else's kitchen? How would small children be cared for when parents worked? How much family labor was required to make a bale of cotton? Other matters seemed

---

[2] That violence would never resurface at the prewar level, and much of what did was transferred to the hands of white men.

straightforward enough. Freedom meant being able to visit extended family and friends without a pass, to attend parties and spend time with lovers without having to sneak away. It meant privacy in the home.

For women who worked in the plantation household, part-time and task work offered the greatest possibility for living freer lives, and they were forms of labor with which black women were familiar. From the outset, therefore, black women favored part-time and task work for the flexibility they offered. Still, it was clear that any hope for any semblance of financial independence lay in the fields that their labor had enriched during slavery. Domestic workers saw this as clearly as field hands. For domestic servants, an additional advantage to field labor was in its physical distance from white homes. When they could choose, freedwomen evinced a decided preference for field work. But it was never as simple a matter as that. Field labor might be more attractive from the standpoint of distance from former owners and in the end more profitable, but black women and their families needed immediate resources to help sustain them as crops were being made.

A multiplicity of arrangements emerged to meet individual and family needs. Some women committed two to three hours per day; some, one, two, or three days per week to waged domestic work, setting aside the remainder of their working hours for work in family fields, the crops of white planters, or for production in their own homes.[3] They fought to keep planters and their wives from encroaching on uncontracted time, just as they fought to maintain a clear understanding of what work they had contracted to do.[4] A woman hired as a cook could find herself having to ward off both threats.

For many, the most logical option under the circumstances was to split their time between field labor and domestic service. This was the decision Lucy and Andrew made, to spend three days in the field and two in paid household work. Another option was to devote a portion of each work day to household labor and field labor. For example, some black women went to the fields after completing their jobs in white homes.[5] The field work might be in their own vegetable gardens, corn or cotton patches, or in planters' fields. Some freedwomen negotiated a day off each week to devote to field labor. Whites who balked at allowing these sorts of arrangements risked losing their domestic workers entirely. Refused the right to go to their corn or cotton fields on their day off, black women often resigned household employment. Employers would then complain that they were setting up for themselves, or that husbands and fathers were carrying them off, saying their wives and daughters were not to work anymore. Former mistresses tried to avoid these sorts of arrangements in the first place, because they gave black women greater independence, making

---

[3] On the two- and three-day system, see Julie Saville, *The Work of Reconstruction: From Slave to Wage Laborer in South Carolina, 1860* (New York: Cambridge University Press, 1996) and Leslie A. Schwalm, *A Hard Fight for We: Women's Transition from Slavery to Freedom in South Carolina* (Urbana: University of Illinois Press, 1997).

[4] Isabelle H. Ward to Mr. [Louis] Manigault, January 26, 1869, Louis Manigault Papers, DU.

[5] Elizabeth P. Porcher to Philip E. Porcher, March 23, 1865, in *World Turned Upside Down*, ed. Towles, p. 452.

them less reliant on household labor. All of this is best understood in the context of black women's determination to decide for themselves what a free life meant.[6]

Former mistresses eventually yielded to the new realities, but not without a fight and often still believing that, in the end, they would be victorious. Esther Simons Palmer unhappily agreed to part-time arrangements in the hope of forestalling the arrival of a domestic revolution on her doorstep. She did not forestall the worst. In 1866 and 1867, freedwomen who had been her slaves for decades left one by one. Palmer tried without success to stay the tide. In March 1865, Lucy had reduced her hours in Palmer's household in order to have more time to work in the field, for herself and her family. In 1867 she left for good.[7]

Without their traditional command of labor seven days a week, former mistresses were forced to accept a quiltwork pattern of labor arrangements to keep house, albeit in "a very unsatisfying way." Esther Palmer found herself making do with a constantly changing staff, trying to convince each in turn to do more than they were hired to do. When Sarah left, Silvy, Lucy's washing assistant, became the cook and Tenny became Lucy's assistant. Esia was brought up from the quarters to make the fires, carry water, and cut wood. Andrew, who in 1865 had negotiated to work for Palmer two days a week and have the rest of his time to work in the field, now offered to work full-time for $100.00 for the year. His wife, Bella, would wash and wait on two of Palmer's nieces (ages 20 and 22) and some younger male relatives for $7 per month. This arrangement, too, was short-lived, for "after a while Bella and Andrew thought they could do better in the field, so the girls got Hester."[8] And so it went.

But the new demands of housekeeping that proved so unsatisfactory to white women did not make for a utopia for freedwomen. The disarray white women charted in their own homes also maps the disarray in black homes. The constant staffing changes white women encountered suggest something of the uncertainty that dogged black women's lives as well. With little in the way of resources at their disposal, beyond control over their labor, freedwomen had no choice but to pursue a patchwork of arrangements. They looked to such arrangements to help them make ends meet and, simultaneously, to secure some degree of autonomy from white households. But there were no guarantees and, certainly, the lives of black women remained fractured and hard.

Black women found that accomplishing their objectives was never as easy as white commentators sometimes made it seem. They had to juggle family obligations and, at the same time protect their children's freedom along with

---

[6] Louisa P. Palmer to Harriet R. Palmer, April 19, 1866; Esther Simons Palmer to Elizabeth P. Porcher, March 11, 1866; Elizabeth Catherine Porcher to Harriet R. Palmer, January 22, 1870, in *World Turned Upside Down*, ed. Towles, pp. 507, 503, and 641.

[7] Esther Simons Palmer to Elizabeth P. Porcher, March 11, 1866, in *World Turned Upside Down*, ed. Towles, p. 503. Lucy left the Palmer household at the end of 1867. (Esther Simon Palmer to Elizabeth Palmer Porcher, December 29, 1867, p. 574.)

[8] Esther Simons Palmer to Elizabeth P. Porcher, March 11, 1866, in *World Turned Upside Down*, ed. Towles, p. 503.

their own. For example, when Lucy decided to stay on as Palmer's washer, she sent her children away with Peggy. Sometimes, however, black women had no choice but to put their children to work elsewhere. In either case, it freed the children from the "yard," where as slaves they had been available to slaveholders' every need and where many former mistresses still counted on having them. Harriet Palmer expressed outrage and exasperation when the mother of two other children decided to remove them from her yard: "This morning Gabriella came to little Peggy and ordered her to go to the field. Did the same to Lizza. What presumption."[9] Single mothers were especially vulnerable. When Hannah, the mother of two children, was hired to take charge of Gertrude Thomas's dairy, she left her oldest child with her former mistress, bringing her two-year-old child with her. She was pregnant with a third child when Thomas hired and fired her.[10] Thomas said she was "sorry for her." For Hannah, it meant loss of income as one of the sacrifices she bore to secure her vision of freedom.

When She Gets Thro With Her Crop

Despite the humiliations and low wages that paid housework entailed, it offered ready, if meager, cash and thus was often vital to fragile black household economies.[11] In the long term, with some employers offering wages for domestic work in allotments of corn or other foodstuffs, and cash wages hovering around two to five dollars per month, domestic workers most often had to work two jobs whether they wished to or not. The need to juggle domestic work with field work (generally better paid) was a major factor in the desire of women domestic workers to work only part-time in white homes. Even though this juggling was a response to the wage differential, and to the need for clear cash, some women nonetheless rejected the small infusion of cash or corn some employers offered for domestic work. They refused such offers, believing that their labor should bring in more than a diet of corn or minimal shelter, no better than they had as slaves. Maria and her husband Robert typified this

---

[9] Harriet S. Palmer Journal, March 15, 1865, Palmer Family Papers, SCL.

[10] Virginia Ingraham Burr, ed., *The Secret Eye: The Journal of Ella Gertrude Thomas, 1848–49* (Chapel Hill: University of North Carolina Press, 1990), June 20, 1869, p. 319. Arranging child care was one of the new dilemmas black women faced. During slavery, the children of domestic slaves usually lived with their mothers "in the yard" or were cared for by relatives or elderly women specifically assigned to this task. Freedwomen with children who hired themselves out as domestic workers had to make their own arrangements for child care. Some white employers saw children as a distraction while others saw them as so many "free" hands to be called on as desired. Domestic workers sometimes still brought their children along. Sometimes they left them in the care of husbands or other family members; sometimes they placed them with former owners in return for mere subsistence. (Burr, ed., *The Secret Eye*, May 14, 1869, p. 316, and June 20, 1869, p. 319).

[11] For an illuminating discussion of the importance of domestic economies in black tenant households, see Sharon Ann Holt, *Making Freedom Pay: North Carolina Freedpeople Working for Themselves* (Athens: University of Georgia Press, 2000).

pattern. They left domestic work, their former mistress explained, because "they could not make out on what I offered." When offered food, clothing, and two dollars a month, another woman refused for the same reason.[12]

In the effort to piece together a livelihood, freedwomen, like freedmen, moved back and forth between "paid" labor and independent labor, establishing patterns that persisted into the 1870s and 1880s and beyond. Mollie Edmonds worked as a washer and ironer three days of the week and in the field three days. "That is what I is done all my life," she stated.[13] When work was required in family fields, whether owned, rented, or sharecropped, black women often left domestic employment temporarily. While some freedwomen secured arrangements upfront that allowed them to devote two to three days to independent labor, others left domestic employment as the crops demanded.

There was little white women could do to prevent black women from leaving to pick cash crops or peas for local planters, or to work land cultivated by their own families.[14] When the sugar cane or cotton crops came in, black women turned to the fields for the higher wages available there. When wages in the Louisiana cane fields hit seventy-five cents a day, three times the most common wage paid to household workers, domestic workers disappeared from white households.[15] Field labor offered another important advantage; it bred the sense of pride and autonomy vividly captured in the message Flora sent to her former mistress. She was "very sorry" to learn that her former mistress was doing her own laundry. She did not, however, offer to go to her aid. She did promise to pay her former mistress a visit "when she gets thro with her crop."[16] Flora had her own priorities, and freedom meant that she could place them above the needs of her former mistress.

While the bargaining power of domestic workers was partly a function of demand, it was also intimately tied to the prevailing terms in staple crop production. Labor shortages in the rice districts of South Carolina forced planters to negotiate contracts more favorable to laborers, and the widespread use of cash wages (as opposed to share wages) as a mode of payment gave workers ready cash and therefore greater control over their household economies. At Gowrie Plantation, James B. Heyward paid in cash, the amount varying according to the difficulty of the task. For 1876, he planned to offer fifty cents per day with no rations, for light labor in the rice fields, such as picking the indigo out of the rice, sixty cents plus rations for work on the thin rice

[12] Quote at Anna Camilla Cordes to Harriet R. Palmer, May 30, 1865; Esther Simon Palmer to Harriet R. Palmer, April 5, 1867, in *World Turned Upside Down*, ed. Towles, pp. 476 and 545, quote at p. 476; Richard N. Côté, *Mary's World: Love, War, and Family Ties in Nineteenth Century Charleston* (Mt. Pleasant, SC: Corinthian Books, 2001), p. 305.

[13] Mollie Edmonds, *Mississippi Narratives*, Supplement Series 1, vol. 7, pt. 2, p. 672.

[14] Henrietta Palmer Smith to Harriet R. Palmer, August 11, 1870; Esther Simons Palmer to Harriet R. Palmer, October 1870, in *World Turned Upside Down*, ed. Towles, pp. 662 and 676.

[15] Wilma King, ed., *A Northern Woman in the Plantation South: Letters of Tryphena Blanche Holder Fox, 1856–1876* (Columbia: University of South Carolina Press, 1993), December 30, 1869, pp. 238–39.

[16] Quote at Marianne Palmer Allston to Catherine Palmer Allston, October 4, 1872, in *World Turned Upside Down*, ed. Towles, p. 760.

fields, seventy cents plus rations for the regular work of cutting, and seventy-five cents plus rations for work in the more difficult acres where the rice was tangled.[17]

At Gowrie, black women could make as much or more in the fields as in domestic work. The system adopted by Heyward also gave "outside hands" (nonresident workers) the option of drawing their rations in cash, which Heyward computed variously at between fifteen and twenty cents per day. The Gowrie system offered the kind of flexibility that reduced reliance on waged domestic work as a source of cash. Black women could draw rations for the days they worked and were permitted to draw on their husbands' accounts as well.[18] Where opportunities were available to earn ready cash, black women were less inclined to take on waged domestic work.

The household economies of black families were projects in the making. Former slave women brought to this task their experience during slavery making and selling products in local markets, growing vegetables on family plots, and working in white women's households. But freedom meant more than just an elaboration of such tasks. It involved as well a reordering of priorities and needs. Black households had no choice but to devote more time and resources to household production of foodstuffs, clothing, furnishings, and so on. This circumstance compelled black women who sought domestic work to seek to do so under conditions that permitted time for gardening, cooking, sewing, and caring for farm animals and fowl.

Whether working part-time as domestic servants or as field hands, or devoting themselves full-time to their own family's crops or animals, the labor of black women and their children made an important contribution to the survival of their households. Children were introduced at an early age to household production, a common pattern among rural working families everywhere. Even a minimum of self-sufficiency required their assistance with such tasks as making butter, milking cows, weeding gardens, and helping to care for sitting hens. When parents removed them from white households, it was a matter of economic survival as well as a means of protecting them from abuse. Former mistresses and masters saw treachery and parental unfitness in these actions. With time, however, the decibel level of the recriminations lowered, even if a

---

[17] James B. Heyward, Jr., to Louis M. Manigault, September 11, 1876; Heyward to Manigault, September 30, 1876, Louis Manigault Papers, DU. On the competition between South Carolina and Georgia planters along the Combahee River, see Heyward to Manigault, September 30, 1876. (The labor shortage was compounded by a yellow fever epidemic.) In addition to paying some workers by the day, Heyward used a variety of other arrangements. One tied wages to the number of acres cut or tied. Some Combahee planters gave $1.50 per acre for both tasks; Heyward never paid more than ninety cents per acre. Fred Blake, on the other hand, planted his crop with workers who took their wages in land rent. Some positions were scaled according to skill, with engineers making two dollars per day; firemen, seventy-five cents; feeders, sixty-two cents; and mill hands, sixty-six cents, all tasks associated with the threshing stage. Interestingly, the rate for trash hands, usually women, was the same as for firemen (Heyward to Manigault, October 5, 1876; ibid, October 11, 1876, Manigault Papers, DU).

[18] Heyward to Manigault, September 30, 1876; October 11, 1876; May 27, 1877, Manigault Papers, DU.

certain possessiveness lingered. Henrietta Smith wrote calmly in 1871: "I am about to lose my girl. Her mother wants to take her with her when she moves away. I am on the lookout again."[19]

The reordering of priorities vital to the building of free black homes brought other kinds of adjustments to black and white households.[20] The putting-out of washing has received a great deal of attention from scholars. The putting-out of other household chores shaped the contours of freedom in similar ways. Besides cooking, cleaning, and washing, there were ancillary chores that domestic workers refused to do as add-ons. These included making butter, tending chickens and hens, and making starch. Like washing, these labors migrated to black households. In addition, former mistresses increasingly depended on the household production of black families, and black families, on the cash that could be earned from household production.

The account books of the Cameron family – North Carolina's wealthiest prewar family – detail this interdependency. Over a two-month period, from September 1883 through November 1883, Rebecca Cameron purchased ten and one-half pounds of butter from one freedwoman along with two chickens and four eggs. During the same period, she made additional purchases from the same community of black women: two chickens from Phil Watkins's wife and eighteen eggs from Eveline. Frances, who sold more than nine and a half pounds of butter, vied with Easter and Liddie Vesey in selling the most butter (nearly ten pounds). Four other women – Hannah, Aunt Mary, Francis (Aunt Mary's daughter), and Lucy – sold smaller amounts of butter and eggs, and fewer chickens during this period. Cameron's "Butter Account" shows black women making and selling butter on a regular basis.[21]

This pattern of purchasing and selling between Rebecca Cameron and black women continued into the late 1880s and expanded to include at least six other black women. Many black families put their first earnings from such sales to the purchase of a cow, pig, or fowl, an investment in household production that signaled faith in the returns to be had from sales of butter and eggs, for example.[22] Accounts for three of the black women who sold to the Cameron household, from September to October of 1883, show the sales indicated in Tables 6.1, 6.2, and 6.3.

[19] Henrietta Palmer Smith to Harriet R. Palmer, August 11, 1870; Henrietta Palmer Smith to Esther Simons Palmer, November 30, 1871, in *World Turned Upside Down*, ed. Towles, pp. 662 and 711, quote at p. 711.

[20] See, for example, Elizabeth Clark-Lewis, *Living In, Living Out: African American Domestics in Washington, D.C., 1910–1940* (Washington, DC: Smithsonian Institution Press, 1994), and Tera W. Hunter, *To 'Joy My Freedom: Southern Black Women's Lives and Labors After the Civil War* (Cambridge, MA: Harvard University Press, 1997).

[21] "Butter Acct. 1883," Cameron Papers, SHC. Cameron paid twelve and a half cents per chicken and fifteen cents per dozen eggs. Some former mistresses also sold goods freedwomen produced within white households.

[22] See A South Carolinian, "South Carolina Society," *The Atlantic Monthly* 39 (June 1877): 678–79. In a famous example, Mary Chesnut and her maid, Molly, made and sold butter "on shares," adapting to household production the terminology of field labor.

TABLE 6.1. *Easter's Account*

Date	Amount of Butter Sold (in ounces)	Number of Chickens Sold
September 11	12	
September 14	0	1/2
September 15	14	
October 10	12	1/2
October 18	16	
October 25	28	
October 30	24	
November 4	16	
November 8	24	
November 22	12	
November 26	12	

TABLE 6.2. *Francis's Account*

Date	Amount of Butter Sold (in ounces)
September 11	20
September 18	16
September 26	20
October 5	12
October 10	20
October 18	23
October 25	18
November 4	16
November 22	16

TABLE 6.3. *Lydia Vesey's Account*

Date	Amount of Butter Sold (in ounces)
September 18	28
September 26 [25?]	16
October 25	36
October 30	25
November 4	20
November 8	32

Butter and egg accounts formed a central part of the cash flow of black and white household economies. The black women who sold butter and eggs to the Cameron household were former Cameron slaves scattered over the various Cameron plantations. Some continued to work in the fields on an irregular basis, at the same time expanding household production destined for the market. Pate Cleamence, for example, worked as a field hand and produced at home for the market.[23]

The vast majority of former slaves failed to achieve the level of subsistence they desired or needed in the years following the Civil War, but its pursuit was not the dead end that some scholars make it out to be. "By 1880," Grace Hale argues, "most ex-slaves and many whites did not have the resources to pursue subsistence and wealthier whites had no need to make what they could more easily and often as cheaply buy. For all classes of southerners, domestic spaces increasingly became places of consumption rather than production."[24] This was probably never the case for rural black people, even after the introduction of mail order catalogs in the late nineteenth century.

Rural black and white workingclass people always depended on the products of their labor, from growing vegetables, keeping fowl and cows, to quilting and making everything from bed linen to clothing. Even if it could not buy a plow, the work and thriftiness of black women helped put meat on the table and purchase other necessities. With the cost of meat around ten cents a pound, the seventy-five cents Willis' wife earned washing clothes for a day was enough to purchase one week's meager supply of meat and avoid a "store bill" with interest.[25] In *The Time of Man*, Elizabeth Madox Roberts, a keen observer of the South's poor, captures how people with "nothing" lived. The fictional Sebe Townley's perspective vividly chronicles the value of women's work.

In another year he expected to be able to rent a place. He knew a good strip of bottom over beyond the creek and corn land. A body could make the store bill off the ducks and geese alone. It was a prime place for ducks, right on the water before the door. He knew a man used to live there and his wife made the store bill every year off the ducks and chickens. A body could do a sight with ducks, a good thrifty wife could. And look what you could do with chickens.... He knew a man had a wife made enough money to buy a disc plow, just off the egg money alone. And there would still be the geese to pay the store bill.[26]

Former mistresses's reliance on the butter, eggs, meat, and other products produced by poor black and white families increased as the pool of afford-able domestic servants available for full-time work decreased. One of the most significant transformations in household production, therefore, was not a trans-formation of domestic spaces from spaces of production to spaces of consump-tion but rather the transformation of black and white homes into expanded and

---

[23] "Butter Acct. 1883," Cameron Papers, SHC. Rebecca Cameron also purchased butter, eggs, and chickens from local white women. Pate Cleamence's name also appears as Pate Clemens.

[24] Grace Elizabeth Hale, *Making Whiteness: The Culture of Segregation in the South, 1890–1940* (New York: Pantheon, 1998), pp. 88–93, quote at p. 89.

[25] "Butter Acct., 1883," Cameron Papers, SHC.

[26] Elizabeth Madox Roberts, *The Time of Man* (1926; reprint, New York: Viking Press, 1963), pp. 50–51.

different spaces of production and consumption.[27] Contemporary and scholarly preoccupation with the notion of black women's "withdrawal" from the fields has, perhaps, contributed to a certain difficulty in seeing this development.[28]

Small but significant incremental advances in wages for domestic workers buttressed the expansion of the black household as a space of consumption and production. By the 1870s, domestic workers earned wages ranging from two dollars and fifty cents per week, plus food, to five to six dollars per month. Demands for five dollars per month seem to have become fairly common.[29] While it is difficult, given the available records, to establish with any precision the advance or retreat of wages for washerwomen in the postbellum South, it does seem clear that those who worked from their own homes had managed by the 1870s to establish a fairly firm baseline for what constituted a washing task or a day's work.

The evidence also points to continued specialization within the trade. In 1870, Esther Simons Palmer hired a washer to whom she sent only the articles she wanted starched. Palmer had the rest of her washing done by a servant on premises. The way in which Palmer doled out her washing confirms price differentials within the washing trade. Starched clothing involved more labor-intensive work – from making the starch to applying it – than clothing that only needed to be washed and folded. It also routinely required ironing. Clear starch washing was considered a specialty. Starched clothing also burned more easily when ironed, thus requiring even more time and care. Further, clothing and other pieces that were usually starched tended to be the more delicate pieces, which again meant greater care and time in handling, and even more time and care if clear starching was requested. Clear starching required several

---

[27] By 1880, as Gavin Wright notes, "self-sufficiency in foods was increasingly crowded out." But farm livestock remained an important component of black people's goal of self-sufficiency. In fact, according to W. E. B. Du Bois, it constituted the largest share of black property values in 1880. Gavin Wright, *The Political Economy of the Cotton South: Households, Markets, and Wealth in the Nineteenth Century* (New York: Oxford University Press, 1978), p. 171; W. E. B. Du Bois, "The Negro Landholder of Georgia," *Bulletin No. 35*, U.S. Department of Labor (July, 1901): 647–777; Arthur F. Raper, *Preface to Peasantry: A Tale of Two Black-Belt Counties* (Chapel Hill: University of North Carolina Press, 1936).

[28] The work of Roger Ransom and Richard Sutch has been of pivotal importance in this debate. See, for example, "The Impact of the Civil War and of Emancipation on Southern Agriculture," *Explorations in Economic History* 12 (January 1975): 13–14 and 22–24. This work is widely cited on the "withdrawal" question. See also Wright, *The Political Economy of the Cotton South*, p. 162.

[29] C. Vann Woodward, ed., *Mary Chesnut's Civil War* (New Haven, CT: Yale University Press, 1981), May 7, 1865, p. 803; Henrietta Palmer Smith to Esther Simons Palmer, November 30, 1871; Samuella J. Palmer to Harriet R. Palmer, May 4, 1872; Thomas Palmer Jerman to John S. Palmer, June 19, 1873, in *World Turned Upside Down*, ed. Towles, pp. 711, 729, and 764; Testimony of Rev. E. P. Holmes, November 20, 1883, U.S. Government, *Report of the Committee of the Senate Upon the Relations between Labor and Capital and Testimony Taken by the Committee*, 5 vols. (Washington, DC: Government Printing Office, 1885), IV: 607; Côté, *Mary's World*, p. 305. Report hereafter cited as *Senate Committee Report*.

additional steps in the process of making the starch and applying it, and was considered a specialty for which washerwomen charged higher rates. This helps to explain Palmer's decision to separate her laundry. She could not afford to send it all out, so she sent her best pieces to an experienced starcher rather than have them done by the washer she employed on site.[30] Ironing was also treated as a special skill worthy of higher pay. One only has to look at the elaborate construction of elite clothing to see why it was justified.

By the 1880s, rates of pay for domestic labor had reached a plateau for the period of Reconstruction. They remained fairly stagnant at the levels achieved in the 1870s, but did so in the face of continued efforts by black women to push them upward. Janie Watkins Palmer was still paying only five dollars per month for her laundry in 1883 when she received notice that her washer planned "to raise on us."[31] But huge spreads could be found in individual cases. At the lower end, Amy Shaw earned only twenty-five cents for a day's work washing in 1884. At the upper end were women like Charlotte, who, working one Sunday per month, earned $96.00 from May 25, 1881 to May 25, 1882 and a total of $263.00 over the three years from December 25, 1880 to December 25, 1883. It is not clear why Shaw worked on Sundays. Conceivably, she did so in order to reserve the other days in the week for labor in her own home or in the field. The high premium of eight dollars per Sunday that she received also suggests that working in white homes on Sunday was a less common practice. Holidays may also have lent themselves to similar arrangements. This may also account for the twenty-five dollars Shaw received for work on Christmas day.[32]

Not only did wages remain stagnant for most women, but by the 1880s those wages had been further depreciated by a gradual shift of the cost of related expenses from white employers to black employees. That shift doubtless reflected a loss in the bargaining power of black women that coincided with the diminution of federal civil rights protections and assaults on black male suffrage. A decade earlier, it was common for employers to supply soap and other supplies, or for washers to receive additional compensation when they (rather than employers) supplied themselves. Some washerwomen, as noted earlier, also demanded payments sufficient to cover the cost of hauling water for the wash. Elizabeth Porcher paid $1.25 for six dozen pieces in 1865 and bore the cost of the wood, soap, and starch. A week after hiring a washer for her starched clothing, Esther Palmer very reluctantly acquiesced when her

---

[30] Esther Simons Palmer to Harriet R. Palmer, September 1870; Harriet R. Palmer to Esther Simons Palmer, October 1870, in *World Turned Upside Down*, ed. Towles, pp. 673 and 675; King, ed., *A Northern Woman*, p. 145; A South Carolinian, "South Carolina Society," p. 679; Hunter, *To 'Joy My Freedom*, p. 57.

[31] Janie Watkins Palmer to Harriet R. Palmer, May 6, 1883, in *World Turned Upside Down*, ed. Towles, p. 922.

[32] Household Account Book of Mrs. Duncan Cameron, pp. 62 and 360, Stagville and Fairntosh, Cameron Papers, SHC. Charlotte received one payment of $50; others were in the amount of $5.

starcher demanded a raise to fifty cents a day, which the starcher justified on the basis of her having to go half a mile for water.[33]

Increasingly washerwomen made and furnished the soap. This was accompanied by no visible increase in their wages even though it greatly increased their investment of time and labor. Making soap, like making starch, was a time-consuming task that now ate into already meager returns. It meant that black women had to furnish the wood ashes, the hog fat for making the lard (cooked-down hog fat), and the wood for cooking the lard and lye.[34] Making and collecting lye was not only dangerous work but took hours. The lard and lye had to be stirred for several hours until it began to harden. The modest rise in the task rate – the rate per dozen pieces – from about twenty-one to twenty-eight cents per dozen to about thirty-five cents per dozen between 1865 and the 1880s – was insufficient to cover the added costs associated with making and supplying their own soap. Rev. E. P. Holmes, who ministered to hundreds of washerwomen, ironers, cooks, and chamber maids throughout the state of Georgia, estimated that, deducting the cost of supplies, washerwomen working at the rate of thirty-five cents per dozen, realized a profit of only ten cents per dozen.[35]

The efforts of black women to juggle the demands of work, family, and personal freedom took their toll. Most of them did not find better pay or, generally, better on-the-job conditions. They took what joy they could find in the freedom to move about, to live with their families and among friends in their own homes, and to enjoy the small fruits of their labor. The need to supplement wages from field labor that had kept black women in domestic service in the first place – whether on a full- or part-time basis – increased rather than lessened over time. With the spread of sharecropping, fewer planters used a cash wage system, thus increasing the pressure on households to find a means to secure clear cash. Working at home retained the advantage of reducing employers' leverage and power. The freedom to leave abusive employers continued to be cherished despite the sometimes prohibitive cost in loss of income. At the same time, white employers were never completely powerless. Just as black women could leave domestic employment when it suited them, white women in turn could fire them, although not without the typical inconveniences. Gertrude Thomas made firing sound simpler than her own experience proved: "I have the satisfaction of knowing when I am not pleased with a servant that I can look out for another."[36]

---

[33] Elizabeth Porcher to Hattie [Harriet R. Palmer], October 1865, Palmer Family Papers; Esther Simons Palmer to Harriet R. Palmer, September 1870; Harriet R. Palmer to Esther Simons Palmer, October 1870, in *World Turned Upside Down*, ed. Towles, pp. 673 and 675; King, ed., *A Northern Woman*, July 15, 1865, p. 145.

[34] The production of lye soap exposed washerwomen to dangerous fumes from lye-water, which can burn the eyes and skin and cause respiratory problems.

[35] Holmes Testimony, *Senate Committee Report*, IV: 605 and 607.

[36] Burr, ed., *The Secret Eye*, May 4, 1871, p. 370.

I Never Liked Extorted Love or Labor

If former mistresses recoiled at having to perform domestic chores and bargain with black women, both considered beneath their dignity, still more insult and injury appeared when black women became their customers. They bought dresses they were not allowed to wear as slaves, and former mistresses now sold to them, sometimes from dire necessity and sometimes to earn enough to buy themselves a new dress. Perhaps the most embarrassing of all such predicaments was having to buy back a dress one had previously discarded as a gift to a slave. Lizzie Neblett faced that dilemma even before the war had ended. In 1864, she "found herself compelled to buy back a dress she had given a slave years before." She paid $3.50. "In her enthusiasm," writes Drew Faust, "she seemed oblivious both to the irony and to the loss of status implicit in purchasing her own cast-off dress from a slave."[37]

Neither the irony nor the loss of status such exchanges marked was lost on Gertrude Thomas. She was insulted when her former slaves came to her with offers to buy her old dresses and mortified to know that not only could they afford to buy them, but that they were familiar enough with her financial circumstances to know that she needed to sell them. Her embarrassed financial predicament was, indeed, public knowledge, but to have it paraded about by former slaves added to her humiliation. By this point, Thomas owned neither a proper carriage nor a proper horse to draw it. On trips to town, she tried to avoid being seen in the only carriage she now owned, an unfashionable thing, by getting out before it reached Augusta's main street where people could see the face attached to the sheriff's sales. She walked the rest of the way.[38]

For three years, Thomas had been wearing "sack cloth and ashes," while her former slaves had money to buy her old, but best, dresses. She could quip that it was a wasteful expenditure of their money and she could refuse to sell to them. She had "never learned to bargain and trade with our old servants" and had no interest in learning. Yet she could not prevent them from obtaining better dresses from other white women of her class who, under the pressure of poverty, were unwilling to hold tightly to appearance for namesake only. But Thomas was determined that even if other white women gave in, she would not, even though she was in desperate straits.[39]

Thomas tried to salvage some remnant of her former self and power by limiting her transactions with freedwomen in the matter of clothing to the form of gifts. She was open to granting "favors," but requests for them had to be put in language that clearly denoted that she rendered a favor, not a service. When a former slave seeking a dress for her daughter's wedding approached

---

[37] Drew Gilpin Faust, *Mothers of Invention: Women of the Slaveholding South in the American Civil War* (Chapel Hill: University of North Carolina Press, 1996), p. 222.

[38] Burr, ed., *The Secret Eye*, May 4, 1869, p. 311; March 6, 1870, p. 331; November 29, 1870, pp. 341–42; December 5, 1870, p. 343; January 2, 1871, pp. 357–58; January 8, 1871, pp. 358–59.

[39] Burr, ed., *The Secret Eye*, July 30, 1870, p. 331; November 29, 1870, p. 341; December 14, 1870, p. 351, quotes at pp. 341 and 351, respectively.

Thomas about purchasing one of hers, she refused. She *gave* her one instead. She would "give" Lily's daughter a wedding dress in memory of old "Aunt Lily" and her family's former "faithful" service as slaves. To sell that dress to Lily was too hardy an acknowledgment of their new relations and too hardy an acknowledgement of black women's right to "take up" their money to dress themselves.[40]

Thomas explained and defended her position on paternalistic and altruistic grounds. The fact that Lily's mother had been her mother's first cook when she married satisfied Thomas that paternalism was the proper response to Lily's request. Moreover, she reasoned, the fact that Lily's house had recently burned down made a handout all the more appropriate, Lily, herself, had not raised either of these matters. Nor had she requested a handout. She had, after all, asked to buy the dress.[41] Like many former mistresses, Thomas revolted really at anything that had to do with black women dressing up and otherwise embellishing their physical appearance unless it was done with her approval and through her giving. When another former slave offered to pay her to cut out a dress, Thomas knew that she could not. To avoid the distasteful dilemma, she quoted a price she knew was out of the woman's reach, and as added insurance, said that she did not have time for such a project. She would not be treated as if she were no more than another hired hand. She would not endorse independent decisions on the part of black women about "articles of dress." Had the woman made the request in the form of a favor and not as a commercial transaction, she would likely have obliged her, she wrote.[42]

Cornelia Shelman, the woman who sought to hire Thomas as a seamstress, was hardly blind to the dilemma her request created for Thomas. In fact, she may have deliberately provoked it. Shelman, after all, had other options. Her mother was a talented seamstress whom Thomas herself employed. And, there were other black women in the community who were capable seamstresses. But Shelman took the job to Thomas anyway. Possibly she wanted to see Thomas squirm, to make her uncomfortable, to confront her. Possibly, she sought revenge for Thomas's past treatment of her when she worked as Thomas' cook. Thomas had fired her only a few months before. Now Shelman, who Thomas had earlier described as dressed in rags, had returned to employ her former mistress.[43] Thomas's refusal did not diffuse the blow she suffered. Not only were ladies' maids dressing up in their former mistresses's gowns before their faces, as many white women complained, they were asking their former mistresses to make them new gowns.

At the same time, Thomas and other employers continued to try to squeeze a bargain by hiring one person to perform tasks previously done by several slaves, or by adding on work. Black women continued to rebuff such propositions.

---

[40] Burr, ed., *The Secret Eye*, December 14, 1870, p. 351.
[41] Burr, ed., *The Secret Eye*, December 14, 1870, p. 351.
[42] Burr, ed., *The Secret Eye*, December 14, 1870, p. 351.
[43] Burr, ed., *The Secret Eye*, May 14, 1869, pp. 315–16; December 14, 1870, p. 351.

Cooks refused to make late suppers for unexpected guests or for the husbands of employers returning home late, or to take on the job of babysitting. When she wanted a servant to perform a task unrelated to the job description for which the person was hired, Gertrude Thomas came to know instinctively that she would have to offer additional compensation in one form or another. When her plans to attend a club party were foiled because the cook and house girl had a social engagement of their own, the wedding of a friend, she was irritated but no longer enraged.[44] Six years of negotiating the terrain of freedom had made her a more perceptive student of free labor, though she still found it hard to reconcile the reality of who she now was with what she had been raised to be, "a golden child and a golden woman," as Nell Painter poignantly put it.[45] She clung stubbornly to a prewar identity that emancipation had eroded. "I never liked extorted love or labour," she wrote. "What I wish now is a sober respectable white woman or colored who will find it in her interest to take an interest in pleasing me and interesting herself in my children."[46] Thomas's desire testified to the forced intimacies of slavery.

By 1880, Thomas had almost reached bottom. Her floors were bare and broken plastering littered her home. But she had something more important, a cook. In this woman, named Dinah Hunter, Thomas thought she had found someone interested in "pleasing" her at last. In Hunter, she invested her sense of who she was. "I believe she likes me," she wrote, "and she mingles with her service so much interest in my welfare that it touches me." Though threatened with another sheriff's sale, the potential loss of a lifetime interest in trust properties inherited from her father's estate, and, besides, forced to use her earnings from teaching to pay the bills her husband could not, she still could not imagine living without a cook; this was more important than repairing her walls.[47] Managing to keep a cook proved another matter. Within months, "Dinah" the "treasure," was "annoying" and "disrespectful." Soon she was gone, only to be replaced by another and another who showed no interest in "pleasing" Thomas.[48]

Thomas ended the decade of the 1880s living as makeshift a life as she had in 1865. She had one house servant, a cook she described as "disrespectful and noisy" but the best she could "command the services of." She hired a washer who did the work off-site. She rented out rooms to pay for dresses and bonnets. She employed black women to sell her old dresses and hats for her. She and a daughter did much of their own housework. Merchants dunned her at home for embarrassingly tiny sums. One was demanding $1.50 for a pair of shoes she had purchased for her daughter and another, thirty-five cents

[44] Burr, ed., *The Secret Eye*, May 4, 1871, p. 369.

[45] Painter, "Introduction," in Burr, ed., *The Secret Eye*, p. 67.

[46] Burr, ed., *The Secret Eye*, May 4, 1871, p. 370.

[47] Burr, ed., *The Secret Eye*, December 31, 1879, p. 391; February 3, 1880, p. 396; May 19, 1880, p. 403.

[48] Burr, ed., *The Secret Eye*, October 1, 1880, p. 412; January 5, 1881, p. 417; October 10, 1882, p. 430.

for a vest. She sent her cook to the market to buy ten cents worth of beef steak. Like their father, three of her children saw no reason to unite with the church.[49] Still, despite her husband's ruinous financial management and her own extravagances, Thomas was able to delay entering the labor force longer than many of her peers; she eventually taught school. She could not put off making other accommodations. Poverty eventually forced her to put aside her pride and bargain and trade with black women.[50]

The realities of life vanquished Thomas's sense of paternalism, *noblesse oblige,* and class and race privilege day by day. Her confident assertion of ten years earlier that she would give but not sell her dresses to black women, gave way under the crush of poverty. By the 1870s, she was selling her old dresses to black women in part to pay the wages of her seamstress, and in part to keep up with her magazine subscriptions. She stopped trying to view those transactions with black women as anything but "selling." Her sons, Jeff and Turner, though destined before the war to stand in the footsteps of their ancestors among the ranks of the South's leading white men, now found themselves without position, power, or wealth. Since at least 1869, Turner had worked as a field hand, plowing alongside the slaves he once expected to inherit. In 1880, Jeff was employed by a Chinese merchant. Thomas considered both situations "degrading."[51]

The financial loss slaves' emancipation had entailed, combined with the resistance of former slaves to the reinstatement of prewar customary norms of subservience, forced radical pecuniary and social changes in the households of all former mistresses. Before the war, Mary Pringle had fourteen slaves in her household and an additional six about her yard and, thus, at her disposal. After her slaves became free people and the war wiped out other forms of her family's wealth, Pringle held her family together financially for a time by renting out the first floor of her home. "By great management," she wrote in the spring of 1867, "I counted up my outside rents at $600, including the housekeeper's room and library." She rented the housekeeper's room to a white couple, enduring a double humiliation: having to rent out her rooms and having to rent them to workingclass white people. The wife in that tenant family was herself a domestic servant and the husband, a policeman. Pringle shortly put them out on the excuse that the woman was a heavy drinker. On top of this she faced her husband's criticism for letting the basement out to "stragglers."[52]

[49] Burr, ed., *The Secret Eye,* March 25, 1880, p. 400; January 5, 1881, p. 417; April 3, 1888, pp. 444–45; September 20, 1884, p. 436.

[50] Burr, ed., *The Secret Eye,* September 2, 1880, pp. 408–9; January 8, 1881, pp. 420–21.

[51] Burr, ed., *The Secret Eye,* February 13, 1871, p. 361; March 25, 1880, p. 400; May 4, 1869, p. 311; September 24, 1880, p. 409; September 27, 1882, p. 428. In 1880, Turner Thomas secured employment as a clerk but continued to work on the farm. Jeff left Chong's in 1883, "a situation" which he, like his mother, found "degrading" and took a job as a railroad express messenger. See also *World Turned Upside Down,* ed. Towles, pp. 639–40.

[52] Côté, *Mary's World,* p. 270.

The following year, Pringle rented out her coach house. The income was an absolute necessity, but her pride was stung. "I am a walking advertisement," she wrote her daughter, "humbly whispering to my friends that my apartments are vacant." She let the coach room for four dollars per month to "the Jew Lewis," who turned it into a store. Pringle and her family quickly regretted the decision, thinking they could have gotten more than double that amount from another Jewish applicant who came forward after the lease had been offered to Lewis.[53] In addition, the store in her yard was further advertisement of her poverty. To help feed her family and pay taxes, Pringle also made orange marmalade, sending some of it to New Haven, where her daughter, Mary Francis, sold it for her. At the same time another daughter, Susan, made floral arrangements, which she sold at the Charleston Hotel, mainly to northerners.[54]

For the first time in their lives, elite women came to understand prudent economy as a way of life, even those like Gertrude Thomas and Mary Pringle, who initially resisted it and held out for as long as they could. It was no longer possible to view pinching pennies as a nice ideal as many had before the war, or to view doing without a new dress or servants on command as a temporary aberration. It was not until 1871 that Mary Pringle gave up the ghost. From her prewar staff of twenty slaves, only three remained in the spring of that year: Amelia (the cook), Thomas (the waiter), and Cretia (the general housekeeper). In July, Pringle decided to fire Thomas. "I give him up," she wrote "as a matter of principle, for people in charity should not keep three servants." People in charity, she apparently imagined, still might keep two. Not of her own volition, she was soon thereafter reduced to one when Cretia left and moved in with her son.[55]

As they struggled to retain at least one servant and, simultaneously, to juggle household finances, former mistresses and those daughters of the old planter class who came of age after the war, learned the necessity of maintaining household accounts. Before the war, the keeping of household accounts was touted as a sign of an accomplished mistress, but then, it was an ideal that most mistresses could comfortably ignore. Now, they could not. Some women, like Grace Elmore, resented the new responsibility and its suggestion of fiscal constraints. "'Tis disgusting," she wrote of her new situation, "to be obliged to calculate so closely."[56] Still, the meticulous account books kept by Margaret B. Mordecai exhibit the new importance white women were forced to attach to domestic economy. Mordecai detailed her expenses for everything, from the purchase of tea and a coffee pot, to fruit, dishes, cheese, medicine, and wages for her washerwoman. So did Mrs. Duncan Cameron in her detailed "Butter

---

[53] Côté, *Mary's World*, pp. 270–71. See also Henry James Trentham, *North Carolina Narratives*, vol. 15, pt. 2, p. 365.

[54] Côté, *Mary's World*, pp. 270–72.

[55] Côté, *Mary's World*, pp. 283–84, quote at p. 284.

[56] Grace Elmore Diary, March 12, 1865, SHC.

Account" and "Washing Account," along with an account of all of her store purchases. In 1882, she recorded her servants' wages and $638.95 in store purchases.[57]

The transition from mistress to employer and worker was wrenching, and the public humiliation, seemingly unending. One source of humiliation was the transformation of mistresses into keepers of plantation stores, an ironic turn from keepers of the keys to the plantation store rooms. Elizabeth Porcher, for example, set herself up as a merchant on her family's plantation, selling and trading with black people a variety of goods from fish to tobacco.[58] The store allowed her to take advantage of the growing opportunities for trade with former slaves. Gertrude Thomas painfully noted her transition from "fashionable lady" to "business woman," and Tryphena Fox, her new role as a "market woman." Performance of this new role fueled other kinds of transformations that brought sweeping changes not only to household economies and but also to relationships between black and white women.[59]

Among the most significant of these transformations was the organization of white women's cooperatives "to assist Ladies who are struggling by their own endeavors to support themselves and families." This is how a handbill circulated by the Ladies Mutual Aid Society of Charleston announced its founding, in 1866. Led by Mrs. George A. Trenholm, wife of the former Confederate Secretary of the Treasury, and boasting a list of officers and a "Board of Managers" representing many of the wealthiest prewar planter families, the organization was established to support its members by taking in orders for such things as needle work, jellies, cordials, wines, and pickles.[60] Women's mutual aid societies were not uncommon in the nineteenth century, but the announced purpose of the Charleston group signaled something dramatically new and different, indeed, a seismic shift in gender and race relations.

In calling on the public to purchase its needle work and preserves, Charleston's elite white women would not necessarily have raised any eyebrows. This, after all, was women's work; and, during the war, both the proliferation of ladies' societies and women's participation as nurses and treasury

---

[57] Account Book of Mrs. M. B. Mordecai, Cameron Papers; "Butter Acct. 1883," Cameron Papers; Household Account of Mrs. Duncan Cameron, Stagville and Faintosh, Cameron Papers, SHC. See also Alice Gaillard Palmer to Harriet R. Palmer, December 9, 1878, in *World Turned Upside Down*, ed. Towles, p. 814.

[58] Elizabeth P. Porcher to Harriet R. Palmer, March 1866, in *World Turned Upside Down*, ed. Towles, p. 498. For examples of the rare cases where antebellum mistresses kept account books, see Joan E. Cashin, *Our Common Affairs: Texts from Women in the Old South* (Baltimore, MD: Johns Hopkins University Press, 1996), pp. 145–46, and Nancy D. Bercaw, *Gendered Freedoms: Race, Rights, and the Politics of Household in the Delta, 1861–1875* (Gainesville: University Press of Florida, 2003), p. 51.

[59] Harriet R. Palmer to Esther Simons Palmer, January 1869; Henrietta Palmer Smith to Harriet R. Palmer, February 9, 1869 in *World Turned Upside Down*, ed. Towles, pp. 610 and 611; Burr, ed., *The Secret Eye*, January 2, 1871, p. 357; King, ed., *A Northern Woman*, February 10, [1870], p. 244.

[60] Ladies Mutual Aid Association (Charleston, S.C.), Handbill, ca. 1866 (43/0996), SCHS.

girls, had introduced the idea of white women's public work to a wide audience. But there, similarities to the past ended. If elite white women were not doing charity work for the first time, it was the first time that they had publicly begged it for themselves. While not strangers to creating fancy needle work and making tasty preserves, elite women had never before had to peddle them. During slavery, they had presided over the production of jams, and their grammatical construction of this work, "made jam today," had erased the labor of bondswomen on whom the actual making had devolved. Now they did all of these, making jellies and needlework by their own hands, and advertising them for sale "to support themselves and families."

The Baltimore Society had its origins in the same financial and social distress. Established as a cooperative to minister to the needs of white women, the organization, headed by Isabella Yates Snowden, operated as a combination workshop and store. Members took their old clothes there to sell along with goods they produced in their homes. The society also operated as a contractor, taking orders for sewing that it subcontracted out to its members. Sometimes it placed large orders and sold the finished products in its store.

Planter women hoping to earn a spot of cash sent cordials and old dresses and shirts to sell. They accepted orders for sewing. A bottle of ketchup sold for fifty cents; a chemise, for eighty cents. Charlestonian Alice Gaillard Palmer, a war widow living with her parents on the reduced income of Wee Nee, the plantation inherited from her husband's estate, noted in August 1869 that she had just completed making aprons for the society and was set to begin work on an order of baby dresses and two gowns for a bridal trousseau. She expected to earn three dollars for each of the gowns. In addition, she taught school.[61]

The organization of the Ladies Mutual Aid Society and the Baltimore Society are small but telling pieces of the larger story of the transformation of southern women's lives in the aftermath of Confederate defeat and slaves' emancipation, and, through these transformations the fundamental rearrangement of southern race and gender relations. The formation of these groups amounted to a startling admission of the failure of southern paternalism and the reality of black freedom. The recognition (however discreet) these groups accorded to women's self-reliance as a value reflected, no doubt, the impact the war had on notions of southern patriarchy. The recognition also doubtless reflected the impact black women had – by turns by their presence and their departures – on the transformation of plantation households and white women's lives. In the aftermath of the war, Charleston's elite white women, like others of their race and class throughout the South, may well have come to

---

[61] On the Baltimore Society, see Elizabeth P. Porcher to Harriet R. Palmer, August 5, 1866, p. 528; Harriet Palmer Smith to Harriet R. Palmer, August 4, 1867, pp. 560–61; Alice Gaillard Palmer to Harriet R. Palmer, September, 25, 1867, p. 565; Alice Gaillard Palmer to Harriet R. Palmer, August 3, 1869, p. 632; Alice Gaillard Palmer to Harriet R. Palmer, July 17, 1870, p. 654; Esther Simons Palmer to Harriet R. Palmer, September 1870, p. 672; Alice Gaillard Palmer to Harriet R. Palmer, April 5, 1871, p. 684; William C. Palmer to Esther Simons Palmer, March 25, 1882, p. 911, in *World Turned Upside Down*, ed. Towles.

understand what Hanna Fambro meant when she predicted at the outset of the Civil War that the war "was goin' to set us free."[62] It is possible to imagine that she had in mind mistresses she knew as well as enslaved women like herself.

Before the Civil War planter women could not have imagined that they or their daughters would one day work for a living making or selling foodstuffs and clothing; that they would weave to pay for their portraits, or work for years as clerks. Those fortunate enough to secure wartime positions had seen them as a temporary sacrifice, not as an entrée into a future occupation. As Judith McGuire explained when she sought a clerk's position in 1864: "They require us to say that we are really in want of the office – rather a work of supererogation, I should say, as no lady would bind herself to keep accounts for six hours per day without a dire necessity."[63] Teaching had never been a strictly forbidden occupation for southern white women, but to be employed as a teacher without raising an eyebrow generally required that one be a spinster or widow. The substantial antebellum market for northern female tutors testified to the constraints on market opportunities for educated elite southern white women. In the postbellum South, poverty and need overrode these constraints. Elite women of the antebellum planter class taught school and worked in other capacities. This necessity, however, made them clamor all the more for black domestic help.

Having to work, white women learned – as black women already knew – left little time or energy for anything else. Isabelle Ward found working incompatible even with writing letters, not a very taxing endeavor, because "we have no servant, & as we teach regularly we have had our hands full in every way."[64] Ward was not only teaching but teaching black children, a job that would have been inconceivable in the prewar South. Janie Watkins Palmer supported herself in part by taking in washing and sewing. Palmer limited the washing she did for wages to the laundry of other white women but made dresses for black women for a fee. On one occasion she wrote:

I made such a pretty dress for a negro this week – a dark blue bunting with a sky blue silk with raised flowers on it. I took it with fear and trembling but as the girl said she thought she wanted something like mine that Lizzie [Anne Elizabeth] Cordes helped me with I thought it was too good a chance to get $1.50 so I tried my best. I did it in less than three days, and it really looked very well made and very pretty. This with my work from the Cordeses brought me $2 this week. If only I could get that much a little oftener it would help us a heap, and I told you it is a tight push to get on after we take out $12 for rent, $5 for washing, $2 to Elsie, and $2 for fuel there is very little left each month to live on. I heard our washer say she means to raise on us, but she won't get

[62] Fambro, *Ohio Narratives*, Supplement Series 1, vol. 5, p. 341.
[63] Alice Gaillard Palmer to Harriet R. Palmer, July 20, 1865, in *World Turned Upside Down*, ed. Towles, p. 480; Judith W. McGuire, *Diary of a Southern Refugee during the War by a Lady of Virginia*, ed. Jean Berlin (1867; reprint, Lincoln: University of Nebraska Press, 1995), November 11, 1864, p. 244. See also King, ed., *A Northern Woman*, February 10 [1870], p. 244.
[64] Isabelle H. Ward to [Louis] Manigault, January 26, 1869, Manigault Papers, DU.

any more for we have not got it to give, as it is frequently we have to do without any kind of meat for dinner and never have it for breakfast.[65]

Unlike Gertrude Thomas, Palmer was unapologetic and betrayed no great embarrassment about sewing for pay for black women. She made nothing of the fact that a former slave would desire a dress like one she owned, much less that she should be asked to make it. Still, she had no intention of giving up her own servant or washer, even though the wages saved would have helped to put meat on her table and eliminated her need to work for black women. Yet, she apparently missed the irony of going to the wash tub herself to earn the money to pay a black woman to wash and clean for her.

White women in the Palmer family slowly conceded the necessity of earning a living even if they fought the necessity of doing without servants. They worked to keep from doing without black help, no matter how minimal that help. They devised creative solutions to their money shortages, but largely to keep themselves in fashion and in servants. They took advantage of the vibrant market in old clothes, selling last year's dresses to black women in order to buy themselves new ones and to have the cash to hire black domestic help. But the women who had once belonged to them could be discriminating customers, as Sarah Palmer Williams learned when she tried to sell an old dress for ten dollars. Her sister-in law, Alice Gaillard Palmer, wisely advised her to lower the price. The trimming and skirt on the dress were "both old fashioned" and would be rejected by the "fastidious ladies of color," especially when they could buy "new marino fabric for one dollar per yard." Sarah's old dress, Palmer warned, stood "little chance of selling for anything" at all.[66]

In addition to their dealings with the Baltimore Society, the Palmer women entered independently into partnerships with black women who sold their former mistresses's old dresses on commission, making ten cents from each sale. Neither were the Palmer women averse to shopping for their domestic servants. On trips to Charleston, Harriet Palmer purchased dresses and other items on behalf of black women, seemingly on a fairly regular basis.[67] On February 9, 1869, she received five dollars from a freedwoman for the purchase of a new dress. Five dollars was a significant sum, and the elderly woman requested that

---

[65] William C. Palmer to Esther Simons Palmer, March 25, 1883, p. 911; Janie Watkins Palmer to Harriet R. Palmer, May 6, 1883, p. 922, in *World Turned Upside Down*, ed. Towles. Conceivably, the washing Janie Palmer took in from the Baltimore Society was done by the black woman she hired to do her own washing. Like other white women, she also had problems retaining her employees. A few months after she wrote her cousin Harriet Palmer of her difficulties, Elsie, the servant she was paying two dollars a month, left (Harriet P. Williams to Harriet R. Palmer, July 28, 1883, p. 929).

[66] Alice Gaillard Palmer to Harriet R. Palmer, January 8, 1868; see also Henrietta Palmer Smith to Harriet R. Palmer, January 9, 1868, in *World Turned Upside Down*, ed. Towles, pp. 579 and 580, quote at p. 579.

[67] Burr, ed., *Secret Eye*, March 25, 1880, p. 400; Harriet R. Palmer to Esther Simons Palmer, January 1869; Henrietta Palmer Smith to Harriet R. Palmer, February 9, 1869; Henrietta Palmer Smith to Esther Simons Palmer, April 1871, in *World Turned Upside Down*, ed. Towles, pp. 607, 610, and 690.

Harriet Palmer use it wisely. She wanted a dress similar to one she had seen but "not as expensive" and requested that any remaining funds be returned to her.[68]

During slavery, black women had used money earned from market sales to buy little extras. Hanna Plummer's mother made bed clothes, bonnets, and dresses to earn cash. Fannie Moore's mother, a field hand, quilted and spun thread at night after working in the fields during the day in order to be able to purchase items her owners did not supply. Betty Deese's master allowed her to raise hogs and chickens. Women used money their husbands earned as well. With freedom, the number of women able to buy fabrics they had not been allowed to wear as slaves dramatically increased. And they could design garments according to their own tastes.[69]

Whether the priority was gaining autonomy in work, maximizing income, caring for children, splurging on extras, and so on down a very long list, in the end, the priorities black women set for themselves and their families and households shaped in fundamental ways the transition to freedom in planter households. Henrietta Palmer Smith was merely blowing at the wind when she bragged, after losing a washer who quit near the end of her pregnancy, that as soon as her husband received a raise she would put her starch clothes out and "make the cook put the house to rights and wait on the table." Rather than improving, her husband's finances steadily worsened over the next decade, and with them the possibility that she would be able to escape cooking her own meals.[70] So, too, her dream that she would be able to make her cook take on additional work cleaning her house and waiting on her table for no extra pay. With a steadily dwindling staff of domestic workers, the Palmer women hired a servant to carry the water and take out the slop, but swept their own rooms and made their own beds. When a servant could not come because of illness or sickness in her own family, they did their own ironing, cooking, and washing. No longer forced to work up to the moment they gave birth, black women also left domestic jobs weeks before they were due.[71]

All across the South, former mistresses, like black women, scraped to make ends meet. But even so, they went on fighting recognition that slavery was over,

---

[68] Harriet R. Palmer to Esther Simons Palmer, January 1869; Henrietta Palmer Smith to Harriet R. Palmer, February 9, 1869, in *World Turned Upside Down*, ed. Towles, pp. 610 and 611. See also Chapter 4.

[69] Hannah Plummer, *North Carolina Narratives*, vol. 15, pt. 2, p. 179; Fannie Moore, *North Carolina Narratives*, vol. 15, pt. 2, p. 129; Betty Deese Deposition, May 26, 1874 before T. W. Parrish, Special Commissioner, ser. 1, S.C., Box 4 [I-81].

[70] Henrietta Palmer Smith to Harriet R. Palmer, August 11, 1871; Henrietta Palmer Smith to Harriet R. Palmer, February 1883, in *World Turned Upside Down*, ed. Towles, pp. 698–99 and 902. Over time, "day work" came to mean the performance of several different tasks by one woman rather the division of domestic work into discrete tasks – washing, ironing, cooking, cleaning – performed by different workers.

[71] Esther Simons Palmer to Elizabeth Palmer Porcher, June 7, 1869; Sarah Palmer Williams to Harriet R. Palmer, May 18, 1871; Henrietta Palmer Smith to Harriet R. Palmer, August 11, 1871, in *World Turned Upside Down*, ed. Towles, pp. 625, 691, and 699.

and they remained rebels. Alice Gaillard Palmer had never retreated from this position. The death of her husband during the war, shortly after their marriage, seemed to give renewed vigor to her faith in the Confederacy, slavery, and black people's inferiority. In the spring of 1865, with the defeat of the South looming, she remained defiant, even arguing that the Palmers should refuse to recognize the power of the North to arbitrate contracts with freedpeople and calling the loyalty oath treason to the South. It would be "humiliating" to the Palmer name, she wrote. Indeed, it would "kill the Palmer name." But by August of 1865, even she stood prepared to take the loyalty oath, though she "hated the idea," in order to protect her property. "I am a greater Rebel than ever," she wrote more than a decade later. A rebel she might still be, but a much different kind of rebel than she was in 1861. And, by 1876, she too was earning a living teaching, a job she found so "irksome" and wrong that she hoped the school would accomplish so little it would be forced to close.[72] This, despite her heavy reliance on the income she received from teaching black children.

Alice Palmer can be counted among those former mistresses who thought that somehow the old and the new might cohabit. Mary Pringle certainly thought that when her servant Cretia left. "It was a great shock to me," Pringle wrote, "for Cretia is the comfort – animal comfort – of my every day life. None of these demoralized negroes would make up my chamber fire at daylight in the morning (Cretia does it, indeed, before day light) or give me as much cold water as I like to bathe in all the year round. I was much startled at her communication, yet endeavored not to show it."[73] Even as they found themselves doing work once unimaginable to them, some mistresses remained unreconstructed in their habits of thought.

The changes elite white women were forced to make in their lives were nonetheless revolutionary. They might criticize black women for taking on "white airs," but it was they who had sold black women last year's dresses, to buy bread or the current year's fashions for themselves.[74] And for some, John S. Palmer's comments were prescient. Palmer placed his hopes on the younger generation, believing they would more easily adapt to postwar changes. Ann P. Porcher was among this group. While her mother and aunts were still fighting to hold on to a servant or two in the 1880s, she, John Palmer's granddaughter, took a job in New York City. As an assistant librarian at the Cooper Institute, she earned her own bread at the rate of sixteen cents an hour.[75]

[72] Journal of Harriet R. Palmer, March 12, 1865, Palmer Papers, SCL; Alice Gaillard Palmer to Harriet R. Palmer, August 2, 1865; Alice A. Palmer to Harriet R. Palmer, July 9, 1876, November 8, 1881, in *World Turned Upside Down*, ed. Towles, pp. 440, 482, 792, and 871, quotes at 440, 482 and 792.

[73] Côté, *Mary's World*, p. 284. Pringle's expression of surprise rings false in light of the fact that she had already concluded that "dear, good Cretia" was "a downright Radical" (p. 281).

[74] See, for example, Elizabeth Palmer Porcher to Harriet R. Palmer, September 30, 1882, in *World Turned Upside Down*, ed., Towles, p. 883.

[75] Elizabeth Palmer Porcher to Harriet R. Palmer, March 4, 1883, in *World Turned Upside Down*, ed. Towles, p. 904; Rable, *Civil Wars*, pp. 265–88.

The transformation of the domestic center of the plantation household was the achievement of freed men and women who challenged the definition of freedom proffered by former masters, mistresses, officers of the Union army and of the Freedmen's Bureau, and northern missionaries. Freedwomen's struggles as domestic workers were part and parcel of the larger struggle of emancipation. When fewer black women opted for domestic service, that choice often reflected the need their families had to put all possible hands "behind the mule," and on family plots. Meanwhile, those who worked in domestic service stood ready to leave when needed in the fields or when working conditions in white homes became intolerable. As Sarah Palmer Williams concluded, "they have all changed."[76] In changing, freedwomen ensured that white women changed, too.

Not surprisingly, former slaves fashioned an understanding of freedom that required the dismantling of antebellum notions of southern white womanhood. The push toward that dismantling could take many forms, from leaving and fighting and even to sassing. When a black woman declared, to her female employer's face that "she cared no more for white folks than she did black ones" and "would take one to the court house just as soon as she would the other," she proclaimed the new order as loudly as if she had demanded better compensation. What she proclaimed aloud also had profound significance. The white woman (Gertrude Thomas) had attempted to intervene in a quarrel between two freedwomen, her employee being the one who spoke up. None of the three could have overlooked that the words announced the readjustment of gender and class relations that was underway in the South. In claiming her right to take white (or black) people to court, the freedwoman challenged Gertrude Thomas's place in southern society and proclaimed her own rights as a citizen. Thomas had no satisfactory recourse. Her options, her husband informed her, were to "dismiss them or shoot them."[77] This was four years after the end of the war.

Contests over the renegotiation of the terms of household labor, and race and class relations, continued into the 1870s. By then, however, white female employers were more likely to opt for some kind of compromise, although even these proved unsatisfactory at best. Black women might show up for work but invoke all manner of precepts about how that work would be accomplished, as Esther Simons Palmer learned one Sunday in the summer of 1870 when she ordered her servant Ellen to kill a chicken and make chicken soup. Ellen

---

[76] Sarah Palmer Williams to Harriet R. Palmer, January 12, 1884, in *World Turned Upside Down*, ed. Towles, p. 938; G. P. Collins to Paul C. Cameron, March 11, 1866, Cameron Papers, DU. Crops raised "behind the mule" were generally those subject to division with the landowner. Crops for which the landlord did not furnish seed or fertilizer, such as sugar cane, watermelon, and sweet potatoes, were generally not divided. On this point, see Thomas J. Edwards, "The Tenant System and Some Changes Since Emancipation," in J. P. Lichtenberger, ed., *The Negro's Progress in Fifty Years: The Annals*, Vol. 69 (Philadelphia, PA: American Academy of Political and Social Science, 1913), p. 41.

[77] Burr, ed., *The Secret Eye*, June 1, 1869, p. 316.

made the soup and served it, but there was not a bit of chicken in it. Palmer dismissed as preposterous Ellen's explanation that "she would not kill chickens on Sunday" and threatened to fire her. Ellen stood her ground. In the end, Palmer's son killed the chicken and Ellen cooked it. The Palmers probably took some small satisfaction in the fact that Ellen had at least cooked the chicken; Ellen, no doubt, reveled in the fact that she had not violated precepts of her own, which forbade killing chickens on the Sabbath.[78]

Tryphena Fox pronounced Milly her most reliable servant – the three years Milly worked for Fox set a record for the length of time Fox had been able to keep a servant. This favorite refused, however, to do the washing. To keep her, Fox agreed to "hire the washing extra." But then Milly inherited two lots and a furnished house in the nearby town of Algiers, Louisiana, from her godmother. This dramatic improvement in her personal fortune gave Milly the resources to reevaluate and change her relationship with Fox. First, she took a personal leave of a little more than a week. When she returned, Fox took comfort in her "broad & smiling face," thinking it meant that Milly was "delighted" to be back. Instead, she let Fox know that she would be taking an additional three weeks off. Having placed her faith in messages Milly had relayed to her, indicating her intention to return, Fox "was *surprised* & very much *displeased* for I have kept her place for her & worked like a darky rather than hire a fresh hand & *teach* them."[79]

Milly's newfound economic independence threatened Fox's sense of identity as much as it interfered with her housework. Indeed, Fox believed Milly acted deliberately to taunt and provoke her, for when she returned, instead of reporting to Fox, she went to the nearby black quarters. "She is too independent," Fox declared, "thinks I cannot get along without her & so stops up there in the Quarters till the 1st of November, knowing I have no one upon whom I can rely to cook my next meal – *working* myself & waiting for her."[80] The woman she had waited for, Fox finally concluded, was like the rest of her race, "*treacherous, difficult & unreliable.*" Worse, her financial independence made her "of no account as a servant anymore."[81]

A year later, Fox was still trying an old shoe, this time thinking to resolve her domestic dilemmas by hiring a black couple and their daughter, all for $300.00 for the year, which averages around one dollar and fifty cents per week, per worker. Letters to her mother in Massachusetts painted a picture

[78] Esther Simons Palmer to Harriet R. Palmer, July 1870, in *World Turned Upside Down*, ed. Towles, p. 633. Another of the Palmers's former slaves, Abraham, refused to work on January 5, the day he believed was the true date of Christ's birth. (See Journal of Harriet Palmer, January 2, 1866.)

[79] King, ed., *A Northern Woman*, October 9, [1868], pp. 227–28, quote at p. 227.

[80] King, ed., *A Northern Woman*, October 9, [1868], p. 227.

[81] King, ed., *A Northern Woman*, October 9, [1868], p. 228. See also King, "Introduction," in *A Northern Woman*, and King, "The Mistress and Her Maids: White and Black Women in a Louisiana Household, 1858–1868," in *Discovering the Women in Slavery: Emancipating Perspectives on the American Past*, ed. Patricia Morton (Athens: University of Georgia Press, 1996), pp. 82–106.

of domestic bliss. Celestine would do the cooking, washing, and ironing while her thirteen-year-old daughter, Rosella, would clean the rooms and serve as the nurse for Fox's young son. Fox was initially happy. Not only did Celestine do her work well but voluntarily pitched in to help her husband, Victor, who was placed in charge of the garden. Fox congratulated herself on having found a black woman who was different from others of her race who "want to do certain things for certain wages & no more," applauding this generous trait.[82] No doubt, the fact that Fox had greatly relaxed her standards of acceptable behavior contributed to the new servant's ability to please her, but, as always, Fox's self-congratulation was premature.

Having braved a litany of her daughter's complaints about the trials of domesticity and black women for more than a decade, Fox's mother made the daring suggestion that her daughter consider doing her own work. Fox retorted that her mother clearly did not understand the work of "such an establishment" as hers; it required help. At the same time, it was clear that her power to order her household as she chose and to order her servants about was no longer effective with Celestine and her family. The new situation that she had bragged was so perfect turned out to be, on closer inspection, as problematic as past experiences with black women. Celestine did indeed volunteer to help in the garden, but habitually served breakfast an hour late. Victor, Celestine's husband, knew Fox liked to have the cows milked at five thirty in order to have fresh milk to serve for her children's supper, but could not seem to get the job done before six thirty or seven o'clock, often after the children were in bed. But Fox stopped fussing about these matters or the other "many curious freaks." She counted herself lucky that she had help at all until the day Celestine *"left suddenly* taking Rosella with her, without any *provocation from* me or *notification* to me." "My baby," she reported to her mother, "lacked a day of being a month old."[83]

Fox's account of her travails as a mistress-turned-employer is tiresome to read, and yet valuable for its insight into the psychology of power.[84] The most salient feature of that psychology, in her case, was blindness to the motives of those she related to as servants. Remarkably, after all that had happened, she still worked to construct a narrative of the good mistress. "I have never had much trouble with any of our servants since I came from the Confederacy," she lied in 1870. Yet, remarkably, true predicaments and genuine fears are revealed

---

[82] King, ed., *A Northern Woman*, February 13, 1869, pp. 229–32, quote at p. 232.

[83] King, ed., *A Northern Woman*, pp. 234–36, 238, and 241–44, quotes at pp. 236, 234, 235, and 238, respectively.

[84] As Nell Painter and Deborah Gray White argue, the question of the psychology of power in southern race and class relations is a vastly understudied subject. A good starting point would be Frantz Fanon's study of mental disorders associated with the Algerian War. See Fanon, *The Wretched of the Earth*, trans. by Constance Farrington (New York: Grove Press, 1963), 249–310. See especially Case No. 5, 267–70. Nell Irvin Painter, "Soul Murder and Slavery: Toward a Fully Loaded Cost Accounting," in Nell Irvin Painter, *Southern History Across the Color Line* (Chapel Hill: University of North Carolina Press, 2002); Deborah Gray White, *Ar'n't I a Woman?: Female Slaves in the Plantation South*, rev. ed. (New York: Norton, 1999), pp. 9–10.

in the very same letter. The household was in much better shape, she wrote, now that she had employed a white English couple. Because they were white people, she could trust them. She could trust the woman with the keys to her store room and with her baby. "I feel so much easier when this woman has the baby than I would trust her to a darky & perhaps a careless one at that." The arrangement, like other such efforts by white women employers to attempt to get from poor white women what they could not get from black women, was short-lived. Fox hired the couple for twelve dollars a month, which she thought was sufficient to pay them for cooking, cleaning, gardening, and child care. In less than a month, Fox fired them for drinking on the job.[85]

Susan Magill's experience was similar. After paying "a white girl $9 a month to cook and do housework.... Mrs. M did nearly everything herself and yet as soon as the month was over the girl left her." Magill had apparently had no better luck with black women. "She can't keep a servant over a month and not that long sometimes," an acquaintance wrote. Fox, too, was also again dependent on the labor of black females, "two helps," two teenage black girls, "both *very* slovenly & careless & prone to be idle & yet very good girls for blacks." Her aim was unchanged: to teach them to be "good" house servants. This time, she thought she stood a better chance because they were young, "*much better* than some old, hard-headed, impudent, stealing woman."[86]

To the end, Delphine Taveau remained unapologetically unreconstructed. When her family in New York and Boston once again balked at supporting her family while her husband seemed forever unemployed and in debt, Taveau continued to plead for support. In fact, she was the victim, she told her brother, and "*thoroughly disgusted* with life of such hardship to which you know I was not brought up to." Her current life was "a very different thing from the agreeable life of *planting* at the South, for to play cook washer & chamber maid all at the same time & that in self-defense, for even if you have money, you can't hire the servants."[87]

Servants were, of course, available for hire, just not on the terms white women believed they deserved. Bella apparently made this clear to a potential employer who found that calling up old relations of power gave her no advantage:

I have not written to Bella to engage her positively yet, but wrote to ask her if she will come to oblige me. She wrote today and would come to oblige me but wants to know what I would give her. I wrote for answer that I had always been in the habit of paying $7 but that she must fix her own price so she wrote today that she would not come for any less than what Miss Lulie had paid her. I will write her again in the afternoon.[88]

[85] King, ed., *A Northern Woman*, February 10, [1870], pp. 242–44 and 246, quote at p. 243.

[86] Sarah Palmer Williams to Harriet R. Palmer, September 19, 1883, in *World Turned Upside Down*, ed. Towles, p. 931; King, ed., *A Northern Woman*, July 10, 1870, p. 247.

[87] Delphine Taveau to Richard T. Sprague, June 29, 1872, Taveau Papers, DU.

[88] Henrietta A. [Palmer] Smith to Harriett R. Palmer, October 1883, in *World Turned Upside Down*, ed. Towles, p. 934. Smith was apparently optimistic that an accord could be reached for in the same letter she asked her sister to loan her "servant pillows."

Assessing the situation from the vantage point of 1877, an ex-master noted that "many ladies, among the aristocrats and the respectable class, have been obliged to do their own cooking. In fact, one is esteemed fortunate to be able to employ a cook.... Most ladies, too, have to be their own house-maids, sweeping out, dusting, and making the beds." These changes encouraged white women to adopt other innovations. Kitchens moved inside, "the ladies, not liking to bring dishes across the yard, as slave women had done when kitchens were detached from the main house." And there was a dramatic increase in the number of white households with stoves: "Not only stoves but sewing machines and other household utensils are much more common than before the war. The whites, having to do their own work, are clamorous for conveniences in which they would not indulge their slaves."[89] Northern merchants did a brisk and profitable business in stoves after the war. William Reynolds, operating out of Alabama on behalf of his uncle, a New York merchant, estimated that he would make an extraordinary profit of $900 to $1000 dollars on a $1300 invoice.[90]

No mechanical conveniences, however, could replace slavery. Before the war, ex-slave John Smith recalled, mistresses had different slaves assigned to the jobs of washing their feet, drying them, and fixing their hair. But, he added, the war and emancipation changed everything: "Some of dese missus atter de war died poor. Before dey died dey went from place to place livin' on the charity of dere friends."[91] Memories such as Smith's suggest the politics that must have informed black women's ideas about what freedom should mean. When Rachel Pearsall's cook claimed that the power of a higher authority, the federal government, made it impossible for her to any longer remain a slave, or to continue to cook for her mistress, her mistress was not fooled. Pearsall believed the cook's main goal was "to have the pleasure of seeing me cook." A Union soldier murdered Pearsall's cook for threatening to kill her mistress. Had she lived, she would have seen Pearsall placed among the ranks of the workingclass. At least for a time, Rachel Pearsall was a field hand.[92] "With

---

[89] A South Carolinian, "South Carolina Society," p. 679. The writer added that black women "are usually rather too uncivilized to be trusted with labor-saving machines requiring any delicacy of management." Black seamstresses, he wrote, unless "reared and trained in cultivated [white] families," did poor work and washer-women and ironers "badly damage the clothes they work on, iron-rusting them, tearing them, breaking off buttons, and burning them brown; and as for starch! – Colored cooks, too, generally abuse stoves, suffering them to get clogged with soot, and to 'burn out' in half the time they ought to last" (Ibid). See also Mary Jones to Mary S. Mallard, January 17, 1866, in *World Turned Upside Down*, ed. Towles, p. 1318; Jane Turner Censer, *The Reconstruction of White Southern Womanhood, 1865–1895* (Baton Rouge: Louisisana State University Press, 2003), pp. 78–82.

[90] William C. Reynolds to H. L. Reynolds, January 16, 1866; ibid., February 17, 1866, Henry Lee Reynolds Papers, SHC.

[91] John Smith, *North Carolina Narratives*, vol. 15, pt. 2, p. 279.

[92] Mathew Page Andrews, comp., *The Women of the South in War Times* (Baltimore: The Norman, Remington Co., 1920), pp. 241–42; see also Jacqueline Jones, *Labor of Love, Labor of Sorrow: Black Women, Work and the Family from Slavery to the Present* (New York: Vintage Books, 1985), pp. 47–48.

the Civil War," DuBois wrote, "the planters died as a class."[93] So too did mistresses, no matter how hard they fought this recognition.

The Duty of the Hour

Former mistresses struggled to hold on to the racial privilege and the paternalistic ethos so central to their sense of self but had less and less room to maneuver. Black women stiffened their terms and white women sometimes felt alone in this battle. Obsessed with their own private and public defeats, former masters continued to show impatience with their wives' troubles, even when they sympathized, and the acrimony between white men and women increased.

The changes that war and emancipation brought to their homes, of course, devastated planter men as much as they did their wives and daughters. They witnessed the physical and emotional toil these changes took on white women; and they, too, complained of black women's "outlandish" behavior. Some, like George A. Holt, went to the aid of their wives. Nancy Johnson was working as a cook, washer, ironer, and dining room attendant earning two dollars a week for six days' labor. One day she accidentally broke the spout of a tea cup. Holt beat her severely. It was not simply the broken tea cup that had enraged him, but Johnson's defense of another employee, a fourteen-year-old girl. The "difficulty," Holt testified, was that Johnson had attempted to undermine his authority by "interfering with my *domestic affairs* exclusively. To wit; Having *occasion to punish* a small girl of about 14 yrs of age – (Ellen) for disobedience of orders or duty – sd Nancy Johnson became very much offended & advised her to leave (A girl that I had raised) and apply to the *Freedmans Beauro* (sic) for redress."[94] But even as white men understood the danger to the entire social order that the displacement of white women as "ladies" signaled, they were equally convinced that only a restoration of the material basis of the plantation household offered former mistresses any hope of regaining any semblance of their former status as ruling women. Unless they could rebuild the agricultural economy, the plantation household would remain shattered. Their immediate priorities were to regain political control and reconstruct plantation agriculture. They gave far less attention to problems within the plantation household.

Jefferson Thomas ridiculed his wife's obsession with domestic labor problems when he did not appear simply nonchalant. Gertrude Thomas's suggestion that they should force unmarried servants to marry drew a reprimand from him and an order that she not interfere lest they lose perfectly good hands.[95] When she insisted that white southerners must "*avoid politics*" and recognize that

[93] W. E. B. Du Bois, *Black Reconstruction in America: 1860–1880* (1935; reprint, New York: Atheneum, 1973), p. 54.

[94] Testimony of Nancy Johnson, March 25, 1867, and Geo. A. Hoke to Col. S. S. English, March 29, 1867, BRFAL, KY, RG 105.

[95] Burr, ed., *The Secret Eye*, May 7, 1869, p. 313.

the "duty of the hour" was family survival, she revealed how very differently he and she understood the question of survival.[96]

Long before the end of the war, former masters began planning their comeback, along with northerners hoping to profit from the reconstruction of the plantation economy. Those who had been able to continue crop cash production during the war or to hoard cotton were best positioned to take advantage of the pent-up demand and high prices that immediately followed the war.[97] The vast majority – made prostrate by the war and emancipation – had nothing to bank on. The position of the largest and wealthiest prewar planters fairly matched that of the overly-ambitious overseer whom a former slave, Lucretia Heyward, remembered less than fondly: "He wuk, he sabe he money for buy slabs [slaves] and land. He gits some slabe, but he nebber git any land – de war come."[98] Without slaves, former masters who were able to retain their land were little better off.[99]

In the main, white women and men continued to see matters pertaining to the plantation household differently. A former mistress testified before the Senate Investigating Committee on Labor and Capital that the problems with black women "were growing worse all the time." A white man at the hearing was of the opinion that she exaggerated conditions. Mrs. George Ward then qualified her remarks in an important way. "I was speaking," she stated "about our household affairs and our relations with our household servants," who were "more incorrigible" than ever.

They leave us at any time they choose; they go from house to house, and we can place no dependence on them at all. That is the way they are doing; and if you dare to correct them or to suggest that their mode of working is not the best, or not the one you approve, they

[96] Burr, ed., *The Secret Eye*, October 22, 1868, p. 293.

[97] See, for example, H. L. Reynolds to the Honorable Secretary of Treasury, [July1866], Henry Lee Reynolds Papers, Ser. 1.2, 1866, Folder 10, SHC.

[98] Lucretia Heyward, *South Carolina Narratives*, vol. 2, pt. 2, pp. 279–81, quote at p. 281.

[99] Since the end of the war, planters had worked feverishly to bring in crops already planted, to secure a labor force, and find the means to finance the 1866 crop. Some turned to antebellum factors newly reopened for business or the few who had been able to hold a position during the war. But technological innovations in shipping, communications, and the adoption of cotton compresses by inland shippers undercut the factors' position and their traditional base in the South. In addition, suppliers of manufactured goods moved to establish direct marketing connections with the growing interior markets. Credit suppliers also moved in. These changes were partly responsible for the weakened position of factors as middle men. At the same time, when they could, planters became furnishing merchants. As well, in cotton production, the South lost market share to Egypt, India, and Brazil. Still, as Gavin Wright notes, "cotton prices were high by historical standards during 1866–79, as American cotton continued to exert a dominant influence on the world price." Harold D. Woodman, *King Cotton and His Retainers: Financing & Marketing the Cotton Crop of the South, 1800–1925* (Lexington: University of Kentucky Press, 1968), pp. 245–94; Thavolia Glymph and John J. Kushma, eds., *Essays on the Postbellum Southern Economy* (College Station: Texas A&M University Press, 1985); Gavin Wright, "Cotton Competition and the Postbellum Recovery of the American South," *Journal of Economic History* 34 (September 1974): 613–20. Quote is from Wright, *The Political Economy of the Cotton South*, pp. 58–59.

will leave you, or else be insolent about it. . . . It is a very hard life that we housekeepers here lead. . . . It is such a makeshift kind of life that it is actually dangerous to invite company three days ahead, because you cannot depend on your servants staying with you so long or doing what you want them to do if they do stay. . . . I have known them to leave when they knew that invitations were out for a dining in the house; they would just leave without any particular reason at all, but simply from some foolish desire for change.[100]

The result, Ward stated, was that few white people still had the same house servants they had before the war.

Senator Henry Blair, a member of the committee, seemed both amused and befuddled by Ward's testimony. After listening patiently, he finally put a question to her, the answer to which he had probably already surmised on the basis of her testimony. What, he asked, was her frame of mind about these things? Ward admitted that it was "a very fractious frame of mind," brought on by annoyance at having to be bothered by the "cares of housekeeping" with free labor. Firing those who displeased her had no effect, for "if you discharge one all you can do is to take another that somebody else has discharged." Perhaps tiring of the script, Senator Blair interjected that it seemed to him that she was a bit confused about who was discharging whom. "From what you say I infer," he remarked, "that, as a rule they discharge you, don't they?" "As a rule, they do," Ward agreed. Still, she stated, she would not know what to do without them. Even if they were "trifling," she would not think of replacing them with white servants. Besides, she added, "We are used to abusing them too."[101]

Former masters generally left to their womenfolk the job of restoring order on the domestic front. This did not mean, however, that they were averse to throwing their own weight against the ambitions of black women. They did in fact intervene in the affairs of the household immediately after the war. That intervention had three important characteristics. First, it usually involved black women whom they, not their wives, had hired. These were women contracted as field hands but called on to do extra work in the homes of planters or their overseers. Second, while planters rarely took part in disputes over pay, hours, or work conditions between white women and the women they hired specifically for house work, when they did, it was often intensely violent. Third, white men kept up their criticism of white women's domestic capacity. The problems white women had managing household servants after the war fueled this criticism. In all these matters, white men's involvement was sporadic, indicating their general alienation from domestic issues. It was the tightness in the labor market for domestic servants that most often brought white men into the picture. Women hired for field labor, but ordered to take on uncompensated additional labor in their employers' households (or in the households of their overseers), might or might not respect the order.

---

[100] Testimony of Henry M. Caldwell and Testimony of Mrs. George Ward, *Senate Committee Report*, IV: 343.

[101] Ward Testimony, *Senate Committee Report*, IV: 344–445.

The staggering losses in property, political, and social power stripped former masters of their accustomed ability to satisfy the requirements of southern paternalism and patriarchy. They watched their wives and children do work previously deemed suitable only for slaves or black people. Further, black men had received the right to vote – the steadfast hallmark of true manhood in the modern world – a right that elite men had long prevented even poor white men from acquiring. Even when white men, like Augustin Taveau and Jefferson Thomas, opined that white women's domestic troubles resulted not only from emancipation but also from their failure, long before the war, to take control of their households, they were not relieved of a sense that they, too, as men, had failed. That feeling could lead them to try to help bring order to the domestic space.

Out of frustration, white men turned to the only source of "captive" labor they had – the women they employed in the fields to do extra ironing or to cook when the cook hired for the purpose quit, fell sick, was just weary of it all, or when they either could not afford a cook or find one to hire. When these women protested, violence often ensued. Eliza Jane Ellison lost her life because she wanted to know how much she would be paid when she was ordered to wash extra clothes "which she was not bound to do by her contract." Her employer's wife considered the question insulting and they argued. She turned to her husband, Dr. L. B. Walton, insisting that he force Ellison to do the extra laundry. Dr. Walton agreed that Ellison's refusal constituted an intolerable insult.

The argument resumed on a subsequent day with Dr. Walton calling Ellison a "God dam bitch" and ordering her to shut up. According to the testimony of her husband, Samuel Ellison, Walton then threatened greater harm and ordered Ellison off the premises. She refused, stating that she would not leave until the expiration of her twelve-month contract, whereupon Walton drew his pistol. Ellison tried to protect herself but the bullet went through her abdomen. Shot on December 12, 1866, she died the following day. Four days later, the court acquitted Dr. Walton of murder. Four Tennessee justices of the peace heard the case of *The State of Tennessee vs. Dr. L. B. Walton*, finding the defendant "not guilty of either murder or manslaughter but that he killed Jane Ellison (col) in his own self defense at the time and place stated . . . and was justifiable in the law in so doing."[102]

Few such disputes over overtime work ended in murder, but violence was not uncommon. When Linda Brown refused a request by her employer's agent to "do a large ironing" for him after she had completed her work in the field, the agent beat her on her head with a hoe.[103] Clary Dean's employer beat her head with a hickory stick. Dean had gone from the field to cook at her

[102] Statement of Justices of the Peace, T. O. Tarpley, James Cook, James N. Thornhill, and James Randolph, Acting Justices of the Peace in the case of the *State of Tennessee vs. Dr. L. B. Walton*, December 17, 1866, enclosing Affidavit of Samuel Ellison, December 17, 1867, TN, ser. 12, Affidavits and Outrages, RG 105.
[103] Affidavit by Sam Brown, July 16, 1866, Letters Received, ser. 933, box 21, GA Sub-Assistant Commissioner, RG 105.

landlord's house when the trouble began. She made biscuits, which he counted both before and after they were baked, and accused her of stealing one, which she denied.[104] Unlike Brown and Ellison, Clary Dean worked regularly as a field hand as well as her landlord's cook and she spun thread at night.[105]

Generally speaking, despite their occasional intervention in household labor disputes, white men proved much less sanguine than white women about the possibility of restoring prewar relations of power. South Carolinian Augustin L. Taveau was certain they could not be. He was finally convinced, he wrote, that black people had never been contented as slaves and would never be satisfied with anything short of freedom. It was foolish to think otherwise, he wrote:

Does the Jew look hopefully for the Messiah? – so has the Negro for forty years been looking for the Man of Universal Freedom; and when his eager ear caught the sounds of his voice thundering at the bars of his prison door, think you that the watchfulness of years was to be drugged into fatal sleep by the well meant kindness of his keeper? Think you that he paused to ponder whether he should starve or fatten in freedom? Nay–he loved us, perhaps not less, but freedom more.... We gave him a plenty of seed, etc. in his cage, but he prefers the privilege of selecting his own food – let him go.... This is language that may grate harshly upon certain ears – but they who have knocked about in camps for four years, and have pondered deeply in the causes, effects, and facts of this awful war, have arrived at conclusions like the foregoing.[106]

Another planter responded similarly when his wife seemed determined to keep a woman enslaved he had informed was free. He, too, invoked the experience of war as a lesson for moving on. The former slave's daughter recalled him saying that "if she had been through wid what he had been through wid she could give mother up as free as takin' a drink of water."[107] John Jones was also ready to move on, and told his sister so in response to her unceasing complaints about servant problems. They must all stop "clinging too much to a race who are more than willing to let us go," he wrote.[108] In this vein, South Carolinian John S. Palmer counseled his married daughter. "We are all now quite disheartened and cast down," he wrote, and the time was "evidently approaching when perhaps the most menial offices will have to be performed by the family.... we must go down to the lowest depths before we can touch bottom and rise again."[109]

---

[104] Affidavit of Clary Dean, July 10, 1866; Letters Received, ser. 933, box 21, GA, Sub-Assistant Commissioner, RG 105.

[105] Affidavit of Clary Dean, July 10, 1866.

[106] Augustin L. Taveau to "Hon. William Aiken," April 24, 1865, Taveau Papers, DU. Taveau titled his letter to Aiken, "A Voice from the South." A nearly identical version of the letter was published in the *New York Tribune*, June 10, 1865.

[107] Jane Anne Privette Upperman, *North Carolina Narratives*, vol. 15, pt. 2, p. 368.

[108] Rev. John Jones to Mary Jones, August 21, 1865, in *The Children of Pride: A True Story of Georgia and the Civil War*, ed. Robert Manson Myers (New Haven, CT: Yale University Press, 1972), p. 1292. See also Nell Irvin Painter, "Introduction: The Journal of Ella Gertrude Thomas: An Educated White Woman in the Eras of Slavery, War and Reconstruction," in Burr, ed., *The Secret Eye*, p. 54.

[109] John S. Palmer to Elizabeth Palmer Porcher, December 29, 1867, in *World Turned Upside Down*, ed. Towles, pp. 575–76.

As he counseled his family on the adjustments in their lives that war and emancipation required, Palmer acknowledged defeat on a number of scores. His family no longer had a washer, but Palmer wrote that former slaveholding families must accept that "old habits and manners" were things of the past, that they no longer owned people who could be made to work for them. Like Taveau and Jones, he had come to the conclusion that black people would move on in total disregard of the needs of white people. White people had to move on, too. He held out hope that "old habits" learned under the radically different circumstance of slavery would dissipate with a new generation of white southerners "with new hopes and new habits." That generation "must live close, work hard, and trust in a good God."[110]

In the Palmer family, some of the women seemed to agree. "What is the use of trying to keep so many servants when there is no money to pay them," concluded Harriet S. Palmer, perhaps the most level-headed of John S. Palmer's children. "The sooner we come down to our means the better."[111] Besides, there was little else many former masters could otherwise do. Emma LeConte's father was useless to help her when he himself "worked like a negro . . . enduring every kind of fatigue," and when he himself was forced to man a flatboat to transport his corn. In general, Confederate men, returning from war neither "exulting" nor "victorious," could marshal little enthusiasm about the problem of missing or insolent cooks.[112]

Paul C. Cameron was not unconcerned for his wife's "constitution" under her "domestic trials," but he, too, tried to spell out to his family the difference they would know in their lives. When one of his daughters asked for money, he explained the toll of taxes, debt, and his continued efforts to educate his children on an estate greatly diminished by the abolition of slavery. He sent her five dollars along with this severe admonition: "Make the most of your money and time – fit yourself for a useful life – I shall have no fortune to bet on my children – all will have to make their own way." It was the same advice – marbled with a dose of racism – he gave to his son, Duncan, in response to a request for a new pair of shoes:

You have very many wants. Your letters hardly ever fail to tell of some want. When I had the money I ever felt glad to furnish my dear children as to anything that they needed – But I am obliged to tell you my dear boy that I have no command of cash and find it difficult to provide my large family with what I know they need. And I look forward this winter to not a little anxiety on the subject of wood and clothing – . . . . We are to have a great revolution in society & social life and those who do not now go to work & make a manly effort to sustain themselves and families will go down. . . . You *will* have

[110] John S. Palmer to Elizabeth Palmer Porcher, December 29, 1867, in *World Turned Upside Down*, ed. Towles, p. 576.

[111] Harriet R. Palmer to Elizabeth Palmer Porcher, December 29, 1867, in *World Turned Upside Down*, ed. Towles, p. 577.

[112] LeConte Diary, January 31, 1864; February 19, 1865; June 27, 1865, SHC; Joseph G. Stockard to P. C. Cameron, December 22, 1865, Cameron Papers, SHC. The work in particular that triggered LeConte's remark, interestingly, involved her father's having merely to carry her Aunt Mary's baggage.

to *labour* to live either by your *head* or by your *hands*!... We are now if possible more than anxious that you are making the *best* use of your time – Have nothing to do with a negro.[113]

Paul Cameron was no doubt distracted by other matters large and small, from trying to get his plantations running again, to facing debts he would have considered insignificant before the war. Trying to fix his wife's servant problem may have paled before the prospect of being dunned for $53.40 for two lots of fruit trees he had purchased in the winter of 1861, just before the war broke out. That his debtor apologized for having to present the bill probably offered little consolation. Only after their political rights and the plantation economy had been restored, former masters believed, could they "take up and dispose of the grand issues in which our welfare as a people are entirely blended." Otherwise, Cameron wrote, "our doom is fixed."[114] Cameron focused on his cash crop and his New York factor drove a hard bargain. For example, in 1870, he was given thirty days to pay for an order of guano or else the factor expected him to ship his "entire crop" to be held to pay advances made to him. As for his experiment with peanuts, the company advised him not to ship because the market was overstocked. "We regret," the agent wrote, "that you had such poor luck in your speculation."[115]

In fact, planters' economic pressures fueled their criticism of their wives' domestic capacity. Deeply in debt and facing the loss of his plantations, William Bull Pringle scolded his wife for spending even small sums. For his wife, Mary Pringle, his criticism stung all the more because she had seen her life reduced to scrounging for cash and taking in boarders. She, no doubt, thought such scolding downright distasteful coming as it did from a man who spent his days crying and seemingly paralyzed by severe depression and alcoholism. In 1870 alone, William Pringle spent $11 on brandy and $157.80 on 128 gallons of whiskey, consuming an average of nearly one and a half quarts of whiskey per day. The following year, crushing debt forced the sale of the family's main plantation, purchased at $160,000, for $10,000.[116]

Once they had accomplished the defeat of black people politically and the restoration of undemocratic governments in the South, white men turned to the household. Their victory paralleled fundamental alterations in southern agriculture. By the last decade of the nineteenth century, the once powerful rice districts of South Carolina and Georgia were in a downward spiral from which they would not recover. Business conglomerates had put down stakes in the

[113] Paul C. Cameron to Pauline [Cameron], May 26 [1865]; Paul C. Cameron to [Duncan Cameron], September 27, 1865, Cameron Papers, SHC. Several months later, Duncan informed his father that he had "resolved to work instead of loafing." (Duncan Cameron to [Paul C. Cameron], January 8, 1866.)

[114] P. C. Cameron to [recipient unclear], September 5, 1865; P.C. Cameron to [Duncan Cameron], February 17, 1865, Cameron Papers, SHC.

[115] Williams, Black & Co. to Thomas Carroll, April 14, 1870; ibid., April 26, 1870; ibid., February 16, 1870, Thomas Carroll Papers, Correspondence, 1865–69, DU.

[116] Côté, *Mary's World*, pp. 274, 284–85.

Mississippi Delta. Advances on credit became harder to get and even harder to repay. Planters and laborers were on the move seeking the best advantage. These changes and disruptions had an impact on the bargaining power black women could wield in negotiating for better wages and working conditions. The extent to which it made a difference is unclear but that black women could no longer call on Union troops or the Freedmen's Bureau to assist them in difficult situations must have made a difference. In addition, Republican office holders sympathetic to their plight had been routed and the spaces to build an independent life though farming severely reduced.

Even these changes, however, were insufficient to completely stop black women from pushing their own agendas, forcing former masters and mistresses to adopt new strategies. In the end, it would take, additionally, a movement of white women, initiated and run by them – grounded in memorial associations buttressed by Lost Cause propaganda and the organization of "home service" courses – to fully return white men to the ideological and practical task of reconstructing white womanhood. Former mistresses like Mary Chesnut contributed by reimagining the past, remembering and disremembering as the need demanded. They memorialized the years of their dispossession, passing off legend as history so successfully that the legend came to be remembered as the history. Still others dressed themselves as rebels even when they could no longer dress themselves as mistresses. Black women did not give up either. Long after the war, as white women dressed in grey and dug in their heels, black women continued to press their rights as a free people entitled to the everyday freedoms of speech, mobility, personal liberty, and to the right to build their families and households according to their own light.[117]

[117] Mary Rowland to Mrs. [Paul C.] Cameron, January 20, 1866, Cameron Papers, SHC; Drew Gilpin Faust, *Mothers of Invention: Women of the Slaveholding South in the American Civil War* (Chapel Hill: University of North Carolina Press, 1996), pp. 252–53; George C. Rable, *Civil Wars: Women and the Crisis of Southern Nationalism* (Urbana: University of Illinois Press, 1989), pp. 238–39.

7

"Wild Notions of Right and Wrong"

From the Plantation Household to the Wider World

I'se Mrs. Tatom now and Hamp is Mr. Sam Ampsey Tatom.

Charity Tatom, ex-slave

The masters disclaimed their paternal responsibilities, but they did not cease, for
many decades, to complain of the "great law of insubordination," the diminution
of deference, that ensued upon the disclaimer....

E. P. Thompson

It often strikes me, as I think of the intense enjoyment of olden times, that perhaps
just as the strongest force in physics is evolved from the greatest consumption of
material, so it is ordained in human affairs that the most exquisite happiness shall
be founded in the intense misery of others.

A South Carolinian

Virginia Newman's first "bought dress" was a "blue guinea with yaler spots."
Two years after emancipation, Nancy Johnson counted up her possessions –
one bed quilt, two calico dresses, three cotton chemises, and one basket.[1] Jane
McLeod Wilborn took the first money she earned as a free woman and bought
some calico cloth and quilts. She was "proud," she said, to have her "own
quilts an' pillows an' things."[2] These material comforts made her home a little
nicer, and, more importantly, they were hers, the small but tangible fruits of
her labor as a washerwoman. Another former slave, Mollie, celebrated her
freedom to put her earnings on her "back."[3] Decades after the end of slavery,
Newman, Johnson, Wilborn, and Mollie remembered these things as concrete
evidence of freedom. In the hands of many of their contemporaries – black
and white, northern and southern – their assessment has been read differently,

[1] Virginia Newman, *Texas Narratives*, vol. 5, pt. 3, p. 151; Affidavit of Nancy Johnson [March
2, 1867], Approved Claims, ser. 732, Southern Claims Commission, RG 217.
[2] Jane McLeod Wilborn, *Mississippi Narratives*, Supplement Series. 1, vol. 10, pt. 5, pp. 2295–96.
[3] Virginia Ingraham Burr, ed., *The Secret Eye: The Journal of Ella Gertrude Thomas, 1848–1889*
(Chapel Hill: University of North Carolina Press, 1990), June 19, 1869, pp. 318–19.

as evidence that black women did not understand what freedom really meant and were decidedly unprepared for it. It has been read further as evidence of a preoccupation with normative white values and a desire to emulate their former mistresses. When one turns to the historiography of emancipation and Reconstruction, the comments by Newman, Johnson, Wilborn, and Mollie pale in significance when set beside those of women like Lucretia Heyward, who used the money from her earnings as a washerwoman for Union soldiers during the Civil War to purchase land in Parris Island, South Carolina.[4]

In the context of the most discussed and familiar history of former slaves, Lucretia Heyward's struggle to buy a piece of land forms part of the great heroic, political contest waged by ex-slaves in the postbellum South. She accomplished the most cherished ambition of freedpeople. In this context, Newman's, Johnson's, Mollie's, and Wilborn's decisions can appear inconsequential, and as unworthy of careful examination. The efforts of black people to secure land, education, mobility, civic and civil rights as citizens, to build schools, churches, and community organizations frames historical scholarship on emancipation and the meaning of freedom, and for good reason. But as vital as these matters were to the construction of new meanings of freedom and the larger project of Reconstruction, alone they could not make for a "whole life." Like human beings everywhere, ex-slaves at the time were surely striving for nothing less than that. Mollie's desire to put her money on her "back" and Wilborn's to own pillows might superficially seem to smack of a lack of political awareness, or even stupidity, rather like buying a doily or damask to dress up a plank board table. But to dismiss these desires as such, however, as too ordinary, too lacking in "real" politics, too ridiculous, and, therefore unworthy of our attention, is to dismiss much of what is important to human beings.[5] Clearly, as well, to understand those desires as mere imitative behavior, as black women trying to be like white women, is to overlook basic and lasting "real" politics in the postwar South.

To dismiss the evidence of this politics as mere imitation is to miss or perhaps overlook the rules of consumption that buttressed slavery by keeping the inequality of black and white women on display, day in and day out, in myriad small facts and acts of denigration. In that context, any move black women made to enlarge their lives could hardly avoid jostling the lives of white women. We can be sure there was nothing "mere" about imitation because white women wrote so much about it. And, it seems reasonably clear that there was nothing "mere" about the imitation white women saw or thought they saw since they wrote so much about it.

The dresses, pillows, and other material purchases black women made testify to the meagerness of black people's lives in slavery and to the promise of fullness in freedom. The signal importance of these purchases is that they were

---

[4] Lucretia Heyward, *South Carolina Narratives*, vol. 2, pt. 2, p. 280.

[5] Rather, as E. P. Thompson suggests, our job is "to prepare for analysis at the points at which it should be made." E. P. Thompson, *Customs in Common* (London: Merlin Press, 1991), p. 43.

not "gifts" from white people, not hand-me-downs. The desire for a pretty dress or a home with kitchen utensils and blankets was a small but central part of freedom's making, of demonstrated control over one's life. They were not purchased or cherished in the hope that they would transform black women into "ladies." Black women had every reason to deplore so many of the habits of white women before emancipation and few reasons in freedom to reconsider that judgment.

Even evidence that seems explicitly imitative deserves deeper study. Ann Drake, for instance, recalled that slave children "wud dress up in mammies dresses, an' play fine ladies," and Ed Williams, his mother telling him that the slaves all "wanted to do like de white folks." Slaveholders, Williams elaborated, "had ebery thing fine an' ebery thing dey wanted, an' cud cum an' go wid out de patroller gittin' dem, but de slaves wanted to do de same thing; dat is de reason dey all wanted to be sot free. When cumpany cum to dat big house, de Judge yelled for sum darky, so mammy sed, to cum an' take de horses an keer fur dem, an' black dem shoes, an' den cooked good things to eat an' loaded de table an' de slaves would git mi'ty little uf it. All de slaves wanted to do like de white folks."[6] It is easy to interpret such remarks simply as a desire to emulate white people. Doing so, however, requires studied inattention to Williams's juxtaposition of the richness of the lives of slaveholders and the scantiness of those of slaves, the "mi'ty little" and the attendant humiliations.[7]

Stores that cropped up on plantations and along rural roadsides after the Civil War became infamous for usurious interest rates and overpriced goods marketed to black farmers and workers. At the same time, they provided hundreds of thousands of rural black people their first opportunity to shop for themselves. The scant provisions provided by slaveholders meant that most former slaves had to acquire the most basic tools for living. Some appropriated their former mistresses's household goods to get their start as free people. Bella, a South Carolinian, carried into freedom a mattress and all of her mistress's cooking utensils.[8] Children who had slept under the dining room tables in planter homes, or, like Frederick Douglass, on the floor of a small closet; and those who had lived in the yards with neither shoes, stockings, jackets, nor trousers, and gone near-naked when the two coarse shirts they were allowed per year wore out, needed beds and clothing.[9]

---

[6] Ann Drake, *Mississippi Narratives*, Supplement Series 1, vol. 7, pt. 2, p. 644; Ed Williams, *Mississippi Narratives*, Supplement Series 1, vol. 10, pt. 5, p. 2308.

[7] For a compelling description of these disparities, see Frederick Douglass, *My Bondage and My Freedom* (1855; reprint, New York: Dover Publications, 1969), pp. 107–8.

[8] Elizabeth R. Porcher to Harriet R. Palmer, October 25, 1865, Palmer Family Papers, SCL. Kitchen supplies for slaves generally do not show up in planter accounts, marking their rarity in the cabins of the enslaved.

[9] Betty Foreman Chessier, *Oklahoma Narratives*, Supplement Series 1, vol. 12, p. 99; Douglass, *My Bondage and My Freedom*, pp. 101 and 87; Leslie A. Schwalm, *A Hard Fight for We: Women's Transition from Slavery to Freedom in South Carolina* (Urbana: University of Illinois Press, 1997), p. 130.

The Civil War had exacerbated existing shortages and longstanding meagerness. Shortages of cooking utensils had forced slaves to adapt big oak leaves to the purposes of pots. Wartime and postwar observers almost routinely noted the arrival of contraband and refugee slaves "wholly destitute of clothing" and their efforts to bring what little property they had with them into Union lines. "It is almost provoking," wrote Col. Thomas Wentworth Higginson, "to see the way in which they cling to their blankets, feather beds, chickens, pigs, and such like.... these things represent the net result of all their labors up to this time."[10]

Some Union officers and soldiers had refused to recognize even the little that black people carried into freedom as their property. In 1862, William T. Sherman famously ordered his soldiers to desist from helping fugitive slaves recover clothing or other articles. Sherman was immediately responding to an order issued by an artillery battery commander that had sent "a party of soldiers" to retrieve clothing and other items claimed by a "fugitive negress." The commander was out of line, Sherman wrote, because slaves could own no property. "The Clothing & effects of a negro are the property of the master & mistress," he asserted with all the authority of the ill-informed. The army had no choice, he opined, but to accept the right of slaves to run away, but to assist in recovering possessions that they claimed to own would be to "sanction theft robbery or violence." He ordered the items returned and the commander to submit a report indicating he had done so. "We must not encourage the negroes in their propensity to steal and be impudent," Sherman ended the order.[11]

In addition to supplying their needs for such basic things as food, kitchen utensils, and beds, former slaves purchased things that they simply enjoyed, the "extras" like jewelry and trinkets, tobacco, liquor, sugar, candy, and fancier (or just plain better-made) clothing. These things they had generally not been permitted to eat, own, or wear as slaves, except by special dispensation of their owners. Former slaveholders now reaped the benefits of their former slaves' ability to make their own purchases, even as they criticized such purchases as unbecoming for black people. Many planters paid in plantation scrip redeemable only at their stores. Whether plantation stores accepted scrip or cash or credit, former masters and mistresses made tremendous profits. On items such as "flour, prints, jewelry, and trinkets," a Louisiana planter reported in 1865, planters charged two to three times their value.[12] Planters

[10] Thomas Wentworth Higginson, Testimony before the American Freedmen's Inquiry Commission, June 1863, ser. 12, RG 94.

[11] Ira Berlin, Thavolia Glymph, Joseph P. Reidy, and Leslie S. Rowland, eds., *Freedom: A Documentary History of Emancipation, 1861–1867*, ser.1, vol. 1, *The Destruction of Slavery* (Cambridge: Cambridge University Press, 1985), p. 297. On slave property, see also ibid., pp. 145 and 153; and Dylan Penningroth, *The Claims of Kinfolk: African American Property and Community in the Nineteenth Century South* (Chapel Hill: University of North Carolina Press, 2003).

[12] Lucy [Chase] "To our folks at home," January 15, 1863, in *Dear Ones at Home: Letters from Contraband Camps*, ed. Henry L. Swint (Nashville, TN: Vanderbilt University Press, 1966), p. 24; Edward King, *The Great South* (Hartford, CT: American Publishing Co., 1875), p. 298; Thomas Wentworth Higginson, Testimony before the American Freedmen's Inquiry

and merchants charged exorbitant interest rates and overpriced goods, all of which made it harder for black people to make ends meet. Those facts are not incompatible with and do not trump the desire to have a ribbon for one's child. Knowing this makes it possible to understand how it was that black women who as slaves "never had over two dresses" could recall with such intense pride their first purchases.[13]

Store-bought dresses, jewelry, sugar, and trinkets formed a comparatively small but not insignificant part of the economic and social transformation of the southern countryside and the plantation household, alongside the return to cash crop production and the restructuring of finance. Ex-slaves' independent purchasing capacity did not escape the attention of merchant firms. *Hunt's Merchants' Magazine* recorded the transformation in 1866, noting the general decline in expenditures in the South both in luxury purchases and in common fabrics formerly purchased for slaves. But for merchants there was an upside. With the freedom to make their own consumer decisions, even within the constraints of their meager budgets, freedpeople dressed "themselves with better fabrics," and consumed more overall.[14]

Northern merchants and manufacturers cheered the change, which promised a greatly expanded consumer base whose aggregate purchases would bring total sales to near pre-war levels. In 1869, *Hunt's* reported that the optimism of 1865 had been born out in "the vastly increased number of independent 'customers' in the Southern States," and in enhanced "demand both in quantity and variety." The "new wants and methods of trade are the direct outgrowth of the new system of labor," the magazine concluded. Like former masters and mistresses, they, too, expected to make a profit from the "new and lucrative enterprise" of selling to black people.[15]

Northern businessmen thus applauded the expansion of the southern market by four million new consumers, and like free labor advocates, saw it as proof that the expansion of black people's wants justified their emancipation in that it ensured the availability of their labor on reconstructed plantations. They would have to go back to the plantations to work to obtain the cash to satisfy these wants. Many northern missionaries, however, derided the trend, seeing it as proof of former slaves' inferiority and inability to understand the meaning of freedom. These missionaries described black women's appreciation for nice clothing in the same language they used to denigrate black people's religious fervor. When a woman, "struck with the beauty of a gay dress" belonging to

---

Commission, June 1863, ser. 12, RG 94; Harold D. Woodman, *King Cotton and His Retainers: Financing and Marketing the Cotton Crop of the South, 1800–1925* (Lexington: University of Kentucky Press, 1968), pp. 308–14; Harold D. Woodman, *New South – New Law: The Legal Foundations of Credit and Labor Relations in the Postbellum Agricultural South* (Baton Rouge: Louisiana State University Press, 1995), p. 88.

[13] Chessier, *Oklahoma Narratives*, Supplement Series 1, vol. 12, p. 100. See also Chapter 6.

[14] As quoted in Woodman, *King Cotton and His Retainers*, p. 320.

[15] Woodman, *King Cotton and His Retainers*, pp. 320–23; quotes at pp. 321 and 322. For a discussion of the efforts of former mistresses to capture a part of this market by establishing and operating their own stores, see Chapter 6.

northern missionary Lucy Chase, expressed her admiration, saying, "I should be ready to die, if I could get that dress," Chase put the compliment down as another sign of black people's backwardness. They "have yet to learn to guard in seemly silence sacred things," she wrote, combining New England pietism and racism. When she gave a woman a piece of gingham with which to make a simple apron with a waist, the woman turned the fabric into a short, fancy apron. When Chase asked for an explanation, the woman responded that aprons with waists were no longer in fashion. Chase found the answer incomprehensible, just as she did the women who arrived "almost universally wear[ing] upon their heads Tubs or Boilers, whether their bodies are clothed or unclothed." She distributed shoes sent from the North and black people "*danced* in them!"[16] For their part, former mistresses saw so many pretenders to ladyhood.

Yet, former mistresses also came to depend on the new market of black consumers. They sold their old frocks to black women and sewed (or purchased on their behalf) new dresses for them. These actions acknowledged white women's diminished control over black women's attire. This coupled with former mistresses's diminished ability to put clothes on their own backs, let alone their servant staff, made it hard for them to even put on a show of superiority. When Alice Palmer discharged a black servant for failing to please her, she retained one of two dresses she had supplied the woman in order to outfit her replacement. Equally embarrassing, she then had to recall the other dress as well.[17]

The ability of freedwomen to purchase cloth or dresses for themselves or to add a piece or two of furniture to their homes was of course circumscribed by meager wages. As well, "home" might be a former chicken shack. None of this should distract us in trying to understand their efforts to make freedom fuller, or lead us to romanticize their poverty. Nor should it lead us to follow white commentators of the time who insisted that black women were merely imitating white women and, that, poorly. The right to an education, to own property, to vote, and to participate fully in civic affairs in other ways are important attributes of freedom. But freedom also means self-definition and self-determination. These are what might be called small rights, in contrast to large ones, like the right to vote for men, or land ownership. This did not make them insignificant. In fact, they are the kinds of rights that get people through

---

[16] Lucy [Chase] to home folks, January 20, 1863, in *Dear Ones at Home*, ed. Swint, pp. 30, 33, and 40. Slave women's head dresses were considered such identifying markers that their absence was as much remarked upon as their presence. A black soldier with the 54th Massachusetts Infantry was struck by the appearance of a group of women who came into Union lines at Jacksonville, Florida. He described them as "the most wo-be-gone set – no shoes, hats or clothing, and, what the most impoverished slave-women seldom fails to possess, turbans" (Sgt. Geo. E. Stephens, March 10, 1864, in *A Grand Army of Black Men: Letters from African-American Soldiers in the Union Army, 1861–1865*, ed. Edwin S. Redkey [Cambridge: Cambridge University Press, 1992], pp. 46–47).

[17] Alice G. Palmer to Harriet R. Palmer, August 7, 1865, Palmer Family Papers, SCL. See also Chapter 6.

the day, that make it possible for them to partake of those larger rights. Small rights can also challenge hierarchies of power. Small rights gain importance when we see them against the background of what could be called small regimes; that aspect of the slave regime that determined where people could go, what they could wear, what rights they had to their children.

Playing the Lady

The right to make, own, and wear a fancy apron that Chase denigrated was a small right. Chase's denigration forms part of an influential narrative that sought to determine *for* former slave women what freedom meant. This narrative was set down by former masters and mistresses, northern missionaries, and agents of the Freedmen's Bureau. It castigated black people's claims to small rights. It turned freedwomen's actions into a caricature, a ludicrous bid to "play the lady." To former mistresses, this bid took shape within the plantation household as black women left to "set up for themselves" and demanded better treatment in general. It was not contained, however, within the plantation household. Former mistresses saw it playing out (outrageously, they believed) in the wider world.

Mary Norcott Bryan, like many white women, penned her reminiscences of slavery, the war, and Reconstruction with the goal of leaving a written record for her descendants. Among the stories she left them was this one: "I was walking along quietly on Broad Street when a fat buxom mulatto wench came up to me, and shaking her fist in my face ordered me off the side-walk." She wrote that she had considered applying for help but immediately recognized that it would be a futile gesture. "I quickly looked up and seeing no white person visible, and the street full of negroes, as a church had just emptied itself into the streets, I stepped aside into the gutter and went home." For Bryan it was figuratively as well as literally a gutter. Stories, Robert Darnton reminds us, provide "meaningful shape to the raw stuff of experience."[18] White women recorded many such stories in their diaries, letters, and postwar memoirs of their confrontations with freedwomen.[19] But the very definition of the word "story," we also know, means that the narration may be true or fictitious; that it may be a report, an allegation of facts, or even a romantic legend.

On June 1, 1865, Eliza Andrews told a story similar to Bryan's. "The last time I went on the street," she wrote, "two great, strapping wenches forced me off the sidewalk. I could have raised a row by calling for protection from the first Confederate I met, or making a complaint at Yankee headquarters, but I would not stoop to quarrel with negroes."[20] Andrews did not stop to

---

[18] Mary Norcott Bryan, *A Grandmother's Recollection of Dixie* (New Bern, NC: Owen G. Dunn, 1912); p. 12; Robert Darnton, *The Great Cat Massacre and Other Episodes in French Cultural History* (New York: Vintage Books, 1984), p. 78.

[19] Schwalm, *A Hard Fight for We*, p. 152.

[20] Eliza Frances Andrews, *The War-Time Journal of a Georgia Girl, 1864–1865*, ed. Spencer Bidwell King, Jr. (1908; reprint, Macon, GA: Ardivan Press, 1960), p. 282.

quarrel with the women or to call for protection for she knew no victory was to be had that day. Whatever humiliation she suffered, there was little to be gained by making it the subject of a public appeal. While redress of some sort might result, further humiliation was certain. Knowledge of the incident would spread, and people would talk. She would likely gain the sympathy of her female peers but she, not the black women, would nonetheless be the loser. Besides, with Union troops holding the town, "the first Confederate" she met, facing his own tattered masculine world, might well have declined the office of protecting her. Taking her complaint to Union officers who were attending balls put on by former slaves and dancing "with the black wenches!" was an equally dubious proposition. Andrews could not hope for redress there.[21] In either place, she might find a sympathetic ear or she might not. And how did a woman of her position talk about such a thing as being forced off the sidewalk by black women, a proposition that just four years earlier would have been considered absurd?

Like Bryan, Andrews got her revenge by different means – in the story she left for posterity. This story is an account of "great, strapping wenches," an image of black womanhood that gained the sympathy and revenge she sought, even if it had to come from future generations of white Americans. Her description of the women aligned neatly with the action she imparted to them. They were large and lewd. The language she chose made them appear the most threatening: in their girth, race, use of brute force, defiled womanhood ("wenches"), their generally "uncivilized" behavior. The story Andrews told certainly gave "meaningful shape" to her experience, but to achieve that, a story can be an exaggeration or even an invention, true only in the sense that fiction is true.

Quite possibly, the black women Andrews encountered did not so much "force" her off the walk – at least not in the manner she implied – but rather, did not remove themselves from the sidewalk, thus leaving Andrews to either go around them or wait for them to pass, options she may not have considered, or been ill-prepared by her former experience as a mistress to consider. The insult to Andrews remained either way; thinking and writing about the incident in the way she did was therapeutic, a way of coping with the revolution that had changed her world. Ultimately, whether the black women had physically "forced" Andrews off the sidewalk or simply refused to give her privileged space by moving aside to make way for her, she was forced to behave as any civilized person should, to wait for them to pass or detour around them. She was not prepared to see or understand this maxim. She could only see the incident as another damning marker of the transformation of her world. Whatever the particulars, the confrontation surely confirmed that transformation.

Andrews's former slaves and the black women she now hired, it turns out, had their own stories to tell, and these, too, bore the weight of fiction and truth. From one of them – who clearly took some delight in the telling – she learned of the dances where black and white people mingled. Another servant,

---

[21] Andrews, *War-Time Journal of a Georgia Girl*, p. 287.

Charity, brought news of a mass marriage ceremony and more. Charity, Andrews relates, "went about her work as usual, but when I stepped into the back porch to get some water, she stopped in the midst of it to tell me that she now had two names, like white folks." Andrews laughed and asked what they were. "'Tatom; I'se Mrs. Tatom now and Hamp is Mr. Sam Ampsey Tatom," Charity replied. Andrews found Tatom's assertion of rights comical and "sad," and a portent signaling an end to the "sweet ties" between slaves and slaveholders.[22]

To former mistresses, even the perception of a slight to their place in the world acquired new meaning in the new South without slaves. In Mary Norcott Bryan's case, the situation was exacerbated by the particular circumstances in her home town of New Bern, North Carolina, where she returned at the end of the war after having spent much of the war as a refugee. In her recollections, Bryan penned a portrait of outrageous black women, highly sexed and violent, so different from her own "black mammy" and all the "fat smiling mammies with red bandanas on their heads singing sweet old Negro melodies, and chopping up sausage meat" she thought that she had known before the war.[23] She did not attempt to explain how mammy had become a "wench." That might have required at least an explanation of mammy's origins, to be followed by another, of her disappearance. Bryan was prepared to give none of this, and none of it suited her designs. The town of New Bern to which she returned was hardly recognizable to her, and this no doubt influenced her judgment. Instead of black mammies, it sheltered free black women who had spent the war fighting for freedom and the success of the Union armies.

New Bern was occupied by federal troops in mid-March 1862. From the outset black women were instrumental in its transformation into a free town. Like Hilton Head Island and its environs, it had become a beacon for fugitive slaves, including slaves refugeed to neighboring Franklin County who swam the river to return "to New Bern and freedom." In New Bern, Hattie Rogers happily exclaimed, the Union army had "rocked the place." Under the banner of the Colored Women's Union Relief Association presided over by Mary Ann Starkey, New Bern's black women had raised hundreds of dollars for black soldiers and their families, and nursed black and white soldiers from Ft. Fisher after the fall of Wilmington. They had worked in tandem with the New England Soldiers Relief Association and the Office of Supervisory Committee for Recruiting Colored Regiments. They had participated in and witnessed the presentation of color standards to black regiments, flags donated through their own efforts and those of black women in the nation's capital. Their "distinguished enterprise" had won them praise from General Edward Wild, northern missionaries at New Bern, Boston philanthropists and abolitionists, and The Supervisory Committee. They had witnessed the enlistment of their husbands, brothers, and fathers into Wild's African Regiment (and

[22] Andrews, *War-Time Journal of a Georgia Girl*, pp. 346–47, quotes at p. 347.
[23] Bryan, *A Grandmother's Recollection of Dixie*, quotes at pp. 12 and 10, respectively.

witnessed the abuse of black enlistees). When a writing school opened in 1863, sixteen of them, "all grown up women," had presented themselves for matriculation.[24] These were the women who represented the real threat to Bryan's sense of self and her place in the world on her return to New Bern in 1865.

A Most Absurd Procession

At emancipation black women took center state, alongside black men, as claimants to power and privilege. But to white Americans, their freedom was the most unearned and their interpretation of it, the most misguided. Black women, the northern white missionary Elizabeth Botume asserted, could have little conception of the meaning of freedom or of their rights as free people. Botume attributed this lack of understanding to their gender and race, but in an interesting way that collapsed the categories. Their sex meant that, unlike black men, they had not fought for their freedom, though Botume would not have questioned her own capacity to understand the meaning of freedom on the grounds of her sex.[25] Botume's judgment reflected the general difficulty white Americans had in seeing black women as women, citizens, the wives and daughters of soldiers, or contributors to the Union cause and freedom. They were mere pretenders to citizenship and womanhood.

If emancipation represented a world turned wrongly on its axis – 'Sternitur,' proclaimed one former master[26] – nothing seemed so thoroughly to present itself as validation than the widely reported "misbehavior" of black women in pretending to be ladies. White people saw the alleged misconduct almost everywhere they looked, from the determination of black women to "set up for themselves" in their own homes, to how they chose to dress themselves and assert their rights of citizenship. Their conduct in all these matters, white southerners believed, entailed most fundamentally a desire to emulate elite white women's behavior, their dress, and relatedly, their privileged social status as nonworkers.[27] Black women with last names and titles; wearing veils;

---

[24] Hattie Rogers, *North Carolina Narratives*, vol. 15, pt. 2, pp. 227 and 231; Mary Ann Starkey to E. W. Kinsley, July 22, 1865; Oscar E. Doolittle to J. W. Sullivan, Esq., July 22, 1863; E. A. Wild to E. W. Kinsley, July 28 [1863]; Andrew J. Holbrook to E. W. Kinsley, September 3, 1863; Joseph E. Williams to Edward W. Kinsley, August 19, 1863; Andrew J. Holbrook to [E. W.] Kinsley, September 12, 1863, Edward W. Kinsley Papers, DU. On the wives of black soldiers in New Bern, see also Horace James to [E. W.] Kinsley, July 4, 1864 and McClary Perkins to [E. W.] Kinsley, April 1, 1865. See also Benjamin Quarles, *The Negro in the Civil War* (Boston: Little, Brown and Company, 1953), pp. 246–47.

[25] Elizabeth Hyde Botume, *First Days among the Contrabands* (1893; reprint, New York, 1968), p. 152.

[26] St. Waddell to Paul Cameron, February 2, 1966, Cameron Papers, SHC.

[27] Andrews, *War-Time Journal of a Georgia Girl*, pp. 288, 306–7; Beth G. Crabtree and James W. Patton, eds., *"Journal of a Secesh Lady": The Diary of Catherine Ann Devereaux Edmondston* (Raleigh: North Carolina Division of Archives and History and Department of Cultural Resources, 1979), May 13, 1865, p. 711 (hereafter cited as Edmonston, *Diary*); Burr, ed., *The Secret Eye*, p. 320.

quitting without notice; refusing to play nursemaid, field hand, and cook all at once; quitting white homes and fields in favor of domestic production, and claiming the right to talk back, constituted the epitome of "'the great law of insubordination,' the diminution of deference."[28] To white observers, all of these things reflected a desire on the part of black women to be what they obviously could not be, ladies.

The term "lady" carried distinct connotations and white southerners had clearly marked and policed its boundaries. Lizzie Bain, the daughter of hotel keepers, was acutely aware of the distinctions and boundaries. In the 1850s, while visiting relatives, she wrote home to her family, "I feel as though I was doing wrong to be playing the lady and you all at work as I know you are."[29] In dressing as they desired or could afford, saying no to unfair and unwanted demands on their time and resources, refusing waged work in preference for vegetable gardens and home-based domestic production for the market and their own families, former slave women challenged the symbolic and material basis of white womanhood.

The subversive function that "playing the lady" served is clear enough. Former slave women, notes Drew Faust, "used the language of clothing to assault the hierarchies of race."[30] In *parading* as ladies, black women struck a deliberately targeted blow at racism and the pedestal of southern white womanhood. The parades, loud and boisterous as parades tend to be, actually began before the war, but it was only in the context of the war and slaves' emancipation that they came to be viewed by more than a minority of white southerners as subversive.[31] With freedom's arrival, the parades became evermore ostentatious, amazing public spectacles acted out in the drawing rooms and yards of planter homes, and in the wider world of southern towns and cities, and country roadways.

Former masters and mistresses indicted black women and men for *parading* as ladies and gentlemen because they understood that its goal was in part to shame and humiliate them, before their very faces. Gertrude Thomas tried to write off the "coloured demoiselle" through caricature: "Numbers of negro

---

[28] Thompson, *Customs in Common*, p. 36.

[29] Lizzie Bain to Sister [Mollie Bain], September 19, 1853; Lizzie Bain to Sister [Mollie Bain Bitting], May 22, 1857, Bain Papers, DU. Bain's parents ran a boarding house in Raleigh, North Carolina. They owned a few slaves and hired others periodically. Bain worked there prior to her marriage and her siblings continued to help manage the place.

[30] Drew Gilpin Faust, *Mothers of Invention: Women of the Slaveholding South in the American Civil War* (Chapel Hill: University of North Carolina Press, 1996), p. 223; Elizabeth Fox-Genovese, *Within the Plantation Household: Black and White Women of the Old South* (Chapel Hill: University of North Carolina Press, 1988), pp. 197, 202–3; Edmondston, *Diary*.

[31] Parades, as several scholars have shown, are important spaces for examining contestations over power. See Simon P. Newman, *Parades and the Politics of the Street: Festival Culture in the Early American Republic* (Philadelphia: University of Pennsylvania Press, 1997); Mary P. Ryan, *Civic Wars: Democracy and Public Life in the American City during the Nineteenth Century* (Berkeley: University of California Press, 1997); and David Waldstreicher, *In the Midst of Perpetual Fetes: The Making of American Nationalism, 1776–1820* (Chapel Hill: University of North Carolina Press, 1997).

women some of them quite black . . . promenading up the streets with black lace veil shading them from the embrowning rays of a sun under whose influence they had worked all their life." Kate Cumming described the freedom parades as a "frolic." "The main portion of the women," she wrote, "do little else than walk the streets, dressed in all kinds of gaudy attire."[32] But it became more and more difficult to laugh at or make light of the celebrations of freedom that followed Lee's surrender. Rebecca Cameron, so unnerved by Lee's surrender that she took to "a darkened room sitting with folded hands" to contemplate "the failure of our cause," found no peace even here. From the darkened room, she sneaked horrified glimpses of the new order. A Union general had taken control of a building for his personal use and that of "two mulatto women." "I kept my curtain down all the time they were here nearly," she wrote, "for I hated them so and couldn't bear to see the insolent whelps strutting around the house."[33]

In Charleston, with final victory secured by Lee's surrender, Union soldiers and black people took to the streets on April 13, 1865, engaging in what one white southerner called "a most absurd procession . . . celebrating the Death of Slavery." On July 4, in Columbia, South Carolina, the celebration of freedom white people had dreaded for the two months it had been in the planning finally took place. As several thousand black people celebrated, white Columbians stayed shut up in their homes but unprotected from the news that seeped in. Emma LeConte heard of the "flag given by the ladies," which had been "decorated with flowers by negro girls," and of the celebration dinner that took place just outside of the city. Listening to the fireworks and the brass band made her feel all the more keenly her diminished position. "It was too humiliating," she wrote. The local newspaper called for police action against the "loud talking, laughing, and whistling of negroes upon the public streets, both in the day and in the night."[34]

The world turned upside down appeared everywhere in the spring of 1865. The fear that black women freed from the oversight of mistresses would openly embrace white men was a partially submerged, but potent, theme. Eliza Andrews was pained at the "sight of our conquerors escorting their negro mistresses" and at their "insolence to walk arm in arm with negro women in our groves." Such behavior, she maintained, accounted for the refusal of white women to admit the "conquering heroes" into their own homes. They would not "stoop to share their attention with our negro maids."[35] Rumors of interracial dating circulated recklessly even as white southerners told competing stories of Union officers' and soldiers' scorn and ridicule of black women.

---

[32] Burr, ed., *The Secret Eye*, May 29, 1865, p. 274; Kate Cumming, *Kate: The Journal of a Confederate Nurse*, ed. Richard Barksdale Harwell (Baton Rouge: Louisiana State University Press, 1959), p. 307.

[33] [Rebecca Cameron] to Sallie [Sarah Cameron], June 3, 1865, Sarah R. Cameron Papers, SHC; LeConte Diary, April 13, 1865; July 5, 1865, SHC.

[34] *Daily Southern Guardian*, September 17, 1863, and April 11, 1864.

[35] Andrews, *War-Time Journal of a Georgia Girl*, pp. 288 and 306–7, quotes at pp. 307 and 288, respectively.

Even knowing that the racism within the Union rank and file was more likely to lead to a defense of white womanhood than black womanhood was of little help. Some, like Gertrude Thomas, worried that the number of relationships between white women and black men would grow and that the offspring of these unions might one day be publicly acknowledged as white and accepted into white families, thus endangering the South's customs and race relations. "I am handling the subject fearlessly," she wrote, "as a great social problem. . . . already I see social equality between our uneducated women & our late servants."[36] Thomas did not oppose the extension of the legal right to marry to black people. She wanted most to be assured that black men and women would only marry *each other*.

While northern white men provided a convenient target in 1865, white southern women's obsession with interracial sex continued long after the war. In 1869, Alice Palmer reacted with disgust to news that South Carolina Governor Robert Scott entertained with "no distinction being made on account of color. White men entered the room with damsels of the dusty color hanging on their arms and black men with white women."[37] Reports of Yankee soldiers and black women mingling "affectionately" became a regular part of white women's conversations and writing. "They lie beside them on the grass," Emma LeConte wrote, "and walk the streets with the negro girls calling them 'young ladies.'"[38]

As Sherman's army made its way north from Columbia, such scenes multiplied subjecting white southerners, in their words, to "enslavement." At Mt. Hope plantation near Ridgeway, South Carolina, Union soldiers dressed a slave girl "in their regimentals and carried her off" as her mistress watched. The streets of small towns appeared "blue with Yankees," who filled their wagons "with loot and Negro wenches," making "a conglomerated mass extending from sidewalk to sidewalk."[39] North Carolina mistresses were not spared. Near Raleigh, Ellen Mordecai experienced the death of the Confederacy as a painful spiral of "Yankee muskets under every window of my house" and slave emancipation. "My yard does not seem to belong to me," she wrote. "Till within the last ten days, it has been a perfect thoroughfare for soldiers, Negroes, and poor white folks. There was *ever* a group at the well, and soldiers hanging around my servants' houses. The nuisance was intolerable."[40]

In parading, freedwomen exercised their newly inscribed right to inhabit public spaces heretofore strictly proscribed, and to do so dressed as they

---

[36] Burr, ed., *The Secret Eye*, June 20, 1869, p. 320.

[37] Alice G. Palmer to Esther S. Palmer, February 13, 1869, in *World Turned Upside Down*, ed. Towles, p. 615.

[38] LeConte Diary, May 18, 1865; April 20, 1865, SHC.

[39] Charles Barnard Fox, *Record of the Service of the Fifty-Fifth Regiment of Massachusetts Volunteer Infantry* (1868; reprint, Freeport, NY: Books for Libraries Press, 1971), p. 64; Katherine M. Jones, ed., *When Sherman Came: Southern Women and the "Great March"* (Indianapolis: Bobbs-Merrill Company, 1964), pp. 216 and 227.

[40] As quoted in Jones, ed., *When Sherman Came*, p. 308.

pleased. In the process, they threatened what remained of the privileged status of white women no less than the parades of black soldiers undermined white men's sense of power and place. In either case, when former slaves appropriated the attire of the slaveholding class, whether military uniform or hoop skirt, the threat became more insufferable. Slave law, after all, had made such self-made transformations illegal. It was precisely in the exercise of this small right that black women got on the nerves of white women. It was calm so long as mistresses had charge of how black women appeared, what they wore. The historiography fails to take notice of this side of female domination and how it fit into the larger repression.

In appropriating the symbols and ceremonies of the ruling class, former slaves mocked them even as they appropriated them in defense of their own humanity.[41] In the ways black people announced their freedom, there was a semblance to carnival but also an important distinction. Carnival historically provided "authorized" occasions for the lower classes to mock the upper classes. Over time, of course, carnival lost its radical edge, becoming in most places a fairly harmless revelry. Unlike peasants or workers of preindustrial Europe, however, former slaves in the U.S. South generally made no pretense to the kind of obliqueness generally associated with the transfigurative realities at the heart of carnival, theater, oral tradition, saturnalia, or charivari, of the kind that, for example, characterized the 1730s cat massacre in Paris. Symbolism triumphed in the journeymen workers' massacre of the cats, including the prized cat of their mistress. In killing their mistress's cat, Robert Darnton writes in his wonderful account of the incident, "the workers ravished the mistress symbolically. At the same time, they delivered the supreme insult to their master. His wife was his most prized possession, just as her *chatte* was hers. In killing the cat, the men violated the most intimate treasure of the bourgeois household and escaped unharmed. That was the beauty of it. The symbolism disguised the insult well enough for them to get away with it."[42]

Symbolism was at work in the postbellum South, but black people did not use it to cloak insults. Rather, they used it to assault small and large regimes of oppression. The common but incorrect assumption that symbolism always works at the level of suggestion partly explains the tendency to equate forms of resistance short of outright military revolt to oblique forms of protest, what some scholars, following James C. Scott, term "hidden transcripts."[43]

---

[41] David Barry Gaspar, *Bondmen and Rebels: A Study of Master-Slave Relationships in Antigua with Implications for Colonial British America* (Baltimore, MD: Johns Hopkins University Press, 1985), p. 249.

[42] Darnton, *The Great Cat Massacre*, p. 99.

[43] James C. Scott, *Domination and the Arts of Resistance: Hidden Transcripts* (New Haven, CT: Yale University Press, 1990); James C. Scott, *Weapons of the Weak: Everyday Forms of Peasant Resistance* (New Haven, CT: Yale University Press, 1985); Peter Kolchin, *Unfree Labor: American Slavery and Russian Serfdom* (Cambridge, MA: Belknap Press of Harvard University Press, 1987), pp. 241–44. Scholars have been eager, for example, to apply James C. Scott's insights regarding peasant societies in Southeast Asia to the experiences of African Americans

Freedwomen's assault on the southern construction of gender fits neither the meaning of "hidden transcripts" nor "silent sabotage." "[E]veryday resistance," James C. Scott argues, "most strikingly departs from other forms of resistance... in its explicit disavowal of public and symbolic goals." It is "off-stage."[44] Examples of this kind of resistance, Scott writes, include Civil War deserters and foot-dragging slaves in the U.S. South. This form of resistance, he adds, is characterized by quiet or covert evasions of authority which are often much more effective in accomplishing a goal than open defiance. But as he and other scholars admit, the accomplishments are limited and do not involve structural change in power relationships.[45]

The open mocking of southern white womanhood by black women and the confrontations (confrontations returned by former mistresses for that matter) that marked interactions in the public sphere *avowed* rather than disavowed public and symbolic goals. The insults were made plainly, openly, "publicly" with announced political goals: a reconstitution of ideologies of race and gender in the U.S. South. This included the destruction of the material basis upon which ideologies of race and gender stood. Black women's actions did not assume the precise posture of "everyday forms of resistance," but that should not dispose us to ignore or trivialize them. Nor should it dissuade us from seeing them as forms of political struggle. Slave resistance to planter hegemony had made that hegemony less than perfect, as had, of course, the inherent ideological constraints and contradictions of human bondage itself.[46] The weapons slaves had at their command to challenge the white South's dominant cultural and ideological constructions of race and gender were tiny compared to those the planter class mounted against them. In the aftermath of slavery's destruction, however, even tiny weapons assumed new political and social meaning and greater force.

The dismantling of the customs of slavery revealed clearly the politics of everyday life. "The negroes have commenced pretty generally to Mr., Mrs., and Miss each other," observed a South Carolinian, and "the whites are very jealous of such innovations." He attributed the "innovations," as many did, to their being "excessively fond of titles," thus, as an apolitical development. Yet the political implications did not fully escape him. Black people's use of the titles, "Brother" and "Sister," he also noted, were now "very ordinary appellations

---

in the United States, and much of his analysis is indeed applicable. Some caution, however, is also necessary.

[44] Scott, *Weapons of the Weak*, pp. 29, 33, 37–41, 273, 284–89, and passim, quotes at pp. 33 and 41.

[45] Scott, *Weapons of the Weak*, pp. 30–34, and 272–303; Eugene D. Genovese, *Roll, Jordan, Roll: The World the Slaves Made* (New York: Vintage Books, 1974).

[46] On hegemony, see Antonio Gramsci, *Selections from the Prison Notebooks*, ed. and trans. Quinton Hoare and Geoffrey Nowell Smith (London: Lawrence and Wishart, 1971); E. P. Thompson, *The Poverty of Theory and Other Essays* (New York: Monthly Review Press, 1978); Nicholas Abercrombie, Stephen Hill, and Bryan S. Turner, *The Dominant Ideology Thesis* (Boston: G. Allen and Unwin, 1980); Genovese, *Roll, Jordan, Roll*; and Scott, *Weapons of the Weak*.

among them," "made fashionable . . . by the Union League." Resistance to the customs of slavery was also evident in the way black people now addressed former masters and mistresses. While the titles, "Massa, Master, Boss, and Miss or Missis (for Mrs.)," were still used by some, "all who are in politics or have money," he wrote, "together with not a few of the more insolent of the common mass, have dropped these titles for Mr. and Mrs."[47] The "insolent" included black children who learned from their parents that it was "a sin" for them to say "sir" to white babies.[48]

White women saw such changes as so flagrantly wrong that some discharged black women who "refused to prefix Master to the names of children."[49] Still, the more common response was ridicule. But even ridicule no longer carried the weight it had during slavery. As slaveholders, white people could enjoy the pretense when they dressed household slaves as decorative elements, provided wedding attire for slave marriage ceremonies that carried no legal or civic weight, or permitted parties and even teas. Ten-year-old Annie Groves Scott was sitting on the front porch of her master's house attired in white muslin, trimmed with blue flounces, and with a blue ribbon in her hair when Union soldiers appeared at her owners' plantation.[50] There had been other lapses. Encountering a large party of about forty slaves returning to Charleston from an all-night party of "dancing and carousing" on Sullivan's Island at 6:00 A.M. one Sunday morning, a white Charlestonian, in a letter to the editor of the local paper, called for an end to the practice: "I wish to know why a stop is not put to the boatmen, plying between this and the Island, carrying negroes from this place to the Island without a pass," he wrote. This party was apparently not the first of its kind.[51]

Slaveholders who had encouraged slaves to "dress up" for special occasions or styled house servants in ribbons, finding the results comical and endearing, could no longer be sure at whose expense the joke lay. "The habits and rituals of race," as Barbara Fields reminds us, "reenacted in a world where slavery no longer established the limits of black people's actions, these became new in essence, even when they persisted in form."[52] No longer masters and

---

47 A South Carolinian, "South Carolina Society," *The Atlantic Monthly* 39 (June 1877): 675.

48 John Hammond Moore, ed., *A Plantation Mistress on the Eve of the Civil War: The Diary of Keziah Goodwyn Hopkins Brevard, 1860–1861* (Columbia: University of South Carolina Press, 1993), April 4, 1861, p. 111.

49 A South Carolinian, "South Carolina Society," p. 675.

50 Annie Groves Scott, *Oklahoma Narratives*, Supplement Series 1, vol. 12, p. 272.

51 A Bye (sic) Stander to the Editor of the *Courier*, [hand dated August 4, 1804], in *Charleston Scrapbook Clippings Chiefly from Charleston Newspapers, 1800–1810*, SCL. On slave dress, see also Helen Bradley Foster, *"New Raiments of Self": African American Clothing in the Antebellum South* (New York: Berg, 1997); and Stephanie M. H. Camp, "The Pleasures of Resistance: Enslaved Women and Body Politics in the Plantation South, 1830–1861," *Journal of Southern History* 68 (August 2002): 534–72.

52 Barbara Jeanne Fields, *Slavery and Freedom on the Middle Ground: Maryland during the Nineteenth Century* (New Haven, CT: Yale University Press, 1985), p. 206; Genovese, *Roll, Jordan, Roll*, pp. 559–60.

mistresses, where former slaveholders had once seen paternalistic and maternalistic largesse, they now saw insult. Some had called it "tomfoolery" all along. On more than one occasion Thomas Chaplin expressed his displeasure with the black women enslaved in his household. He complained most frequently when illness kept slave women out of the fields. But he also voiced his displeasure with the elaborate feasts provided for slave weddings, believing they tore at the fabric of slave society, prompting slaves to mistake "gifts" for rights.[53]

Before the war, Ella Gertrude Thomas, like Chaplain's wife and other mistresses, seemed oblivious to the dangers Chaplin railed against. In her diary, Thomas recorded in the most matter of fact way an invitation received by three of her slaves, two women and a man, to attend a "tea party" given by a slave on another plantation. Prior to her own marriage, she attended the lavish wedding her family put on for a favored slave woman's nuptials to "Mr Joseph Watts," a slave from a neighboring plantation. On another occasion, she joined her husband and Dr. Augustus Longstreet, author of *Georgia Scenes,* and his wife and other local white notables, in attending a slave wedding. Before the war, she could note without comment the assertion of a recently married slave that her husband's name was "Mr Washington." Her own slaves gave dinner parties to which they invited notable black people from the larger community like the minister Sam Drayton.[54]

Yet, even Thomas discerned the difference emancipation made. "I remember," she wrote in 1869, "that it was an uncommon thing to hear a servant addressed by any other title than that of their master, I do not remember the 'ontitles' as they called them of more than half dozen servants we owned before the war. 'Trimmings to his name' & 'handle to his name' is another favorite style of alluding to their titles.... My cook is called Cornelia Shelman."[55] Unlike most former mistresses and masters, however, Thomas could tolerate freedpeople having last names that were not their masters' and even refer to them by their titles, but she could not see them as equals.

Despite emancipation and trying financial times, Thomas still defined herself as a mistress. That was her identity, and when the basis for its creation and existence was destroyed, maternalism was all she had left. But without slavery,

[53] Theodore Rosengarten, *Tombee: Portrait of a Cotton Planter with the Plantation Journal of Thomas B. Chaplin (1822–1890)* (New York: William Morrow & Company, Inc., 1986), May 28, 1850, June 10, 1851, pp. 499 and 535.

[54] Burr, ed., *The Secret Eye,* October 7, 1855, p. 135; June 10, 1852, p. 107; April [10], 1855, p. 121; April 6, 1856, p. 137; August 20, 1865, p. 146. Thomas was an enthusiastic supporter of Drayton, who officiated at many slave weddings. She described him as "one of the most intelligent negroes I have ever met with," praised his "decidedly fine command of language" and often went to hear him preach. She also had high praise for his wife, "one of the most ladylike persons I have ever seen" (Ibid., April [10] 1855, p. 121; June 24, 1855, p. 129; June 12, 1855, p. 131). Several of the Thomas's slaves frequented Augusta. Some married men from the city and participated in the black community life of antebellum Augusta, which boasted several black churches (Ralph Betts Flanders, *Plantation Slavery in Georgia* [Chapel Hill: University of North Carolina Press, 1933], pp. 174–75).

[55] Burr, ed., *The Secret Eye,* May 7, 1869, p. 313.

even that was a shabby vessel in which to reconstruct her life. The women who worked in her household were no longer her slaves, but she tried to reconstruct the customs of slavery. She happily furnished cards and envelopes in order that a hired female servant could send invitations to her wedding "in a more formal style" and household furnishings to decorate the bride's room for her wedding night. The groom's white female employer sent flowers.[56]

Gertrude Thomas's proslavery ideology provided a near-perfect vehicle for her postbellum racism. She favored marriage for black people. It remained hard, though, for her to relinquish the idea that it was her own largesse, in the form of wedding cakes, announcement cards, dresses, and veils, that sanctified marriage between black people. She struggled to accept the fact that the marriages of black people were no longer white-arranged affairs legitimized by ownership, but rather law. She had trouble seeing former slaves' desire for autonomy and self-identification as legitimate. She would give women who had once belonged to her a dress or a ribbon for a special occasion, but she would never sell such things to them. Any other understanding she feared, contributed to an erosion of white supremacy. Without the borders of permissibility strictly monitored by white people, chaos would certainly ensue.

Gertrude Thomas might hold on to notions that could only make black women's dressing *themselves* up appear illegitimate, but she did not doubt the ambitions of black people. That black men would vote the radical ticket, she thought perfectly reasonable. The vote, she acknowledged, would allow them to secure their own rights and those of their descendants. She might ridicule it, but she understood it. A conversation between her daughter, Mary Bell, and Mac, one of her servants and a known Republican activist, repulsed her on one level but on another confirmed her thinking about such matters. Mary Bell had asked Mac whether he had voted in the November 1868 elections; he replied that he had and for the Republican ticket. Everything had gone "Beautifully mam beautifully," he told her.[57] Thomas gave serious thought to assertions of freedom by black people. She took seriously their strivings.

While a staunch believer in white supremacy, Thomas's keen intellect nonetheless rebelled at the seemingly neat categories that framed southern race and gender ideals. She chafed at the notion that black and white women shared much in common. Yet, at the same time, her thinking betrayed a sense that she knew they were like her, human and mothers, sisters, and daughters. And like her, they had ambitions for themselves and their children. But she feared these things, nonetheless. Had it been possible for Thomas to take a public stand, her political views might have commanded a substantial following among white southerners. A passage from her diary, written June 26, 1869, places her in the advance of segregationist thinking:

Sometimes I think our people are blind. They do not see the handwriting on the wall. . . . The boys of our country poor as well as rich must be educated, must be instilled

---

[56] Burr, ed., *The Secret Eye*, September 16, 1866, p. 281.
[57] Burr, ed., *The Secret Eye*, November 3, 1868, p. 298.

and ever kept before them the idea of social & mental superiority & *this must be no imaginary idea of caste* but a real substantial fact. I commend industry but parents are making (many of them) a great, a very great mistake in having their boys plough daily side by side with the Negro who perhaps works for his victuals & clothes.... can this go on without degradation?... I look around & I see worthy men who talk about their sons being indispensable in the field, 'hands are scarce' and to obtain a hand the boy's head suffers and he grows up an ignoramus while negro women toil and strive, labour and endure in order that their children may have schooling.... We have the superiority of race by nature & education. Let us see that we maintain it and then all laws concerning marrying or giving in marriage will be useless. As it is the law is almost an insult to Southern women.... Our girls require no training. Natural feminine instinct will be their guide, as it ever has been.[58]

The "unprovoked" declarations of independence by black women, caricatured as "playing the lady," were intended to undermine black women's personal sense of self-worth and dignity, and their political ambitions. Criticizing black people for wanting to "copy, as far as they could, the habits of whites," in particular by sending their children to public schools, served only to make them more determined opponents of illiteracy. "The whites," admitted one white southerner, "have a violent prejudice, nay, hatred, against these laudable efforts at civilization, and take every opportunity to insult such negroes as make them. 'Your wife and children had better be in the field,' is a remark frequently heard." Still, he was not able to let go of the belief that such feelings were justified, indeed, provoked by offensive behavior on the part of black people. "The airs which the negroes assume often interfere with their efficiency as laborers, and give them a demeanor insolent and presumptuous; and to such novelties the whites are not yet accustomed." Signing himself anonymously as "A South Carolinian," the writer attacked black families but returned again and again to the theme of freedpeople's larger ambitions "to increase the comforts of life, as well as to give leisure to their females and education to their children."[59]

It was against these ambitions and aspirations to equality, for which "negro women toil and strive," that white women lashed out, even when they pretended, like Mary Chesnut, neither to notice nor care. Chesnut feigned nonchalance at the suggestion that her maid Ellen would soon be her social equal, "a lady and driving about in your carriage." To admit concern was to be "of the

[58] Burr, ed., *The Secret Eye*, June 26, 1869, pp. 320–21 and 322. Thomas pointed to Aaron A. Bradley, the Georgia black Republican, as a case in point, an example of the danger of educating freedpeople and of interracial relations. Her tirade was directed at her own husband as well, and his poor management of their finances. Thomas's conclusion that miscegenation laws were "almost an insult to Southern women" would be echoed in the decades to follow by Ida B. Wells-Barnett (Ida B. Wells-Barnett, *Southern Horrors: Lynch Law in all Its Phases* [1892; reprint, Salem, NH: Ayer Company, Publishers, 1987]). Her call for white people to firm up their place as the racial superiors of black people would eventually be taken up by white men in such organizations as the Commission on Southern Race Questions. Augustin Taveau was an early white male proponent of her views. See, especially, his letter, "A Voice from the South."
[59] A South Carolinian, "South Carolina Society," pp. 677–84, quotes at pp. 677 and 678.

crybaby kind" and Chesnut would have none of that. A refugee surrounded by other similarly placed mistresses in the aftermath of Sherman's march through South Carolina, she listened more than indulged in the "women's chatter" around her, but the chatter often struck a chord.[60] She, too, was witness to the small but vital struggles of daily life that were ushering in a revolution in social relations just as they were in the region's political and economic affairs.

It has been easy to declare that former masters, mistresses, Freedmen's Bureau agents, and other transplanted northerners were right when they insisted that black people, once free, measured freedom in large part by the degree to which they were able to absorb or adopt nineteenth-century ideas of domesticity and patriarchy.[61] That historiography has a deep past. When freedom came, historian E. Merton Coulter wrote, "the first great ambition" of black women "was to wear a veil and carry a parasol," a rendering he perhaps considered a less noxious arrangement of the grammar of the "lady-like appearing" white woman encountered by Sidney Andrews at a Salisbury, North Carolina, hotel, who, putting it a bit differently, stated: "The chief ambition of a negro wench seems to be to wear a veil and carry a parasol."[62] The "nasty niggers," a white woman fumed to him, "must have a parasol when they ha'nt got no shoes." A Freedmen's Bureau agent informed Andrews that the "wearing of veils by young Negro women has given great offense to the young white women" so much so "that there was a time earlier in the season when the latter would not wear them at all." White women, Andrews concluded, were "bitter, spiteful women." The taking on of "airs" by black women, he observed, was considered a not insignificant matter. "I have," he wrote, "one way or another, heard so much about it, that I am not at liberty to suppose it a mere matter of local or temporary grievance." Satirizing white women's obsession with the matter, Andrews wrote: "Wretched negro girls, you of sprawling feet and immense lips and retreating foreheads and coal-black color, cease from your vagaries! Cease from such sore troubling of the placid and miasmatic waters of good society."[63]

In their actions and words, black women further undid the web of pride and prejudice so central to the cornerstone of slavery. What else were white women to make of "lady's maids dressing themselves in their mistresses's *gowns before their very faces* and walking off?"[64] "If the spectacle of black marriages

---

[60] C. Vann Woodward, ed., *Mary Chesnut's Civil War* (New Haven, CT: Yale University Press, 1981), February 26, 1865, quotes at pp. 737 and 735, respectively.

[61] See, for example, Jim Cullen, "'I's a Man Now': Gender and African American Men," in *Divided Houses: Gender and the Civil War*, ed. Catherine Clinton and Nina Silber (New York: Oxford University Press, 1992), p. 90.

[62] E. Merton Coulter, *The South During Reconstruction, 1865–1877* (Baton Rouge: Louisiana State University Press, 1947), pp. 52–53; Sidney Andrews, *The South Since the War* (1866; reprint, New York: Arno Press, 1969), p. 186; Mary Elizabeth Massey, *Women in the Civil War* (1966; reprint, Lincoln: University of Nebraska Press, 1994), pp. 278–79.

[63] Andrews, *The South Since the War*, pp. 186–87.

[64] Woodward, ed., *Mary Chesnut's Civil War*, p. 833.

amused former masters and mistresses, the inclination of black women," as Leon Litwack writes, "'to play the lady' did not, particularly when it made it more difficult for white women to do so." Their "cries of despair reflected, both physical exhaustion and psychic humiliation."[65]

Had they read Sidney Andrews's account, white women would not have shared the humor he found in their fascination with sidewalks and veils or agreed with his analysis. Black women were not merely making it "more difficult" for white women to "play the lady," they were making it impossible. Their movements constituted an assault on one of the white South's most cherished ideals, indeed, contravened it, as white women correctly perceived. In their hour of tribulation, white women would find no comfort in the reassuring words that had sent white southerners marching off to war. "We are contending for all we hold dear – our property – our institutions – our honor," wrote William Grimball. "A stand must be taken for African slavery or it is lost forever."[66] Southern white women in the main, of course, had been no less confident.

White women worked to reclaim as much of the ideological terrain as possible even as they struggled to comprehend the meaning of black women's actions and mocked what they considered to be their pretensions to the status of "ladies." The seeming contradiction is not at all incomprehensible. On the one hand, white women were protesting a challenge to their race and class status; on the other, the raw stuff of experience taught them that black women's ambitions and actions projected a sense of self radically at odds with their own.

Black women's political engagement and participation after the war provided one kind of evidence of the different ambitions and notions of citizenship on the part of black and white women.[67] Their politics worried their employers. Some white women employers fired black women who spoke openly of politics and especially of their support for the Republican Party. Mary Pringle even directed her servants to boycott "Radical Nigger" purveyors of meat in the city.[68] Politics were an inevitable part of every aspect of the relations between white and black women.

Gertrude Thomas's former slaves and the female servants she hired after the war gave her several lessons on the subjects of gender roles and gender relations, lessons that left no doubt that black women's understanding of such matters differed fundamentally from her own. In a diary entry on October 22, 1868, she wrote that white southerners must *avoid politics* and focus on

---

[65] Leon F. Litwack, *Been in the Storm So Long: The Aftermath of Slavery* (New York: Vintage Books, 1979), p. 245; Leon F. Litwack, "The Ordeal of Black Freedom," in *The Southern Enigma: Essays on Race, Class and Folk Culture*, ed. Walter J. Fraser, Jr. and Winfred B. Moore (Westport, CT: Greenwood Pub. Co., 1983), p. 9.

[66] William Grimball to Elizabeth Grimball, November 20, 1860, John Berkeley Grimball Papers, DU.

[67] Julie Saville, *The Work of Reconstruction: From Slave to Wage Laborer in South Carolina, 1860–1870* (Cambridge: Cambridge University Press, 1994); Elsa Barkley Brown, "Negotiating Community and Freedom: African American Political Life in the Transition from Slavery to Freedom," *Public Culture* 7 (Fall 1994): 107–46.

[68] Richard N. Côté, *Mary's World: Love, War, and Family Ties in Nineteenth Century Charleston* (Mount Pleasant, SC: Corinthian Books, 2001), p. 281.

family survival. A few days later, politics intruded directly into her life when Dinah hosted a political meeting in her room. At least two of several men in attendance were known to be active Republican partisans. Thomas learned of the meeting and of alleged plans to burn her home and others in the neighborhood from a black teenager and from her husband, who had adopted the habit of sneaking under the cabins of black people at night in order to eavesdrop on their conversations.[69]

Following the meeting at Dinah's, Bob, a former slave, sent for Thomas's husband, who he learned had accused him and his wife of conspiring to burn down the Thomas's house. Gertrude Thomas went in place of her husband. Thomas trusted Patsey, Bob's wife, who was one of the first slaves her father had given her and the only one of her former house slaves who had remained at the end of the war. "I took a seat and talked with them awhile," Thomas wrote, "told them that the white people were anxious to avoid a difficulty but that if forced to it they would fight and fight well – that I did not feel uneasy &c." Without hesitation, Patsey staked her position on the opposing ground. Thomas remembered her saying, "Well I want to be where Bob is." If there was going to be a fight, she let Thomas know that neither was she anxious and that they would be enemies to each other. Patsey's comment unnerved Thomas. If Patsey was willing to take up arms, she was not. "I do not wish to be where Mr. T is," she retorted, "for I would want him to be in the fight." When Bob joked (perhaps) in reply that "Miss Trudy would be a good soldier herself," Thomas replied, "I would not be a good soldier Bob . . . but I cannot imagine myself as being a coward."[70]

Also present at the meeting was Warren, a Republican activist who Thomas characterized as "very independent and impertinent." He and Bob were "both radicals." Dinah, who had hosted the political meeting that had taken place earlier in the evening, where, supposedly, there was talk of war between black and white people, was also present. Thomas had intruded on a meeting intended to confront her husband. But she knew, when the message from Bob came for her husband, that something was amiss. It was, she wrote, "an unusual proceeding for him to send for Mr T instead of coming." The presence of Dinah and the terse speeches by Patsey and Thomas marked the divide that separated black and white women. If she had thought so before, Thomas could no longer believe that black women aspired to be like her.[71]

[69] Burr, ed., *The Secret Eye*, October 22, 1868; November 1, 1868, pp. 293–94, quote at p. 293.

[70] Burr, ed., *The Secret Eye*, November 1, 1868, pp. 294–95, quote at p. 295. Bob and Patsey left the Thomas's place the following month (ibid., December 3, 1868, p. 300).

[71] Burr, ed., *The Secret Eye*, June 19, 1869, pp. 317–19; Fox-Genovese, *Within the Plantation Household*, pp. 298, 329, and 373. The words of Mabel John in the 1970s echoed those of rural black women in the postbellum South. John had a difficult time understanding that her employer had to get her husband's permission for every purchase she wanted to make. As for herself: "Now, I just couldn't be so bothered with all that. I am a grown woman, so I buy what I think I should. . . . my husband . . . was a man and I was a woman, so we didn't neither of us have to raise the other." (John Langston Gwaltney, ed., *Drylongso: A Self Portrait of Black America* [New York, 1980] p. 167).

In the 1930s, Sarah F. Babb reminisced about her "mammy." She remembered her thus: "A plodding life, whose sameness was never varied by divine flashes of joy or saddened by deep sorrows that try the soul – hers was not a soul great enough for that. Her sorrows were petty trials and griefs quickly dispelled, her greatest happiness consisted in a dress of a gay pattern, a bow of ribbon and a green feather in her hat, 'year bobs,' a brass ring, and a strand of beads."[72] On the ground of slavery and the ground of freedom, Sarah Babb's "mammy" was more fiction than not. Slaveholding women misread the meaning of a "bow of ribbon" on both grounds.

---

[72] Sarah F. Babb, *Mississippi Narratives*, Supplement Series 1, vol. 9, pt. 4, p. 71.

Epilogue

> I would stand for hours on the doorsteps of neighbors' houses listening to their talk, learning how a white woman had slapped a black woman, how a white man had killed a black man.
>
> Richard Wright, *Black Boy*

Plantation mistresses were slaveholders. They were slaveholders whether they held slaves in their own names or not, and this status gave them virtually unrestricted power over the slaves who labored in their homes. Black women who labored in the antebellum plantation household were enslaved workers. They were enslaved workers despite the intimacies inherent in the household. The plantation household was a site of work during and after slavery, and it was that despite the ideologies of white male patriarchy, white female subordination, and private versus public spheres, that circulated within and around its precincts. These are the simple facts that lie submerged in the historiography. Submerged along with them is the story of what those simple facts meant for the lives of black and white women in slavery and freedom. Yet this history is far from simple.

Over the past three decades, historians have worked imaginatively to re-interrogate a host of political and social conventions whose impact was to deny black people active roles in the making and remaking of slavery, emancipation, and the postemancipation world. The reward has been a more sophisticated understanding of the dynamics that this entailed. As a result of path-breaking scholarship in the field of southern women's history over the last twenty years, in particular, the history of southern women and of the relations between white and black women in the nineteenth-century South has taken on sharper contours. Clearly indebted to this scholarship, this book has sought to contribute to the process of re-conceptualizing the way we understand the history of slavery and freedom, especially as it concerns southern women. My particular focus has been the power relations between white and black women during and after slavery. The constant construction, destruction, and reconstruction of certain kinds of power relations allow us to see more clearly how struggles over land and political power were linked to struggles within households and among women.

Within this broad context, this book has focused on the transformation of the plantation household and slaves' unfree homes into free homes, and women, black and white, into free women. This choice of focus has allowed me to document the gilding of privacy that encased the plantation household and to lay bare the injuries that took place within it. It brings into view transformations, initiated by black women, that began during slavery and continued into freedom in the plantation household. These transformations spoke to the very meaning of womanhood, as much as they did to the very meaning of freedom and citizenship.

Writing the history of southern women is difficult. If excavating the part enslaved women played in this history is harder still, one reason, to borrow a phrase from Laura Stoler and Karen Strassler, is the "density of the archives" about them.[1] Produced by slaveholders, those archives are full of references to black women, yet full of distortions and misdirecting clues to the historian. To the extent that power has been treated as a dynamic of the plantation household, therefore, it comes into view as power exercised by masters – and, remarkably, by black women. Patriarchy has explained the power of masters. How the power of black women has been explained is by a curious inversion. In this narrative, the slave woman is in control and holds power. But that power cannot be imagined, in retrospect, as self-liberating and worthy to be remembered as such. Instead, it is apolitical and destructive. This powerful servant manages to keep mistress out of "her" kitchen, or humiliates mistress by allowing a speck of dust to escape the broom, or breaks things. She is powerful, but incompetent, and in all ways a menacing presence, a dozing tiger. The real black woman with her own life is not there.

The common currency of many archival sources, this narrative took shape in the complaints of white women about the domestic albatross of having to play "lady" and mistress: having to manage and care for slaves in the household over whom they had to keep a constant eye else black women would revert to slovenly work habits or do no work at all. It explained away white women's resort to violence, their unladylike use of beatings and lockdowns with chains.[2] Unless the mistress was "gifted in human relations," says this narrative, she was doomed to suffer "constant problems with recalcitrant, defiant, slovenly slaves, some of whom were skilled at intimidating their mistresses."[3] It has, thus, been

---

[1] Ann Laura Stoler with Karen Strasser, "Memory-Work in Java: A Cautionary Tale," in *Carnal Knowledge and Imperial Power: Race and the Intimate in Colonial Rule*, ed. Ann Laura Stoler (Berkeley: University of California Press, 2002), p. 162; see also p. 8.

[2] J. Carlyle Sitterson, "A Planter Family of the Old and New South," *Journal of Southern History* 6 (August, 1940): 350.

[3] Anne Firor Scott, *The Southern Lady: From Pedestal to Politics, 1830–1930*, 25th Anniversary ed. (Charlottesville: University Press of Virginia, 1995), p. 37.

possible to conclude that "as a class," mistresses "earned their reputation for graciousness and ladylike accomplishments while having to perform the grubbiest of chores."[4]

This book has told a different history of the relations of power within the plantation household and of the efforts by former mistresses and masters to circumscribe the efforts of black women to build free and private lives, and homes that challenged prevailing gender ideals grounded in notions of race. Black women's attempts to "set up for themselves," in the jargon of white southerners, threatened to remove their labor and the labor of their children from the complete control of former slaveholders. In contemporary accounts and in the historiography, these attempts have been essentially characterized in two interrelated ways: On the one hand, as bids by black women to emulate their former mistresses; on the other, as moves demanded by black men intent, as free men, on taking on the mantle of patriarchal authority. Both portray former slaves as most interested in establishing within their own homes notions of domesticity copied from their former owners.

But it was not in order to emulate white women that black women moved to withdraw their labor from white homes. When they pushed to move jobs like washing and ironing to their own homes, and demanded changes that would allow them to do domestic work part-time, they were also devoting as much of their laboring hours as possible to subsistence activities and to work in the fields. They took these steps not because their husbands or fathers demanded it, but because these were choices integral to becoming free. The conclusion of mere emulation thus collapses under the weight it is asked to bear. Furthermore, the history of black women goes beyond their efforts to help reconstitute families and re-shape labor arrangements, however interpreted against the background of the plantations. It is also about their own economic relations and cultural forms, and about the social and political conflicts that engaged them as laboring women.

The history of white women in the South, too, is about struggles for human liberation. White women, too, were part of a larger reality of class and gender formation and re-formation. These circumstances are easy to overlook when black women's activities and their actions are cast primarily as contests over hearth and home, as struggles that concerned a private, domestic sphere. Equally, they fade from view when white women are cast simply as suffering victims of patriarchy, or black men as rising patriarchs. The central fact, absolutely not to be overlooked, is that the plantation household was in fact transformed, despite white women's insistence that this transformation would not and should not endure. The turbulence with which this transformation proceeded did not give rise to the belief that "gender based experiences might

---

[4] Eugene D. Genovese, *Roll, Jordan, Roll: The World the Slaves Made* (New York: Knopf, 1974), p. 81.

join women" of different races or classes into a sisterhood.[5] Instead, the history of white women's work to corral a labor force of black domestic workers is evidence of a much different belief, and a response to the on-going resistance of black women to the coercive intimacy of the antebellum notion, "one family, black and white."

In 1933, the Richmond Urban League and the Richmond, Virginia branch of the Southern Woman's Educational Alliance (SWEA) joined forces to inaugurate a new era in domestic work in the South. They came together to co-sponsor the "Home Service Course for General Maids." The twelve-week program was declared a success and expanded in its second year to twenty-four weeks.[6] On May 10, 1934, "twenty colored girls" received certificates of graduation. Mrs. Albert Sidney Johnston, member of the Confederate Daughters of America, and chair of the YMCA's Committee on Employer-Employee Relationships, was the featured speaker, taking as her subject, "the improvement of employer-employee relationships in the field of domestic service."[7]

The graduates had endured a detailed immersion in the intricacies of cleaning, bed-making, table-setting, infant care, care of the pre-school child, home care of the sick, cooking, the use of electrical household appliances, personal hygiene, appropriate dress, general cleanliness, correct dining room service, proper use of the telephone and, arguably, most important of all, the best sort of attitude to bring to one's job.[8] Like their antebellum and postbellum predecessors, elite white women in the 1930s held the contradictory beliefs that black women were "naturally" suited to domestic labor and, at the same time, that they required training to be made suitable. Sufficiently pliant and docile women were made, not born. The goals and strategies of the Richmond project thus bore witness to the continued resistance of black women to the demeaning and exploitative aspects of domestic work, the only choice, of employment, beyond agricultural work, available to the vast majority of black women.[9]

---

[5] Marli F. Weiner, among others, concludes that gender united black and white women. The quote is from Weiner, *Mistresses and Slaves: Plantation Women in South Carolina, 1830–80* (Urbana: University of Illinois Press, 1998), p. 150; see also pp. 146–54.

[6] "Home Service Course for General Maids," Given Cooperatively by the Richmond Urban League and the Richmond Branch of the Southern Woman's Educational Alliance, 1933–34; Certificate, Introductory Course on General Maid Service, 1933. Alliance for the Guidance of Rural Youth Records, DU (hereafter referred to as Rural Youth Records).

[7] "Certificate to Be Awarded to Colored Girls and Women in Domestic Training," Press Release sent to *News Leader*, May 4, 1934, Home Service Course of General Maids, 1933–34, Rural Youth Records, DU.

[8] HOUSEHOLD MANAGEMENT COURSE, RICHMOND URBAN LEAGUE, Rural Youth Records, DU. Household appliances became much more widely available in the 1920s as technologies developed for hotels and restaurants were tailored to home use.

[9] In Durham, North Carolina, for instance, 24 white women worked in domestic service (18 of them as cooks) as compared to 1,283 black women in 1930. Vernon Benjamin Kiser, "Occupational Change among Negroes in Durham," Masters Thesis, Duke University, 1942, pp. 76–77. What makes these figures all the more significant is that Durham was a factory town, and although black women were generally excluded from mill employment, many found employment in local tobacco factories.

The Richmond project responded to that resistance. It represented an alliance of conservative "up-lift" black politics, Progressive Era reform ideology, and white racism that sought to bring "order" to domestic labor relations and, by turn, to "race relations."[10]

The evidence of the tremendous importance white women attached to these goals is visible in the proliferation of projects and organizations devoted to the "servant question." The Housekeepers' Alliance, organized in 1924, initially brought together "about 100 earnest homemakers endeavoring to solve the difficulties of housekeeping." The Domestic Efficiency Association (DEA), organized in Baltimore in 1920, and the National Association of Wage Earners (NAWE), organized the following year and led by prominent black leaders Nannie H. Burroughs and Mary McLeod Bethune, had helped pave the way.[11]

---

[10] In the United States, the domestication movement began in earnest with the publication of Catherine Beecher's *Treatise on Domestic Economy* in 1841. In the following decades, northern educated middleclass women led the campaign to remake the geography of the domestic space. Some championed cooperative kitchens as a means to relieve the drudgery of housework. In the end, however, middle- and upperclass women in the North fell back on the hire market for domestic workers. The results of an essay contest in 1923 on "the future of the American home" published in the pages of *Woman Citizen*, edited by Carrie Chapman Catt, confirmed the continued preference for domestic workers. Contestants were asked to consider the following options as suitable paths for the future: cooperative housekeeping, the simplification of housework through time- and labor-saving devices, and changes to improve the social and economic status of domestic work. The latter was the overwhelming favorite. See Delores Hayden, *The Grand Domestic Revolution: A History of Feminist Designs for American Homes, Neighborhoods, and Cities* (Cambridge, MA: MIT Press, 1981), pp. 286–88. On nineteenth-century domestic feminism, see Kathryn Kish Sklar, *Catherine Beecher: A Study in American Domesticity* (New Haven, CT: Yale University Press, 1973) and Hayden, *The Grand Domestic Revolution*, 55–89. These notions were translated in the South most prominently by the influential work of O. Latham Hatcher, president of the Southern Woman's Educational Alliance, and Staff Associates and a former professor of English at Bryn Mawr College. Hatcher was primarily concerned with rural young women who migrated to urban areas. See, for example, O. Latham Hatcher, *Rural Girls in the City for Work: A Study Made for the Southern Woman's Educational Alliance* (Richmond: Garrett & Massie, 1930); O. Latham Hatcher, *Guiding Rural Boys and Girls: Flexible Guidance Programs for Use by Rural Schools and Related Agencies*, ed. Emery N. Ferriss (New York: McGraw-Hill, 1930); O. Latham Hatcher, ed., *Occupations for Women, being the Practical Information Obtained by a Study Made for the Southern Woman's Educational Alliance* (Richmond: Southern Woman's Educational Alliance, 1927). See also Marguerite Stockman Dickson, *Vocational Guidance for Girls* (Chicago: Rand McNally & Co., 1919). On the rise of scientific management and the adaptation of "Taylorism" to the home, see Katzman, *Seven Days a Week*, pp. 179–81 and 253–56; Christine Frederick, *Scientific Management in the Home: Household Engineering* (London: G. Routledge & Sons, 1922); and Janice Williams Rutherford, *Selling Mrs. Consumer: Christine Frederick & the Rise of Household Efficiency* (Athens: University of Georgia Press, 2003).

[11] The following summary is from the Housekeepers Alliance Papers, Anna Kelton Wiley Papers, LC. See especially, "Aims and Purposes of the Domestic Efficiency Association" and Nannie H. Burroughs's "A Domestic Practice House." An even earlier precursor was The Society for the Encouragement of Faithful Domestic Servants, founded in New York in 1825. Calls for domestic worker educational programs took off in the late nineteenth century with public school programs and domestic science programs at women's and black colleges. The trend was assisted by the proliferation of campaigns sponsored by women's magazines (the *Better Homes*

These and other similar organizations worked to develop courses of study for domestic workers. They ran employment bureaus, euphemistically called "intelligence offices," for domestic workers. And, they opened the door, even if ever so gently, for white women to begin to publicly address the problem of the abuse of domestic servants. The DEA gently broached the matter. A white woman desiring to use its "intelligence office" was required "to sign a card of rules by which she pledges to be just, kind, and considerate to her employees." The DEA also required employees and employers who used its services to give a week's notice if quitting or terminating the employment, and black women to pay for the training it offered.

A "girl" accepted into the program paid a tuition fee of $5.00 per week. Those who could not afford the fee could arrange to have it deducted from their wages at the "rate of at least $2.50 per week" from their first job after training. Leaders of the DEA seemed shocked to find that the "colored girls" were reluctant to enter such a bargain and called on leaders of the black community to lobby these women on its behalf, "asking their leaders to teach them that this training, with the stamp of the school, will give them an advantage lasting all their lives." It sought to convince women who knew better that there was "nothing degrading in domestic service well done." The NAWE launched, besides, its own Domestic Service Center that included a "practice house" for actual training. Brandishing race uplift ideology, the NAWE weighed in with the pronouncement that unless black women consented to formal training, white women would be forced to hire women "*green* from the streets or *greasy* from employment agencies," thus endangering "the strongest link in the chain of race relationship."[12]

Throughout the late nineteenth century and into the twentieth, black rural women had held on tightly to the hard-won victories of the emancipation era amidst a worsening, even deadly, political and economic climate. Attempts by white women in the nineteenth century to score an advantage through informal agreements to set wages and hours all employers would abide by had failed to bring about the transformation in black women they sought. Now, white women had re-grouped amid a congenial political climate of racial fears and reform ideologies that lent themselves to support of the kind of repressive regimes and agendas that are documented in these projects.

To former mistresses, their daughters, and granddaughters, teaching black women such practical matters as how to dress a bed was as important as bringing a certain kind of "order" to the field of domestic work. The lessons in humility that black women received as part of the educational program stood out as central to this objective. An important part of the program's ideological

Campaign, for example), household guides, and the work of the U.S.D.A. Department of Home Economics. See also David M. Katzman, *Seven Days a Week: Women and Domestic Service in Industrializing America* (New York: Oxford University Press, 1978), pp. 104–5, 116, and 135–37, and Elizabeth Clark-Lewis, *Living in, Living Out: African American Domestics in Washington, D.C., 1910–1940* (Washington, DC: Smithsonian Institution Press, 1994).

[12] Nannie H. Burroughs, "A Domestic Service Practice House," Nannie H. Burroughs Papers, LC.

underpinnings were the twin notions that domestic work was honorable, and that white women were doing God's work in making it available. White women employers saw their project as an means to improve relations between black women workers and themselves, and as "a Christian undertaking," an "effort of the strong to help the weak." Besides, they insisted, their objective was "ultra-economic." It was "essentially a project in Race Relations" transcending such matters as better pay.[13]

This project in "race relations" admitted, indirectly, that black women continued to suffer violent abuse in domestic employment. Its literature veiled this abuse in the polite language of a "too often strained lack – of concord" in the workplace. Its call on white women to practice patience and a good nature was a polite way to frame this abuse. The seriousness of the problem emerges from the lessons in working conditions, hours, and general treatment, and in the call for the "elimination of mental cruelty." Still, it placed the burden for the elimination of this cruelty on black women. According to that instruction, it was not that their prospective employers might be inclined to beat and berate them, but that they might incite violence and verbal assault against themselves. It was black women's failure to be punctual, loyal, "docile," and diligent that invariably was used to explain the cruelty. They did not "safeguard family secrets" but gossiped about their employers. They did not engage in "fly control" and "swat every fly soon." They did not present themselves without "runs" in their stockings. They were not "economical" with their employers' food or their own time. They were not "ambitious" enough in forging forward in the "vocation" of domestic service. The syllabus for the Richmond program's course of instruction even included this: Black women could not be trusted to know "Why, How, When and With What to Clean" their bodily cavities (eyes, ears, mouth, nose, armpits, vagina, etc.), thereby jeopardizing the health of their employer and her family.[14] The indictment goes on in week after week of guest lectures. The resemblance to the antebellum rebukes could not be more striking.

Despite the religious underpinnings and the often polite language of this campaign to make "better girls"of black women, black women remained in the view of white women alien, women whom they might reform to some degree but who were inherently different, and therefore difficult. Thus, as white women set about teaching black women how to clean their homes, cook their meals, nurse their children, set their tables, launder their silk clothes, and use electrical appliances, they reminded their black servants that segregation extended to the domestic sphere. "Each maid should have her own drinking

---

[13] "CHRISTIAN ATTITUDES IN HOME-SERVICE RELATIONSHIPS," Rural Youth Records, DU.

[14] Ibid.; Wiley A. Hall, "INTRODUCTION – PURPOSE OF THE COURSE," Home Service Course for General Maids," Given Cooperatively by the Richmond Urban League and the Richmond Branch of the Southern Woman's Educational Alliance, 1933–34, Rural Youth Records, DU.

cup and hand towel for use in the kitchen." Each maid was also to learn how to change her employer's pillowcases without breathing on them.[15]

Like former masters, former mistresses became not only employers but also laborers. They found themselves working inside and outside of their homes. From that fundamental fact, Jane Turner Censer, in her recent study of white women in Virginia and North Carolina, draws this conclusion: "In many ways the chronicle of privileged white women after the war is a success story." According to this view, former mistresses not only adapted well but demonstrated "some willingness on their part" to shoulder the drudgery of domestic work in their own homes.[16] But such willingness as may be found was born of dire need. It should not confuse the picture that emerges from so many diaries, letters, and narratives. Privileged white women simply did not believe this household drudgery was theirs to do. A different reality and spirit drove them. After the war, and into the twentieth century, they devoted themselves to ridding themselves of the drudgery of housework. They attended the countless home economics courses and read the countless books and journal articles, devoted to the "servant question": how to get and keep domestic laborers. A contest sponsored by *Good Housekeeping* magazine in 1885 offered $200 for the best article on the "Vexed Servant Girl Question." The winner was a Texas housewife, whose contribution was serialized in six issues in 1886 as "Mistress Work and Maid Work. Which is Mistress and Which is the Servant?"[17] White women never gave up the idea that they should have black maids and cooks and laundresses. And in the twentieth century this belief came to be shared even by white mill workers.

While the Richmond project was set in an urban area, its concerns reflected the problems of rural areas as well as the impact of black migration to urban areas in the South and the North. World War I, the Great Depression, and World War II each had its impact on migration and the availability of domestic help in the South, and each opened up new employment and other opportunities for black women. "Numerous are the rumors about high and mighty ways displayed by previously apparently docile colored girls on the basis of economic emancipation from their former owners," wrote one federal government official.[18] The "defection" of black domestics was put in terms that would have been easily understood by former mistresses in 1865. As one employer

[15] Mrs. E. J. Wampler, "HYGIENE AND THE KITCHEN"; Mrs. John Palmer Lea, "BED MAKING"; Dr. Z. G. Gilpin, "PERSONAL HYGIENE AND THE JOB: Proper Cavity Cleansing"; Rural Youth Records, DU. See also Patricia Yeager, *Dirt and Desire: Reconstructing Southern Women's Writing, 1930–1990* (Chicago: University of Chicago Press, 2000), pp. 61–87; and Susan Tucker, *Telling Memories among Southern Women: Domestic Workers and Their Employers in the Segregated South* (New York: Schocken Books, 1988).

[16] Jane Turner Censer, *The Reconstruction of White Southern Womanhood, 1865–1895* (Baton Rouge: Louisiana State University Press, 2003), pp. 8 and 64.

[17] Katzman, *Seven Days a Week*, p. 175; see also pp. 189–97.

[18] Edgar A. Schuler, "Tension Area Analysis: Racial Problems," January 22, 1943, Edgar Schuler – Field Reports, RG 44, Box 1824, NA. Schuyler also documented the power of white southerners in the 1930s to get WPA payments to black women reduced in order to bring them down to

reported her tribulations in hiring domestic labor: "We were considered by a colored maid the other day."[19] The reality was always more complicated.

By the end of the 1880s, black women's vision of freedom and their actions to attain it had brought about the transformation of the plantation household. Black women had ensured that it remained a space of contested labor and gender relations even though, outwardly, it sometimes appeared unchanged. It is difficult to see this transformation without understanding the nineteenth-century plantation household as a political space and a site of labor, and without turning our attention as much to domestic economies as to agricultural ones.[20] Otherwise, the labor of black women in white homes in the rural South seems supra-historical, unchanging over time and space, "settled into a pattern that remained virtually unchanged," as one scholar writes, after the first year of freedom.[21] The picture that has emerged from this close examination is by no means a story of sameness.

I have tried in this book to insist on the importance of attending to relations of power between women, and contests over that power. Once "home" is understood as a political space, those contests, once silent and unseen in the historiography become visible and public. Black women were determined to take control of their whole lives. They challenged the authority of former masters and mistresses to order them about any longer, speak for them, or to cheat them of their earnings. They made a public matter of what one planter called "my *domestic affairs* exclusively."[22] Many paid a dear price for doing so, but the memory of the struggles that had gone before continued to inform black women's resistance to racism and discrimination. Meanwhile, despite the calls to Christian charity and reform, physical violence and mental abuse remained entrenched in domestic work.

In 1935, Mrs. Andrew Williams, with her husband and son, was still trying to live out the promises of freedom. Like so many black women before her and at the time, Mrs. Williams helped out on the family's small two-acre farm and worked outside the home as a cook. When her employer reduced her wages by more than half, to $2.00 per week, she quit. Her employer went to her house, forced her to return to work, and to leave her family permanently. When her husband protested, he was ordered to leave their home and never return. In a letter to President Franklin D. Roosevelt seeking his help, her son said that

the going wage rates for domestic work, and the authority white southerners took to cut the number of hours black women could work for the WPA (ibid., March 20, 1943).

[19] Tensions Involving Two Minority Groups, Special Services Division, Report No. 109, March 15, 1943, Bureau of Intelligence, Office of War Information, Box 1718, RG 44, NA; "Opinions About Inter-racial Tension," August 25, 1943, Division of Research Report No. C 12, Office of War Information, RG 44, NA.

[20] An important exception is Tera W. Hunter, *To 'Joy My Freedom: Southern Black Women's Lives and Labors after the Civil War* (Cambridge, MA: Harvard University Press, 1997), whose focus is the urban environment of Atlanta, Georgia.

[21] Weiner, *Mistresses and Slaves*, p. 207.

[22] Testimony of Nancy Johnson, March 25, 1867 and Geo. A. Hoke to Col. S. S. English, March 29, 1867, KY, RG 105, KY.

his mother quit when her wages were reduced "and as she had work at home it did not pay to work away for so little." For this her employer had forcibly removed her from her home and forced her "to say she does not want to come back for fear of harm to my father." "I hope," he wrote, "you president (sic) can make it safe for us to go back home where we made our living and have our crops to gather."[23] In this way, Mrs. Williams's role as cook did not at all belong to "domestic affairs exclusively." It was anchored within the public architecture of agricultural work and the political power that denied her right to choose, and that of her family, for many seasons thereafter. The system of peonage gave added weight to white women's efforts to regain power over their households and the women who labored in them, and it prolonged the struggle for free homes and women.

[23] George Williams to Mr. president, Oct. 3, 1935, Box 1282, Central Files and Related Records, 1904–67, General Records, Records of the Department of Justice, RG 60, NA. Mrs. Williams was a victim of peonage. On peonage, see Pete Daniel, *The Shadow of Slavery: Peonage in the South, 1901–1969* (Urbana: University of Illinois Press, 1972).

Bibliography

Primary Sources

Archives and Manuscript Collections

Rare Book, Manuscripts, and Special Collections Library, Duke University, Durham, NC
  Alliance for the Guidance of Rural Youth Records
  William T. Bain Papers
  John Ball and John Ball, Jr. Papers
  Samuel Simpson Biddle Papers
  Thomas C. Carroll Papers
  Maria Dyer Davis Papers
  Lucy Muse Walton Fletcher Diary
  John Berkeley Grimball Papers
  Edward William Kinsley Papers
  Louis Manigault Papers
  William Slade Papers
  Augustin Louis Taveau Papers
  Isaac B. Youngman Papers
  Manchester Ward Papers
  District Conference Records, 1866–1897, Methodist Church Papers
South Carolina Department of Archives and History
  Clarendon County Freeholders & Magistrates Court Records
  Pendleton/Anderson District Magistrates and Freeholders Court Records
  Spartanburg District Court of Magistrates and Freeholders Records
Southern Historical Collection, Manuscript Department, Wilson Library, University of North Carolina, Chapel Hill, North Carolina
  North Carolina Collection
  Cameron Family Papers
  Sarah Rebecca Cameron Papers
  Grace Elmore Papers

Charles Iverson Graves Papers
Grimball Family Papers
Emma LeConte Diary
Margaret Ann Meta Morris Grimball Dairy
George Nelson Hill Diary and Account Book
Belle Kearney Papers
Manigault Family Papers
Morris Manigault and Grimball Family Papers
James S. Milling Papers
Pettigrew Family Papers
William Renwick Papers, 1850–1869
Henry Lee Reynolds Papers
Roach and Eggleston Family Papers
Cordelia Lewis Scales Family Papers
Jane Sivley Papers
South Carolina Historical Society, Charleston, South Carolina
    Ladies Mutual Aid Association
    Langdon Cheves Papers
    Manigault Family Papers
    Mitchel & Smith Papers
    Frederick A. Porcher Papers
    Ravenel Family Papers
South Carolinian Library, Manuscripts Division, University of South Carolina, Columbia, South Carolina
    Charleston Scrapbook Clippings Chiefly from Charleston Newspapers, 1800–1810
    Palmer Family Papers
        John S. Palmer Family Letters, November 1860–June 1865
        Palmer Family Journal
        Harriet R. Palmer Diary
    Kedeziah Goodwyn Hopkins Brevard Diary
    Manigault Family Papers
Mississippi Department of Archives and History, Jackson, Mississippi
    Joseph E. Davis and Family Papers
Library of Congress, Washington, D.C.
    Nannie Helen Burrough Papers
    Mary Virginia Montgomery Diary
    Anna Kelton Wiley Papers
National Archives, Washington, D.C.
    General Records of the Department of Justice, Record Group 60
    Records of the Adjutant General's Office, Record Group 94
    Records of the Bureau of Refugees, Freedmen, and Abandoned Lands, Record Group 105
    Records of the Office of Government Reports, Record Group 44
    Records of the Treasury Department, Record Group 366
    Records of the United States Army Continental Commands, 1821–1930, Record Group 393
    Records of the United States General Accounting Office, RG 217
    Records of the United States House of Representatives, Record Group 233

Government Documents, Official Proceedings, and Addresses

Cases Argued in the Court of Chancery of South Carolina, June 1869

U.S. Government. *Report of the Committee of the Senate Upon the Relations between Labor and Capital and Testimony Taken by the Committee.* 5 vols. Washington, DC: Government Printing Office, 1885.

———. *Official Records of the Union and Confederate Navies in the War of the Rebellion.* Washington, DC: Government Printing Office, 1894–1922.

———. *The Statutes at Large, Treaties, and Proclamations.* Boston, MA: Little, Brown, 1863–69.

———. *The War of the Rebellion: A Compilation of the Official Records of the Union and Confederate Armies.* Washington, DC: Government Printing Office, 1880–1901.

Diaries, Letters, Articles, Slave Narratives, and Travel Accounts

Advertisement, Nashville Healing Institute, *Confederate Veteran* 1 (September 1893): 287.

A South Carolinian. "South Carolina Society." *The Atlantic Monthly* 39 (June 1877): 670–84.

Alston, J. Motte. *Rice Planter and Sportsman: The Recollections of J. Motte Alston, 1821–1909.* Ed. Arney R. Childs. Columbia: University of South Carolina Press, 1953.

Andrews, Eliza Frances. *The War-Time Journal of a Georgia Girl, 1864–1865.* New York: D. Appleton and Co., 1908.

Andrews, Matthew Page, comp. *The Women of the South in War Times.* Baltimore: Norman, Remington, Co., 1920.

Andrews, Sidney. *The South Since the War.* 1866. Reprint, New York: Arno Press, 1969.

Baer, Elizabeth, ed. *Shadows on My Heart: The Civil War Diary of Lucy Rebecca Buck of Virginia.* Athens: University of Georgia Press, 1997.

Ball, Charles. *Slavery in the United States: A Narrative of the Life and Adventures of Charles Ball, a Black Man.* 1836. Reprint, New York: Negro Universities Press, 1969.

Barrow, Bennett H. *The Plantation Diary of Bennett H. Barrow.* In *Plantation Life in the Florida Parishes of Louisiana, 1836–1846.* Ed. Edwin Adams Davis. New York: Columbia University Press, 1943.

Beecher, Catherine E. and Harriet Beecher Stowe. *The American Woman's Home.* Ed. Nicole Tonkovick. 1869. Reprint, New Brunswick, NJ: Rutgers University Press, 2002.

Beeton, Mrs. [Isabella]. *Mrs. Beeton's Book of Household Management.* Ed. Nicola Humble. 1861. Abridged Edition, New York: Oxford University Press, 2000.

Blackford, Susan Leigh, comp. *Letters from Lee's Army or Memoirs of Life In and Out of the Army in Virginia During the War Between the States.* 1947. Reprint, New York: A. S. Barnes & Co., 1962.

Blassingame, John W., ed. *Slave Testimony: Two Centuries of Letters, Speeches, Interviews, and Autobiographies.* Baton Rouge: Louisiana State University Press, 1977.

Bleser, Carol, ed. *Secret and Sacred: The Diaries of James Henry Hammond: A Southern Slaveholder.* New York: Oxford University Press, 1988.

————, ed. *Tokens of Affection: The Letters of a Planter's Daughter in the Old South*. Athens: University of Georgia Press, 1996.

Botume, Elizabeth Hyde. *First Days among the Contrabands*. 1893. Reprint, New York: Arno Press, 1968.

Brockett, L. P. and Mary C. Vaughan, eds. *Woman's Work in the Civil War: A Record of Heroism, Patriotism and Patience*. Philadelphia: Zeigler, McCurdy, & Co., 1867.

Bruce, H. C. *The New Man. Twenty Years a Slave. Twenty Nine Years a Free Man: Recollections of H. C. Bruce*. 1895. Reprint, New York: Negro Universities Press, 1969.

Bryan, Mary Norcott, *A Grandmother's Recollection of Dixie*. New Bern, NC: Owen G. Dunn, [1912].

Burke, Emily. *Pleasure and Pain: Reminiscences of Georgia in the 1840s*. Savannah, GA: Beehive Press, 1982.

Burr, Virginia Ingraham, ed. *The Secret Eye: The Journal of Ella Gertrude Thomas, 1848-1889*. Introduction by Nell Irwin Painter. Chapel Hill: University of North Carolina Press, 1990.

Byrd, William. *The Secret Diary of William Byrd of Westover, 1709–1712*. Ed. Louis B. Wright and Marion Tinling. Richmond, VA: Dietz Press, 1941.

Carter, Christine Jacobson, ed. *The Diary of Dolly Hunt Burge, 1848–1879*. Athens: University of Georgia Press, 1997.

Carter, Landon. *The Diary of Colonel Landon Carter of Sabine Hall, 1752–1778*. 2 vols. Ed. Jack P. Greene. Charlottesville: University Press of Virginia, 1965.

Catterall, Helen Tunnicliff, ed. *Judicial Cases Concerning American Slavery and the Negro, 1926–1937*. 1926. Reprint, New York: Negro Universities Press, 1968.

Child, Mrs. [Maria] *The American Frugal Housewife*, 12th ed., 1833. Reprint, Bedford, MA: Applewood Books, N.D.

Clifton, James M., ed. *Life and Labor on Argyle Island: Letters and Documents of a Savannah River Rice Plantation, 1833–1867*. Savannah, GA: Beehive Press, 1978.

Crabtree, Beth G. and James M. Patton, eds. *"Journal of a Secesh Lady": The Diary of Catherine Ann Devereaux Edmondston*. Raleigh: North Carolina Division of Archives and History and Department of Cultural Resources, 1979.

Cumming, Kate. *Kate: The Journal of a Confederate Nurse*. Ed. Richard Barksdale Harwell. Baton Rouge: Louisiana State University Press, 1959.

Dawson, Frances W., ed. *Our Women in the War: The Lives They Lived, the Deaths They Died*. Charleston, SC: News and Courier, 1885.

Dawson, Sarah Morgan. *A Confederate Girl's Diary*. Ed. James I. Robertson, Jr. 1913. Reprint, Bloomington: Indiana University Press, 1960.

Deas, Anne Simons. *Recollections of the Ball Family of South Carolina and Comingtee Plantation*. [Summerville], SC: Privately Published, 1909.

De Forest, John William. *A Union Officer in the Reconstruction*. Ed. James H. Croushore and David Morris Potter. New Haven, CT: Yale University Press, 1948.

Dennett, John Richard. *The South as It Is: 1865–1866*. Ed. Henry M. Christman. New York: Viking Press, 1965.

De Saussure, Nancy B. *Old Plantation Days: Being Recollections of Southern Life Before the Civil War*. New York: Duffield & Company, 1909.

Douglass, Frederick. *My Bondage and My Freedom*. 1855. Reprint, New York: Dover Pub. Inc., 1969.

Eaton, John. *Grant, Lincoln and the Freedmen: Reminiscences of the Civil War*. In Collaboration with Ethel Osgood Mason. 1907. Reprint, New York: Negro Universities Press, 1969.

Elmore, Grace Brown. *The Civil War Diary of Grace Brown Elmore, 1861–1868*. Ed. Marli F. Weiner. Athens: University of Georgia Press, 1997.

Emerson, Nancy. Diary of Nancy Emerson (1862–1864). http://etext.lib.virginia.edu/ etcbin/toc . . . diaries&tag+public&part=25&division=div1.

Everson, Guy R. and Edward L. Simpson, Jr., eds. *"Far, Far From Home": The Wartime Letters of Dick and Talley Simpson, Third South Carolina Volunteers*. New York: Oxford University Press, 1994.

Fields, Mamie Garvin with Karen Fields. *Lemon Swamp and Other Places*. New York: Free Press, 1983.

Fishel, Leslie H. and Benjamin Quarles, eds. *The Negro American: A Documentary History*. New York: Scott, Foresman, and Co., 1967.

Foner, Philip S. and Ronald L. Lewis, eds. *The Black Worker: A Documentary History from Colonial Times to the Present*. 8 vols. *The Black Worker to 1869*. vol. 1. Philadelphia: Temple University Press, 1978.

Forten, Charlotte L. *The Journal of Charlotte L. Forten*. Ed. Ray Allen Billington. New York: W. W. Norton and Co., 1981.

Fox, Charles Barnard. *Record of the Service of the Fifty-Fifth Regiment of Massachusetts Volunteer Infantry*. 1868. Reprint, Freeport, NY: Books for Libraries Press, 1971.

Galbraith, William and Lorretta Galbraith, eds. *A Lost Heroine of the Confederacy: The Diaries and Letters of Belle Edmondson*. Jackson: University Press of Mississippi, 1990.

Grant, U.S. *Personal Memoirs of U.S. Grant*. Ed. E. B. Long. 1885–86. Reprint, New York: Grosset & Dunlap, 1962.

Gwaltney, John Langston, ed. *Drylongso: A Self-Portrait of Black America*. New York: Vintage Books, 1981.

Hague, Parthenia. *A Blockaded Family: Life in Southern Alabama During the Civil War*. 1888. Reprint, Freeport, NY: Books for Libraries Press, 1971.

Harris, Joel Chandler. "The Women of the South," Reprinted in *The Women of the Confederacy*. Ed. J. L. Underwood. New York: Neale Pub. Co., 1906.

Harris, Robert F. and John Niflot, eds. *The Civil War Letters of the Brothers Gould*. Westport, CT: Praeger, 1998.

Higgins, Henry and Connie Cox with Jean Cole Anderson, eds. *Journal of a Landlady: A Personal Account of Life in the Deep South During the Civil War by a Loyal Family, Marietta, Georgia, 1857–1883*. Privately Published. Chapel Hill, NC: Professional Press, 1995.

Hunt, Dolly Sumner (Mrs. Thomas Burge). *A Woman's Wartime Journal: An Account of the Passage over a Georgia Plantation of Sherman's Army in the March to the Sea, as Recorded in the Diary of Dolly Sumner Hunt*. New York: Century Co., 1918.

Inman, Myra. *A Diary of the Civil War in East Tennessee*. Ed. William R. Snell. Macon, GA: Mercer University Press, 2000.

Jacobs, Harriett. *Incidents in the Life of a Slave Girl, Written by Herself*. Ed. Jean Fagan Yellin. Cambridge, MA: Harvard University Press, 1987.

Johnson, Clifton H., ed. *God Struck Me Dead: Religious Conversion Experiences and Autobiographies of Ex-Slaves*. Philadelphia: Pilgrim Press, 1969.

Johnston, Frontis W., ed. *The Papers of Zebulon Baird Vance*. vol. 1, 1843–1862. Raleigh: State Department of Archives and History, 1963.

King, Edward. *The Great South*. Hartford, CT: American Publishing Co., 1875.

King, R. "On the Management of the Butler Estate." *Southern Agriculturalist* (December 1862): 523–29.

King, Wilma, ed. *A Northern Woman in the Plantation South: Letters of Tryphena Blanche Holder Fox, 1856–1876*. Columbia: University of South Carolina Press, 1993.

Le Guin, Charles A., ed. *A Home Concealed Woman: The Diaries of Magnolia Wynn Le Guin, 1901–1913*. Athens: University of Georgia Press, 1990.

Lewis, G. *Impressions of America and the American Churches from the Journal of the Rev. G. Lewis, One of the Deputation of the Free Church of Scotland to the United States*. 1848. Reprint, New York: Negro Universities Press, 1968.

Lines, Amelia Akehurst. *To Raise Myself a Little: The Diaries and Letters of Jennie, a Georgia Teacher, 1851–1886*. Ed. Thomas Dyer. Athens: University of Georgia Press, 1982.

Livermore, Mary A. *My Story of the War: The Civil War Memoirs of the Famous Nurse, Relief Organizer and Suffragette*. 1887. Reprint, New York: Da Capo Press, 1995.

Longstreet, A. B. *Georgia Scenes: Characters, Incidents &c. in the First Century of the Republic*. 1835. Reprint, New York: Sagamore Press, 1957.

McDonald, Cornelia Peake. *A Woman's Civil War: A Diary, with Reminiscences of the War from March 1862*. Ed. Minrose C. Gwin. Madison: University of Wisconsin Press, 1992.

McGuire, Judith W. *Diary of a Southern Refugee During the War by a Lady of Virginia*. Ed. Jean Berlin. 1867. Reprint, Lincoln: University of Nebraska Press, 1995.

Manigault, Arthur Middleton. *A Carolinian Goes to War: The Civil War Narrative of Arthur Middleton Manigault*. Ed. E. Lockwood Tower. Columbia: University of South Carolina Press, 1983.

Markham, Gervase. *The English Housewife*. Ed. Michael R. Best. 1615. Reprint, Kingston: McGill-Queen's University Press, 1986.

Martineau, Harriet. *Society in America*. 3 vols. 1837. Reprint, New York: AMS Press, Inc., 1966.

Mason, Mary Ann. *The Young Housewife's Counsellor and Friend: Containing Directions in Every Department of Housekeeping including the Duties of Wife and Mother*. New York: E. J. Hale & Son, 1875.

Mathew, William M., ed. *Agriculture, Geology, and Society in Antebellum South Carolina: The Private Diary of Edmund Ruffin, 1843*. Athens: University of Georgia Press, 1992.

Maury, Betty Herndon. *The Civil War Diary of Betty Herndon Maury (June 3, 1861–February 18, 1865)*. Ed. Robert A. Hodge. Fredericksburg, VA.: Privately Printed, 1985.

Moore, John Hammond, ed. *A Plantation Mistress on the Eve of the Civil War: The Diary of Keziah Goodwyn Hopkins Brevard, 1860–1861*. Columbia: University of South Carolina Press, 1993.

Morgan, Sarah. *Sarah Morgan: The Civil War Diary of a Southern Woman*. Ed. Charles East. New York: Simon & Schuster, 1991.

Myers, Robert Manson, ed. *A Georgian at Princeton*. New York: Harcourt Brace Jovanovich, 1976.

———, ed. *The Children of Pride: A True Story of Georgia and the Civil War*. New Haven, CT: Yale University Press, 1972.

O'Brien, Michael, ed. *An Evening When Alone: Four Journals of Single Women in the South, 1827–67*. Charlottesville: University of Virginia Press, 1993.

Olmstead, Frederick Law. *The Cotton Kingdom: A Traveler's Observations on Cotton and Slavery in the American Slave States*. 2 vols. New York: Mason Brothers, 1861.

Pennington, Patience. [*Elizabeth Allston Pringle*] *A Woman Rice Planter*. 1913. Reprint, New York: Macmillan Co., 1928.

Percy, William Alexander. *Lanterns on the Levee: Recollections of a Planter's Son*. New York: Alfred A. Knopf, 1941.

Perdue, Charles L., Jr., Thomas E. Barden, and Robert K. Phillips, eds. *Weevils in the Wheat: Interviews with Virginia Ex-Slaves*. Charlottesville: University Press of Virginia, 1976.

Phillips, Wendell. *Speeches, Lectures, and Letters*. Boston: James Redpath Pub., 1863.

Pringle, Elizabeth Allston. *A Woman Rice Planter*. 1913. Reprint, Columbia: University of South Carolina Press, 1992.

Putnam, Sallie Brock. *Richmond During the War: Four Years of Personal Observation*. 1867. Reprint, Lincoln: University of Nebraska Press, 1996.

Rawick, George P., ed. *The American Slave: A Composite Autobiography*. Westport, CT: Greenwood Press, 1977–1979.

Redkey, Edwin S., ed. *A Grand Army of Black Men: Letters from African-Americam Soldiers in the Union Army, 1861–1865*. Cambridge: Cambridge University Press, 1992.

Ruffin, Edmund. *The Diary of Edmund Ruffin*. vol. 2. *The Years of Hope, April 1861– June 1863*. Ed. William K. Scarborough. Baton Rouge: Louisiana State University Press, 1976.

Russell, William Howard. *My Diary North and South*. Boston: T. O. H. P. Burham, 1863.

Sherman, William T. *Memoirs of General William T. Sherman*. 2nd Ed. 2 vols. 1914. New York: D. Appleton and Co., 1931.

Sims, William Gilmore. *Sack and Destruction of the City of Columbia, South Carolina: To Which is Added a List of the Property Destroyed*. Columbia, SC: Power Press of Daily Phoenix, 1865.

Smedes, Susan Dabney. *Memorials of a Southern Planter*. Ed. Fletcher M. Green. 1887. Reprint, New York: Alfred A. Knopf, 1965.

State Agricultural and Mechanical Society of South Carolina. *History of the State Agricultural Society of South Carolina from 1839 to 1845, Inclusive of the State Agricultural Society of South Carolina from 1855 to 1861, Inclusive of the State Agricultural and Mechanical Society of South Carolina from 1869–1916, Inclusive*. Columbia, SC: R. L. Bryan Co., 1916.

Steedman, Carolyn Kay. *Landscape for a Good Woman: A Story of Two Lives*. 1986. Reprint, New Brunswick, NJ: Rutgers University Press, 2000.

Stewart, Austin. *Twenty-Two Years a Slave, and Forty Years a Freeman*. 1856. Reprint, New York: Negro Universities Press, 1968.

Stone, Kate. *Brokenburn: The Journal of Kate Stone, 1861–1868*. Ed. John Q. Anderson. Baton Rouge: Louisiana State University Press, 1995.

Sutherland, Daniel E., ed. *A Very Violent Rebel: The Civil War Diary of Ellen Renshaw House*. Knoxville: University of Tennessee Press, 1996.

Swint, Henry L., ed. *Dear Ones at Home: Letters from Contraband Camps*. Nashville: Vanderbilt University Press, 1966.

Taylor, Susie King. *Reminiscences of My Life in Camp with the 33rd U.S. Colored Troops, Late 1st South Carolina Volunteers*. Ed. Patricia Romero. 1902. Reprint, New York: Markus Weiner Pub., 1988.

Towles, Louis P., ed. *A World Turned Upside Down: The Palmers of South Santee, 1881–1881*. Columbia: University of South Carolina Press, 1996.

Two Diaries: From Middle St. John's Berkeley, South Carolina, February–May, 1865: Journals Kept by Miss Susan B. Jervay and Miss Charlotte St. J. Ravenel, at North-hampton and Poshee Plantations, and Reminiscences of Mrs. (Waring) Henagan, with Contemporary Reports from Federal Officials. [St. John's Island, SC]: St. John's Hunting Club, 1921. Reprinted as *Diaries of '65* (1994).

Underwood, Rev. J. L. *The Women of the Confederacy.* New York: Neale Pub. Co., 1906.

Wagstaff, H. M., ed. *The James A. Graham Papers, 1861–1884.* Chapel Hill: University of North Carolina Press, 1928.

Warren, Rev. Joseph D. D., comp. *Extracts from Reports of the Superintendent of Freedmen.* Vicksburg, MS: Freedmen Press Print, 1864.

Weld, Theodore. *American Slavery as It Is: Testimony of a Thousand Witnesses.* 1839. Reprint, Westport, CT.: Negro Universities Press, 1970.

Wells-Barnett, Ida B. *Southern Horrors: Lynch Law in all Its Phases.* 1892. Reprint, Salem, NH: Ayer Company, Publishers, 1987.

———. *On Lynchings: Southern Horrors, A Red Record, Mob Rule in New Orleans.* 1892, 1895, and 1990. Reprint, New York: Arno Press, 1969.

Weschler, Lawrence. "Inventing Peace." *The New Yorker.* November 29, 1995, p. 59.

Wiley, Bell Irvin, ed. *This Infernal War: The Confederate Letters of Sgt. Edwin H. Fay.* Austin: University of Texas Press, 1958.

Wood, W. Kirk, ed. *A Northern Soldier and a Southern Wife: The Civil War Reminiscences and Letters of Katherine H. Cumming, 1860–65.* Augusta, GA: Richmond County Historical Society, 1976.

Woodward, C. Vann, ed. *Mary Chesnut's Civil War.* New Haven, CT: Yale University Press, 1981.

Woodward, C. Vann and Elisabeth Muhlenfeld, eds. *The Private Mary Chesnut: The Unpublished Civil War Diaries.* New York: Oxford University Press, 1984.

Yacovone, Donald, ed. *A Voice of Thunder: The Civil War Letters of George E. Stephens.* Urbana: University of Illinois Press, 1997.

Fiction

Chamoiseau, Patrick. *Texaco.* Trans. Rose-Myrium Rejouis and Val Vinokurov. New York: Pantheon Books, 1997.

Faulkner, William. *Absalom, Absalom!* 1936. New York: Vintage Books, 1978.

Mitchell, Margaret. *Gone With the Wind.* New York: Macmillan, 1936.

Morrison, Toni. *Beloved.* New York: Knopf, 1987.

Roberts, Elizabeth Madox. *The Time of Man.* 1926. Reprint, New York: Viking Press, 1963.

Secondary Sources

Aaron, Daniel. *The Unwritten War: American Writers and the Civil War.* London: Oxford University Press, 1973.

Abbott, Shirley. *Womenfolks: Growing Up Down South.* New Haven, CT: Ticknor & Fields, 1983.

Abercrombie, Nicholas, Stephen Hill, and Bryan S. Turner. *The Dominant Ideology Thesis.* Boston, MA: G. Allen and Unwin, 1980.

Aiken, Charles S. *The Cotton Plantation South Since the Civil War*. Baltimore, MD: Johns Hopkins University Press, 1998.

Amin, Shahid and Dipesh Charabarty, eds. *Subaltern Studies IX: Writings on South Asian History*. Delhi: Oxford University Press, 1996.

Anderson, James D. *The Education of Blacks in the South, 1865–1935*. Chapel Hill: University of North Carolina Press, 1988.

Anderson, Jean Bradley. *Piedmont Plantation: The Bennehan-Cameron Family and Lands in North Carolina*. Durham, NC: Historic Preservation Society of Durham, 1985.

Aptheker, Herbert. *American Negro Slave Revolts*. New York: Columbia University Press, 1943.

Ariès, Philip. "Introduction." In *Passions of the Renaissance*. vol. 9. *A History of Private Life*. Ed. Roger Chartier. Cambridge, MA: Harvard University Press, 1989.

Ash, Steven V. *When the Yankees Came: Conflict and Chaos in the Occupied South, 1861–1865*. Chapel Hill: University of North Carolina Press, 1995.

Attie, Jeanie. "Warwork and the Crisis of Domesticity in the North." In *Divided Houses: Gender and the Civil War*. Ed. Catherine Clinton and Nina Silber. New York: Oxford University Press, 1992.

Ball, Edward. *Slaves in the Family*. New York: Farrar, Straus, and Giroux, 1998.

Ballantyne, Tony and Antoinette Burton, eds. *Bodies in Contact: Rethinking Colonial Encounters in World History*. Durham, NC: Duke University Press, 2005.

Banta, Martha. *Taylored Lives: Narrative Productions in the Age of Taylor, Veblen, and Ford*. Chicago: University of Chicago Press, 1993.

Bardaglio, Peter W. *Reconstructing the Household: Families, Sex, and the Law in the Nineteenth-Century South*. Chapel Hill: University of North Carolina Press, 1995.

Barton, Keith. "'Good Cooks and Washers': Slave Hiring, Domestic Labor, and the Market in Bourbon County, Kentucky." *Journal of American History* 84 (September 1997): 436–60.

Beckles, Hilary McD. "Taking Liberties: Enslaved Women and Anti-Slavery in the Caribbean." In *Gender and Imperialism*. Ed. Clare Midgley. Manchester, UK: Manchester University Press, 1998, pp. 137–57.

_____. "White Women and Slavery in the Caribbean." *History Workshop Journal* 36 (Autumn 1993): 66–82.

Bercaw, Nancy D. *Gendered Freedoms: Race, Rights, and the Politics of Household in the Delta, 1861–1875*. Gainesville: University Press of Florida, 2003.

Berlin, Ira. "Who Freed the Slaves? Emancipation and Its Meaning." In *Union and Emancipation: Essays on Politics and Race in the Civil War Era*. Ed. David W. Blight and Brooks D. Simpson. Kent, OH: Kent State University Press, 1997, pp. 105–21.

Berlin, Ira, Thavolia Glymph, Steven F. Miller, Joseph P. Reidy, Leslie S. Rowland, and Julie Saville, eds. *Freedom: A Documentary History of Emancipation, 1861–1867*. ser. 1, vol. 3. *The Wartime Genesis of Free Labor in the Lower South*. Cambridge: Cambridge University Press, 1990.

Berlin, Ira, Thavolia Glymph, Joseph P. Reidy, and Leslie S. Rowland, eds. *Freedom: A Documentary History of Emancipation*. ser. 1., vol. 1. *The Destruction of Slavery*. Cambridge: Cambridge University Press, 1985.

Berlin, Ira, Joseph P. Reidy, and Leslie Rowland, eds. *Freedom: A Documentary History of Emancipation*. ser. 2. *The Black Military Experience*. Cambridge: Cambridge University Press, 1982.

Bernhard, Virginia, Betty Brandon, Elizabeth Fox-Genovese, and Theda Purdue, eds. *Southern Women: Histories and Identities*. Columbia: University of Missouri Press, 1992.

Best, Joel. *Random Violence: How We Talk about New Crimes and New Violence*. Berkeley: University of California Press, 1999.

Blassingame, John W. "Using the Testimony of Ex-Slaves: Approaches and Problems." *Journal of Southern History* 41 (November 1975): 473–92.

Bleser, Carol K., ed. *In Joy and in Sorrow: Women, Family, and Marriage in the Victorian South, 1830–1900*. New York: Oxford University Press, 1991.

————. "Southern Planter Wives and Slavery." In *The Meaning of South Carolina History: Essays in Honor of George C. Rogers, Jr.* Ed. David R. Chestnut and Clyde N. Wilson. Columbia: University of South Carolina Press, 1991.

Bleser, Carol and Frederick Heath. "The Clays of Alabama: The Impact of the Civil War on a Southern Marriage." In *In Joy and in Sorrow: Women, Family, and Marriage in the Victorian South, 1830–1900*. Ed. Carol Bleser. New York: Oxford University Press, 1991.

Blight, David W. and Brooks D. Simpson, eds. *Union and Emancipation: Essays on Politics and Race in the Civil War Era*. Kent, OH: Kent State University Press, 1997.

Boles, John B. and Evelyn Thomas Nolen, eds. *Interpreting Southern History: Historiographical Essays in Honor of Sanford W. Higginbotham*. Baton Rouge: Louisiana State University Press, 1987.

Boritt, Gabor S., ed., *Why the Civil War Came*. New York: Oxford University Press, 1996.

Boydston, Jeanne. *Home and Work: Housework, Wages, and the Ideology of Labor in the Early Republic*. New York: Oxford University Press, 1990.

————. "To Earn Her Daily Bread: Housework and Antebellum Working-Class Subsistence." *Radical History Review* 35 (April 1986): 7–25.

Brown, Elsa Barkley. "Negotiating Community and Freedom: African American Political Life in the Transition from Slavery to Freedom. *Public Culture* 7 (Fall 1994): 107–46.

Brown, Kathleen M. *Good Wives, Nasty Wenches, and Anxious Patriarchs: Gender, Race, and Power in Colonial Virginia*. Chapel Hill: University of North Carolina Press, 1996.

Brubaker, Rogers and Frederick Cooper. "Beyond 'Identity.'" *Theory and Society* 29 (February 2000): 1–47.

Bujra, Janet M. "Men at Work in the Tanzanian Home: How Did They Ever Learn?" In *African Encounters with Domesticity*. Ed. Karen Tranberg Hansen. New Brunswick, NJ: Rutgers University Press, 1993, pp. 242–65.

Burr, Virginia. "A Woman Made to Suffer and Be Strong: Ella Gertrude Clanton Thomas, 1834–1907." In *In Joy and In Sorrow: Women, Family, and Marriage in the Victorian South, 1830–1900*. Ed. Carol Bleser. New York: Oxford University Press, 1991.

Burton, Orville Vernon. *In My Father's House are Many Mansions: Family and Community in Edgefield, South Carolina*. Chapel Hill: University of North Carolina Press, 1985.

Bynum, Victoria. "Reshaping the Bonds of Womanhood: Divorce in Reconstruction North Carolina." In *Divided Houses: Gender and the Civil War*. Ed. Catherine Clinton and Nina Silber. New York: Oxford University Press, 1992.

Camp, Stephanie M. H. *Closer to Freedom: Enslaved Women and Everyday Resistance in the Plantation South*. Chapel Hill: University of North Carolina Press, 2004.

———. "The Pleasures of Resistance: Enslaved Women and Body Politics in the Plantation South, 1830–1861." *Journal of Southern History* 68 (August 2002): 534–72.

Cashin, Joan, ed. *Our Common Affairs: Texts from Women in the Old South*. Baltimore, MD: Johns Hopkins University Press, 1996.

———. "'Since the War Broke Out': The Marriage of Kate and William McClure." In *Divided Houses: Gender and the Civil War*. Ed. Catherine Clinton and Nina Silber. New York: Oxford University Press, 1992.

———. "Structure of Antebellum Southern Families: 'The Ties That Bound Us Was Strong.'" *Journal of Southern History* 56 (February 1990): 55–70.

Censer, Jane Turner. *The Reconstruction of White Southern Womanhood, 1865–1895*. Baton Rouge: Louisiana State University Press, 2003.

———. *North Carolina Planters and Their Children, 1800–1860*. Baton Rouge: Louisiana State University Press, 1984.

Chakrabarty, Dipesh. "The Difference – Deferral of a Colonial Modernity: Public Debates on Domesticity in British Bengal." In *Tensions of Empire: Colonial Culture in a Bourgeois World*. Ed. Frederick Cooper and Ann Laura Stoler. Berkeley: University of California Press, 1997.

———. *Rethinking Working Class History: Bengal 1890–1940*. Princeton, NJ: Princeton University Press, 1989.

Clark-Lewis, Elizabeth. *Living in, Living Out: African American Domestics in Washington, D.C., 1910–1940*. Washington, DC: Smithsonian Institution Press, 1994.

Clinton, Catherine. *Tara Revisited: Women, War & the Plantation Legend*. New York: Abbeville Press, 1995.

———. "Reconstructing Freedwomen." In *Divided Houses: Gender and the Civil War*. Ed. Catherine Clinton and Nina Silber. New York: Oxford University Press, 1992.

———. "Southern Dishonor: Flesh, Blood, Race, and Bondage." In *In Joy and In Sorrow: Women, Family, and Marriage in the Victorian South, 1830–1900*. Ed. Carol Bleser. New York: Oxford University Press, 1991.

———. "Caught in the Web of the Big House." In *The Web of Southern Social Relations: Women, Family, and Education*. Eds. Walter J. Fraser, Jr., R. Frank Saunders, Jr., and Jon Wakelyn. Athens: University of Georgia Press, 1985.

———. *The Other Civil War: American Women in the Nineteenth Century*. New York: Hill & Wang, 1984.

———. *The Plantation Mistress: Woman's World in the Old South*. New York: Pantheon, 1982.

Clinton, Catherine and Nina Silber, eds. *Divided Houses: Gender and the Civil War*. New York: Oxford University Press, 1992.

Cooper, Frederick. *Colonialism in Question: Theory, Knowledge, History*. Berkeley: University of California Press, 2005.

Cooper, Frederick, Florencia E. Mallon, William Roseberry, and Steven J. Stern, eds. *Confronting Historical Paradigms: Peasants, Labor, and the Capitalist World System in Africa and Latin America*. Madison: University of Wisconsin Press, 1993.

Cooper, William J., et al., eds. *A Master's Due: Essays in Honor of David H. Donald*. Baton Rouge: Louisiana State University Press, 1985.

Cornish, Dudley Taylor. *The Sable Arm: Negro Troops in the Union Army, 1861–1865*. New York: Longmans, Green and Co., 1956.

Côté, Richard N. *Mary's World: Love, War, and Family Ties in Nineteenth Century Charleston.* Mt. Pleasant, SC: Corinthian Books, 2001.

Cotterill, R. S. *The Old South.* Glendale, CA: Arthur H. Clark, Pub., 1937.

Coulter, E. Merton. *The South During Reconstruction, 1865–1877.* Baton Rouge: Louisiana State University Press, 1947.

Crawford, Stephen C. "Punishments and Rewards." In *Without Consent or Contract. Technical Papers: The Rise and Fall of American Slavery.* 2 vols. *Conditions of Slave Life and the Transition to Freedom.* vol. 2. Ed. Robert William Fogel and Stanley L. Engerman. New York: W. W. Norton, 1992, pp. 536–50.

Cross, J. Russell Cross. *Historic Ramblin's through Berkeley County.* Columbia, SC: R. L. Bryan Co., 1985.

Cullen, Jim. "'I'se a Man Now': Gender and African American Men." In *Divided Houses: Gender and the Civil War.* Ed. Catherine Clinton and Nina Silber. New York: Oxford University Press, 1992.

Da Costa, Emília Viotti. *Crowns of Glory, Tears of Blood: the Demerara Slave Rebellion of 1823.* New York: Oxford University Press, 1994.

Daniel, Pete. *The Shadow of Slavery: Peonage in the South, 1901–1969.* Urbana: University of Illinois Press, 1972.

Darnton, Robert. *The Great Cat Massacre and Other Episodes in French Cultural History.* New York: Vintage Books, 1984.

Davidoff, Leonore. "Gender and the 'Great Divide': Public and Private in British Gender History." *Journal of Women's History* 15 (Spring 2003): 11–27.

Davis, David Brion. *From Homicide to Slavery: Studies in American Culture.* New York: Oxford University Press, 1986.

———. "The American Family and Boundaries in Historical Perspective." In *From Homicide to Slavery: Studies in American Culture.* Ed. David Brion Davis. New York: Oxford University Press, 1986.

———. *The Problem of Slavery in the Age of Revolution, 1770–1823.* Ithaca, NY: Cornell University Press, 1975.

Davis, Edwin Adams. *Plantation Life in the Florida Parishes of Louisiana, 1836-1846 as Reflected in the Diary of Bennett H. Barrow.* New York: Columbia University Press, 1943.

Degler, Carl N. *At Odds: Women and the Family in America from the Revolution to the Present.* New York: Oxford University Press, 1980.

De Groot, Joanna. "Sex and Race: The Construction of Language and Image in the Nineteenth Century." In *Cultures of Empire: Colonizers in Britain and the Empire in the Nineteenth and Twentieth Centuries: A Reader.* Ed. Catherine Hall. Manchester, UK: Manchester University Press, 2000.

Delfino, Susanna and Michelle Gillespie, eds. *Neither Lady nor Slave: Working Women of the Old South.* Chapel Hill: University of North Carolina Press, 2002.

Dennis, Samuel. "Meaning and Materiality: The Racialized Landscape of Antebellum Georgia." Paper in possession of the author.

Denzer, LaRay. "Domestic Science Training in Colonial Yoruba Land, Nigeria." In *African Encounters with Domesticity.* Ed. Karen Tranberg Hansen. New Brunswick, NJ: Rutgers University Press, 1992, pp. 116–92.

Dickson, Margaret Stockman. *Vocational Guidance for Girls.* Chicago: Rand McNally & Co., 1919.

Dillman, Caroline Matheny, ed. *Southern Women.* New York: Hemisphere Pub. Corp., 1988.

Dirks, Nicholas B., ed. *Colonialism and Culture.* Ann Arbor: University of Michigan Press, 1992.

Dodd, William E. *The Cotton Kingdom: A Chronicle of the Old South.* New Haven, CT: Yale University Press, 1920.

Du Bois, W. E. B. *Black Reconstruction in America: An Essay Toward a History of the Part Which Black Folk Played in the Attempt to Reconstruct Democracy in America, 1860–1880.* 1935. Reprint, New York: Atheum, 1973.

———. "The Negro Landholder of Georgia." *Bulletin No. 35.* U.S. Department of Labor (July 1901): 647–777.

Eaton, Clement. *The Waning of Old South Civilization, 1860–1880s.* Athens: University of Georgia Press, 1968.

———. *The Mind of the Old South.* 1964. Rev. Ed., Baton Rouge: Louisiana State University Press, 1967.

———. *A History of the Southern Confederacy.* New York: MacMillan, 1954.

Edwards, Laura F. *Gendered Strife and Confusion: The Political Culture of Reconstruction.* Urbana: University of Illinois Press, 1997.

Edwards, Thomas J. "The Tenant System and Some Changes Since Emancipation." In *The Negro's Progress in Fifty Years: The Annals.* vol. XLIX. Ed. J. P. Lichtenberger. Philadelphia, PA: American Academy of Political and Social Science, 1913. pp. 38–46.

Ellison, Mary. "Resistance to Oppression: Black Women's Response to Slavery in the United States." *Slavery and Abolition* 4 (May 1983): 56–63.

Emilio, Luis F. *A Brave Black Regiment: The History of the Fifty-Fourth Massachusetts Volunteer Infantry, 1863–1865.* 1894. Reprint, New York: Da Capo Press, 1995.

Escott, Paul D. *Many Excellent People: Power and Privilege in North Carolina, 1850–1900.* Chapel Hill: University of North Carolina Press, 1985.

Evans, David. *Sherman's Horsemen: Union Calvary Operations in the Atlanta Campaign.* Bloomington: Indiana University Press, 1996.

Fanon, Franz. *The Wretched of the Earth.* Trans. by Constance Farrington. New York: Grove Press, 1963.

Farnham, Christie Anne. *The Education of the Southern Belle: Higher Education and Student Socialization in the Antebellum South.* New York: New York University Press, 1994.

Faust, Drew Gilpin. "The Civil War Soldier and the Art of Dying." *Journal of Southern History* 67 (February 2001): 3–38.

———. *Mothers of Invention: Women of the Slaveholding South in the American Civil War.* Chapel Hill: University of North Carolina Press, 1996.

———. *Southern Stories: Slaveholders in Peace and War.* Columbia: University of Missouri Press, 1992.

———. "'Trying to Do a Man's Business': Gender, Violence, and Slave Management in Civil War Times." In Drew Gilpin Faust. *Southern Stories: Slaveholders in War and Peace.* Columbia: University of Missouri Press, 1992.

———. "Altars of Sacrifice: Confederate Women and the Narratives of War." *Journal of American History* 76 (March 1990): 1200–28.

———, ed. *The Ideology of Slavery: Proslavery Thought in the Antebellum South, 1830-1860.* Baton Rouge: Louisiana State University Press, 1981.

———. "Culture, Conflict, and Community: The Meaning of Power on an Antebellum Plantation." *Journal of Social History* 14 (Autumn 1980): 83–97.

Faust, Drew Gilpin, Thavolia Glymph, and George C. Rable. "A Woman's War: Southern Women in the Civil War." In *A Woman's War: Southern Women, Civil War, and the Confederate Legacy*. Ed. Edward D. C. Campbell, Jr. and Kym S. Rice. Charlottesville: University Press of Virginia, 1996.

Fernandes, Leela. *Producing Workers: The Politics of Gender, Class, and Culture in the Calcutta Jute Mills*. Philadelphia: University of Pennsylvania Press, 1997.

Fields, Barbara Jeanne. "Slavery, Race, and Ideology in the United States of America." *New Left Review* 181 (May–June 1990): 95–118.

_____. "Who Freed the Slaves?" In *The Civil War: An Illustrated History*. Ed. Geoffrey C. Ward. New York: Knopf, 1990.

_____. *Slavery and Freedom on the Middle Ground: Maryland During the Nineteenth Century*. New Haven, CT: Yale University Press, 1985.

_____. "Ideology and Race in American History." In *Region, Race, and Reconstruction: Essays in Honor of C. Vann Woodward*. Ed. J. Morgan Kousser and James M. McPherson. New York: Oxford University Press, 1982.

Fischer, David Hacker. *Albion's Seed: Four British Folkways in America*. New York: Oxford University Press, 1989.

Flanders, Ralph Betts. *Plantation Slavery in Georgia*. Chapel Hill: University of North Carolina Press, 1933.

Fleming, John E. "Slavery, Civil War, and Reconstruction: A Study of Black Women in Microcosm." *Negro History Bulletin* 38 (August/September 1975): 403–33.

Fogel, Robert William and Stanley L. Engerman, eds. *Without Consent or Contract. Technical Papers: The Rise and Fall of American Slavery*. 2 vols. *Conditions of Slave Life and the Transition to Freedom*. vol. 2. New York: W. W. Norton, 1992.

Foner, Eric. *Reconstruction: America's Unfinished Revolution, 1863–1877*. New York: Harper and Row, 1988.

_____. *Nothing But Freedom: Emancipation and Its Legacy*. Baton Rouge: Louisiana State University Press, 1983.

Forbes, Ella. *African American Women During the Civil War*. New York: Garland Pub., Inc., 1998.

Foster, Helen Bradley. *"New Raiments of Self": African American Clothing in the Antebellum South*. New York: Berg, 1997.

Fox-Genovese, Elizabeth. "Contested Meanings: Women and the Problem of Freedom in the Mid-Nineteenth Century United States." In *Historical Change and Human Rights: The Oxford Amnesty Lectures, 1994*. Ed. Olwen Hufton. New York: Basic Books, 1995.

_____. "To Be Worthy of God's Favor: Southern Women's Defense and Critique of Slavery." 32d Annual Fortenbaugh Memorial Lecture. Gettysburg College. 1993.

_____. "Family and Female Identity in the Antebellum South: Sarah Gayle and her Family," In *In Joy and In Sorrow: Women, Family, and Marriage in the Victorian South, 1830-1900*. Ed. Carol Bleser. New York: Oxford University Press, 1991.

_____. *Within the Plantation Household: Black and White Women of the Old South*. Chapel Hill: University of North Carolina Press, 1988.

_____. "The Ideological Basis of Domestic Economy: The Representation of Women and the Family in the Age of Expansion." In Elizabeth Fox-Genovese and Eugene D. Genovese. *Fruits of Merchant Capital: Slavery and Bourgeois Property in the Rise and Expansion of Capitalism*. New York: Oxford University Press, 1983.

Fox-Genovese, Elizabeth and Eugene D. Genovese. *The Mind of the Master Class: History and Faith in the Southern Slaveholders' Worldview.* New York: Cambridge University Press, 2005.

_____. *Fruits of Merchant Capital: Slavery and Bourgeois Property in the Rise and Expansion of Capitalism.* New York: Oxford University Press, 1983.

Frankel, Noralee. *Freedom's Women: Black Women and Families in Civil War Era Mississippi.* Bloomington: Indiana University Press, 1999.

Franklin, John Hope. *The Emancipation Proclamation.* 1963. Reprint, Wheeling, IL: Harlan Davidson, 1995.

_____. "Mirror for Americans: A Century of Reconstruction History." In John Hope Franklin, *Race and History: Selected Essays, 1938-1988.* Baton Rouge: Louisiana State University Press, 1989.

_____. *The Militant South.* Cambridge, MA: Harvard University Press, 1956.

Franklin, John Hope and Loren Schweninger. *Runaway Slaves: Rebels on the Plantation.* New York: Oxford University Press, 1999.

Fraser, Walter J., Jr. and Winfred B. Moore, eds. *The Southern Enigma: Essays on Race, Class and Folk Culture.* Westport, CT: Greenwood Press, 1983.

Frederick, Christine. *Scientific Management in the Home: Household Engineering.* London: G. Routledge & Sons, 1922.

Friedman, Jean E. *The Enclosed Garden: Women and Community in the Evangelical South, 1830-1900.* Chapel Hill: University of North Carolina Press, 1985.

Gallagher, Gary W. *The Confederate War: How Popular Will, Nationalism, and Military Strategy Could Not Stave Off Defeat.* Cambridge, MA: Harvard University Press, 1997.

Gardner, Sarah E. *Blood Irony: Southern White Women's Narratives of the Civil War, 1861–1937.* Chapel Hill: University of North Carolina Press, 2004.

Garner, James Wilford. *Reconstruction in Mississippi.* 1901. Reprint, Baton Rouge: Louisiana State University Press, 1968.

Gaspar, David Barry. "Working the System: Antigua Slaves and their Struggles to Live." *Slavery and Abolition: A Journal of Comparative Studies* 13 (December 1992): 131–55.

_____. *Bondmen and Rebels: A Study of Master-Slave Relationships in Antigua with Implications for Colonial British America.* Baltimore, MD: Johns Hopkins University Press, 1985.

Genovese, Eugene D. "'Our Family, White and Black': Family and Household in the Southern Slaveholders' World View." In *In Joy and In Sorrow: Women, Family, and Marriage in the Victorian South, 1830–1900.* Ed. Carol Bleser. New York: Oxford University Press, 1991.

_____. "Toward a Kinder and Gentler America: The Southern Lady in the Greening of the Politics of the Old South." In *In Joy and In Sorrow: Women, Family, and Marriage in the Victorian South, 1830–1900.* Ed. Carol Bleser. New York: Oxford University Press, 1991.

_____. *From Rebellion to Revolution: Afro-American Slave Revolts in the Making of the Modern World.* Baton Rouge: Louisiana State University Press, 1979.

_____. *Roll, Jordan, Roll: The World the Slaves Made.* New York: Vintage Books, 1974.

Gilmore, Glenda E. "Gender and Origins of the New South." *Journal of Southern History* 67 (November 2001): 769–88.

Glattnar, Joseph T. *The March to the Sea and Beyond: Sherman's Troops in the Savannah and Carolinas Campaign*. New York: New York University Press, 1985.

Glymph, Thavolia. "The Civil War Era." In *A Companion to American Women's History*. Ed. Nancy A. Hewitt. Oxford: Blackwell Pub., 2002.

_____. "African American Women in the Literary Imagination of Mary Boykin Chesnut." In *Slavery, Secession, and Southern History*. Ed. Louis Ferlegher and Robert Paquette. Charlottesville: University Press of Virginia, 1999.

_____. "'This Species of Property': Female Slave Contrabands in the Civil War." In *A Woman's War: Southern Women, Civil War, and the Confederate Legacy*. Ed. Edward D. C. Campbell and Kym Rice. Charlottesville: University Press of Virginia, 1996, pp. 55–71.

Glymph, Thavolia and John Kushma, eds. *Essays on the Postbellum Southern Economy*. College Station: Texas A&M University Press, 1985.

Gramsci, Antonio. *Selections from the Prison Notebooks*. Ed. and Trans. by Quinton Hoare and Geoffrey Nowell Smith. New York: International Pub., 1971.

Gray, Richard. *Writing the South: Ideas of an American Region*. New York: Cambridge University Press, 1986.

Greenberg, Kenneth S. *Honor and Slavery*. Princeton, NJ: Princeton University Press, 1996.

Guimond, James. *American Photography and the American Dream*. Chapel Hill: University of North Carolina Press, 1991.

Gutman, Herbert G. *The Black Family in Slavery and Freedom, 1750–1925*. New York: Pantheon, 1976.

Haggis, Janet. "White Women and Colonialism: Toward a Non-Recuperative History." In *Gender and Imperialism*. Ed. Clare Midgley. Manchester, UK: Manchester University Press, 1998.

Hagler, D. Harland. "The Ideal Woman in the Antebellum South: Lady or Farmwife?" *Journal of Southern History* 46 (August 1980): 405–18.

Hahn, Steven. *A Nation Under Our Feet: Black Political Struggles in the Rural South from Slavery to the Great Migration*. Cambridge, MA: Harvard University Press, 2003.

_____. "'Extravagant Expectations' of Freedom: Rumour, Political Struggle, and the Christmas Insurrection of 1865 in the American South," *Past and Present* 157 (November 1997): 122–58.

_____. "Class and State in Postemancipation Societies: Southern Planters in Comparative Perspective." *American Historical Review* 95 (February 1990): 75–98.

Hale, Grace. *Making Whiteness: The Culture of Segregation in the South, 1890–1940*. New York: Pantheon, 1998.

Hall, Catherine. *Civilising Subjects: Metropole and Colony in the English Imagination, 1830–1867*. Chicago: University of Chicago Press, 2002.

Hall, Jacqueline Dowd. "Partial Truths: Writing Southern Women's History." In *Southern Women: Histories and Identities*. Ed. Virginia Bernhard, Betty Brandon, Elizabeth Fox-Genovese, and Theda Purdue. Columbia: University of Missouri Press, 1992, pp. 11–29.

Hall, Jacqueline Dowd and Anne Firor Scott. "Women in the South." In *Interpreting Southern History: Historiographical Essays in Honor of Sanford W. Higginbotham*. Ed. John B. Boles and Evelyn Thomas Nolen. Baton Rouge: Louisiana State University Press, 1987, pp. 454–509.

Hansen, Karen Tranberg, ed. *African Encounters with Domesticity*. New Brunswick, NJ: Rutgers University Press, 1992.

Harley, Sharon and Rosalyn Terborg-Penn, eds. *The Afro-American Woman: Struggles and Images*. New York: Kennikat Press, 1978.

Harley, Sharon and the Black Women and Work Collective, eds. *Sister Circle: Black Women and Work*. New Brunswick, NJ: Rutgers University Press, 2002.

Harris, George E. *A Treatise on the Law of Contracts by Married Women, Their Capacity to Contract in Relation to Their Separate Statutory Legal Estates, under American Statutes*. Albany, NY: Banks and Brothers, 1887.

Harris, William C. *The Day of the Carpetbagger: Republican Reconstruction in Mississippi*. Baton Rouge: Louisiana State University Press, 1979.

Hartman, Saidiya V. *Scenes of Subjection: Terror, Slavery, and Self-Making in Nineteenth Century America*. New York: Oxford University Press, 1997.

Hatcher, O. Latham. *Rural Girls in the City for Work: A Study Made for the Southern Woman's Educational Alliance*. Richmond, VA: Garrett & Massie, 1930.

————. *Guiding Rural Boys and Girls: Flexible Guidance Programs for Use by Rural Schools and Related Agencies*. Ed. Emery N. Ferriss. New York: McGraw-Hill, 1930.

————, ed. *Occupations for Women, being the Practical Information Obtained by a Study Made for the Southern Woman's Educational Alliance*. Richmond, VA: Southern Woman's Educational Alliance, 1927.

Hayden, Delores. *The Grand Domestic Revolution: A History of Feminist Designs for American Homes, Neighborhoods, and Cities*. Cambridge, MA: MIT Press, 1981.

Haygood, Margaret Jarman. *Mothers of the South: Portraiture of the White Tenant Farm Woman*. 1939. Reprint, Charlottesville: University Press of Virginia, 1996.

Heilbrun, Carolyn G. *Hamlet's Mother and Other Women*. New York: Columbia University Press, 1990.

Hesseltine, William B. *A History of the South, 1607–1936*. New York: Prentice-Hall, 1936.

Hill, Christopher. *The World Turned Upside Down: Radical Ideas during the English Revolution*. London, UK: Temple Smith, 1972.

Hine, Darlene Clark. *A Shining Thread of Hope: The History of Black Women in America*. New York: Broadway Books, 1998.

————. *Hinesight: Black Women and the Re-Construction of American History*. Brooklyn, NY: Carlson Pub. Co., 1994.

————. "Rape and the Inner Lives of Black Women: Thoughts on the Culture of Dissemblance." In *Hinesight: Black Women and the Re-Construction of American History*. Ed. Darlene Clark Hine. Brooklyn, NY: Carlson Pub. Co., 1994.

Hirsh, Jerrold. "Toward a Marriage of True Minds: The Federal Writers' Project and the Writing of Southern History." In *The Adaptable South: Essays in Honor of George Brown Tindall*. Ed. Elizabeth Jacoway, Dan T. Carter, Lester C. Lamon, and Robert C. McMath, Jr. Baton Rouge: Louisiana State University Press, 1991, pp. 148–75.

Hobsbawm, Eric. *Revolutionaries*. 1973. Reprint, New York: Free Press, 2001.

Holt, Sharon Ann. *Making Freedom Pay: North Carolina Freedpeople Working for Themselves*. Athens: University of Georgia Press, 2000.

Holt, Thomas C. *The Problem of Freedom: Race, Labor and Politics in Jamaica and Britain, 1832–1938*. Baltimore, MD: Johns Hopkins University Press, 1992.

Hunter, Tera W. *To 'Joy My Freedom: Southern Black Women's Lives and Labors After the Civil War*. Cambridge, MA: Harvard University Press, 1997.

Isaac, Rhys. "Communication and Control: Authority Metaphors and Power Contests on Colonel Landon Carter's Virginia Plantation, 1752–1778." In *Rites of Power:*

Symbolism, Ritual and Politics Since the Middle Ages. Ed. Sean Wilenz. Philadelphia: University of Pennsylvania Press, 1985.

Isaacman, Allen F. "Peasant and Rural Social Protest in Africa." In *Confronting Historical Paradigms: Peasants, Labor, and the Capitalist World System in Africa and Latin America.* Ed. Frederick Cooper, Florencia E. Mallon, William Roseberry, and Steven J. Stern. Madison: University of Wisconsin Press, 1993, pp. 205–317.

Jaynes, Gerald David. *Branches Without Roots: Genesis of the Black Working Class in the American South.* New York: Oxford University Press, 1986.

Johnson, Walter. *Soul By Soul: Life Inside the Antebellum Slave Market.* Cambridge, MA: Harvard University Press, 1999.

Johnston, Frances B. *The Hampton Album.* New York: Museum of Modern Art, 1966.

Jones, Gareth Stedman. *Languages of Class: Studies in English Working Class History, 1832–1982.* New York: Cambridge University Press, 1983.

Jones, Jacqueline. *Labor of Love, Labor of Sorrow: Black Women, Work, and the Family from Slavery to the Present.* 1985. Rev. Ed., New York: Vintage Books, 1995.

Jones, Katherine M., ed. *When Sherman Came: Southern Women and the Great March.* Indianapolis: Bobbs-Merrill Co., 1964.

Jones, Norrece T., Jr. *Born a Child of Freedom Yet a Slave: Mechanisms of Control and Strategies of Resistance in Antebellum South Carolina.* Hanover, NH: University Press of New England, 1990.

Jordan, Weymouth T. *Hugh Davis and His Alabama Plantation.* University: University of Alabama Press, 1948.

Jordan, Winthrop D. *Tumult and Silence at Second Creek: An Inquiry into a Civil War Slave Conspiracy.* Baton Rouge: Louisiana State University Press, 1993.

Joyner, Charles. "The World of the Plantation Slaves." In *Before Freedom Came: African American Life in the Antebellum South.* Ed. Edward D. C. Campbell, Jr. with Kim R. Rice. Charlottesville: University Press of Virginia, 1991.

Kahn, Charles. "An Agency Theory Approach to Slave Punishments and Rewards." In *Without Consent or Contract. Technical Papers: The Rise and Fall of American Slavery.* 2 vols. *Conditions of Slave Life and the Transition to Freedom.* vol. 2. Ed. Robert William Fogel and Stanley L. Engerman. New York: W. W. Norton, 1992, pp. 551–65.

Kaplan, Sidney. "The 'Domestic Insurrections' of the Declaration of Independence." *Journal of Negro History* 61 (July 1976): 243–55.

Katzman, David M. *Seven Days a Week: Women and Domestic Service in Industrializing America.* New York: Oxford University Press, 1978.

Kerber, Linda. "Separate Spheres, Female Worlds, Woman's Place: The Rhetoric of Women's History." *Journal of American History* 75 (June 1988): 9–39.

King, Wilma. "The Mistress and Her Maids: White and Black Women in a Louisiana Household, 1858–1868." In *Discovering the Women in Slavery: Emancipating Perspectives on the American Past.* Ed. Patricia Morton. Athens: University of Georgia Press, 1996.

_____. *Stolen Childhood: Slave Youth in Nineteenth Century America.* Bloomington: Indiana University Press, 1995.

Kiser, Vernon Benjamin. "Occupational Change Among Negroes in Durham." Masters Thesis, Duke University, 1942.

Kolchin, Peter. *Unfree Labor: American Slavery and Russian Serfdom.* Cambridge, MA: Harvard University Press, 1987.

_____. *First Freedom: The Responses of Alabama's Blacks to Emancipation and Recon-struction.* Westport, CT: Greenwood Press, 1972.

Krowl, Michelle A. "'Her Just Dues': Civil War Pensions of African American Women in Virginia." In *Negotiating Boundaries of Southern Womanhood: Dealing with the Powers that Be.* Ed. Janet L. Coryell, Thomas H. Appleton, Jr., Anasta-tia Sims, and Sandra Gioia Treadway. Columbia: University of Missouri Press, 2000.

LaDurie, Le Roy. *Carnival in Romans.* Trans. Mary Feeney. New York: George Barziller, 1980.

Landes, Joan B. *Women and the Public Sphere in the Age of the French Revolution.* Ithaca: Cornell University Press, 1988.

Lebsock, Suzanne. *The Free Women of Petersburg: Status and Culture in a Southern Town, 1784–1860.* New York: W. W. Norton, 1984.

Lerner, Gerda. "Women and Slavery." *Slavery and Abolition* 4 (December 1983): 173–98.

Litwack, Leon F. *Trouble in Mind: Black Southerners in the Age of Jim Crow.* New York: Knopf, 1998.

_____. "The Ordeal of Black Freedom." In *The Southern Enigma: Essays on Race, Class and Folk Culture.* Ed. Walter J. Fraser Jr. and Winfred B. Moore. Westport, CT: Greenwood, 1983.

_____. *Been in the Storm So Long: The Aftermath of Slavery.* New York: Vintage Books, 1979.

Lockridge, Kenneth A. *On the Sources of Patriarchal Rage: The Commonplace Books of William Byrd and Thomas Jefferson and the Gendering of Power in the Eighteenth Century.* New York: New York University Press, 1992.

_____. *The Diary, and Life, of William Byrd II of Virginia, 1674–1744.* Chapel Hill: University of North Carolina Press, 1987.

Lohrenz, Mary Edna and Anita Miller Stamper. *Mississippi Homespun: Nineteenth Century Textiles and the Women Who Made Them.* Jackson: Mississippi Department of Archives and History, 1989.

Lomax, Alan. *The Land Where the Blues Began.* New York: Pantheon, 1993.

Lonn, Ella. *Desertion During the Civil War.* New York: Century Co., 1928.

Martin, Bessie. *Desertion of Alabama Troops from the Confederate Army: A Study in Sectionalism.* New York: Columbia University Press, 1932.

McCurry, Stephanie. "Producing Dependence: Women, Work, and Yeoman House-holds in Low-Country South Carolina." In *Neither Lady nor Slave: Working Women of the Old South.* Ed. Susanna Delfino and Michele Gillespie. Chapel Hill: University of North Carolina Press, 2002, pp. 51–71.

_____. *Masters of Small Worlds: Yeoman Households, Gender Relations, and the Political Culture of the Antebellum South Carolina Low Country.* New York: Oxford University Press, 1995.

_____. "The Politics of Yeoman Households in South Carolina." In *Divided Houses: Gender and the Civil War.* Ed. Catherine Clinton and Nina Silber. New York: Oxford University Press, 1992, pp. 22–41.

McDonald, Roderick A. *The Economy and Material Culture of Slaves: Goods and Chattels on the Sugar Plantations of Jamaica and Louisiana.* Baton Rouge: Louisiana State University Press, 1993.

McFeely, William S. *Sapelo's People: A Long Walk into Freedom.* New York: W. W. Norton, 1994.

McGlynn, Frank and Seymour Drescher, eds. *The Meaning of Freedom: Economics, Politics, and Culture After Slavery*. Pittsburgh, PA: University of Pittsburgh Press, 1992.

McMillen, Neil R. *Dark Journey: Black Mississippians in the Age of Jim Crow*. Urbana: University of Illinois Press, 1990.

McMillen, Sally G. *Motherhood in the Old South: Pregnancy, Childbirth, and Infant Rearing*. Baton Rouge: Louisiana State University Press, 1990.

McPherson, James M. *For Cause and Comrades: Why Men Fought in the Civil War*. New York: Oxford University Press, 1997.

_____. *Battle Cry of Freedom: The Civil War Era*. New York: Oxford University Press, 1988.

McPherson, Tara. *Reconstructing Dixie: Race, Gender, and Nostalgia in the Imagined South*. Durham, NC: Duke University Press, 2003.

Massey, Mary Elizabeth. *Women in the Civil War*. 1966. Reprint, Lincoln: University of Nebraska Press, 1994.

_____. *Ersatz in the Confederacy: Shortages and Substitutes on the Southern Homefront*. 1952. Reprint, Columbia: University of South Carolina Press, 1991.

Mbembe, Achille. "Necropolitics." Trans. Libby Meintjes. *Public Culture* 15 (Winter 2003): 11–40.

_____. *On the Postcolony*. Berkeley: University of California Press, 2001.

Mbembe, Achille and Janet Roitman. "Figures of the Subject in Times of Crisis." In *The Geography of Identity*. Ed. Patricia Yeager. Ann Arbor: University of Michigan Press, 1996.

Merrill, Michael. "'Cash is Good to Eat': Self-Sufficiency and Exchange in the Rural Economy of the United States." *Radical History Review* 4 (Winter 1977): 42–71.

Midgley, Clare, ed. *Gender and Imperialism*. Manchester, UK: Manchester University Press, 1998.

Mintz, Sidney W. "Pangloss and Pollyanna; or Whose Reality Are We Talking About?" In *The Meaning of Freedom: Economic, Politics, and Culture After Slavery*. Ed. Frank McGlynn and Seymour Drescher. Pittsburgh, PA: University of Pittsburgh Press, 1992.

Mitchel, Reid. *The Vacant Chair: The Northern Soldier Leaves Home*. New York: Oxford University Press, 1993.

Mohr, Clarence. *On the Threshold of Freedom: Masters and Slaves in Civil War Georgia*. Athens: University of Georgia Press, 1986.

Montgomery, David. *The Fall of the House of Labor: The Workplace, the State, and American Labor Activism, 1865–1925*. New York: Cambridge University Press, 1987.

_____. *Beyond Equality: Labor and the Radical Republicans, 1862–1872*. New York: Knopf, 1967.

Moore, Albert B. *Conscription and Conflict in the Confederacy*. New York: Macmillan Co., 1924.

Moore, Frank. *Women of the War: Their Heroism and Self-Sacrifice*. Hartford, CT: S. S. Scranton, 1966.

Morgan, Edmund S. *American Slavery, American Freedom: The Ordeal of Colonial Virginia*. New York: W. W. Norton, 1975.

Morris, Thomas D. *Southern Slavery and the Law, 1619–1860*. Chapel Hill: University of North Carolina Press, 1996.

Morton, Patricia, ed. *Discovering the Women in Slavery: Emancipating Perspectives on the American Past*. Athens: University of Georgia Press, 1966.

Muhlenfeld, Elisabeth. *Mary Boykin Chesnut: A Biography.* Baton Rouge: Louisiana State University Press, 1981.

Nevins, Allan. *Ordeal of the* Union. 8 vols. *The War for the Union: The Organized War, 1863–1864.* vol. 3. New York: Charles Scribner's Sons, 1971.

Newman, Simon P. *Parades and the Politics of the Street: Festival Culture in the Early American Republic.* Philadelphia, PA: University of Pennsylvania Press, 1997.

Norton, Mary Beth. *Founding Mothers and Fathers: Gendered Power and the Forming of American Society.* New York: Vintage Books, 1996.

Oakes, James. *Slavery and Freedom: An Interpretation of the Old South.* Chapel Hill: University of North Carolina Press, 1990.

————. "The Political Significance of Slave Resistance." *History Workshop* 22 (Autumn 1986): 89–107.

Odum, Howard W. *Race and Rumors of Race; Challenge to American Crisis.* Chapel Hill: University of North Carolina Press, 1943.

Orser, Charles E., Jr. *The Material Basis of the Postbellum Tenant Plantation: Historical Archeology in the South Carolina Piedmont.* Athens: University of Georgia Press, 1988.

Orvin, Maxwell Clayton. *Historic Berkeley County, 1671–1900.* Charleston, SC: Comprint, 1973.

Owens, Harry P., ed. *Perspectives and Irony in American Slavery.* Jackson: University of Mississippi Press, 1976.

Painter, Nell Irvin. "The Journal of Ella Gertrude Thomas: A Testament of Wealth, Loss, and Adultery." In Nell Irvin Painter. *Southern History Across the Color Line.* Chapel Hill: University of North Carolina Press, 2002, pp. 40–92.

————. "Soul Murder and Slavery: Toward a Fully Loaded Cost Accounting." In Nell Irvin Painter. *Southern History Across the Color Line.* Chapel Hill: University of North Carolina Press, 2002, pp. 15–39.

Paludan, Phillip Shaw. *A People's Contest: The Union and Civil War, 1861–1865.* 1988. Reprint, Lawrence: University Press of Kansas, 1996.

Patterson, Orlando. *Slavery and Social Death: A Comparative Study.* Cambridge, MA: Harvard University Press, 1982.

Patton, James Welch. *Unionism and Reconstruction in Tennessee, 1860–1869.* Chapel Hill: University of North Carolina Press, 1934.

Pease, Jane H. and William H. *Ladies, Women, & Wenches: Choice and Constraint in Antebellum Charleston & Boston.* Chapel Hill: University of North Carolina Press, 1990.

Perreault, Melanie. "To Fear and to Love Us: Intercultural Violence in the English Atlantic." *Journal of World History* 19 (March 2006): 71-93.

Perrot, Michelle, ed. *Writing Women's History.* Trans. Felecia Pheasant. 1984. Reprint, Oxford: Basil Blackwell, Ltd., 1992.

Phillips, Ulrich B. *American Negro Slavery: A Survey of the Supply, Employment and Control of Negro Labor as Determined by the Plantation Regime.* 1918. Reprint, Baton Rouge: Louisiana State University Press, 1966.

Pollock, Linda A. "Living on the Stage of the World: The Concept of Privacy Among the Elite of Early Modern England." In *Rethinking Social History: English Society and Its Interpretation, 1570–1920.* Ed. Adrian Wilson. Manchester, UK: Manchester University Press, 1993, pp. 78–96.

Powell, Lawrence N. *New Masters: Northern Planters during the Civil War and Reconstruction.* New Haven, CT: Yale University Press, 1980.

Proctor, Nicholas W. *Bathed in Blood: Hunting and Mastery in the Old South*. Charlottesville: University Press of Virginia, 2002.

Quarles, Benjamin. *The Negro in the Civil War*. Boston, MA: Little, Brown and Co., 1953.

Rable, George C. "'Missing in Action': Women of the Confederacy." In *Divided Houses: Gender and the Civil War*. Ed. Catherine Clinton and Nina Silber. New York: Oxford University Press, 1992.

———. *Civil Wars: Women and the Crisis of Southern Nationalism*. Urbana: University of Illinois Press, 1989.

———. *But There Was No Peace: The Role of Violence in the Politics of Reconstruction*. Athens: University of Georgia Press, 1984.

Ramsdell, Charles W. *Behind the Lines in the Southern Confederacy*. Baton Rouge: Louisiana State University Press, 1944.

Ransom, Roger L. and Richard Sutch. *One Kind of Freedom: The Economic Consequences of Emancipation*. Cambridge: Cambridge University Press, 1977.

———. "The Impact of the Civil War and of Emancipation on Southern Agriculture," *Explorations in Economic History* 12 (January 1975): 1–28.

Raper, Arthur F. *Preface to Peasantry: A Tale of Two Black-Belt Counties*. Chapel Hill: University of North Carolina Press, 1936.

Raymond, Ida. *Southland Writers: Biographical and Critical Sketches of the Living Female Writers of the South with Extracts from their Writings*. 2 vols. Philadelphia: Claxton, Remsen & Haffelfinger, 1870.

Reidy, Joseph P. *From Slavery to Agrarian Capitalism in the Cotton Plantation South: Central Georgia, 1800–1900*. Chapel Hill: University of North Carolina Press, 1992.

Rice, C. Duncan. *The Rise and Fall of Black Slavery*. New York: Harper and Row, 1975.

Roark, James L. *Masters Without Slaves: Southern Planters in the Civil War and Reconstruction*. New York: W. W. Norton, 1977.

Robinson, Armstead L. *Bitter Fruits of Bondage: The Demise of Slavery and the Collapse of the Confederacy, 1861–1865*. Charlottesville: University Press of Virginia, 2005.

———. "The Difference Freedom Made: The Emancipation of Afro-Americans." In *The State of Afro-American History: Past, Present, and Future*, Ed. Darlene Clark Hine. Baton Rouge: Louisiana State University Press, 1986.

———. "'Worser dan Jeff Davis': The Coming of Free Labor During the Civil War, 1861–1865." In *Essays on the Postbellum Southern Economy*. Ed. Thavolia Glymph and John J. Kushma. College Station: Texas A&M University Press, 1985.

———. "In the Shadow of Old John Brown: Insurrection Anxiety and Confederate Mobilization, 1861–1863." *Journal of Negro History* 65 (Autumn 1980): 279–97.

Rogers, William Warren and Robert David Ward. *August Reckoning: Jack Turner and Racism in Post-Civil War Alabama*. Baton Rouge: Louisiana State University Press, 1973.

Roland, Charles P. *Louisiana Sugar Plantations during the Civil War*. Leiden: E. J. B. Brill, 1957.

Rollins, Judith. *Between Women: Domestics and their Employers*. Philadelphia, PA: Temple University Press, 1985.

Rosaldo, Renata. *Culture and Truth: The Remaking of Social Analysis*. Boston, MA: Beacon Press, 1989.

Rose, Willie Lee. *Rehearsal for Reconstruction: The Port Royal Experiment*. London: Oxford University Press, 1964.

Rosengarten, Theodore. *Tombee: Portrait of a Cotton Planter with the Journal of Thomas B. Chaplin (1822–1890)*. New York: William Morrow & Co., Inc., 1986.

Royster, Charles. *The Destructive War: William Tecumseh Sherman, Stonewall Jackson, and the Americans*. New York: Knopf, 1991.

Rutherford, Janice Williams. *Selling Mrs. Consumer: Christine Frederick & the Rise of Household Efficiency*. Athens: University of Georgia Press, 2003.

Ryan, Mary P. *Civic Wars: Democracy and Public Life in the American City during the Nineteenth Century*. Berkeley: University of California Press, 1997.

Sansing, David G., ed. *What Was Freedom's Price?* Jackson: University Press of Mississippi, 1978.

Saville, Julie. "Rites and Power: Reflections on Slavery, Freedom and Political Ritual." In *From Slavery to Emancipation in the Atlantic World*. Ed. Sylvia R. Frey and Betty Wood. London: Frank Cass, 1999, pp. 88–102.

———. *The Work of Reconstruction: From Slave to Wage Laborer in South Carolina, 1860–1870*. Cambridge: Cambridge University Press, 1994.

Scarborough, William K. *Masters of the Big House: Elite Slaveholders of the Mid-Nineteenth Century South*. Baton Rouge: Louisiana State University Press, 2003.

———. "Slavery – The White Man's Burden." In *Perspectives and Irony in American Slavery*. Ed. Harry P. Owens. Jackson: University Press of Mississippi, 1976.

Schmidt, Elizabeth. "Race, Sex, and Domestic Labor: The Question of African Female Servants in Southern Rhodesia, 1900–1939." In *African Encounters with Domesticity*. Ed. Karen Tranberg Hansen. New Brunswick, NJ: Rutgers University Press, 1992, pp. 221–41.

Schwalm, Leslie A. *A Hard Fight for We: Women's Transition from Slavery to Freedom in South Carolina*. Urbana: University of Illinois Press, 1997.

Schwartz, Marie Jenkins. *Born in Bondage: Growing Up Enslaved in the Antebellum South*. Cambridge, MA: Harvard University Press, 2000.

Scott, Anne Firor. *The Southern Lady: From Pedestal to Politics, 1830–1930*. 1970. 25th Anniversary Ed., Charlottesville: University Press of Virginia, 1995.

———. "On Seeing and Not Seeing: A Case of Historical Invisibility." *Journal of American History* 71 (June 1984): 7–21.

———. *Making the Invisible Woman Visible*. Urbana: University of Illinois Press, 1984.

———. "Women's Perspective on the Patriarchy in the 1850s." *Journal of American History* 61 (June 1974): 52–64.

Scott, James C. *Seeing Like a State: How Certain Schemes to Improve the Human Condition Have Failed*. New Haven, CT: Yale University Press, 1998.

———. *Domination and the Arts of Resistance: Hidden Transcripts*. New Haven, CT: Yale University Press, 1990.

———. *Weapons of the Weak: Everyday Forms of Peasant Resistance*. New Haven, CT: Yale University Press, 1985.

———. *The Moral Economy of the Peasant: Rebellion and Subsistence in Southeast Asia*. New Haven, CT: Yale University Press, 1976.

———. *Political Ideology in Malaysia: Reality and Beliefs of an Elite*. New Haven, CT: Yale University Press, 1968.

Scott, Joan. "Gender: A Useful Category of Analysis." *American Historical Review* 91 (December 1986): 1053–75.

Scott, Rebecca J. "Defining the Boundaries of Freedom in the World of Cane: Cuba, Brazil, and Louisiana after Emancipation." *American Historical Review* 99 (February 1994): 70–102.

Shammas, Carole. "The Domestic Environment in Early Modern England and America." *Journal of Social History* 14 (Autumn 1980): 3–24.

Simkins, Frances Butler and James W. Patton. *Women of the Confederacy*. Richmond: Garret and Massie, 1936.

Sitterson, J. Carlyle. "A Planter Family of the Old and New South." *Journal of Southern History* 6 (August 1940): 347–67.

Sklar, Kathryn Kish. *Catherine Beecher: A Study in American Domesticity*. New Haven, CT: Yale University Press, 1973.

Smith, Mark M. *Mastered by the Clock: Time, Slavery and Freedom in the American South*. Chapel Hill: University of North Carolina Press, 1997.

Spender, Dale. *Man Made Language*. Boston, MA: Routledge and Kegan Paul, 1980.

Spruill, Julia Cherry. *Women's Life and Work in the Southern Colonies*. New York: W. W. Norton, 1972.

Stampp, Kenneth M. *The Peculiar Institution: Slavery in the Antebellum South*. New York: Vintage Books, 1956.

Stanley, Amy Dru. *From Bondage to Contract: Wage Labor, Marriage, and the Family in the Age of Slave Emancipation*. Cambridge: Cambridge University Press, 1998.

Sterkx, H. E. *Partners in Rebellion: Alabama Women in the Civil War*. Rutherford, NJ: Fairleigh Dickinson University Press, 1970.

Stevenson, Brenda E. "Distress and Discord in Virginia Slave Families, 1830–1860." In *In Joy and In Sorrow: Women, Family, and Marriage in the Victorian South, 1830–1900*. Ed. Carol Bleser. New York: Oxford University Press, 1996.

———. "Gender Convention, Ideals, and Identity among Antebellum Virginia Slave Women." In *More than Chattel: Black Women and Slavery in the Americas*. Ed. David Barry Gaspar and Darlene Clark Hine. Bloomington: Indiana University Press, 1996, pp. 168–90.

———. *Life in Black and White: Family and Community in the Slave South*. New York: Oxford University Press, 1996.

Stewart, Mart A. *"What Nature Suffers to Groe": Life, Labor, and Landscape on the Georgia Coast, 1680–1920*. Athens: University of Georgia Press, 1996.

Stoler, Ann Laura. *Carnal Knowledge and Imperial Power: Race and the Intimate in Colonial Rule*. Berkeley: University of California Press, 2002.

Stoler, Ann Laura with Karen Strasser. "Memory-Work in Java: A Cautionary Tale." In *Carnal Knowledge and Imperial Power: Race and the Intimate in Colonial Rule*. Ed. Ann Laura Stoler. Berkeley: University of California Press, 2002.

Stowe, Steven M. *Intimacy and Power in the Old South: Ritual in the Lives of the Planters*. Baltimore, MD: Johns Hopkins University Press, 1987.

Strickland, John Scott. "Traditional Culture and Moral Economy: Social and Economic Change in the South Carolina Low Country, 1865–1910." In *The Countryside in the Age of Capitalist Transformation: Essays in the Social History of Rural America*. Ed. Steven Hahn and Jonathan Prude. Chapel Hill: University of North Carolina Press, 1985.

Sutherland, Daniel E. "A Special Kind of Problem: The Response of Household Slaves and Their Masters to Freedom." *Southern Studies* 20 (Summer 1981): 158–162.

Tague, Ingrid H. *Women of Quality: Accepting and Contesting Ideals of Femininity in England, 1690–1760*. Suffolk, UK: Boydell Press, 2002.

Taliaferro, Frances. *A Portrait of Historic Athens and Clarke County.* Athens: University of Georgia Press, 1992.

Tatum, Georgia Lee. *Disloyalty in the Confederacy.* Chapel Hill: University of North Carolina Press, 1934.

Taussig, Michael. "Culture of Terror – Space of Death: Roger Casement's Putamayo Report and The Explanation of Torture." In *Colonialism and Culture.* Ed. Nicholas B. Dirks. Ann Arbor: University of Michigan Press, 1992.

Taylor, Alrutheus A. *The Negro in South Carolina during the Reconstruction.* 1924. Reprint, New York: Russell and Russell, 1969.

Taylor, Joe Gray. *Louisiana Reconstructed, 1863–1877.* Baton Rouge: Louisiana State University Press, 1974.

Tebbutt, Melanie. "Women's Talk? Gossip and 'Women's Words' in Working Class Communities, 1880–1939." In *Workers' Worlds: Cultures and Communities in Manchester and Salford, 1880–1939.* Ed. Andrew Davies and Steven Fielding. Manchester, UK: Manchester University Press, 1992, pp. 49–73.

Thompson, E. P. *Making History: Writings on History and Culture.* New York: New Press, 1994.

———. *Customs in Common.* London: Merlin Press, 1991.

———. *The Poverty of Theory and Other Essays.* New York: Monthly Review Press, 1978.

———. "Patrician Society, Plebian Culture." *Journal of Social History* 7 (Summer 1974): 382–405.

———. *The Making of the English Working Class.* New York: Vintage Books, 1966.

Thorne, Susan. *Congregational Missions and the Making of an Imperial Culture in Nineteenth Century England.* Stanford, CA: Stanford University Press, 1999.

———. "Fungusamongus; Or, An Imperial Idea without Enemies." *Journal of British Studies* 33 (January 1994): 110–17.

Tindall, George Brown. *South Carolina Negroes, 1877–1900.* 1952. Reprint, Columbia: University of South Carolina Press, 2003.

Titus, Mary. "The Dining Room Door Swings Both Ways: Food, Race, and Domestic Space in the Nineteenth-Century South." In *Haunted Bodies: Gender and Southern Texts.* Ed. Anne Goodwyn Jones and Susan V. Donaldson. Charlottesville: University Press of Virginia, 1997.

Tucker, Susan. *Telling Memories among Southern Women: Domestic Workers and their Employers in the Segregated South.* New York: Schocken Books, 1988.

Upton, Dell. "White and Black Landscapes in Eighteenth Century Virginia." *Places* 2 (1985): 59–72.

Van Onselen, Charles. *The Seed Is Mine: The Life of Kas Maine: A South African Sharecropper, 1894–1985.* New York: Hill and Wang, 1996.

———. "Race and Class in the South African Countryside: Cultural Osmosis and Social Relations in the Sharecropping Economy of the South-Western Transvaal, 1900–1950." *American Historical Review* 95 (February 1990): 99–123.

Varon, Elizabeth R. *We Mean to be Counted: White Women and Politics in Antebellum Virginia.* Chapel Hill: University of North Carolina Press, 1998.

Vickery, Amanda. *The Gentleman's Daughter: Women's Lives in Georgian England.* New Haven, CT: Yale University Press, 1998.

Vlach, John Michael. *Back of the Big House: The Architecture of Plantation Slavery.* Chapel Hill: University of North Carolina Press, 1993.

Waldstreicher, David. *In the Midst of Perpetual Fetes: The Making of American Nationalism, 1776–1820*. Chapel Hill: University of North Carolina Press, 1997.

Warren, Joseph. "Husband's Right to Wife's Services." *Harvard Law Review* 38 (February 1925): 421–46.

Way, Peter. *Common Labour: Workers and the Digging of North American Canals, 1780–1860*. Cambridge: Cambridge University Press, 1993.

Weiner, Jonathan M. "Female Planters and Planters' Wives in the Civil War and Reconstruction." *Alabama Review* 30 (April 1977): 135–49.

Weiner, Marli F. *Mistresses and Slaves: Plantation Women in South Carolina, 1830–80*. Urbana: University of Illinois Press, 1998.

Wesley, Charles H. *Collapse of the Confederacy*. Washington, DC: Associated Pub., 1937.

White, Deborah Gray. *Ar'n't I a Woman?: Female Slaves in the Plantation South*. Rev. Ed., New York: W. W. Norton, 1999.

———. *Ar'n't I a Woman?: Female Slaves in the Plantation South*. New York: W. W. Norton, 1985.

Whites, Lee Ann. *The Civil War as a Crisis in Gender: Augusta, Georgia, 1860–1890*. Athens: University of Georgia Press, 1995.

———. "The Civil War as a Crisis in Gender." In *Divided Houses: Gender and the Civil War*. Ed. Catherine Clinton and Nina Silber. New York: Oxford University Press, 1992.

Wiley, Bell Irwin. *Confederate Women*. Westport, CT: Greenwood Press, 1975.

———. *Plain People of the Confederacy*. Baton Rouge: Louisiana State University Press, 1943.

———. *Southern Negroes, 1861–1865*. New Haven, CT: Yale University Press, 1938.

Williams, David, Teresa Crisp Williams, and David Carlson. *Plain Folk in a Rich Man's War: Class and Dissent in Confederate Georgia*. Gainesville: University Press of Florida, 2002.

Williamson, Joel. *The Crucible of Race: Black-White Relations in the American South Since Emancipation*. New York: Oxford University Press, 1984.

Wilson, Adrian, ed. *Rethinking Social History: English Society and Its Interpretation, 1570-1920*. Manchester, UK: Manchester University Press, 1993.

Wilson, Joseph T. *The Black Phalanx: African American Soldiers in the War of Independence, the War of 1812 and the Civil War*. 1887. Reprint, New York: Da Capo Press, 1994.

Wilson, Woodrow. *A History of the American People*. 5 vols. New York: Harper and Brothers, 1901-2.

Wood, Betty. *Women's Work, Men's Work: The Informal Slave Economies of Low Country Georgia*. Athens: University of Georgia Press, 1995.

Woodman, Harold D. *New South—New Law: The Legal Foundations of Credit and Labor Relations in the Postbellum Agricultural South*. Baton Rouge: Louisiana State University Press, 1995.

———. "Economic Reconstruction and the Rise of the New South." In *Interpreting Southern History: Historiographical Essays in Honor of Sanford W. Higginbotham*. Ed. John B. Boles and Evelyn Thomas Nolen. Baton Rouge: Louisiana State University Press, 1987.

———. "The Reconstruction of the Cotton Plantation in the New South." In *Essays on the Postbellum Southern Economy*. Ed. Thavolia Glymph and John J. Kushma. College Station: Texas A&M University Press, 1985.

_____. "Sequel to Slavery: The New History Views the Postbellum South." *Journal of Southern History* 43 (November 1977): 523–54.

_____. *King Cotton and His Retainers: Financing and Marketing the Cotton Crop of the South, 1800–1925*. Lexington: University of Kentucky Press, 1968.

Woodruff, Nan Elizabeth. "African American Freedom Struggles for Citizenship in the Arkansas and Mississippi Deltas in the Age of Jim Crow." *Radical History Review* 55 (Winter 1993): 33–52.

Woodward, C. Vann. "History from Slave Sources." *American Historical Review* 79 (April 1974): 470–81.

_____, ed. *Mary Chesnut's Civil War*. New Haven, CT: Yale University Press, 1981.

Woodward, C. Vann and Elisabeth Muhlenfeld, eds. *The Private Mary Chesnut: The Unpublished Civil War Diaries*. New York: Oxford University Press, 1984.

Woofter, J. J., Jr., *Black Yeomanry*. New York: Henry Holt and Co., 1930.

Wright, Gavin. *The Political Economy of the Cotton South: Households, Markets, and Wealth in the Nineteenth Century*. New York: Oxford, 1978.

Wright, Richard. *Twelve Million Black Voices: A Folk History of the Negro in the United States*. New York: Viking Press, 1941.

Wyatt-Brown, Bertram. *Southern Honor: Ethics and Behavior in the Old South*. New York: Oxford University Press, 1982.

Yaeger, Patricia. *Dirt and Desire: Reconstructing Southern Women's Writing, 1930–1990*. Chicago: University of Chicago Press, 2000.

_____. "Introduction: Narrating Space." In *The Geography of Identity*. Ed. Patricia Yaeger. Ann Arbor: University of Michigan Press, 1996, pp. 1–38.

Index

CPSIA information can be obtained
at www.ICGtesting.com
Printed in the USA
LVOW01s1622030216

473536LV00003B/27/P